# Hebrew Prophets and Sages in Ancient Israel

And Their Relevance to Contemporary Dalit Prophets and Sages

# Hebrew Prophets and Sages in Ancient Israel

## And Their Relevance to Contemporary Dalit Prophets and Sages

**Kondasingu Jesurathnam**

Christian World Imprints

First Published in 2025 by

**Christian World Imprints**
*Christian Publishing & Books from India*
A-71 Group, Wazirpur Industrial Area
**Delhi-110052**
cwidelhi2017@gmail.com
www.ChristianWorldImprints.com
Phone: +91 11 41526079

ISBN: 978-93-6065-390-3 (HB)
ISBN: 978-93-6065-558-7 (PB)

Cover Design: Ms. Denin Sweety, Dharapuram, Tamilnadu



Printed in India.

# Contents


| | | |
|---|---|---|
| *Preface* | | vii |
| *Abbreviation* | | ix |

**Part-I: An Introduction to the Hebrew Prophetic Thought and Literature of the Old Testament**

| | | |
|---|---|---|
| Chapter 1: | General Introduction | 3 |
| Chapter 2: | Pre-Monarchic and Monarchic Prophets and their Ministry | 15 |
| Chapter 3: | Prophecy in the Eighth Century BCE (Amos, Hosea, Isaiah of Jerusalem & Micah) | 25 |
| Chapter 4: | Seventh Century Prophecy (Jeremiah, Zephaniah, Nahum & Habakkuk) | 57 |
| Chapter 5: | Prophetic Ministry During the Exilic Period (Ezekiel and Deutero-Isaiah-Chaps. 40-55) | 73 |
| Chapter 6: | Prophetic Ministry During the Post-Exilic Period (Trito-Isaiah, Haggai, Zechariah and Malachi) | 103 |
| Chapter 7: | Prophecy in the Ancient West Asia | 125 |
| Chapter 8: | Formation of the Prophetic Books | 131 |
| Chapter 9: | Exegetical Study on the Selected Texts of Isaiah 40-55 | 139 |
| Chapter 10: | Prophecy in India | 175 |
| Chapter 11: | Hebrew Prophets and Dalit Prophets: A Comparative Analysis | 189 |

**Part-II: An Introduction to Poetic and Wisdom Literature of the Old Testament**

| | | |
|---|---|---|
| Chapter 1: | Extent and Characteristics of Hebrew Poetry | 207 |
| Chapter 2: | Extent and Characteristics of Hebrew Wisdom | 217 |
| Chapter 3: | Poetry in Ancient West Asia | 229 |
| Chapter 4: | Wisdom in Ancient West Asia | 235 |
| Chapter 5: | Literary Types of Psalms and their Traditions | 241 |

| | | |
|---|---|---|
| Chapter 6: | Literary Types of Wisdom and their Traditions | 251 |
| Chapter 7: | Survery of the Content and Theology in Poetic and Wisdom Books of the Old Testament | 263 |
| Chapter 8: | Dalit Sages and their Relevance to the Ancient Hebrew Sages | 325 |
| Chapter 9: | Exegetical Study on the Selected Psalms | 331 |
| Chapter 10: | General Conclusion | 373 |
| *Selected Bibliography* | | 377 |
| *Author Index* | | 379 |
| *Biblical Index* | | 381 |

# Preface

Prophets are the backbone of any progressive society both in the ancient and in the modern times. They offer constructive criticism both to the individuals and to the oppressive and corrupt regimes in order to keep them on right track when things get bad to worse in skewed social, political and economic systems. On account of their intervention at right and appropriate time many kingdoms and systems were redeemed from great disasters. When justice was and is denied even to an individual, on account of prophetic oracle justice was executed. When brutal wars are fought warning signs are given to the regimes to mend their ways and repent. In times of fear and discouragement, prophets, through their message of comfort and consolation restored the communities to a normal situation. The prophets on the whole give lifeline to the perishing communities both then and now so that despite grim and dark situations, people can live in hope.

The sages in ancient Israel as well as in our contemporary society play pivotal role like prophets to guide and steer the societies with their timely guidance and wise instructions. Even when the sages emerge from an elite social location, their support for the downtrodden and marginalized communities is highly appreciable. On account of their sharp observations and wise instructions both the rulers and common people are warned and are directed to the right path towards progress. The sages on account of their keen observations of personal and social life as well as the nature good lessons are taught to the community as well as the individuals to steer their lives in accordance with the creator and the created order. By listening and following the wisdom instruction of the sages the entire human and non-human creation is restored towards peace and justice in the whole cosmos.

In the light of the above discussion, the present project combines both the work of the Hebrew prophets and sages and see their relevance to our contemporary Dalit prophets and sages. We must be careful not to equate the ancient prophets and sages with that of contemporary figures. We can only look at the wider converging points between the ancient and the present figures and communities in the light of their overall vocation and purpose. If this idea is clear, then we have achieved our major goal behind this project.

The book has three major parts. The first part deals with the history, literature and theology of ancient Hebrew prophets that culminated in an exegetical analysis of the selected texts from Deutero-Isaiah. The second section consists of the materials on ancient Hebrew wisdom literature covering the historical background and a detailed study of Hebrew poetic and wisdom books and their theology. This section concludes with the exegetical analysis of selected psalms. The final section of this book deals with examples of contemporary Dalit prophets and sages and to see their converging points between ancient and contemporary situations. In all these three parts, care is taken to include the latest material possible as resource material and as many as relevant biblical references are added at appropriate places mostly from the New Revised Standard version. In the case of contemporary Dalit situation more recent illustrations are provided to keep the material up to date. At certain places only brief examples are provided which will give scope for the readers to expand the materials with more similar examples on their own.

Several people must be thanked and acknowledged for their invaluable support and assistance towards this project. I thank God for God's enabling grace who strengthened me to work on this material over a period of several months. I would like to thank all my postgraduate and doctoral students, who through their interaction on various topics covered in this book have sharpened my thinking and perspective. I also thank my colleagues in the department of Old Testament and colleagues at SBSI for their deliberations at various times through different fora which helped me to focus on my work in this project. I would like to thank Mr. Samson Wilson Naveen Kumar, MTh student who helped me to draw biblical index and author index and other aspects of formatting the draft. I also thank Rev. Mede Jeevan Sagar for his help in formatting and timely help at various stages of this project. I am thankful for his hard work on the entire draft. I would like to thank Ms. Denin Sweety BD student who designed a beautiful cover art depicting the biblical and the Dalit context. I would like to thank my son David Sunil and wife Beatrice Veena for their support and encouragement.

I hope and pray that this book will be of immense help to all those biblical students and scholars along with pastors as a supporting backdrop document to the study of Old Testament and to preach the Gospel message. The message of Hebrew prophets and sages is unfathomable and what we have presented is only a glimpse of such a great personality. The work of contemporary Dalit prophets and sages is also huge and vast and we have only given small portion of their honorable cause and commitment for the shalom of the entire creation.

Bangalore 560 046
June 2025

# Abbreviations

| | |
|---|---|
| Amos | Am |
| 1 Chronicles | 1 Chr |
| 2 Chronicles | 2 Chr |
| Daniel | Dn |
| Deuteronomy | Dt |
| Ecclesiastes | Eccl |
| Esther | Est |
| Exodus | Ex |
| Ezekiel | Ez |
| Ezra | Ezr |
| Genesis | Gn |
| Habakkuk | Hb |
| Haggai | Hg |
| Hosea | Hos |
| Isaiah | Is |
| Jeremiah | Jer |
| Job | Jb |
| Joel | Jl |
| Jonah | Jon |
| Joshua | Jo |
| Judges | Jgs |
| 1 Kings | 1 Kgs |
| 2 Kings | 2 Kgs |
| Lamentations | Lam |
| Leviticus | Lv |
| Malachi | Mal |
| Micah | Mi |

| | |
|---|---|
| Nahum | Na |
| Nehemiah | Neh |
| Numbers | Nm |
| Obadiah | Ob |
| Proverbs | Prv |
| Psalms | Ps (plural Pss) |
| Ruth | Ru |
| 1 Samuel | 1 Sm |
| 2 Samuel | 2 Sm |
| Song of Solomon (Songs of Songs) | Sg |
| Zechariah | Zec |
| Zephaniah | Zep |

# Part-I

# An Introduction to the Hebrew Prophetic Thought and Literature of the Old Testament

Chapter 1

# General Introduction

***Introduction:*** Prophecy and wisdom are twin related concepts and those who practice both phenomena are very vital for the growth and development of any society. Both these can also be practiced independently although there is intrinsic relationship exist between them. Before, during and after Israelite settlement in the Promised Land both the above mentioned phenomena were seen as significant. After the Torah and its cardinal principles, prophecy and wisdom traditions stand vital for the society of Israel for all their walks of life. Even when we see the complexity of both these phenomenon, they have grown and developed and took many shapes as the time progressed in ancient Israelite society. At the same time both these have been developed and took shape under the influence of their ancient West Asian counterparts. It is this influence that makes our study of ancient Israelite prophecy and wisdom interesting and exciting. More details will be presented in this direction as we venture and move forward in this discussion.

In the above light we can also see contemporary Dalit discourse based on what we may freely call as Dalit prophets and sages transcending the barriers of religion and language even when they worked in a particular context of ancient Israel. While the times that we draw parallels between Israelite and Dalit entities are far and wide, their functional and performative dimensions are quite close to each other. On account of this we dare to venture into this attempt of putting Old Testament phenomena of prophecy and wisdom with the contemporary Dalit discourse based on their frontline warriors of justice, peace and order in human communities and in the entire cosmos. On this point we shall make available more detailed information in the course of our discussion below. But unlike Hebrew tradition, Dalit discourse has no well-organized literary collections. So our attempt in this direction will stand as a pioneering attempt and thus very challenging. What we have in the Dalit prophetic and wisdom tradition is mostly limited to oral tradition found in the form of popular sayings, case studies, oral stories circulated from older to younger generations. We have also taken into consideration the stories from the ground reality, the intimidating accounts of oppression of Dalits and the voices of solidarity and support to the Dalits by the prophetic and wisdom figures.

When we speak of prophecy and the prophets in the Old Testament, we are generally thinking of the fifteen books (former and latter Prophets) attributed to Prophetic authors in the midsection of the Hebrew Bible. Yet these books by no means exhaust the phenomenon of prophecy in Israel. According to a rabbinic dictum there were forty-eight prophets and seven prophetesses in Israel, and based on the head count in the entire Hebrew Bible. None of the books accepted as canonical is ascribed to a prophet who lived before the eighth century BCE. Yet the earliest of these canonical prophets, Amos and Hosea, not only knew of prophetic predecessors but stood quite consciously within a prophetic tradition (Amos 2:11-12; Hos. 6:5; 9:7-8, 12:10,13). By the eighth century, in fact, Israelite prophecy had a history of some three centuries behind it.

The purpose of this volume however, is not to go into all the details of the early stages of the history of prophecy (we may do it at some relevant places) but to trace out few important elements on the nature of Hebrew prophecy, and certain concepts relate to it. This will be done briefly in the introduction, followed by the detailed historical study of individual prophets in their context.

***Terminology Concerning Prophet and Prophecy:*** The term prophet: The basic and common Hebrew word for Prophecy in the Old Testament is nabhi. In Arabic same root word for the prophet is: naba'a means "to proclaim or announce". Hence, the Hebrew noun nabhi', "Prophet" means literally a "spokesman" or "speaker." According to C. H. Cornil, the Arabic root for Prophet does not have simply the general sense of speaking, as in the Assyrian Babylonian, but has the special sense of a deputed speaker. Thus the speaker discourses not of himself/herself, but as an agent of another who has some special communication to deliver. The verb nabha also refer to the meaning, "to flow, build up, bubble forth", hence, "to pour forth words." William Gesensius rightly pointed out, "the prophets when under the power of inspiration, appear to have been greatly agitated affections and to have exhibited writings and spasmodic of the body like delirious persons.

The noun "prophet" is also derived from an Akkadian root. According to Albright, the correct meaning of the term prophet is not speaker, announcer, but "one who is called (by God), one who has a vocation (from God)." This is almost always the sense of the verb nabu "to call" in Akkadian. The king is styled a nibitu (the noun The biblical prophets in the Old Testament being from the verb), meaning "the one called" by the God's, the verbal adjective nabi means 'called' in the code of Hammurabi.

Exodus 7:1-2, clarifies the meaning of nabhi as the one who speaks for God: Here the function of the Prophet is to speak forth the divine message (cf. Exod. 4:19f, Jer. 1:17, 15:19, Isa. 1:20, Zech. 7:12, Amos 3:8 et.al).

There are certain other terms used to refer to prophet:

**(i)** ***Seer:*** this is used synonymous for nabhi, (roe'h and hozeh) both are translated as "seer." Their verbal roots mean "to see". 1 Sam. 9:9 indicates that the offices of prophet and seer were substantially identical. While nabhi has the objective or active work of the messenger of the lord in speaking forth God's word, whereas the terms roe'h and hozeh ("seer") emphasized the subjective element, namely, the mode of receiving divine revelation, by "seeing". In other words, we may roughly say that the term "seer" speak of the receptive aspect, whereas the term for "prophet" points up the communicative function.

**(ii)** ***Man of God:*** This was a common and general term for the prophet of Israel which emphasised his/her holy calling, moral character and divine ministry. The term is used quite early for instance, of Moses, Samuel, Elijah and Elisha (Deut. 33:1, I Sam. 9:6, II Kings 4:9 etc.).

**(iii)** ***Servant of the Lord:*** This title stresses the close and holy relationship between God and his faithful messengers. It is used of the prophet Ahijah in 1 Kings 14:18.

**(iv)** ***Messenger of the Lord:*** The same Hebrew term (mal'ak) is used for both messenger and angel. As the angels of the lord are his spiritual messengers, so too his prophets were the messengers of his revealed word. This term defines more exactly what the servant of the lord was employed to do. namely, deliver the messages of God (Haggai 1:13, Isa 44:26).

***A Brief Outline and Survey of the Prophetic Literature in the Old Testament:*** In this section, the students are expected to know and read the Bible and get familiar with the following prophetic literature, especially the literature on the former prophets. However, in the following section on the study of the life and teachings of the prophets, we shall make a detail study on the major and minor prophets as they are placed in their respective historical milieu.

The following is the traditional division on the prophetic literature:

I Former Prophets: Joshua, Judges, 1,2 Samuel, 1,2 Kings.

II Latter Prophets: (A) Major Prophets: Isaiah, Jeremiah & Ezekiel
(B) Minor Prophets: Hosea, Joel, Amos, Obadiah, Jonah, Micah, Nahum, Habakkuk, Zephaniah, Haggai, Zechariah & Malachi

Based on their historical milieu the following division can be made on the prophets and prophetic literature.

I Pre-Monarchic Prophets: Moses, Deborah and Samuel, Early Prophetic Guilds.

II Monarchic Period:
- (a) United Monarchy: Nathan
- (b) Divided Monarchy:
  - (i) 9th century: Ahijah, Elijah, Elisha, Micaiah ben Imlah.
  - (ii) 8th century: Amos, Hosea, Isaiah (1-39), Micah, Jonah and Joel
  - (iii) 7th century: Jeremiah, Zephaniah, Nahum, Habakkuk.
- (c) Exilic period: Ezekiel, Isaiah (40-55)
- (d) Post-exilic period: Isaiah (56.66), Haggai. Zechariah, Malachi.
- (e) Unnamed prophets in the history of Israel:

While the above classification of the Hebrew prophets is based on the chronological order, there is another classification that exists based on the Hebrew canon as mentioned above like former prophets and latter prophets. The former prophets are classified based on few prophetic insights and prophetic figures associated with few historical events. The latter prophets are also classified based on their historical context. However canonically and based on their content or material collected, they are further divided into major and minor prophets. On the whole we may argue that the prophetic literature plays a major and significant role in the ancient society of Israel.

Before we venture into the prophetic traits and figures in the books of the former prophets, we may also see Moses as prophet par excellence as there are number of qualities of prophets appear in him.

***Moses, the Prophet Par Excellence:*** Moses has a special place in redemptive history, Moses occupied a unique position in God's covenant administration. He ministered to Israel as the Servant of the Lord and was exalted by his special relationship with the Lord (Numb. 12:6-8: Deut. 34:10-12). When Aaron and Miriam complained about Moses' exalted position as mediator between Yahweh and Israel, Moses did not respond to their charge (Numb 12:3). Instead, the Lord spoke to defend his servant, (Numb. 12: 6~8). The Lord confirmed Moses' authority to be his chosen vehicle of communication. "Israel... I speak to him..." (Numb.12:6, cf. I reveal Deut. 18:18). He set Moses apart as his servant (Exod. 14:31, Deut. 34:5)—a relationship of confidence and friendship between a superior and an inferior. The last words of the Pentateuch testify to the importance of Moses as a prophet of God (Deut. 34:10-12).

As fountain head of the prophetic tradition, Moses saw more of God's glorious self-revelation than anyone else in the Old Testament (Exod. 33:18, 34:29-35). He spoke by God's authority. Whoever questioned Moses challenged the Lord. Israel could find comfort, grace, and blessing because in Moses the role of covenant mediator and intercessor (Exod. 32:1,34:10: Num. 14:13-25) came together. He prayed for Israel, spoke boldly as their advocate in the presence of the Lord, and encouraged them to look beyond himself to Yahweh. When his leadership role was challenged he confronted those who opposed or resisted him in boldness with confidence and more so with compassion.

In a dialogue between Moses and God some important theological message is set. God is revealing and not hiding. Throughout its history Israel looked back to the events of this period when they learned who God was and what he was to be to them. In the sequel to the revelation of the divine name, Moses continues to object to his call. In Exod. 4:10ff, Moses observes that he is not eloquent but slow of speech and tongue. To help Moses Aaron is sent as an assistant. This paradigm of the prophetic role shows clearly that the task primarily to bear the message, submerging one's own ideas, interests and decisions beneath those of the sender: Exod 4:14-23; 5:1. There is a commission to Moses by God to say: "Thus says the Lord": Here Moses role is characterized in the "messenger formula" by which the prophetic word is authorized as the word of God, "Thus says the Lord." Although prophecy in Israel's history does not reach its fullest development until the period of monarchy, its form emerges full blown in the call, commission, and task by Moses, prophet of God par excellence. Moses sets a good example of the expectations of a prophet of God as envisaged in Deuteronomy 18 and stands as an exemplary forerunner of all the prophets yet to come in ancient Israel.

Prophetic traits and figures in other books of former prophets: In the case of few prophetic figures appear sporadically in the books of former prophets, we do not have a detailed information about them. In the book of Joshua for instance, although no prophetic figure as such appears Joshua in chapter 24 appears and exhibits prophetic character. The primary story line of both Joshua and Judges is that while God's chosen people are repeatedly rebellious against God, turning to serve other gods and forgetting God's covenant with them, God is always ready to respond to their crises and deliver them. Only when they cease even to desire God's blessings do they fall into misery and social devastation. This is a remarkably contemporary message, as well. We often find ourselves drifting away from God as we decide how to handle the many opportunities and challenges that arise in our work. We discover that we have elevated other concerns above receiving his love and loving and serving him through our work. The message of Joshua and Judges is that God is ready, now and here, for us to return to him and receive his blessings in our life and work.

The renewal of God's covenant with Israel concludes the book of Joshua. The high point occurs in the very last chapter, when Joshua inspires the people with a rousing challenge to their commitment to serve God alone. His speech is a model of communication. First, he recounts God's amazing acts on Israel's behalf in Egypt, the wilderness and the Promised Land. Why then, Joshua asks, are they still carrying idols and false gods with them? Using what today we might call reverse psychology, he challenges them, "Now if you are unwilling to serve the Lord, choose this day whom you will serve" (Josh. 24:15).[1] This gets their attention. "Far be it from us that we should forsake the Lord to serve other gods" (Josh. 24:16). But Joshua challenges them further. "You cannot serve the Lord," he tells them, "for he is a holy God" (Josh. 24:19). "If you forsake the Lord and serve foreign gods, then he will turn and do you harm, and consume you, after having done you good" (Josh. 24:20). This brings them to a point of actual decision, and they resolve, "No, we will serve the Lord!" (Josh. 24:21) Let's put it in writing, Joshua says, and he has the people sign and witness their commitment (Josh. 24:15-27). In more recent times, John Wesley published a covenant renewal service that is widely used today, and many churches have developed their own approaches to renewing the covenant. Thus Joshua plays a significant prophetic role here at the end of the book by making a covenant in written form to ensure the people keep their words and follow them in letter and spirit.

When people seem to be wavering in their commitment, leaders can be tempted to minimize the task at hand or mislead people into thinking things will be easier than they actually are. Perhaps there are times when this technique can gain compliance for a while. But as Ronald Heifetz argues in *Leadership Without Easy Answers*, misleading followers rapidly diminishes a leader's authority. This is not only because followers eventually discover the deception, but because it prevents them from contributing to solving the group's challenges. Unless the leader knows the solution to every

---

1 All Scriptural quotations used in this book are taken or adapted from New Revised Standard Version unless otherwise quoted from another version/s.

challenge—an extremely unlikely possibility—solutions will have to come from the creativity and commitment of group members. But if the leader has misled the people about the nature of the challenges, the people cannot contribute to finding a solution. This all but guarantees that the leader will fail. Instead, leaders who are honest with their followers about the difficulty of the challenges have an opportunity to involve their people in creating solutions. Joshua, through his relationship with God, provides an excellent model for leaders seeking to build commitment toward a difficult course of action through honesty and transparency rather than secrecy and false hope.

***Prophetic figures in the books of Judges and Samuel:*** The books of Judges and Samuel mentions few important prophetic figures while they still act and perform their administrative role as judges. Apart from this few collective activities of sons of prophets are also noted during and after the time of judges in ancient Israel. The book of Samuel also describes the activity of prophet Nathan in a brief record of his appearance in different intervals during the time of Kings David and Solomon. We shall now discuss the significant contribution of each of them as appeared in the biblical books. We shall include our discussion on the prophet Nathan in the next chapter at an appropriate place.

***A) Deborah:*** The prophetess and judge (Judges chapters 4-5), who belonged to the tribe of Issachar (Judg 5:15) and directed the affairs of tribes from a spot between Ramah and Bethel, later known as *Tomer Deborah*, i.e., the Palm tree of Deborah. Deborah successfully mobilized the Israelite militia, whose deeds are variously recalled, evaluated and celebrated in the book of Judges. The activity of Deborah wife of Lappidoth ('flashes') is admiringly recounted in prose (Judges chp. 4) and celebrated in song (Judges chp. 5). Introduced as Prophetess, Deborah was available for oracular consultation at "Deborah's Palm." This was a time of severe oppression sponsored by Jabin, King of Canaan reigning at Hazor, and executed by Sisera, commander of 900 chariots.

Consulted by Israelites in the face of Sisera's aggression, Deborah's "Judgement" is to summon Barak, field commander of Israelite militia from Kadesh in Naphtali, together with forces from Zebulun and Naphtali.

The song of Deborah and Barak (Judg 5:21-31) is much older than the received from of the prose account, to Judge form the evidence of archaic language and poetic structure. Here the main concern is at the time of the problem, the ten tribes had a league. Ephraim, Benjamin, Machir (Manasseh), Zebulun, Issachar and Naphtali; or they are admonished for their non-participation Reuben, Gilead (i.e, Gad). Dan and Asher. This victory song is in many ways comparable to victory hymns of Egyptian and Assyrian kings. It celebrates both process of Yahweh's peasantry and the reciprocal intervention by Yahweh, when "the start in their courses fought against Sisera." The concluding irony contrasts Deborah, "a mother in Israel" who rose up, with Sisera's anxious mother and the wisest of her ladies (Judg 5:28-30), both of whom are confident that the victory celebration had delayed the return of the troops.

Thus Deborah combined three functions in her service to the Israelites, legal and military functions as well as the prophetic role. Thus she was key person in a strategic battle mentioned above for control of central and northern Palestine. Deborah had demonstrated her prophetic vision by guiding Israelite army at a critical juncture and saved the nation from the onslaught of the power and might of the Canaanite army. Deborah's motherly care helped to united many tribes of Israel to make a joint and united effort to fight against the enemy which was a great need of the time of Canaanite domination and oppression. What is most significant in Deborah is that at a time when hardly a woman played any role in the national affairs of Israelites, Deborah as a woman, through her wise and courageous advises.

***Prophecy Israel:*** Samuel was the last of the judges of Israel, and the guiding light in the establishment of kingship, he served Israel in the crucial period of Israel's history when the external pressures brought upon Israel by the Philistines called for far-reaching social and political changes.

The childhood of Samuel has a background in his mother Hannah, who shows piety and family loyalty to God which indicates a positive side at this time of trouble. Even though there are other sanctuaries, there seems to be a central shrine at Shiloh from the time of the settlement until the destruction of the Philistines in Samuel's day. Hannah's pledge before God seems to indicate that she would consecrate her son as a Nazirite, although she mentions only the most obvious prohibition "no razor shall touch this head." This view is particularly appropriate for Samuel who stood firmly for Israel's ancient standards, which were solely tested by compromise and indifference.

***The Name Prophet Samuel Means:*** "El is his name", "name of El", or "Name of God", Hannah's explanation (I Sam. 1:20) is a popular etymology. Perhaps she connected Samuel with the phrase: "asked of God" (*shaal el*) because of the similar sound. At the age of three Hannah brought Samuel to Eli and dedicated him to the service of the Lord with what was probably a thank offering (Lev. 7:11).

Eli's wicked sons (1 Sam. 2:12-36), are the symbolic of the toll Canaanite corruption had taken on Israel's values were Phinehas and Hophni. They were involved in fornication with the women attendants at the shrines, which brought a shocking report to Eli (I Sam. 2:22-25). The doom of these wicked sons was announced to the old priest by a nameless prophet called "a man of god" (I Sam 2:27-28), perhaps a member of one of the bands of itinerant prophets active during this period (1 Sam. 10:5 m, only the gist of his message is given.

The prophetic influence discernible in the life of Samuel is seen in various parts of. I Sam. chapter 3:1-21, especially in the emphasis of the word of the lord (vv. 1,7, and 19-21). Samuel was dedicated to priestly service by his mother, in accordance with Israel's ancient custom of consecrating the firstborn to the Lord in commemoration of the preservation of the first born during the final plague in Egypt (Exod. 13:2,15). Perhaps because of the impracticality of this practice, the Mosaic legislation substituted the tribe of Levi for the first born of all the tribes (cf. Numb 3:11 ff), Hannah, however, felt her obligation to God so keenly that she conformed to the tradition literally.

I Sam. chapter 3 explains the expansion of Samuel's ministry from mere priestly apprenticeship to full prophetic office. The first oracle he uttered (1 Sam. 3:11-14) was a renunciation of the house of the Eli, whose sons had corrupted the cult of Yahweh (cf: I Sam. 2:12-17). This marked the beginning of Samuel's career as a prophet (cf: I Sam. 3:19-4:l). The story of the voice which Samuel mistook for Eli's shows that Samuel had a direct call from God to be a prophet. H. H. Rowley has stressed the importance of this sense of vocation: "It is clearly held that what made him a genuine prophet was not parental dedication, but the fact that when he was still a child the Word of God came to him by divine initiative" (*The Servant of the Lord*, (pp. 112f). This experience, which ushered in a new era of prophetic activity, must be compared with Moses' burning bush or the visions of Isaiah, Jeremiah, and Ezekiel, Samuel heard the voice of God, he was never the same afterwards, and Israel knew it (1 Sam. 3:20).

Samuel functioned as such a prophet when he authorized Saul to attack Amalek (1 Sam. 15:1-13); but he sharply rebuked the King for sparing the Amalekite King Agag and the best of his livestock in violation of the laws (I Sam. 15:13-23). As a result of his disobedience, Samuel announced that Yahweh had rejected Saul as King (vv. 23,26) When Saul tore Samuel's robe he was trying to leave, the prophet informed him that Yahweh had torn the Kingdom of Israel from Saul and given it to a "neighbour of yours, who is better than you." (vv. 27f, cf. 28:17).

Later biblical tradition highlights Samuel's role as intercessor (Jer 15:1, Psa 99:6) and associates him with David in the establishment of the office of gate keepers (I Chr. 9:22). The New Testament often refers Samuel as the first prophet (Acts 3:24, 13:20), and his prophetic career is summarized in the apocryphal book of Sirach (46:13-20).

The biblical narrative presents Samuel as the last of the heroes of the Pre-monarchial age and the first of the prophets who stand alongside the

Kings. Samuel is presented as the ideal prophetic leader, in whom all types of authority: military, judicial, and sacerdotal are combined.

***B) Early Prophetic Guilds:*** During the time of Samuel, in the eleventh century, BCE, a new institution arose in Israel in connection with her Spiritual and religious life (I Sam. 10-5-13). Samuel indicated few words after he anointed Saul in I Sam. 10:5. This is the first mention of such; group of prophets in the Old Testament. The band of prophets could be Nazirites and Rechabites. R.B.Y. Scott considers them as forerunners of the prophets. However, these people have no affinity with the prophetic tradition, but they maintained a constant protest against religion and culture of Canaan, II Kings 10:1-28. The Rechabites and Nazirites. They made significant contribution during the early stages of prophetic activity in ancient Israel. Their involvement can be summarized in the following manner: First, these early prophetic guilds lived and moved in the entire country in groups rather than as individuals. Second: they prophesied together on many concerns of the nation at that time. Third: they dwelt in sanctuaries and shrines in groups and while uttering their prophetic words and These prophetic guilds lived at a time when the nationalism was undermined in the context of growing domination of Canaanite religion. These prophetic guilds were critical about the people and the nation when their moral and ethical values were at the lowest level. The guilds wanted to encourage everyone in the nation to be the true follower of Yahwism. It is the highly patriotic commitment of the prophetic guilds that sustained the nation from further deterioration of moral and ethical principles before the emergence of prophets. These guilds of prophets instilled a sense of strong nationalism among the entire population. Therefore, these prophetic guilds may be rightly called as the forerunners of the actual prophets working from the tenth century BCE in ancient Israel. They abstained from wine and continued to live in tents as nomads even after Israel had settled in houses and cities in Canaan. They protested against corrupt influences of Canaanite civilization. Prophet Jeremiah commended these people for their principles (Jer 35:10).

According to Numbers 6, the Nazirites were also members of an ancient institution. The Nazirite was an individual who had taken special religious vows. Even prophet Amos would seem to link the Nazirites with the old prophets (Amos 2:11-12). However, according to Amos, the Nazirites would have existed side by side with prophetic tradition.

There is no indication in scripture prior to I Sam. 10 as to when the organized bands or so called "schools of prophets" originated. Since it was, however, the custom of great prophets to gather disciples around them, the "schools of the prophets" may have been originated in this way, as disciples of the prophet Samuel. This way of gathering the disciples around them was also practiced by the prophets Elijah and Elisha (1 Kings 2-6).

Julius Wellhausen and his school is of the opinion that prior to Samuel's time, there was a host of prophets in Israel, and Samuel simply organized them and made himself their head. In I Sam. 19:18-20, Samuel was pictured as "standing as head over them" at Ramah and Gibeah (1 Sam. 10:5,10). After this, this sort of group, is not mentioned in Samuel's time. But they appear quite suddenly during the time of Elijah and Elisha and for the first time they are designated as "sons of prophets" (1 Kings 20:35). According to 2 Kings 4:38, 42-43, approximately one hundred sons of prophets sat before Elisha at Gilgal and ate their meal together (cf: 2 Kings 2:7, 16-17; 6:1-2).

These nabis interceded for the people during some religious ceremony: they come down from some sacred hill, for example in Ramah, which was valued as a sanctuary in the days of Prophet Samuel (1 Sam. 10:19). There are supposed to have been 400 prophets (and at another time even 450) at the North Israelite court, and they appeared together in order to prophesy for public religious ceremonies (I Kings chaps 18-22). Probably they also practiced meditation and trained in ecstasy and inspiration. In fact, the meaning of the term "sons of prophets" (*bene-ha-nebi'im*) means, not the children, but the pupils or disciples of the prophets.

Sons of prophets arose as a result of political conditions of the day and that their chief purpose was patriotic. They were bands of religious devotees moving throughout Palestine awakening the patriotism of the people.

Three-fold function and character of these sons of prophets is evident: (i) they are residing together in common dwellings of religious centers like Gilgal, Bethel and Jericho: (ii) They were prophesying together (I Sam. 10:5 ff; I Chr 25:l-3); (iii) They also acted as spiritual messengers in important matters pertaining to Israel (1 Kings 20:35-43).

What was the divine purpose for the rise of these bands of Prophets? The actual situation in which these prophetic bodies arose is clearly indicated in the historical narrative. The early zeal for Yahwistic faith, particularly during the time of conquest of Canaan had waned. During the time of Elijah, Baalism became a serious threat to Israel's very existence as a theocentric nation under the sole authority of Yahweh. Thus, these sons of prophets were raised up by God in this period of spiritual crisis to stem the tide of religious and moral declension and to call the nation to repentance.

Prophetic figures in other books and centuries of the Old Testament: An overview: In this section we shall briefly make few comments on the overall prophetic phenomena and prophetic figures in ancient Israel. Few general remarks are in order: first, as we will see below, through centuries the prophetic activity took various forms and shapes and prophets served in general as champions of justice in order to set right the social and religious as well as political degradation. Second, when all institutions of election, covenant, temple seem to have failed prophets reminded the community about their gross failure to recognize and accept Yahweh's sovereignty and authority in their lives and thus they alone are responsible for their present predicament. Third, at the same time the prophets preached a lasting message of hope in the midst of hopelessness so that the people of Israel would continue to impact other communities in the entire world. All the prophets by and large adhere to the message of judgment and salvation that God would bring to God's people as appropriate which is directly proportional to their deeds.

***Concluding Remarks:*** On the basis of what has been discussed in this chapter the following concluding observations can be made: first, the prophetic phenomena in ancient Israel in the early stages prior to the well-established centuries of prophetic activity was rather sporadic and mixed with other offices like priestly and judges. This was necessitated as leaders emerged through charismatic activity. Second, Moses as an exceptional leader of ancient Israel had an exceptional quality of a prophet and intercessor. Moses, in fact, serves as an exemplary prophetic model and a forerunner of a great leadership. Third, prophets and prophetess Samuel and Deborah served at a critical juncture to steer the nation from further degenerating religious apostasy. Fourth, the sons of the prophets as a whole worked together to lay foundation towards a strong as against the Canaanite religious influences. Fifth, the early prophetic activity reveals how the prophetic figures in their limited way laid strong foundations for the more intense and rigorous prophetic activity in the coming centuries. In the chapters that follow we will look for more details on the prophetic phenomena and prophetic figures and many more prophets discussed in this chapter.

Chapter 2

# Pre-Monarchic and Monarchic Prophets and their Ministry

***Introduction:*** Pre-monarchic prophets can be seen as the prophets who laid a strong foundation for the long years of prophetic activity prevailed in ancient Israelite society. In fact, these years of prophetic activity may be rightly seen as formative years of prophecy for the future hears to come. As was discussed in the introductory chapter we had a brief discussion on prophetic personalities like: Moses, Samuel, Deborah and sons of the prophets (prophetic guild) who made tremendous impact and also pioneered the prophetic activity in ancient Israel that has a long lasting impact for several centuries to follow. We will not repeat what has already been discussed in the introductory chapter concerning the pre-monarchic prophets, but we shall briefly mention about prophet Samuel who worked during the transition between pre and monarchic times in ancient Israel.

## 1) United Monarchy (Samuel and Nathan)

We have already discussed on the ministry of Samuel who also come under pre-monarchic period. We noted that Samuel was a guiding light in establishing the monarchy. He was entrusted by God to choose a king for Israel and he chose and anointed Saul as a King of Israel. In the same vein Samuel also replaced Saul by anointing David as King. As noted above Samuel ruled Israel as a judge and guided in their affairs of the kingdom as a prophet. Perhaps Samuel was the last among the judges ruled Israel before the monarchy was established. In this section we shall, at the outset, make few remarks concerning the nature and character of the prophecy during this time, then we shall move on to discuss on prophet Nathan.

Under the united monarchy in Israel and Judah we find, nevertheless, a type of court prophecy similar in some respects to that of the Mari (in Mari: the content of the Mari prophecy is delivered to the king. Most of them have to do with military affairs, warnings about revolt and the possibility of assassination, injunctions against undertaking certain expeditions or entering into certain alliances: this was done by an ecstatic *muhhum* fem *muhhutum* or oracle given otherwise also called as: *apilum,* fem *appiltum,* employed in a temple especially the Dagon, chief God of the area, in the city of Terqa near Mari.

In some instances, the warning is about fortifying a gate or not rebuilding a house are accompanied by threats of unpleasant consequences.

The God of Aleppo, where Zimrilim, had taken refuge before returning to re-establish his father's kingdom in Mari, gave him a dynastic oracle not unlike that of Nathan to David (2 Sam.7).

"Am I not Adad lord of Kallassu who reared him between my thighs and restored him to the throne of his father's house? After restoring him to the throne of his father's house, I again gave him a dwelling place. Now, since I restored him to the throne of his father's house, I should receive from him an hereditary property (for a temple)."[2]

Wishing to build a temple to Yahweh in Jerusalem, David consulted with Nathan, his court seer, who at first gave a favorable reply but then, after a night vision forbade him to do so (2 Sam. 7:4-17). In keeping with a conservative aversion to Canaanite cult places, the original form of this oracle opposed the building of a temple without qualification. All these points indirectly are found in the case of Mari court prophecy, i.e., prophets played a significant role in the Kings court, to determine the proceedings of the court, etc.

Samuel, Nathan and Ahijah were the prophets who arose at the time of what was in the Deuteronomic view the triple constellation of Saul, David and Solomon. These prophets did not merely help to put their respective rulers on the throne, but also threatened them later with the end of their government. Nathan's speech, attacking David indirectly prompted Absalom's insurrection, that, at least, is the way the books of Samuel see things.

***Nathan:*** A prophet of David's time who figured prominently in events at three critical junctures in David's life:(i) he delivered the dynastic promise to David (ii) he confronted David about his sin involving Bathsheba and

---

2 Antti Laato, "Second Samuel 7 and Ancient Near Eastern Royal Ideology." *The Catholic Biblical Quarterly*, 59: 2, (1997), pp. 244–269. *JSTOR*, www.jstor.org/stable/43722940. Accessed 1 June 2021.

Uriah; (iii) and he intervened on Solomon's behalf in the struggle for succession to David's throne.

Nathan first appears with no introduction, and no pedigree, in the crucial and much discussed 2 Sam. 7 (parallel passage in 1 Chr. 17) in which he delivers to David the important promise of a perpetual dynasty. Nathan delivers the message to David using the classical prophetic formula ("Thus says Yahweh": 2 Sam. 7: vv 5,8,17).

Nathan's greatest moments came in his confrontation with David after David's two great sins (2 Sam. 12). Here, he boldly and courageously confronted the King of gross sin involving Bathsheba and Uriah.

Nathan next appears as Bathsheba's and Solomon's ally in the struggle for succession to David's throne. He helps Bathsheba to plan for a strategy for having Solomon installed on the throne of David (1 Kings 1:11-14).

Nathan appears in these three instances as a court prophet with a free access to the king, yet as the one who spoke with the authority and boldness of the classical prophets of 8th century BCE. He appears also as a historian "in the Chronicles of Nathan" as mentioned in 1 Chr. 29:29; 2 Chr. 9:29. His prophetic activity and authority appears again later, when Hezekiah installed Levites with musical instruments in the temple, according to Yahweh's command, "David and Gad the King's seer and Nathan the Prophet" (II Chr. 29:25), also was likely the Nathan of I Kings 4:5.

In all his short and brief appearances, Nathan was portrayed as a bold and courageous prophet from the court of King David is in no way less important to any other classical prophets appeared in the following centuries. More important about Nathan was that being a sponsored court prophet was a fearless and with a great vision worked at critical junctures in the united monarchy of the ancient Israelite kingdom.

### *Prophecy in the Ninth Century (Ahijah, Elijah, Elisha and Micaiah ben Imlah)*

In the previous section we have discussed on the prophecy that was in general characterised in the prophecy of monarchical times, especially in the time of united monarchy. We have also noted that much of it is like a court prophecy as also found in the case of Mari or elsewhere in the ancient West Asia. While in the case of Nathan, the relationship between the king and prophet was more of cordial in nature, there are other prophets like Elijah, Micaiah who had a different personality during 9$^{th}$ century BCE who rather confronted the kings and the result was disastrous even to risk their life. We shall attempt in this section to look into such prophets like: Ahijah, Elijah, Elisha and Micaiah ben Imlah, prior to that consideration we shall briefly trace the political and social background of 9th century BCE that prompted the developments of prophecy during this century.

During two centuries from the death of Solomon (925 BCE) to the fall of Samaria (722 BCE) references in the history to the prophets and prophecy are restricted entirely to the Northern Kingdom. The dictum was: if you ignore your prophets as they did theirs, the same will happen to you (2 Kings 17:7-18). It should be noted, however, that the idea of charismatic leadership, which remained strong in the territory of Northern Kingdom, acted as a counter force to hereditary kingship. This left more room for the involvement of prophets in public affairs, and we shall find them playing an important role in the making and unmaking of rulers, especially in the half century preceding the establishment of the Omrid dynasty.

After the death of Solomon, his son Rehoboam duly betook himself to Shechem, the ancient shrine of the Joseph tribes, to seek renewal of the agreement with the elders of Israel. This time, however, the tribal leaders were no longer content to go through with a purely formal ratification but laid down conditions which Rehoboam unwisely rejected out of hand (1 Kings 12:1-15). The outcome was the accession of Jeroboam, one of Solomon's officials, as ruler of a separate kingdom to the north. The revolt against Solomon was, in effect, a reaffirmation of the traditional pattern of tribal separation as against the innovation of hereditary and dynast kingship. The result was that, Judah lasted for three centuries, North witnessed rapid rise and full of petty dynasts, with army playing dominant role. In this situation the old war prophecy continued to flourish while in Judah it was, in effect, demilitarization and forced to take different directions. Prophecy has a very less role in Judah during ninth century BCE.

***A) Ahijah:*** in describing the rise to power of the Ephraimite Jeroboam, son of Nebat, the historian assigned a role of the greatest importance to a Shiloh prophet named Ahijah, who, following the example of Samuel, a designated Jeroboam, king of the ten tribes (1 Kings 11:29-39). After enjoying prophetic support, possibly also from Judah (1 Kings 12:22-24), he was condemned by Ahijah, who also predicted the death of his son who was sick (1 Kings 14:l-16).

Ahijah, the prophet from Shiloh (1 Kings 11:9) supported Jeroboam's abortive coup against Solomon. He played a crucial role in the Deuteronomistic Historian's portrayal of the split between the southern and northern kingdoms during the reign of Rehoboam. Ahijah meets Jeroboam, Solomon's overseer over compulsory labour, outside Jerusalem and through symbolic action and prophetic utterance provides the theological justification for the division of the kingdom after Solomon's death. The rending of Ahijah's cloak into 12 pieces and the giving of 10 to Jeroboam is reminiscent of Samuel's rejection of Saul in 1 Sam. 15 (however, LXX differs in details than MT including the claim that this action was carried out by Shemiah and not Ahijah). It was made clear that, although the socioeconomic reasons for the division stem from the oppression of the Davidic monarchy brought to a head by the policies of Rehoboam (1 Kings 12), the theological justification offered in the apostasy of Solomon. Ahijah promises Jeroboam a "sure house" (1 Kings 11:38), echoing the dynastic promise of David in 2 Sam. 7. The final break brought about by the heavy tax levied by Rehoboam was presented in typical Deuteronomistic terms as the fulfilment of the prophecy of Ahijah (1 Kings 12:15).

Later when Jeroboam sent his wife to the prophet to enquire of his son Abijah's survival of his childhood sickness (1 Kings 14:1-18), the prophecy delivered by Ahijah was the fulcrum for deuteronomistic rejection of all northern kings. Jeroboam was rejected for his apostasy, particularly the setting up of the rival northern shrines at Bethel and Dan. The dynastic promise, which was couched in conditional terms in 1 Kings 11:38,39 was withdrawn. The fulfilment of the prophecy of Ahijah was fulfilled in the death of the child, and in slaughter of the house of Jeroboam by Baasha (1 Kings 15:29). Ahijah represents sign of the Deuteronomistic prophet whose words are fulfilled as he prophesied (see also Deut. 18). According to M. A. Cohen, Ahijah represents a Shilonite priestly faction who supported Jeroboam's struggle with Rehoboam. This faction was thought to represent the pre-monarchic religious specialists, identified with Abiathar, who had become increasingly marginalised by the centralizing policies of Solomon.[3] According to Martin Noth, although Ahijah was in favour of political break with south, he was not in favour of a break with Jerusalem cult.[4] According to Robert Wilson,[5] Ahijah was a typical peripheral: prophet from Ephraim: he represents the view of group outside of and opposed to the royal establishment. His support group was presumably drawn from Ephraimites and probably from the old Shilonite priesthood ousted by Solomon. Ahijah challenged royal establishment in an attempt to redress the balance in this struggle for power.

***B) Elijah:*** He was a prophet in north Israel during 9th century BCE. The stories of Elijah, the prophet are found in 1 Kings 17-19, 21 and 2 Kings 12. Their most frequent theme is the conflict between Elijah and the royal house of Israel over syncretistic worship. The prophets' ministry is set in Israel during the Omrid dynasty (9th Cent. BCE), a period marked by relative

---

3 Martin A. Cohen, "The Role of the Shilonite Priesthood in the United Monarchy of Ancient Israel," *Hebrew Union College Annual* 36 (1965), pp. 59-98.

4 Martin Noth, *The Deuteronomistic History*, JSOT sup. 15 (Sheffield: The University of Sheffield, 1981).

5 Robert Wilson, *Prophecy and Society in Ancient Israel* (Philadelphia: Fortress Press, 1980), pp. 184-87.

peace and prosperity in the northern kingdom of Israel. Elijah was presented as the powerful champion of Yahweh against the royally-patronized worship of Baal portrayed with characteristics drawn from throughout Israel's prophetic tradition.

According to 1 Kings 17:1, Elijah not only come from a remote area of Gilead, east of Jordon, but also belonged to the class of small tenant farmers (toshab) who owned no land of their own. He shows how people of lowly origin could, through their prophetic activity come to play a decisive role for the whole of society. Perhaps we may assume that as a man of God, Elijah-like the slightly younger Elisha--was at the same time the recognized master of a guild of nabis (see also Numb. 12, 1 Sam. 19:1ff).

The main context in which Elijah's ministry begins is by putting down to the first persecution of Yahwistic nabis in Israel by notorious Jezebel, a Phoenician princess who, with missionary zeal, spread the cult of Baal of Tyre (the God of her native country) and whose efforts met with great success in the country. At that time Tyre was enjoying an economic heyday; its merchants dominated the shipping trade in the Mediterranean. Phoenician colonization spread as far as Spain. The deity who was at work in all this could be no minor God! At the royal court of Samaria people, no doubt put the Tyrian Baal on the same level as Yahweh and therefore simply used the title of dignity, 'Lord and Master' (*ba'a*l), and not the proper name (Melkart) under which the god was worshipped in Tyre.[6]

But Elijah expressed the conscience of the old Yahwistic religion on Israel's soil there can only be one worship that is worship of Yahweh. Every alien god who exerts his influence from outside makes people and country taboo (Heb. Word: *'akar*: 1 Kings 18:17) and destroys the healthy condition of its life both the religious as well as societal.

The struggle between Yahwism and Baalism supplies dramatic unity to the events recounted in 1 Kings 17-19 chapters. Elijah speaks a word of power to withhold rainfall and thus posing a direct challenge to Baal's claim of authority, over storms and fertility. The result was drought, but Ahab thinks it as Baal's displeasure that Elijah's "blasphemy" has gone unpunished (1 Kings 18:17-18). When prophets of Baal defeated by Yahwism, Jezebel threatens to avenge the murder of her favorites, and Elijah escapes to Southern desert, where he undertakes a pilgrimage to Horeb to complain of the failure of Yahwism in Israel.

The act of Elijah on Mount Carmel even though looks cruel and violent, it was necessary undertaking at that time. If Elijah had not been victorious, he would have been killed. (1 Kings 18:19-46). Moreover, Elijah

6 For more details, see Klaus Koch, *The Prophets: Vol 1: The Assyrian Period* (Philadelphia: Fortress Press, 1983).

had maintained that the country was being defiled by cults and that its vital power was being sapped. Because the deity declares that Elijah is right. It is essential that the religious pollution should be eradicated by means of some impressive act.

Elijah's stories also show that the prophet engaged in disputes, not merely about cultic sites and rites as in 1 Kings 18:19-46 and in 2 Kings 1 but also about the right of the individual Israelite to the land which is his ancestral heritage (1 Kings chp. 21, the story of Naboth's vineyard) The central focus of 1 Kings 21 is the juridical murder of Naboth and the royal confiscation of his land (cf: 1 Kings 21:26). Elijah confronts the king for his social injustice. The prophets' role in this chapter in particular seems to have been modelled to some extent on that later classical prophets.

The motif of the "word" in chp. 17 of 1 Kings reveals a well-developed theology of prophetism. The prophet is the one who speaks an authoritative word of power (17:11), obeys Yahweh's word (vv. 5,10), commands human obedience and conveys divine promise (vv. 13, 15, 16), speaks a word of miraculous intercession that Yahweh heeds (v. 22), and is ultimately acknowledged as chosen bearer of Yahweh's own word (v. 24).

It is no exaggeration to say whenever Elijah appears, there is an eruption like the outbreak of a volcano. No other prophet of the early period of the monarchy approaches him in effectiveness, or in his readiness for complete involvement in Yahweh's cause.

***C) Elisha:*** According to the description of the biblical story Elisha was a prophet and a wonder-worker of the Kingdom of Israel who was active during the reign of Joram, Jehu, Jehoahaz, and Jehoash (Joash). Elisha was the son of Shaphat, a wealthy land-owner of Abel-meholah; he became the attendant and disciple of Elijah. He was a follower and the designated successor of Elijah (1 Kings 19:16-21: 2 Kings: 2).

The extensive narratives which preserved numerous stories about the prophet Elisha can be found in the Deuteronomistic Historian. (1 Kings 19; 19-21, 2 Kings 2-13). This narrative complex is constructed from a number of legends or miracle stories which have been classified and analyzed. The general conclusion is that many of these stories achieved their form prior to their inclusion in the Deuteronomistic History. It is conjectured that extensive hagiographical material about Elisha was collected and preserved by the prophetic groups closely associated with him in 2 Kings, this material about Elisha establish the fact that he was the prophet of Yahweh: his authority is confirmed by his ability to part the waters of the Jordan (2 Kings 2:19-22), and to fatally curse the children that taunted him (2 Kings 2:23-25). These prophetic acts repeated throughout the narrative complex: he helped the widow of one of the prophetic guilds to pay her debts (2 Kings

4:1-7). Other acts recorded are in the following passages: 2 Kings 4:8-37, 4:38-41, 42-44:2 Kings 5:1-19, 20-27: 6:1-7, 8-23:2 Kings 13:20-21.

It is difficult on the basis of these stories to identify, with any certainty, historical information about Elisha. However, based on the recent analyses of the social roles of Israelite prophets reveals that despite Deuteronomic editing these narratives preserve important information about the activities of Ephraimite northern prophets. It is argued that these stories were originally collected and preserved by northern prophetic groups closely associated with Elijah and Elisha. Elisha was a son and acted as a leader of a prophetic guild, "the son of the prophets." Elisha was frequently addressed as *'is' e l - o h i m,* "man of God," in addition to nabi," perhaps the other title is a designation for a holy man as depicted in legends. However, both terms appear to be synonymous. According to Robert Wilson, Elisha was considered as a peripheral prophet. His support group "the sons of the prophets" was also composed of peripheral prophets removed from the religiously, economically, and politically dominant groups at the centre of society. They may have a minimal support in Ephraimite society (2 Kings 4:8-17, 42-44).[7]

Elisha was depicted as constantly in conflict with the Omride dynasty, and it culminated in his central role in legitimizing the rebellion of Jehu (2 Kings. 9:1-10), who massacred Ahab and the remaining Omrides in a palace coup. Robert Wilson feels that Elisha's role as peripheral to central prophet changed, after Jehu's assumption of power, now Elisha became more closely associated with the royal court, particularly in the military sphere (2 Kings 6:8-7:20; 13:14-19).[8]

***D) Micaiah ben Imlah:*** He was an Israelite prophet who appears in the narrative describing oracular inquiries made by the kings of Israel and Judah (1 Kings 22:4-28: 2 Chronicles: 18:3-27). Ahab suggests an alliance with Jehoshaphat to go and war against Ramoth Gilead. While Jehoshaphat agrees insists Ahab first to seek oracular guidance from the prophets of the Lord (v. 5) Gathering about 400 prophets, Ahab inquires whether or not to engage the Syrians in battle (v. 6), their advice is unanimous-the Lord will deliver Syria into their hands. Jehoshaphat, however, asks if there are any other prophets Ahab can consult (v. 7), Ahab admits there is one prophet left-Micaiah-but grudgingly insists Micaiah never prophesies anything good where Ahab is concerned (v. 8). At Jehoshaphat's insistence, Ahab sends for Micaiah (v. 9). While Micaiah is being summoned, Zedekiah, son of Chennanah, appears before the kings. By symbolic action and oracle,

7 Robert Wilson, *Prophecy and Society in Ancient Israel* (Philadelphia: Fortress Press, 1980), pp. 184-87.

8 Ibid.

Zedekiah predicts Syria's defeat (vv. 11-12). On the whole 1 Kings chp. 22 is more like prophetic activity through symbolic acts, acted signs (cf. Isa 20:3) or prophetic drama; Zedekiah, son of Channanah, who had made for himself iron horns, symbols of strength and aggression (Ps. 18:2, Deut. 3:17). It is something like a sympathetic magic, but no such phenomena are found in biblical narratives.

Micaiah's answer has two parts: First, illustrates a second technique by which the prophet with "second sight," 'sees' in an everyday object or scene, some hidden reality relevant to the occasion. Here Micaiah sees a flock of sheep scattered on a hillside without a shepherd, and this picture of leaderless valor necessarily tells him that Israel will certainly be defeated if they go to war with Syria, they have no leader, a directed and pointed insult to the kings in his audience. Second, Micaiah's second answer is even more explicit. This time he recounts a visionary experience of a kind. His glimpses into the workings of the heavenly court ('I saw the Lord sitting in his throne' 22:19) not only authenticate his prophetic word to Israel, but also reveals to him (and to us) the complexity and diversity of the prophetic process. The Lord controls all the spirits that possess human beings, good and evil. False prophets, like Zedekiah, are possessed by lying spirits, sent by God to trick people, leading them, as in the case of Ahab, to their death. This narrative is certainly the product of later speculation on the phenomenon of prophecy, in line with the Deuteronomic theology and legislation on pagan divination and wizarding.

Micaiah's prophetic activity in 1 Kings 22 reveals how a prophet convinced of his vision received from Yahweh cannot surrender or compromise to the occasion to please those in power and authority. The prophetic judgment pronounced by Micaiah even risked his life to his imprisonment and death. Micaiah demonstrates the guts and courage a prophet of God can express as against the court or traditional prophets compromising their prophetic voice for the sake of their survival.

***To Make Few Concluding Remarks on the Ninth Century Prophecy:*** first, it was limited to the activity of prophets in the northern kingdom, mostly related to the Omrid dynasty. Second, prophets of ninth century went more on confrontation mode with those in administration and power, even risking their lives to the point of death. Third, due to the intense involvement of the prophets in the ninth century Israel, drastic religious and political changes took place which will have long lasting impact in the centuries that follow. Fourth, ninth century prophets, even though are popular due to their prophetic activity, are still considered as peripheral or marginal prophets since their works are not a collection of literary compositions and they are mostly considered as anti-establishment prophets.

***Conclusion:*** Based on our discussion of the ancient Hebrew prophets from the pre-monarchic and monarchic times, major prophetic activity took place in ancient Israel. We now make the following concluding observations: First, the prophetic activity during the pre-monarchic times started in a low key but has become intense. Initially it was limited to small circles gradually spread as a main activity among the nation and its ruling quarters. Second, when we moved from pre-monarchic to ninth century BCE the prophetic activity was more focused in the Northern Kingdom of Israel. These prophets either established or supported the new kingdoms and their prophetic oracles are very sharp and pointed towards the royal establishment.

Chapter 3

# Prophecy in the Eighth Century BCE (Amos, Hosea, Isaiah of Jerusalem & Micah)

***Introduction:*** During eighth century BCE the prophecy and prophets played a vital role in the life of Israel. This period was important than 9th century because we have what may be termed as 'literary sources/evidence' for the prophetic writing from now onwards. Moreover, the neighboring countries of Israel like Assyrian annals do furnish some details fairly well concerning this period. Before we talk about individual prophets of this century, let us briefly look into the eighth century condition (economic, political and historical) as seen in the background information in the ministry of prophet Amos.

After the military successes in the early part of Jeroboam II's reign, Israel experienced a period of economic prosperity which was assumed in many of Amos' and his contemporary prophets' oracles. Commerce became extremely active (Amos 8:5a), and trade was practiced on an international scale (Amos 3:9). Deceitful business practices increased profits (8:5b). Building activity flourished (3:15). Houses became more numerous and more substantial than ever before in Israel (Amos 3:15b; 5:11; 6:8), and they were elaborately furnished (Amos 3:10,12b,15b:6:4a). Viniculture and cattle raising became geared to demanding customers (Amos 5:11b; 6:4b) since the thirst for pleasure manifest in rollicking feasts had to be accommodated (Amos 4:1; 6:4,6). New music was composed (Amos 6:5). Sexual immorality increased (Amos 2:7b). The cults directly reflected in the economic boom; sacrificial offerings proliferated (Amos 4:24-25; 5:21-22); the feasts were celebrated with ebullient singing and instrumental music (Amos 5:23).

The converse (opposite) of this development was social upheaval. The rich became richer while the poor became poorer. Such early capitalism quickly led to expropriation of the holdings of the smaller landowners. The ancient Israelite land rights were superseded by Canaanite practice. Slavery for debt took on vicious forms (Amos 2:6:8:6). The socially underprivileged were exploited (Amos 2:7-9; 4:1; 8:4). Their rights were violated through intimidation of witnesses and bribery of judges (Amos 2:7a; 5:10, 12).

Jeroboam II (786-746 BCE) effectively exploited internal Assyrian weakness. He extended the borders of Israel ("from the entrance of Hamath to the Sea of Arabah 2 Kgs 14:25) engaged in significant military expansion of border forts and armories, and transformed the socioeconomic system.' Archaeological remains document the prosperity of the period. Excavations throughout north Israel show splendid and expansive buildings, buildings possessing costly imported goods." However, as noted above, this socioeconomic boom carried tragic consequences. If we accept the prophetic records as reliable witnesses to the period, we realize that the prosperity was not equally distributed. Rather, this period saw the rise of a wealthy merchant class, a class enriched at the expense of the poor! As one small sector of Israelites grew richer, a major sector became increasingly impoverished. Intriguingly, the death of Jeroboam II roughly coincides with the reemergence of Assyria.[9]

Thus in the shadow of world politics following the great foreign policy successes of Jeroboam II, luxury and injustice alike abundantly flourished; in the east, border incidents had once again begun to occur. The impending attack of Assyrian king Sennacherib in Judah is fast approaching was also a warning sign for Israel. With all its prosperity Israel had to face a great disaster by the Assyrian campaign. Quick political developments both internally and major resurgence of Assyrian power externally led to the destruction of Israel shortly from now.

After a brief surge forward in the 9th century, the Assyrians experienced a half century of decline during which the Syro-Palestinian states were able to pursue, their own policies unmolested. The dynasty founded by Jehu was therefore able to consolidate itself, reaching a high water mark of political successes and economic expansion under Jeroboam II (786-746). In Judah the same situation obtained during the long reign of Uzziah (786-742). The assassination of Jeroboam's son and successor Zechariah after less than a year's reign coincided with the accession of Tigllath-Pileser III and may not have been unconnected with it. Thereupon the dynasty came to an end and

9 Rick R. Marrs, "The World of Eighth Century Prophets," *Leaven (Pepperdine University)* 11:2 (2003), pp. 63-68. Can be accessed on: https://digitalcommons.pepperdine.edu/leaven/vol11/iss2/3.

there followed in the Northern Kingdom a period of chaos (745-722) during which five kings ascended the throne, of whom three were assassinated and another, the last, was deported by the Assyrians.

The accession of the usurper Tiglath-Pileser III ushered in a century of achievement that brought Assyria to the apogee of its power. The Assyrian success was built on a highly organized standing army. In warfare, they were technologically far ahead of anything seen previously, especially in the art of siege warfare. They were also the first we know of to use atrocities against civilian populations as a deliberate instrument of policy and in the event of rebellion, mass deportations. The "king of the world" as Tiglath-Pileser III modesty called himself, began to campaign in North Syria in 738 BCE, occupying Hamath and reducing Damascus and Israel to vassalage, other details concerning the influence of Assyrians on Judah and Israel will be considered later as and when we deal with individual prophets.

With all the complex national and international politics eighth century Israel saw a modest prophetic activity. During this century Israelite prophets picked up issues and concerns from both north and south. All issues related to religious, social and political matters were addressed by the prophets in order to offer their critique on behalf of God. The prophets of eighth century by and large communicated the message of doom although the message hope was also proclaimed by them along with sharp oracles concerning other nations.

***A) Amos:*** The first prophet whose sayings have been gathered together in a book of their own in Amos. When Amos was born and when he died, we do not know. How old he was at the time of his appearance around 760 BCE, all such details are hidden from us. He had been attentive to affairs faraway (1:3-8; 13:2:3; 3:9:6:2:9:7). His verdict concerning Israel was well founded and conclusive (2:6-9, 5:18-24; 7:11,16-17). His speech at times took on a sharpness and boldness which appears youthful (4:1; 5:5; 6:12).

It is likely that Amos stirred-up unrest among Israel in at least two localities, and perhaps three places of the northern kingdom, i.e., Samaria (3:9; 4:1; 6:1); Bethel (7:10-17) and Gilgal (5:5). Amos was not a native of northern kingdom but a Judean (7:12) come from Tekoa, which was situated at an altitude of 825 meters directly south of Jerusalem, approximately seventeen lineal kilometers from the city of Jerusalem. Further, Amos declined to be addressed as a professional prophet, since he made his living raising livestock and as a tender of mulberry (sycamore) trees. As a sheep breeder (and as such to be distinguished clearly from a lowly shepherd) he was probably not exactly poor. If a sheep breeding had not been enough to take him into town and oasis markets to sell animals and wool, then tending sycamores at least demanded a wide range of travel for that tree does not grow on the hills around Tekoa and the Mediterranean. Thus he became a farsighted, well informed Israelite. The instruction of ancient Israel, in the form of clan wisdom, had been taught to him by the clan elders in the gate, perhaps this wisdom had been preserved more zealously in Tekoa than elsewhere. Amos brought home from his travels a rich knowledge of events among the neighboring people (1:3-8; 1:13-2:3; 3:9; 6:2; 9:7). Thus Amos may have come to know the particular ills of the northern kingdom, evident especially in Samaria and Bethel.

It was the hand of Yahweh which uprooted him temporarily from his familiar realm and made him break the silence of the wise in evil times (5:13). To the priest Amaziah in Bethel Amos says that it was Yahweh's grasp and call alone which took him away from tending the flock (7:15). Amos does not proclaim judgement as a consequence of legal reasoning, based on the infraction of ancient divine decrees; rather, because he has been constrained by Yahweh to proclaim his judgment, Amos also exposes Israel's guilt as a reason for this judgment.

***The Time of Amos:*** When Amos came to the northern kingdom of Israel to prophecy, the king of Israel (north) was Jeroboam ben Joash (i.e., Jeroboam II). Since Jeroboam II reigned from 786-746 BCE, Amos' prophetic activity must be dated within these limits in the middle decades of the eighth century BCE. The title of the book in 1:1 indicates the reign of Uzziah died in 742 BCE; but because he had become a leper, his son Jotham had been regent since about 750 BCE. If the composers of superscription reckoned Jotham's assumption of regency as the end of Uzziah's reign, it was their opinion that Amos appeared in Israel before then, the title also specifies a precise year for Amos, 'two years before the earthquake. The earthquake may have occurred about 760 BCE, if this was so Amos was placed in the fourth decade of the eighth century BCE.

The record of Jeroboam II appears in 2 Kings 14:23-29. The account is typical of the Deuteronomistic Historian's treatment of Israel's kings in its single-minded interest, in classifying along the long list of rulers who made Israel to sin. The historian does, however, observe that Jeroboam II restored the northern and southern borders of Israel east of Jordan and even concedes that Yahweh saved Israel by Jeroboam. Behind this observation there is an important point to make. Under Jeroboam II, Israel knew her best years of prosperity and peace. The international situation was auspicious. Assyria's power has waned under a succession of inept rulers who could only manage in defending themselves against the kingdom of warriors until the accession of Tiglath-Pileser III (745 BCE), Syria-Palestine was free from that quarter. The Kingdom of Damascus had not yet fully recovered from her earlier defeats by Assyria and was locked in a crippling struggle with Hamath in north. Therefore, at long last there was peace with Judah taking advantage of these favorable circumstances, Jeroboam had pursued a vigorous policy of expansion east of Jordan with great success. Reflections of an ebullient confidence among Israelites appear in the speeches of Amos (6:1,8,13). Along with political success, many people were prosperous in the nation. The older homogenous economic structure of Israel gave way to sharp distinctions of wealth and privilege. The excavations at Tirzah (Tellel-Farah) uncovered evidence of social revolution that had occurred. While the city's houses in the tenth century had been uniform in size, in the eighth century by contrast there was a quarter of large, expensive houses, and one of small huddled structures (R. de Vaux, *Ancient Israel,* 1961, pp. 72ff). The result was the sharp contrast between the luxury of the rich and the misery of the poor which Amos repeatedly indicts. The rich enjoyed an indolent, indulgent existence (4:1f; 6:1-6) in winter and summer houses (3:13; 6:11). The poor were a tempting target for legal and economic exploitation (2:6-8; 4:1:5:10-12; 8:4-6). Meanwhile religion flourished in the nation. The populace thronged the shrines at festival time (4:4f; 5:5f) to practice and elaborate sacrificial ritual (5:21-24). Yahweh was trusted and patronized with presumptuous arrogance (5:14; 18-20; 6:3). To such a nation Amos was commissioned to announce the word of the Lord.

The Forms of Speech in Amos' oracles: It is surprising that Amos displays a wealth of rhetorical forms. We will consider few important types of speech forms under the following main categories.

***Commission-bound Message or Speech:*** When Yahweh comes to the fore in the messenger speech, it is consistently as the first person speaker. For important types of formulae are used by the prophet as follows:

(i) The "messenger formula": which derives from the language of diplomatic exchange (cf. 7:11) is used most frequently by Amos. Eleven of his oracles contain the introductory messenger formula "thus Yahweh had said" (*ko 'mar Yahweh*: 1:1,6,13; 2:1, 6; 3:11,12; 5:3,4,16; 7:17), and five of these also show the corresponding concluding formula "Yahweh has said" (*'mar Yahweh*: 1:5,8,15; 2:3; 5:17). In seven instances the messenger formula is placed at the head of the entire oracle; four times it appears only at the head of the announcement of punishment (3:11, 5:3,16; 7:17).

(ii) The "divine oracle formula" - (oracle/utterance of Yahweh): is found in few places: 2:16, 3:15; 4:3,5; 9:7a. In these places it stands at the end of an oracle in order to distinguish it in a solemn way as a speech of Yahweh in comparison with the speech of the prophet.

(iii) The "oath formula": is introduced by the statement: "Yahweh has sworn by", which intensifies the usual messenger formula. Its function is related to that of the messenger formula. In two places it serves to introduce, (after a preceding accusation) the announcement of judgment as a divine oracle (4:2; 8:7); in a third place (6:8) it opens an oracle in which the announcement of punishment and the motivation are intertwined. Thus oath formula fundamentally emphasizes the message of judgment as Yahweh's word and thereby underscores the certainty of judgment beyond any doubt.

(iv) The "proclamation formula": (hear!), it does not always immediately introduce an oracle of Yahweh (4:1, 8:4), but it is 7:16-17 shows, is tied less strictly to Yahweh's word of judgment. When the call to "hear" immediately introduces an oracle of Yahweh, the affected party is also addressed in the subsequent speech of Yahweh (3:la).

***Free Witness-Speech:*** The first characteristic of this type is the absence of all framework formulas that designate Yahweh as the speaker. Three further sub-types can be classified under this section as follows:

(i) Prophetic prologue to the word of Yahweh: (Eg. 3:1a), "Hear this word!"; The prophet arouses attention in preparation for the oracle of Yahweh that follows (4:1, 5:1). In 4:1, there first follows a detailed characterization of those who are addressed and whose crimes are listed. Only after that is the word of Yahweh issued, separately introduced by the oath formula (*if.* 8:4-6,7). In 5:1 it becomes even clear that the call is first of all challenge to hear the prophet's own word ("Hear this word which I take up..."); the reference here is to the funerary lament in 5:2 which receives its motivation in the subsequent word of Yahweh (5:3). This combination of the proclamation formula with the prophet's own utterance corresponds to a simple form of "pedagogical introduction" of the wisdom teacher.

(ii) Didactic Questions: Disputation concerning the prophet's commission can also appear in an independent sequence of oracles: 3:3-6,8. A series of questions unfold. Each one is formulated in such a way the hearer is brought to the conviction that calamity must also be recognized as the result of Yahweh's acting (3:6b), and the activity of the prophet as a result of the Yahweh's speaking (3. 8b), other examples of this type can be found in 5:19 20; 6:12; 9:7.

(iii) The "Woe-cries": These has a primary didactic function in a pedagogical setting. Within the clan pedagogy, the woe cries belong more to the style of basic catechetical instruction. Eg: 5:18-20; 5:7,10; 6:1,3-6. Woe is constructed in series. It is always followed by a plural participle. Direct address is usually not present. Instead, deeds defined in a general way are placed under the woe. The woe-cries indicate the intensity of the situation and the grave Judgment that will be due to come upon the people.

***Vision Reports* (7:1-3, 4-6, 7-8 and 8:1-3):** These were perhaps literary compositions from the outset, though they may have been orally transmitted to us. Everywhere in these reports prophetic 'I' is used, except in 7:14-15, where it is Amos' autobiographical account. "Thus the Lord Yahweh showed me" are the words which introduce every vision and which are followed by mysterious voices, the voices count far more than the vision. What they say is fixed for the future. The vision, reports are developed basically as conversations evoked. In the first pair by Amos' intercession and in the second pair by Yahweh questions. Just as the vision proper opens each resort, the words giving Yahweh's decisions always close it. Although the issue is indeed Israel's fate, not once does Israel figure in the scenes as the recipient of a message which the prophet. is being commissioned to deliver, in contrast to the situation as we find in 1 Kings 22:20-23; Isa 6:8-10; Jer 1:4-10 and Ezek 2:3-3:11.

***Other Types:*** In addition to the important forms of speech used by Amos as mentioned above, there are certain other types of speech forms used by Amos. We will consider few of them:

(i) The "graded numerical saying": (1:3,6,13; 2:1,6) These sayings are against foreign nations focusing only one crime. He employs this sayings, not for instructional purpose but to motivate Yahweh's irrevocable announcement of punishment.

(ii) In the judgment those who are indicted, a casting in participial style is immediately apparent. The participial forms are always found in plurals. Eg: 5:18, 6:1,3-6.

(iii) Antithesis occur especially as structural features of admonitory speech (5:4-5: "seek me...do not seek Bethel ...!") They are widespread in the language of sapiential counselling (5:4-5).

(iv) Wordplays are often found in oracles of Amos. The message of "end" was impressed upon Amos himself by means of the alliteration (*Qayis*: summer fruit and *Qēs*: end) other examples of this word play are: 6:1,6,7; 6:1 and 3-7.

The riches of imagery show Amos' desire to communicate clearly, a desire shaped by wisdom. The scope of his comparisons reflects the prophet's breadth of education. Certainly he knows the life of a simple shepherd and his legal obligations (3:12a), and his fear of the lion (3:4,8; 5:1a). Catching birds and other hunting experiences are familiar to him (3:5), from the vantage point of the steppe he longs for the blessing of streams that flow perennially (5:24).

***The Message of Amos:*** The first answer to the question concerning the proclamation of Amos must be, in keeping with his own perspective, that it is the message from Yahweh. For he himself has basically defined it as such (3:8; 7:15; 7:1-8; 8:1-2; 9:1-4). We can summarize the main message of Amos under the following points: each point is discussed briefly for clarification.

a) How does Amos speak of Yahweh? At the outset Amos says that Yahweh is at work with humanity. He speaks neither of Yahweh's justice or faithfulness, nor of Yahweh's covenant or Yahweh's law. Nor once does Amos use any fixed expression to say that Yahweh is "Israel's God." In contrast to the listing's fullness of affirmation, the most extreme simplicity in speaking "Yahweh" is Amos' own way to express his deep emotion and reverence.

No Baal competes with Yahweh for Israel's affections as we find in the situation to be in Hosea. But neither is there a God apart from Yahweh responsible for foreign nations (1:3-8, 13-15; 2:1-3; 3:2; 9:7). Thus Amos offers no polemic against any cult of foreign gods. That Yahweh is the only God of Israel and of the world of nations and is not a theme of his message but its self-evident presupposition.

If Yahweh has chosen Israel before all nations and for Amos election must be seen in connection with the giving of the land, and not with the exodus from Egypt (compare 2:9 with 9:7b) then this election establishes, for Amos, only the divine judgment (3:2). Thus Amos is remarkably laconic (given to such a speech) and theologically independent with regard to the traditions of salvation history.

Amos often declares that Yahweh's speaking has frighteningly and powerfully overwhelmed him (3:8; 7:15). Amos presents the message of Yahweh by affirming that Yahweh himself intervenes in the situation. By using first person speech form Amos communicates the message of Yahweh thus: "I will send fire..., I will break..., I will cut off" (1:4-5,7-8,14; 2:2-3); "I will turn my hand against" (1:8); "I will wreck" (3:15); "I will pass through your midst" (5:17b); "I will send you into exile" (5:27); I abhor..., I hate..., I will deliver up" (6:8); "I will raise up against you" (6:14) etc.

Death is brought to Israel not by Yahweh's absence, but precisely by Yahweh's undesired new advent (5; 16-17). Thus Amos never speaks of Yahweh as such, but only of Yahweh's dealings with humanity, of Yahweh's speaking to and through the prophet, and in all this, especially, of Yahweh's advent which Israel will experience as a destructive blow.

***The Exploitation of the Poor:*** Amos' social criticism: In his prophecies Amos develops what the visions only suggest: the guilt of Israel's leaders as the reason for the downfall: the very first saying (2:4-8) against Israel in the book gives a detailed picture of this idea:

The sale of men and women is condemned - a gross inhumanity for modern readers. In fact, the sale of men and women was permitted according to ancient oriental and Israelite law, if debts could not otherwise be paid. Amos does not oppose the existing law in principle, such as the unreasonable seizure of clothing as security, or of wine from a debtor, it was the sign of a fatal tendency in contemporary society. Under the pretext of justice, the *derek* (way: means the unity of a person's conduct and the course of his life) of a particular class of people is being 'turn aside'; this means meaningful living is made impossible. Amos here is concerned, not with individual events, but with their background and consequences. For his Derek anthropology (and this is true of pre-exilic Israel as a whole), the ties between human beings and the God who confers salvation are inextricably linked with the economic freedom given by possession of one's own land. Derek on one's own land, given to the patriarchs (Israel's ancestors) by God, counts as the precondition which makes a successful and harmonious life possible. A person has to be able to stand up straight on his own inherited ground. If he is bent down to the earth, then his/her vital hope is extinguished. He/she is, for all practical purposes, dead.

In another example of Amos 4:1-3, Amos sharply brings out his social criticism on Israel and her condition. This passage talks about a heedless, luxurious life led by an exploitative ruling class. This is the picture of the capital city on northern kingdom of Israel, Samaria. He calls the elegant ladies 'cows'—cows of Bashan, which were a much valued breed of cattle at that time. Like replete cattle, they willfully trample down their pastures, the lower classes of the people, on whom their existence in fact depends. Their fate will meet them on the same level. Amos may be mockingly picking up a cultic name the woman gave themselves, since they imagined themselves to be the worshippers of the mighty bull of Samaria (Hos. 8:5f), a north Israelite manifestation of Yahweh. Again Amos puts the relation between people and land in the foreground. The women will not be raped or killed, but they will be driven out of the land that nourishes them.

In 5:11f, Amos talks about the injustice m the realm of tax payment. In reality in the gateway of township of this kind, in the portico behind the one gateway in the town walls, the free, adult men of the community assembled. They alone had legal status and were empowered to take part in cultic ceremonies and to bear arms. The communal village democracy has legal and administrative competence. It decided on questions of inheritance and even pronounced judgment in the case of capital crimes. It probably also had the task of allotting to individual members of the community the taxes or compulsory labour which the state imposed on the local community. It looked after the local hilltop sanctuary; which its members visited. In spite of this democratic constitution, influential families gained upper hand since it was they who were able to provide members for the local council. It was a great temptation to use a majority vote to distribute taxes in such a way that families which were small and economically weak bore an undue burden. In this process, small and economically poor families are at the receiving end. The rich and upper class families imposed heavy taxation on the poor and landless farmers. This led Amos to rebuke the rich class in 5:11f.

***Amos Criticism of the Cult and the Search for God*:** In three or four sayings the prophet condemns the religious places and ceremonies of his people who took such practices granted as if they are in true devotion to God.

When a sacrifice was offered at an Israelite sanctuary, the priest usually provided a declaratory formula. This generally declared the act to be 'well pleasing to God' and only exceptionally as 'Yahweh's abhorrence'. Amos dares to express a wholesale rejection of cultic offerings in Yahweh's name. (5:21-22):

> 21 I hate, I despise your festivals,
> and I take no delight in your solemn assemblies.
> 22 Even though you offer me your burnt offerings and grain offerings,
> I will not accept them;
> and the offerings of well-being of your fatted animals
> I will not look upon.

Attending divine worship seems to be worse than questionable practices in dealings with the peasant farmers! If we know that the pre-exilic Israel was a religious and worshipping community, then what Amos was saying, if the listeners heard these words a cold shudder ran down their spines.

The sanctuaries of Bethel and Gilgal are named in horrifying terms. Amos' listeners believed that they will find Yahweh and life there. In Bethel Jacob once heard a divine voice (Gen 28:13). At that very place, Jeroboam I set up a cult for God who "led up Israel out of the land of Egypt (1 Kings 12:28). Gilgal was the first stage in the Promised Land, the beginning of the consummation of salvation history in the early period. It was there Joshua gave the word of Yahweh to his people (Josh 3:10). These places are considered to be sacral than any other in the northern kingdom. Yet it is precisely these places which Amos declared were the breeding places of sacrilege. What Amos attacks is not idolatrous cultic practices, or the number of altars everywhere in the country as his contemporary Hosea does. The object of his polemic are practices, which in the opinion of his listeners, were absolutely enjoyed by Yahweh on every Israelite. His listeners sought Bethel that they might live, expecting their physical existence (*chayim*) to be revitalized there, probably especially through the sacrament of the sacrificial feast (*zebach*: 4:4; *shēlēm*: 5:22). Added to this was the strong thumbing of their faith; the faith that Israel would never again loose this land into which Yahweh had once led them: "Yahweh is with us" (5:14) was the formula coined for this. Amos turns this assurance upside down by proclaiming the downfall of Gilgal and Bethel, Amos was forced to bring down the pillars of traditional religion, especially Amos attacked the sacrificial meals and the sanctuaries because these the indulgent luxury of the rich was at the expense of the poor people (cf. 6:l-7, where an extravagant cultic celebration in Samaria was probably being castigated).

Amos also hints at alternative: a sincere search for Yahweh (5:14f). What Amos is hinting here is not feast of jubilation but a rite of repentance, which did not require the splendor of ceremonies in Bethel and Gilgal. A rite of repentance (*som*) was an unusual ceremony. The people appeared before God with gestures of self-humiliation-torn clothes ashes in their hair, general hymns of lament-in order to hear an oracle showing that their prayers had been heard, or that collective doom had or had not averted. The prayer 'restore us' (Ps. 80:19), belongs to this context. In Amos the search for God is bound up with the same aim. A pre-exilic Israelite was probably unable to conceive of repentance like this without some external rite. Thus Amos avoids the lofty word 'repentance,' this is also indicated in the visible community relationships established by Yahweh.

***Misphat and Sedaqa:*** Their reversal and Pésa: The words misphat and sedaqa is translated as, "justice and righteousness" are the key words in the preaching of Amos to Israel. These words occur at several places. We shall take one or two examples to express the mind of Amos in his message to Israel.

The paired concepts are used in 5:23-27. They represent the highest values of human behaviour and the human condition; and Amos can only declare that they are totally lacking at the present time. Because these values have been lost, Yahweh is incensed against Bethel and Joseph and sends an occupying power into the country. Amos' God emancipates himself from men and women and from their ritual worship.

***The Down Fall of the Neighboring Nations:*** When Yahweh wants to bring to an end the wickedness of Israel, Amos takes up all the neighboring people one after another—the Philistines, the Phoenicians, the Edomites the Ammonites, and Moabites. A burden of rebellion has been gathered on them in the course of history, which Yahweh was no longer prepared to ignore. Yahweh will send a cleansing, destroying fire on them. All that Amos said about Israel's neighbours came to its fulfilment. All over Syria-Palestine the main cities and their places will be destroyed by fire. In the case of Ammonites, the government will be deported, and in Moab both army and government will be exterminated. The Aramean senders will be exterminated; whereas the people will be deported. The Philistines, Israel's old enemy, are to have the hardest fate. There the remnant of the people will be destroyed as well.

For Amos, the foreign nations are guilty before Yahweh because they have mistreated weaker human beings (1:3,6, 13,2:1) just as Yahweh at one time led the Philistines and the Arameans (9:7) and judged the Amorites (2:9), so he determines the future of the Arameans and the Philistines, the Moabites and the Amorites.

In describing the foreign nations, Amos' message has two important and specific elements: (i) Amos testifies that Yahweh alone is the God of Israel as well as the nations; the origin and future of both are freely determined by Yahweh; (ii) Amos equalizes nations with Israel and Israel with nations. The nations-need-nations stand was taken by Amos, just as does Israel, under Yahweh's guidance.

***B) Hosea:*** The prophet of northern kingdom, son of Beeri, was active in the last days of northern kingdom. During the peaceful period under Jeroboam II, shortly after Amos, indeed with some overlap, Hosea was the second prophet appeared in the northern kingdom. In his proclamation, Hosea too points to the same unconditional catastrophe as Amos. He too, foresees the downfall of state and people, the advance of Assyrian power, military defeat and deportation. Behind political and military events there was a divine impulse. In the message of Hosea, the primary concern of the prophet was: Yahweh afflicts his people and cuts himself loose those who had been intimately linked with him for centuries.

Neither his place of birth nor his office is mentioned, to say anything of his age (cf: Jer 1:6), the year of his call (cf. Isa 6:10), or similar details of his personal life. Our remaining knowledge of Hosea, we owe exclusively to the fact that particulars of his life become the subject of his prophetic commission.

The most important of these is Hosea's marriage. The prophet's marriage was to expose the guilt of contemporary Israel, who had succumbed to the Canaanite fertility rites. Thus "the whore" Gomer was probably no exception in her own day; rather, she was simply one of many Israelite women who had submitted to the bridal rites customary among the Canaanites. We can only infer that one-day Gomer, having committed adultery, left Hosea and became the legal wife of another part of his proclamation of Yahweh's will in Israel (3:1f).

We have not direct evidence of the places in which Hosea lived and worked. We are however, certain that he was active in the northern kingdom. The cities he named are located chiefly in the regions of Ephraim and Benjamin. He most frequently mentions: the royal city of Samaria (7:1. 8.5f; 10:5; 7; 14:1); the sanctuaries of Bethel (4:15; 5:8; 10:5; 12:5) and Gilgal (4:14, 9:15, 12:12). He also mentions the valley of Achor (2:17), Adam on the Jordan (6:7); Ramah and Gibeah (5:8).

According to the content of his sayings Hosea's public orations were most likely delivered in Samaria (5:1-7) or in the area of Bethel and Gilgal (4:4-19). We can say where and when Hosea spoke in these cities only by examining the manner he chose to express himself. He primarily used the speech forms of the legal dispute (*rib* in 2:4; 4:1; 12:33) or of the "watchman" of Ephraim (9:8; 5:8; 8:1). It is therefore easily conceivable that he addressed public gatherings for example, at the city gate (4:1-3; 5:1-7; 5:8-8:14; 12:1-14:1) or even at the cultic places (2:4-17; 4:4-19; 9:1-9).

We need not think that Hosea was a solitary figure in his opposition to Israel's conduct. He considered himself thoroughly allied with other prophets, a link in the chain of Yahweh's messengers that reached back to Moses (6:5; 9:7; 12:11,14). In addition, Hosea presents a clear picture of the pure priest in Israel, which was presumably kept alive in the Levitical circles of his own time (4:6; 6:6: 8:12).

The Historical Period of Hosea: No other prophet says "now" as often as Hosea (4:16; 5:3-7; 7:2; 8:8,10,13; 10:2,3; cf 13:13). To be sure, we possess very little biographical information about him. Yet it is possible to date his sayings with a high degree of accuracy. At the most, the exact year may be disputed, but not the decade. Hosea's initial activity coincides with the last years of Jeroboam II, presumably at least five years before the king's death (741-46 BCE)—752 at the latest. Not only is the threat in 1:4 directed at the Jehu's dynasty, but the entire chapter is also to be dated at the time of Jeroboam II. Chapter 1, which describes "how Yahweh began to speak through Hosea" already covers a period of at least five years. Chap. 2:4-17 and chap. 3:1-5 also reflect a time of political security and economic plenty. There, as in 4:1-5:7, a major concern was the flourishing cult. The great political difficulties which began with the catastrophe of Jehu's dynasty first appear in the prophet's threats (1:4; 3:4).

The second major period of Hosea's proclamation was linked with the crucial events of the Syro-Ephraimite War (5:8-11) and the subjugation by Tiglath-Pileser III of extensive territory in Israel in the year 733 BCE (5:14; 7:8f). At that time Hosea could look back upon a long series of palace revolts (7:7; 8:4); political vacillation between Egypt and Assyria (7:11); Hoshea ben Elah's submission to Assyria (5:13); and payment of heavy tribute (8:9f).

The sayings contained in chaps 9-12 are related to the quiet period before and after the accession to the throne of Shalmaneser V in 727 BCE. To be sure, the mention of Shalman in 10:14 was not an allusion to Shalmaneser of Assyria, but more probably to the Moabite king Shalamanu, whom Tiglath-Pileser III named among his tribute-paying vassals in the year 728 BCE, perhaps 9:3 and probably 11:5 and 12:2 presuppose Israel's mission to Egypt in 727 BCE, during the reign of Hoshea ben Elah (2 Kings 17:4), the same may be said of 13:15, "where then is your king, that he may save you?" (13:10) likewise points to this final period, when king Hoshea already had been taken captive at the beginning of Assyria's attacks. Hence the latest group of texts which can be dated with a fair amount of certainty has its origin around 725-24 BCE, immediately preceding or at the beginning of the siege of Samaria.

The forms of speech used by the Prophet: A large majority of Hosea's sayings have the basic form of the divine speech. In these sayings Yahweh speaks in the first person. (eg: 1:4f, 6, 9; 2:4-23; 4:4-9; 5:1-3, 8:1-12; and 9:10-13 etc). A smaller number of sayings are clearly formulated as prophetic speech. Here Yahweh is spoken of in the third person (3:5, 4:1-3; 5:4-7; 9:1-9; 10:1-8; 12:3-7,13-15; 13:15-14:14). It should be noted that Yahweh's personal speech is found in extensive contexts, especially in sections which introduce a complex of sayings having a unified theme. However, the "disputation style," with Yahweh in the third person, may appear in the midst of these complexes. This can result in a lively alternation from divine to prophetic speech (eg: 4:10-15; 8:11-13; 12:1-15).

Conscious of the fact that he is Yahweh's messenger, the prophet most often utilizes the personal form divine speech; he is the announcer of God's message. Other forms of divine speech are analogous to the language of the cult:

(i) Yahweh's self-introduction ("I am "Yahweh"), in connection with the proclamation of divine law (cf: 12:9,10; 13:4); (ii) the announcement of assurance that a prayer has been granted. (oracle of salvation) within the framework of the lamentation liturgies (6:1-3; 8:1-3; 14:5-9). Most of Hosea's prophetic sayings are reminiscent of those speech forms which have their *Sitz im Leben* (life setting) in the legal dispute between two parties, especially when they bring their case before the elders at the city gate. This explains the connection between the prophets' accusations and the announcements of judgment. (eg: 4:1-3; 8:1-3; 13:1-3); one hardly occurs without the other. Hosea's use of the key word *rib* ("to countered, accuse in 2:4, 4:4; law suit" 4:1,12:2-3) clearly indicate that his proclamation of the divine word is modelled after the legal procedure, in the city gate.

Three others features are prominently found in the sayings of Hosea based on the form critical analysis: (i) Words of genuine lament and complaint may be interspersed among the threats and accusations (4:6, 5:11; 7:8f; 8:8), they attest to the compassion of Israel's God and God's prophet for their people. (ii) In the book of Hosea the exhortations have their origin in the form of the "proposal to reach a settlement" in the law suit (2:4f; 4:15; 8:5; 14:2 cf. 9:1; 10:12; 12:6) and (iii) to a lesser extent defined forms peculiar to the law teacher: didactic exhortations (5:1) and precept (6:6; 8:6).

In addition, Hosea independently creates numerous metaphors. No other prophet indeed, uses as many similes as Hosea does. He may take one metaphor and develop it in detail (11:1-4; 2:4-17); or more frequently he clothes the thought of each succeeding sentence in new imagery (eg: 5:11-15; 7:4-12; 13:3,15; 14:6-8). The most provocative are his similes for Yahweh and Israel. He pictures Yahweh allegorically as a husband (2: 4ff.); a father (11:1f), a physician (14:5; 7:1; 11:3 cf. 5:13; 6:1f), as shepherd (13: 5f) and fowler (7:12). Even Hosea uses stranger similes for Yahweh and Israel like: a lion (5:14; 3:17), a leopard (13:7) and a she-bear (13:8), as dew (14:6 cf. dawn and downpour in 6:3) and a luxuriant tree (14:9), as pus and rottenness (5:12). Corresponding to the first Yahweh similes named above, Israel appears as the wife (2:4f), as son (11:1f) a sick person (5:13; 7:1, 9; 14:5), a herd (13:5-8), a flighty dove and other birds of the air (7:11f; 9:11); Israel is said to be like a trained (10:11) as well as a stubborn heifer (4:16), a grapevine (10:1; 14:8), the early fig (9:10), the wine of Lebanon (14:8), and the lily (14:6), the forest of Lebanon and the olive tree (14:6), a mother in labour as well as an unborn son (13:13) Israel is like a cake of bread (7:8), a slack bow (7:16), morning mist and dew (13;3a cf 6:4), chaff blown from the threshing floor, and smoke that rises from the window (13:3-6). Thus, Hosea's audience are amazed by the number and variety of metaphors he employs, he omits no sphere of life; but the imagery is drawn from the vegetable and animal world and from family life clearly demonstrates the wealth and richness of metaphorical language employed by the prophet.

Hosea often employs parallelism in his poetic texts, at times Hosea's enthusiastic manner of speech is a step like parallelism (eg: in 8:11:13:6) seems to build to a climax.

***The Message of Hosea:*** Hosea names "Yahweh" (occurs about 45 times or more) much more often than God (*elohim*: occurs 26 times or more) when he specifically mentions the one he serves as messenger. For Hosea knows only the God who, since the time of Moses (12:13-14) has revealed himself in a proclamation of his law and through his liberating acts: "I am Yahweh, your God from the land of Egypt" (12:10; 13:4). Nor does Israel know another as God and saviour besides Yahweh (13:4b). Hosea was familiar with the interpretation of Yahweh's name in Exod 3:14, as he indicates in his negation of the old covenant formula. Yahweh, the ancient God of Israel, is the God who Hosea proclaims anew.

Since this Yahweh is God not only of the past but of the present as well, the prophet can use new, extremely bold expressions in referring to God. He speaks of Yahweh, the judge of Israel, only once as "his Lord" (12:1-15). Some of the similes used by Hosea for Yahweh sound very strange to his audience. For example, Yahweh has Hosea describe him as "pus to Ephraim" and "rottenness to the house of Judah" (5:12) or as a lion that rends and carries off his prey, from whom none shall rescue (5:14). The prophet's language itself strikes in the hearts of his audience the terror of Yahweh's presently burning anger (5:10; 13:11). Subordinating all consideration of pious tradition and aesthetic sensitivities, the prophet sought to bear witness to Yahweh's awesome, over powering strength and present action.

Hosea uses extreme imagery in his announcement of salvation. The power of God's saving deeds was elucidated by metaphors of the "dew" in I4:5-6 and of the "luxuriant fruit tree" in vv. 8-9.

Hosea talks about Yahweh as Israel's husband had its roots in the prophet's recognition of Israel's specific guilt: the people have given themselves to "whoredom" (1:2; 2:4-7; 3:3; 4:10-18; 5:3f; 6:10; 9:1). By her cultic practices and her dependence upon Canaanite mythology and thought, Israel has become unfaithful to Yahweh. The metaphor of the "first husband" (2:9,18 thus has the purpose of elucidating the accusation that Israel is guilty of whoredom and adultery. This metaphor also emphasizes that Yahweh is the exclusive provider of all the gifts of the arable land (2:7,10). Hosea's adaptation of the divine husband concept to Yahwism presents Yahweh as the only God and thus states Yahwism's claim of exclusiveness.

Two important observations show how Hosea's use of mythical elements is dominated by his polemic against the Baal myth, and how the myth is broken precisely 1n the marriage parable. *Firstly*, it is Yahweh who provides the gifts of the arable land and who is free to take them back again (2:10, 11, 17). Here the concept of conjugal union completely recedes and Yahweh attests that he is -in contrast to Baal-Lord over devastation and wilderness. In spite of Hosea's use of certain mythical fragments, his certitude that Yahweh alone is God disallows any suggestion of a plurality of divinities or even of a sexually differentiated pantheon. *Secondly*, Yahweh's partner in the marriage parable was not some goddess, but historical Israel. The legal categories of covenantal thought replace the mythic-cultic fertility concepts that are rooted in the sacral marriage (cf 1:9, 2:4,21f). This unfolding of Hosea's theology in polemical dialogue with the cults and mythology of Canaan provides us with a fundamental example of faith's dialogue with contemporary ideology. In spite of Hosea's daring usage of certain key words from Canaanite mythology, the idea remains dominant that the Yahweh who acts in the present and future is none other than the one who has begun his covenant history with Israel at the time of her youth, with the Exodus from Egypt (2:17; 11:1; 13:4); with the making of the covenant (1:9; 6:7; 8:1); and with the gift of divine law (2:21f; 8:12;13:4f). Hosea views Israel's present and future together with her history.

It is remarkable to see how thoroughly Israel's history is embedded in Hosea's proclamation He looks back over the last decade when kings were murdered and the throne usurped (7:7; 8:4); over the last century, with the crimes of Jehu's dynasty in 844 BCE (1:4); on to the beginnings of kingship under Saul, where he locates the roots of the present kingship's transgression (13:10f; 9:15). Beyond this he reaches back even more comprehensively to the period of the conquest (2:10; 9:10; 10:11f; 11:1f; 13:5f). For Hosea the conquest tradition was to be separated neither from the deliverance from Egypt (2:17; 11:1; 12:14; 13:4) nor from the wilderness traditions (9:10; 13:5; 2:5,16). The period of conquest saw Israel's early encounter with the Baal cult (9:10) and with it the apostasy— determinative for Israel's present—from the God who had begun his saving history with her in Egypt and in the wilderness. Hosea's longest step basic into history takes him to the Jacob traditions (12:4-5,7,13). They especially serve to lay bare Israel's present deceit against God and neighbor.

Hosea's use of traditions is more significant than arbitrary collection of examples from the past. Three reasons for this can be identified:

(i) The historical retrospect discloses early, fundamental connections within Israel's history. Her apostasy to the Baal of Peor was an abominable transgression in view of the previous election of the fathers in the wilderness (9:10). Theologically speaking, in the light of Israel's beginnings, her present transgression was revealed as transgressions against the God of love and election, against the Lord of saving history.

(ii) The historical retrospect shows how God's intensive struggle with Israel reach from her past down to Hosea's present time. Yahweh's great lawsuit with his wife—turned—whore (2:4-17) and his accusing speech against the rebellious son (11:1-7) indicate how much the prophet was interested in the continuity of the defendant's previous life.

(iii) It is not accidental that Hosea gives especially close attention to various beginnings: Jehu-the first king of the present dynasty (1:4); Gilgal and Saul the beginning of the present kingship (9:15; 13:10t); Baal-Peor-the beginning of the cult of Shamel (9:10); the wandering in the wilderness and the deliverance from Egypt—the initial saving acts of Yahweh (2:17; 9:10; 11:1; 12:10,14; 13:4-6); the Jacob story—when Israel's deceitfulness began (12:4f, 13f). Whenever Israel's beginnings are examined, her present immediately appears indeed, the present is the end of ancient saving history now has actually begun. The most impressive statement in this regard is found in the recasting of the old covenant formula as a formulae of divorce (1:9; cf. 2:4); but it is also expressed in the sayings which threaten Israel's return to Egypt, whereby the gift of the land is taken back (8:13; 9:3,6).

Hosea brings his accusation particularly against two groups within the nation: the priests and political leaders. He measures the priestly sacrifices and oracles and also the activities of the priests in the festivity cult against a remarkably positive ideal of a "knowledge of God". Thus he expects them to cultivate and use this knowledge in order to maintain people's attitude in God's saving action and justice (4:1,6; 6:6; 13:4-6; 2:10-15,21f). He charges the political leadership with zealous revolutionary intrigues and constant charges of direction in foreign policy which they pay out without ever seeking the will of Yahweh, the God of Israel (5;1f,11f; 7:3-16; 8:1-4,7-10; 10:13-15; 13:10-14:1).

We find the following expression in Hosea in order to explain the rebellious attitude of Israel; Israel's "no longer knows" (2:10; 5:4; 11:3) Yahweh, "forgets" (2:15; 4:6; 8:14; 13:6), "forsakes" (4:10) him; leaves him "to go after her lovers" (2:7,15 cf.11:2); "disregards the instructions of his covenant" (6:7; 8:1); "turns to other gods" (3:1); "is unfaithful to him" (5:7;6:7); "becomes stubborn" (4:16; 9:15).

Hosea describes how God feels profound sorrow, laments the apostasy of his people; how God himself suffers under the distress their estrangement prepares them. In bringing correction on Israel numerous threats are used on "Israel to announce impending judgment." Hosea first depicted it in terms of natural catastrophes (11:5; 7:16; 8:3; 10:14f; 14:1) and then later as military catastrophes (1:5; 7:16; 8:3; 10:14f; 14:1). It is more characteristic of Hosea when he announces Yahweh will personally draw near to execute his punishment (5:12,14:7:12,15; 12:10; 13:7f) and that Yahweh will act not only as requite (4:9; 12:3; 9:7) but also as teacher (5:2,9 cf. 10:10). The most peculiar feature of Hosea's proclamation we find in the lawsuit speeches in which his God not only struggles with Israel but with himself as well; indeed, he calls his own decisions into question (2:4-17; 6:4; 11:8f). Thus according to Hosea, Yahweh's judgment in essence is his struggle for his people. In the beginning of his proclamation, Hosea's exhortations to repent become ultimatums (2:4f); later, they still appear occasionally (4:15; 8:5), though they are met with stubborn resistance (4:16), refusal (11:5b), and the complete inability to return, since the actions of the people have rendered them incapable of conversion (5:4; 7:2).

The message of salvation is also seen in the oracles of Hosea in the midst of his severe judgment speeches After Israel had broken the covenant (1:9), the new beginnings was to come only as a result of the preconditions which God himself created: in his Judgment God would block Israel's path to her idols (2:8) and bring her a new to the wilderness, the place where his saving history had begun (2:16). There Israel would turn her thoughts to Yahweh (2:9), listen to Yahweh's wooing words of love (2:16f) and return to him and his goddess (3:5).

In the later part of Hosea's ministry, when it became clear that Yahweh's words of judgment could not bring Israel to obedience God's unqualified love is expressly represented as the only precondition for healing Israel's apostasy and for giving her new life (11:8f).

***Isaiah of Jerusalem (8th Century Prophet):*** It is beyond question that behind chs. 1-39 of the book of Isaiah there stands one of the greatest figures of the religious and political story of ancient Israel. Equally however, is the fact that we have very little information about this man and the personal circumstances in which he lived and worked. We are left entirely to a process of making inferences from features preserved in his sayings.

Isaiah was called to be a prophet in the year of Uzziah's death (736 BCE) which also effectively marked the beginning of the Syro-Ephraimite crisis. Isaiah clearly had a wife, who was called prophetess (8:3) and at least three children (8:18). He was known to the king (7:3), and was evidently familiar with the work and planning of the king. Beyond this he was well known to the rulers and priests of Jerusalem (see 28:7,14), and appears to have had remarkably prompt and full information about the most intimate details of the king and planning that took place in the inner circles of government in Jerusalem (see especially 29:15).

This deep insight into the inner life of government and the court has given rise to a widely adopted view concerning the person of Isaiah: that he was himself a nobleman of high birth and high education among the wealthy and aristocratic leaders of his people. Isaiah was undoubtedly a highly educated man, with an expert mastery of the skills of rhetoric and persuasion. No other figure of the Old Testament literature shows so commanding a control of the use of irony and subtle word-play.

Another important area of particular importance to the prophet was the royal court, and the distinctive traditions associated with the Davidic dynasty assume a very special prominence with him. It appears strongly in the prophecies relating to the Syro-Ephraimite crisis, and most strongly of all in the well-known 'messianic' prophecy of 9:2-7. Here it appears that Isaiah was deeply committed to the royal Davidic tradition, the possibility that he himself contemplated, or even directly prophesied, the ending of the long period of Davidic rule from Jerusalem (see 7:9), must be considered.

***The Historical Background:*** The superscription in Isaiah 1:1 asserts that Isaiah prophesied during the days of Uzziah, Jotham, Ahaz and Hezekiah, kings of Judah. But this superscription is quite later addition to the composition of the book. Since Isaiah did not receive his call to be a prophet until, the year that king Uzziah dies" (6:1), it was in only case evident that little could have derived from that same year and none at all from it, as was most probable, Uzziah was already dead when the call came. While the dates of the other kings are a dispute among scholars more or less the following dates can be agreed upon: Uzziah (Azariah). 787-736 BCE; Jotham (co-regent) 756-741 BCE; Ahaz (co-regent); 741-736 BCE; Ahaz (sole ruler); 736-725; Hezekiah: 725-697 BCE.

Unfortunately, yet another major point of uncertainty over dating emerges with regard to the year in which Hezekiah came to the throne. The evidence of 2 Kings 18:1f,9, asserts that Hezekiah had already assumed the throne of Judah for some years when Samaria fell to the Assyrians in 722 BCE. This contradicts with the evidence of 2 Kings 18:13 that it was only the 14$^{th}$ year of Hezekiah when Sennacherib marched into Judah and attacked Jerusalem, an event which can be placed in 701 BCE. Therefore, several scholars tend to propose that Hezekiah's accession did not take place until 715 BCE. But R. E. Clements makes a proposal by suggesting Ahaz's death probably occurred in 726/5 and that Hezekiah's accession took place in 725. From these conclusions we can then proceed to Isaiah's prophesying between these two reigns. The prophets' call may be located in 736 BCE, and the latest prophecies which have been preserved from him in the year 701, or very shortly thereafter (1:4-8; 22:1-4, 12-14).

The major political events which affect the entire period of Isaiah's activity were those occasioned by the military and political threat posed to Israel and Judah by the Assyrians. Four rulers of Assyrian empire were involved in this regard: Tiglath-Pileser III: 744-727 BCE; Shalmaneser V: 726-722 BCE; Sargon II: 721-705 BCE; Sennacherib: 704-681 BCE. We shall now turn to examine briefly the events and political developments that occurred in Judah ultimately shared by Isaiah in his oracles and prophetic ministry in this regard we shall briefly look into Isaiah's relationship to the court.

It is understood Isaiah must have acted as adviser to two kings of Judah: Ahaz and Hezekiah (Isa 7:3-17; 37:2-7,21-35), and that his prophetic message contains much directly political advice, Isaiah seems to have had ready access to the king (7:3,10) and according to the narrative of chs. 36-39 the king sent to consult him when the Assyrians invaded. J. Fichtner and J. W. Whedbee argued that Isaiah was a 'wise man' in the technical sense, someone educated in the schools of ancient Israel, which are widely thought to have trained civil servants to work in the chancelleries of the royal courts in Jerusalem and Samaria.[10] When Isaiah condemned the ruling classes of Jerusalem, and commented on the country's foreign policy, he was criticizing members of the social class he himself belonged to.

Isaiah lived in the period when the growing might of Assyria increasingly threatened the stability and independence of the small states of Syria-Palestine. In the ninth century these states had been quite successful in containing Assyrian expansionism, and in 853 BCE had beaten off Shalmaneser III at the battle of Qarqar; Ahab of Israel was among the successful allies.

But the 745 BCE was usually regarded as the crucial turning point, the year in which Tiglath-Pileser III took the throne of Assyria and began a series of conquests which would effectively wipe out Israelite and Judean independence. Isaiah began to Prophesy at a time when both the aggressive incentives and the various kings of Judah as they tried to handle the complexities of a situation from which, in the end, no one was likely to come to Palestine as happened to other kingdoms.

There are four important issues we need to consider briefly in order to examine the role of Isaiah in his historical and political situation:

***The Syro-Ephraimite Crisis:*** The Syro-Ephraimite crisis had its beginning in the early conquests of Tiglath-Pileser, who captured Hamath in northern Syria as early as 738 and then quickly took tribute from the cities of Phoenicia and from Damascus, the immediate neighbour of northern kingdom of Israel (Ephraim) and the leading Aramean (Syrian) state, Israel soon paid tribute in turn. Paying tribute was the least of the kind of vassal Dom enforced by the Assyrians and involved no invasion or 'conquest' in the physical sense it is not unlike paying protection money. By these means the Assyrians spread their influence and control by the threat of military

10 For more details on this point see, William J. Whedbee, *Isaiah and Wisdom* (Nashville: Abingdon Press, 2016), Revised Edition.

invasion, without needing to expend forces on its army, paying tribute also had the effect of weakening the national economy, and consequently also the political institution leaving the country an easier prey if the Assyrian king later decided on a more aggressive.

At this stage Judah was not affected. However, in 734 BCE Tiglath-Pileser moved west and terrorized the Philistine pentapolis. Judah was thus threatened to both north and west of Assyria, on the other hand, may have looked slightly overstretched. At all events in 733 BCE Israel and the Arameans of Damascus decided to try to revive the old alliances of the ninth century and oppose the Assyrians through a 'Syro-Ephraimite' coalition. They failed to see how immensely Assyrian power had increased, and how weak they themselves now were. Razon (biblical Rezin) of Damascus and Pekah son of Remaliah of Israel invited Ahaz, who had just succeeded Jotham, to join the coalition. They intended if he refused to depose him, and place on the Judaic throne someone called 'ben Tabeel, his personal name was unknown, as was everything about him. As the northern armies prepared to march on Judah to implement this unwise plan (Hos 5:8-9 may describe their route), Ahaz decided to send the Assyrians the tribute they had not (yet) asked for to persuade them to intervene on his behalf. Whether on his behalf or not, the Assyrians certainly did crush the rebellion, which in any case they could not have afforded to ignore. Samaria was sacked in 733, Damascus in 732 BCE, Isa. 17:1-6 predicted both events.

This period was the setting for Isaiah 7 and 8. Isaiah goes to meet Ahaz 'at the end of the conduit of the upper Pool' on the highway to the Fuller's Field, perhaps implying that the king was inspecting the city's water supply in case of siege.

Isaiah's message to Ahaz had two aspects. The first was the symbolic prediction in his son's name, Shear-jashub ('a remnant will return'). The other was the advice given to the king, which bears directly on the political decision he had to make. The adverse appears clear: Do not fear, because God can deliver his people; take no action to prevent by the coalition (8:4).

What was the action Ahaz contemplated, and which Isaiah warned against? At the face value of the text, it may appear that Isaiah was warning the king Ahaz not to prepare for siege or war rather to put his trust in God. But there was another possibility; and that Isaiah was opposing not Ahaz's preparations for war, nor his plans for fortifying the city, but his intention of sending tribute to Tiglath-Pileser. Isaiah could have been saying that Ahaz had no need to do anything but 'keep quiet.' A small indication that this may be what was meant is Isaiah's advice not to fear Rezin and Pekah. Ahaz sending to Assyria for help would indeed show fear, and it may be this that Isaiah opposes.

The oracle which Isaiah gives to Ahaz seems to have both unconditional and conditional promise. On the one hand, Isaiah was saying that the king had no need to fear, since God will confirm him on his throne? Isa. 8:1-14 might tend to support this: "Before the child (the prophet's son, Maher-Shalal-Hash-Baz knows to cry "My father" or "My mother," the wealth of Damascus and the spoil of Samaria will be carried away before the king of Assyria; or it could be conditional promise, and also a conditional threat. Isa. 7:4 and 7:9a suggests the conditional promise, but 7:9b, the climax of the oracle may mean in the sense: unless you are prepared to stand firm, you will not be confirmed or upheld in your position.

Thus the whole oracle was probably meant as a conditional promise of deliverance: only by not "fearing" only by being "quiet" (cf. Ps 76:9), will Ahaz be showing faith in Yahweh, and thus deserves Yahweh's protection. Paradoxically, to be afraid, and therefore to seek help from Assyria, was the one certain way of not obtaining help from the genuine source of help—the God of Israel.

***The Fall of Samaria:*** The aftermath of the Syro-Ephraimite coalition was disastrous for the northern kingdom of Israel, which effectively became an Assyrian province, with only Samaria and its immediate surroundings left as a nominally independent but tribute-paying vassal state. Israel had long had a stronger tendency to insurrection and internal strife than its smaller southern neighbour, and in the years following the defeat of the coalition the monarchy there became highly unstable This is the situation reflected in the book of Hosea (eg: 6:11-7:7; 8:4). On 722 BCE, Samaria revolted against Assyrian rule, and the city was besieged, falling in 722 to Shalmaneser V. Judah was not implicated in this revolt, and so retained its status as a vassal but with its own monarchy and administration.

***Alliances with the Philistines and the Egyptians:*** The third phase of Isaiah's life saw Judah preoccupied with intrigues and alliances involving the Philistine cities and the Egyptians. From about 720 BCE, a couple of years after Samaria fell, Syria-Palestine experienced stirrings of rebellion against Assyrian domination. There were revolts in Hamath, the first state to fall to the Assyrians, and in Gaza, the farthest point of the empire from their Mesopotamian power-base. The Egyptians saw advantage for themselves in getting involved, but nevertheless the king of Gaza was captured, and the revolt fizzled out.

But in 713-711 there was a further serious bid for freedom when the city of Ashdod tried to break the Assyrian's hold on the Philistine pentapolis (five cities). This time the Egyptians, under Shabaka were deeply entangled; there were also negotiations with the more easterly Palestinian states, Edom and Moab, and Judah was certainly part of the alliance. This is widely agreed to be the background to the oracles of Isaiah 18 and 19. It is also the contest for the story of Isaiah walking naked and barefoot through Jerusalem in ch. 20, dated to 'the year that the Tartan came to Ashdod,' that is, 711 BCE—the year when the Assyrians under Sargon II finally stepped in to put the rebellion down. Ashdod was completely crushed, and the Egyptians willingly handed over the king of Ashdod, who had fled to them for asylum, to the Assyrians; but there was no record of any reprisals against Judah, Edom or Moab.

Isa 19:16-24 consists of five oracles about Yahweh's future purpose for Egypt, culminating in the extraordinary promise that the day Israel will be the third with Egypt and Assyria' (v. 24) - one of the most universalistic oracles in the Old Testament. Isaiah's political advice was again that Judah should rely on God, not on human beings, and he interprets this to mean that no alliances should be made with Egypt. Isaiah's message in this crisis was thus completely consistent with his attitude in the earlier days when it was the alliance with Assyria that he condemned.

***The Assyrian Crisis:*** The final phase of Isaiah's 'political' prophecy was also the most complex and the most discussed. The accession of Sennacherib to the Assyrian throne in 705/04 BCE evidently seemed to the Palestinian states to herald a weakening of Assyrian power, or at least a time when determined vassals could exploit possible tensions and uncertainties at the heart of the empire. Along with the Philistine cities of Ekron and Ashkelon, Hezekiah withheld tribute, perhaps in consultation with Babylon, then ruled by Marduk-apal-iddin II (biblical Merodach-baladan), with who he said to have had diplomatic dealings (see Isa. 39; 2 Kings 20:12-19). Once again Egypt was heavily involved, its promises of help as crucial as empty as ever. Thus Sennacherib was faced with rebellion at the extreme western and eastern ends of his empire. Since it took him four years to put down the Babylonian rebellion and turn his attention to that in the west, the allies had probably judged their moment well: if there ever would be a moment for rebellion, this was it.

Nevertheless, in 701 BCE Sennacherib was at last in a position to involve Judah, and to involve the Judeans in what is usually called 'the Assyrian crisis.' It drew from Isaiah a number of prophecies, broadly in line with his utterances in the earlier periods. The main sources for Isaiah's oracles are 28-31 chapters; 36-38 chapters and 1:2-9. The last passage gives a graphic description of the state of Judah once Sennacherib's army had invaded, leaving Jerusalem the only unconquered city in a devastated country, which was comparable to Sennacherib's own account of this campaign.

As to Hezekiah the Jew, he did not submit to my Yoke. I laid siege to 46 of his strong cities, walled forts, and countless small villages in their vicinity, and conquered (them) by means of well-stamped (earth) ramps, and battering rams...Himself I made a Prisoner in Jerusalem, his royal residence, like a bird in a cage (cf. Isa. 10:14).[11]

In 28:1-6 we find the main contents are on the northern kingdom and its fall, its concerns the social morality of the north (specifically its leaders habitual drunkenness) rather than its political attitudes. But the chapter continues (vv. 7-13) with what seems to be an attack on Judah ('there also...'), reapplying the early, anti-Israel oracle to the southern kingdom during the Assyrian crisis. A similar use of the fall of northern Israel as a warning to Judah can be found in Micah and in 2 Kings 17:7-41. Isaiah saw the leadership as so befuddled that they believe they can defeat the superior power of Assyria.

In Isa 28:14-22 the core of political message of Isaiah is found: 'he who believes will not be in haste' (v. 16). It apparently condemns the alliance with Egypt as an attempt to make a 'covenant with death'-Death is a notoriously hard bargaining Partner. The only true security comes horn Yahweh, who Provides a secure rock in Zion for those who trust him, but rejects those who Prefer to seek safety in Egypt. It Piled-up metaphors experience when the Assyrians come and sweep away all Possibility of security: hail, rising flood-waters, a scourge, boots to trample them down, as they try in vain to rest on a bed too short to lie down on, under sheets too narrow to cover them.

How far did the events of 701 BCE vindicate Isaiah's words? Two things are virtually certain. Firstly, Jerusalem was not actually captured by Sennacherib. The Assyrian troops went away without sacking the city, and an oracle in Isa. 22:12-14 Probably refers to the Population's reaction: 'Joy and gladness slaying oxen and killing sheep, eating flesh and drinking 'wine', But secondly, the context in which the city was thus 'delivered' was such as to make these celebrations 'the unforgettable day of Jerusalem's complacency as R. E. Clements calls it.

There is a much more difficult historical Problem about the Assyrian crisis. It arises from the Puzzling inconsistencies and duplications in the biblical narratives. The short account of the events of 701 in II Kings 18:13-18 does not appear in Parallel account in Isa. 36-37, except for the introductory verse ('In the fourteenth Year of King Hezekiah, Sennacherib King of Assyria came up against all the fortified cities of Judah and took them'). This account is broadly confirmed by Sennacherib's own annals (ANET. PP. 287-88). The account which does appear, which is also in Kings, is along and rambling one. It cultimates in a miraculous deliverance

11 James B. Pritchard, *Ancient Near Eastern Texts Relating to the Old Testament* (Princeton: Princeton University Press, 1950).

of Jerusalem and the death of the Assyrian army through the agency of the angel of Yahweh' (Isa. 37:36). The Assyrian official, the Rabshakeh, makes two Speeches in very Similar words (Isa.36:4-20 and 37:10-13), Hezekiah twice consults Yahweh through Isaiah (37:1-4 and 37:14-20), and Isaiah twice Prophesies the deliverance of the city (37:5-7 and 37:21-35).

The events of Isaiah's life were complex, as the political allegiances of the State of Judah shitted and adapted to accommodate the realities of Assyrian Power. His message, however, was remarkably simple and unchanging. It concentrated on a pure trust in Yahweh; which they believed must exclude all human attempts at self-defense and self-determination-whether these took the form of military Preparations or appeals for help to one of the great Powers.

Theology and Preaching of Isaiah: A study of the background to the Preaching of the Prophet has already raised a number of matters concerning his Particular theology. That he was a citizen of Jerusalem, born and brought up in the city, has clearly Pointed us to the main setting of his understanding of God and his relationship to Israel. His favourite title for God is 'the Holy one of Israel' (1:4 etc.), and this immediately draws our attention a major feature of his whole outlook. Yahweh was the God of 'Israel' and by this the Prophet quite evidently understood both Kingdoms, Ephraim and Judah to be referred to (cf. 5:7; 8:14), so that the Prophet is concerned about both Israel and Judah. Isaiah began his ministry at a time when the relationship between Judah and Israel was hostile than any other time (of. 7:17). He found himself confronted with a King, Ahaz who was bent on betraying this historic unity between the two Kingdoms still further by appealing to Assyria to rescue him from the sister Kingdoms in the north.

It is not surprising therefore that Isaiah should have felt able to affirm that the People Whom God had once owned as 'my People' had become a band of rebels, whom he only describes as 'this People' (cf. 629). Even the reigning King of Judah, in whose days he began to Prophesy, had the Davidic heritage of ruling with a regard for all Israel. He Played Politics against the interests of God's People. Especially was this true Ahaz, whom Isaiah regards as having betrayed the very foundation of the throne of David. He had greater hopes for Hezekiah (cf. 9:2-7), although these were destined never to be realized so far as the remains of the Northern Kingdom were concerned (cf. 9:8). Nonetheless, the sense that in God's eyes both 'houses' of Ephraim and Judah formed only one People Israel established a basis for all Isaiah's Preaching. In his eyes the royal claims of the Davidic family belonged within this 'all Israel' perspective.

It is within this broader Perspective that we must understand the special significance with both the temple Jerusalem and the Davidic royal dynasty had for Isaiah. They were institutions which belonged to the entire nation. At no Point does Isaiah appear to have considered either of them to be entirely indispensable to the Purposes of God with Israel. So we must dismiss completely any suggestion that he regarded Jerusalem as inviolable on account of the Presence of God in the temple there, or the Davidic dynasty as irreplaceable. They each fulfilled a purpose in the plans of Yahweh, but this was open to the realities of each historical situation, as God made his intentions known regarding it.

Isaiah's theology therefore operating within this Place, primarily looks critically at the making of foreign alliances. We have already presented a detailed picture on this in our discussion on the historical background. From this point on the reader is expected to consult the material on previous section in Isaiah.

***C) Micah:*** The book of Micah reflects the turbulence of several centuries, for only a small Part of the Prophetic saying it Presents to its readers are from Micah of Moresheth, who saw of clouds of doom on the horizon as early as the neo-Assyrian era.

Only his name and the Place of his original and work are mentioned. Neither his father's name nor his profession is noted, neither his call nor his encounter with other Persons is narrated. According Micah 1:1, the name of the Prophet is a Popular name in the Old Testament; the meaning of it is "who is like Yahweh" (also it is mentioned in Jer. 26:18).

The home of Micah is Moresheth, situated in the foothills of south-western Judah, the Shepelah (1:13-15), Probably located in the modern Tell-el-Judeiah about 35 km south-west of Jerusalem, 400 meters above the sea level. Micah also appeared in Jerusalem (3:10,12) to preach his message of Prophecy. According to H. W. Wolff, Micah functioned as a local leader (Zqen), or as a head of a clan (ro's), in Moresheth, before and during the time when the office of the charismatic Prophet was bestowed upon him. He never calls himself a Prophet, but he was surely dominated by the specific authority of the Prophet who acts as spokesman for Yahweh, beginning with the time he became certain of the doom that was approaching Samaria, Judah and Jerusalem (1:69). This was Probably indicated in 2:3f, but the messenger speech against the authorities whom he indicated m 2:1-2 (also 2:6f, 11); it becomes clearer by the way he Presents himself in 3:8 in his direct confrontation with the Prophets (3:5-7) and "heads" (3:1, 9:11) in Jerusalem (3:5,11). It is noticeable that Micah never calls People for whom he concerns himself the "poor" ('e b y o n) "oppressed" (d a l) or "needy" ('a n i); it is the husband (Gerber) and citizen ('is), whose family and Property he defends (2:2), the chief opponents in the Shephelah are hardly the greedy estate owners (as in Isa 5:8), but rather the officials, officers and soldiers from the garrison in the region. As the "authorities" (2:1b) they have confiscated houses and land and have degraded free persons by turning them into working slaves.

It has been often noted that the book contains no record of Micah's call to be a Prophet; however, we cannot conclude that there was no such call, nor 3:8 can be substitute for it, because here there is no reference to Yahweh. However, the Phrase "with the spirit of Yahweh" may be a later addition indicate the ministry of Micah received from Yahweh. Micah came before them authorities fearlessly with inner superiority. Within the simple social relationship of the Provincial towns, the elder is at once and the same time a teacher of Justice and Wisdom.

***Historical Period:*** As noted in our introduction, the book of Micah contains sayings of several centuries even though the Prophetic activity is limited to a certain Period. The book contains sayings of neo-Assyrian, neo-Babylonian as well as the sayings from a period in which an Israelite remnant in the Persian empire was gathered together.

It is certain however, based on the majority of his sayings, Micah of Moresheth appeared in the second half of the eighth century. But the words transmitted to us in the book are related to people from the most desperate Phases of history, from the second half of eighth century to around the first half of the fifth century BCE. We are however, unable to date certain original Prophecies of Micah due to some reasons; for example:

(i) In Jer. 26:18 Micah of Moresheth is mentioned only once Micah is mentioned as a Prophet who appeared in the days of Hezekiah, King of Judah. Hezekiah reigned 29 years from third year of Hoshea northern King (II Kings 18:1f) thus Probably from 729 to 700. "In Micah 3: 12 often Placed in proximity to the siege upon the city made by the Assyrian Sennacherib in the Year 701 BCE. However, in the motivation (3:9-11) for the disaster no connection with Political matters or military actions is to be recognized, as we find for Eg. in Isa 30:1-5; 31:1-3. Instead this text of Micah speaks only of injustice in the city (v. 9), mainly rooted in the building activity. Therefore, Jerusalem will become a "heap of ruins" (vv. 10-11). (ii) According to Micah 1:1, Prophet works not only under Hezekiah but also works under his two Predecessors, Jotham and Ahaz; (iii) According to 1:6-16, a different date is suggested Micah, especially in 1:6, a reference is made against Samaria which was under siege for three years (725-722 BCE).

In light of those considerations, we can say 722 BCE. is the *terminus ad quem* for the entire text in 1:6-16 originally from Micah.

The texts contained in the book of Micah extend far beyond the final quotation of Micah 3:12 in Jer. 26:17-19 already indicates. The historical background of all the Prophecies contained in the book of Micah comprehends, therefore a span of time of about three hundred years.

### *The Language of Micah*

***D) Style:*** Micah carefully follows the order of events and with a lively interest, notes their details and features. Even when Micah uses Parallelism, he moves quickly from fact to fact. He sometimes emphasizes the climax of a speech by using alliteration. eg: 1:16 "Make large your baldness like a buzzard (vulture)..."

Micah's Passionate accusations can also be expressed crudely and dramatically. For eg: what the construction workers must suffer in Jerusalem he Portrays with metaphors borrowed from the butcher shop. What the farmer in the Shephelah routinely does only to his cattle the leaders in the capital city do to human beings "remove the hide" - "break the bones" - "devour their flesh" (3:2f,10). Micah's usage becomes lively by this frequent use of quotations (cf. 2:3 f; 2: 1 f): "we are completely ruined; our fields are divided." We always find in Micah the forms of direct address (2nd Person Plu. cf. 2:3b-4a, 8-10, 3:12a). Questions also Promote his contact with his audience; he formulates questions with his audiences Quotations (2:7a, 3:11a). questions he himself Poses (2:7b), counter questions to the authorities (3:1b).

### *Genre: Three Important Genres are Prominent in Micah's Speech*

***(i) The Judgment Speeches*****:** found in 1:6f, 2:2-4; 3:1-4; 8,9-12 They all exhibit a taunt form, usually of two Parts, in which the accusation, as a rule, precedes (2:11f; 3:1-3,5,9-11), and is often more detailed than, the announcement of disaster (2:3f; 3:4,6-7, 12). The announcement of disagter, usually attached to the announcement by la ken ("therefore" - 2:3; 3:6-12 except 3:4 where 'a z "then' is used) is the proof of guilt which provides the motivation for divine announcement. Only in 1:6,7b is the announcement followed by the accusation with a "because" or "for" clause gives the motivation for divine punishment. The simple form of two-part judgment speech accords with the manner method of the elders who, sitting in the legal gate of the Villages, made their indictments, brought attention to legal infringements, and explained their legal decisions.

This parallels describe our attention, because Micah usually introduces the Punishment as the direct consequence of the guilt (a wisdom connection) to which he has pointed, without presenting the punishment as though it were brought on by the special direction of Yahweh (cf. 3:4,6,12) only one saying is given with messenger formula (2:3a).

***(ii) By contrast, the judgment speech in 2:1-4 exhibits an element that is central to the funerary lament:*** Sentences of the accusations are introduced with the use cry from the death lament. The woe cry belongs to the mourning ceremonies of the clan, and thus Micah as clean elder would be familiar with it. In 1:8-16, many other elements of the mourning rites (weeping, rolling in the dust, lamentation, shaving the head bald in vv. 8,10,11) devastating war and capitulation (vv. 11-15), also symbolic action of "barefoot and naked."

The summons to lament do not speak of the guilt of Judah or Jerusalem, where the reports of disaster led to serious actions besides mourning rites, nevertheless at no point do they summon the People to pray to repent, or some act of worship, Micah is in no way connected with cultic functions, he speaks in 'a religious' manner, this too is true in the light too of his office as an elder from Judah.

***(iii) The disputation speech:*** Probably belongs as well to the rhetorical forms of the elders at the city gate: the form occurs in 2:6-11. It begins with a quotation of Micah's opponents, who register their Protest (v. 6) and then asks questions (v. 7a), a reply is then given, which, formulated as direct address (2nd Person), immediately shifts from a general accusation (v. 7a) reply is than given, which formulated as direct address (2nd Person), immediately shifts from a general accusation (v. 8a) to concrete reproaches (vv. 8b-10) Micah's rejection of his opponents concludes with a sarcastic picture of the kind of accommodating Prophet desired by the People (v. 11), Yahweh is mentioned once by the protesters (v. 7a). The alteration between direct address (2nd Person), and report (3rd Person) reflects the course of, disputation speech: at first, in the style of a report (3rd Person v. 6a). Micah quotes his opponents (Probably before the assembly before the city gate), next, in the course of indictment he addresses them directly (2n Person vv. 11) refers to them as "this People over there" as he hands them over to the assembly for sentencing.

***Message of Micah*****:** The heart and the centre of Micah's message can be stated briefly: Yahweh is bringing inexorable doom on Samaria, Jerusalem and the cities of Judah. The guilt for this rests with the authorities and the leading citizens, such as Judges, Prophets, and Priests.

Prophet is concerned about his home town. Village after village is exposed to the doom (2:1-11) but at the same time Micah is concerned about Jerusalem (3:1-12).

What is the origin of the approaching disaster? while the destructive elements are clearly scotched out, all of which point to military conquest, nevertheless "the conquest" (l;15a) is not mentioned by name. "Assyria" is mentioned in 5;5b (6b) by a late of voice. The Prophet expresses that Yahweh as the author of imminent catastrophe (1:12b, 2:3). For Micah,

Samaria will be demolished (1-6), Jerusalem will be completely destroyed, and even the temple mount will become a wilderness (3:12), the Present authorities become enslaved, losing their Property (2:3f), the children of the People will be carried into exile (1:16), there are also hints of military occupation and flight (1:15).

***Motivation for the Disaster:*** it is Yahweh's judgment that terrifies Micah (2:3), the guilty are not the individual members but "Jacob" and Israel, with its wickedness and sin, i.e., the same entity for which he holds the heads and leaders of Jerusalem responsible, according to 3:1,19. Micah places the guilty before a court of Justice which is not ministered in the gate of the village; rather, it is Yahweh who, comprehensively and conclusively executes justice over Judah and Jerusalem.

If more precisely we ask to whom in particular Micah accuses in his judgment speeches, then clearly it is not the People of Judah and Jerusalem as a whole; rather, it is exclusively the leaders in positions of responsibility; the authorities (2:1b), especially the heads, overseers, judges, priests and prophets in Jerusalem (3:1,5,9,11).

***Why does he Accuse them of Guilt?*** because they transgress against one people whom Micah considers himself so responsible-a responsibility which they are supposed to carry out. What for Micah is the decisive criterion of his accusation? Justice (misphat) i.e. the orders and institutions of justice which guide and orient Israel, and to which the heads and judges of Jerusalem should equally consider themselves obligated but which they abhor (cf. 3:1b, ab with 3:8a). Accordingly, Micah can formulate his accusation against the leading circles in general terms: "They hate the good and love the evil" (3:2a) or "They twist all that is straight." When Micah expresses himself in concrete terms, he appreciates catchwords for guilt from Israel's legal tradition: "covet", "role", "Oppress" (2:2 cf. Exod. 20:17a, b; Lev. 19:13 etc.).

***Conclusion:*** The prophetic activity in ancient Israel during eighth century was one with radical change and we make the following concluding remarks.

First eighth century Israel was the result of a change from tribal background to well-developed socio-economic and political system. Prophets of this period had to address those issues drastically creating a wide gap between the rich and poor. Second, the economic system had also moved from tribal-egalitarian to business oriented market economy in which the poor and the underprivileged communities were further marginalized. The production of crops was geared towards profit and market. The staple food products became expensive making the poor farmers further poor. Third, the religious system was also moving towards syncretism due to the influence of Canaanite-Baal religion.

Chapter 4

# Seventh Century Prophecy (Jeremiah, Zephaniah, Nahum & Habakkuk)

***Introduction:*** In the previous section we have noted in most details the situation of 8th century Prophecy both in its historical Period as well as in its Prophetic involvement. We have Pointed out that the northern Kingdom had disintegrated quickly and most of the religious situation of the southern Kingdom too was not up to the expectation. When we come to the seventh century the situations in the southern Kingdom is further deteriorated. We shall examine this situation in the light of four Prophets as mentioned above. To begin with we shall consider Jeremiah's Prophetic ministry because Jeremiah delivered several oracles belonging to this turbulent Period.

***Jeremiah:*** One of the major Prophets in ancient Israel whose dates corresponds roughly to the last half-century of Israel's nation-hood, i.e., 640-587 BCE. Jeremiah survived, however the destruction of Jerusalem in 587 BCE. and lived out the final years of his old age in Egypt where he was taken by refugees who sought exile there. Jeremiah roughly worked during the Period of late seventh and early 6th century BCE during which time many events in the world history surrounding Judah took place which had direct impact upon the Kingdom of Judah that led to its final destruction.

On Jeremiah's early life very little is known besides What is mentioned in the superscription to his book (1:1)., His father was very glad the day he was born (20:15), and he too was Joyful earlier in life (8:18 "My Joy is gone"). Jeremiah was born the son of Hilkiah, a Priest at Anathoth. Anathoth was a village 2-3 miles north of Jerusalem in the old territory of Benjamin. The family of Jeremiah possessed land (32:9) and may have been one of some means.

Jeremiah was called to be a Prophet in the 13th year of Josiah (1:2,4). This was 627 BCE, the same year Assurbanipal died, in his account of the call, Jeremiah lay stress on his young age, i.e., somewhere around 18 and 25 years of age. Based on this calculation, Jeremiah must have been 12 or 13 when he began his ministry as in the case of boy Samuel (1 Sam. 2:11,18,21). So Jeremiah's birth can be dated in ca. 640 BCE.

Jeremiah gives no indication of accepting Yahweh's call when it comes, despite the impression made upon him that he was chosen for prophetic office before he was born and now on the day of visitation has heard that choice continued (1:5,10). But Yahweh, too, is clear that the call must await a future fulfilment; "I am watching over my words to Perform it" (1:12).

***Historical Period of Jeremiah:*** Jeremiah's historical Period, and all the events revolved around him can be better understood at two stages. We shall briefly consider them.

***a) Jeremiah's Early Career (622-605 BCE):*** Jeremiah accepts the call in 622 BCE. after the temple scroll is found. In a later confession he reflects on the importance of this event Personally, saying,

"Your words were found, and I ate them and Your words became to me a joy and the delight of my heart for I am called by your name of Yahweh, God of hosts" (15:16).

If Jeremiah was thirteen, say, when the call came, he would now be 18. No Prophetic Preaching, in any event, should be dated before the year 622 BCE.

According to 1:13-19, soon after his call, Jeremiah was given mandate to begin his ministry. Yahweh's word was conveyed to him in a vision: "kettle of Boiling water tipped away from the north, its contents almost read to spill out." The vision spoke of a foe who was balanced to attack Judah from the North. When this message to Jerusalem is conveyed, People may hate Jeremiah, but those who fight against him will not Prevail for Yahweh Will be with him and see that his life is spared (1,19).

During Josianic reform (622 BCE), Jeremiah was actively pursuing his vocation as a Prophet: Preaching Yahweh's word, attending temple worship, and associating with many of the nation's leading citizens (eg: 19:1). He supported to some extent the national reform Program. The Persecution which he experienced early from Priestly kin at Anathoth (11:18-12:6) is fully understandable if Jeremiah gave support to the reform Program of centralized worship at Jerusalem (cf. 3:12-14; 31:2-14), for that would have had the Practical effect of closing down the Anathoth sanctuary. His preaching on obedience to the Covenant (11:11-8) and his call for a more rigorous Sabbath observance (17:19-27) also fit well into the period after 622 BCE.

Jeremiah reflects nationalistic ideas when he wants Judah divested of its vassalage to Assyria and Egypt (2:18,36; 13: 1-11) and when he calls for a return of the exiles taken away to Assyria in 722 BCE (3:12-14; 30:31). The same can be social for his support of political union between North and South, a reform idea tied in closely with Josiah's Plan for single sanctuary in Jerusalem.

Neither People of high nor low status escaped Jeremiah's indictment (2:8; 5:4-5; 8:8), thus he faced tremendous opposition from everyone. Jeremiah's frustration over a lack of preaching success is espoused in 6:16-17, a passage that also Provides a focus on the early career:

*"Thus says the lord: stand by the roads, and look, and as for the ancient Paths, where the good way is; and walk in it, and find rest for your souls. But they said, 'we will not walk in it'. I set watchmen over you, saying, 'Give heed to the sound of the trumpet!' But they said, 'we will not give heed!"*

When his reform Preaching failed to move People to true repentance, Jeremiah turned his attention to the coming foe. Though the identity of Judah's foe is never given, it has to be Babylon; some would like to identity this foe with Scythians, but it is unlikely at this point. Jeremiah was full apprised of this foe shortly after 622 at, a time when he was still a relatively young man. Yahweh's command, that he not marry (16:2) is already predicted on the certainty of war and national destruction.

If the foe Poems are correlated with Babylon's rise in Mesopotamia, they begin then 614-612 BCE Prophet Habakkuk announces the rise of this same foe, earliest date assigned to his Preaching is 615 BCE. The laments of Jeremiah show his deepest level of involvement. The dialogues and trilogues contain rapid alternation between divine word, human terror, and the Prophet's own expression of Personal grief (eg: 8:13-17, 18-22).

The death of Josiah was a national tragedy, and Jeremiah's silence about the Megiddo adventure remains as an enigma in his early Career. He laments this good King (II Chr 35:25), although soon after he says the greater tragedy for Judah is the Permanent departure of Young Jehoahaz (Shallum) from the land (22:10). Jeremiah's remembrances of Josiah are Positive, particularly when the comparison is made between him and his son Jehoiakim (22:13-17).

The years from 609 to 605 were difficult for the Prophet as the earliest dated Price in the book makes all too clear. When Pharaoh Neco installed Jehoiakim, the Political climate in Jerusalem changed. During this time Jeremiah delivered the so called "Temple Sermon" (7:1-15) in the Jehoiakim's accession Year (26:1). Jeremiah here makes a scathing indictment of the People's 'shallow religiosity and duplicity before Yahweh. They seem content just to know that the temple sits on Zion and that salvific liturgies are spoken in worship; they care nothing for the weightier matters of executing justice and living in accordance with covenant demands. Jeremiah says that the Place is rife with every imaginable evil, the real nerve is struck when Jeremiah announces that Yahweh will destroy the temple as he destroyed his first sanctuary at Shiloh. When the sermon is over, the court is called into session at the New gate in the temple in Present. The Priests and the Prophets who were the most offended, demanded that Jeremiah be Put to death. The Princes in attendance are more allied with the defense. In the end they decide the case, acquitting Jeremiah on the strength of his testimony that Yahweh had sent him with his message. Jeremiah has passed the test of a true Prophet (Deut. 13:1-5). Many of the confessions fit well into the early years of Jehoiakim's reign. These are glimpses into a Prophets interior life show that bedrock tenets of Jeremiah's faith were being called into question (15:15-18; 10:14-18; 20:7-10). But once the heart is let out, assurances are renewed (15:19-21) and Jeremiah too is 'renewed, enough in one case that he able to sing about Yahweh's deliverance (20:11-13).

The year 605 was Pivotal for the nation and for Jeremiah Personally. The Battle of Carchemish left Egypt weakened and Babylon emerged as the new Power in the world affairs. Jeremiah addressed the Egyptian defeat with an oracle (46:2-12). Jeremiah also decided in this year to Prepare the first written scroll of his oracles. After the scroll was read Publically, Jeremiah and Baruch were forced to go into hiding, for they were now in direct conflict with the King (chap. 36).

***(b) Jeremiah's later Career (604-586 BCE):*** These years are remarkably well documented compared to the Previous years in his early career. Nevertheless, these are two periods of roughly seven years each, 604 597, and 596-588, during which we have no definite knowledge of Jeremiah's activities. When Jeremiah and Baruch disappeared from Public view in 604, they had most recently Preoccupied with scroll writing It is possible that in the years following, particularly when the two of them were out of public view, more time was spent in this Pursuit. We are told that when the first scroll had been destroyed was written, it contained added material (36:32). It is unlikely that Jeremiah had any Public ministry during Jehoiahim's remaining years. He certainly had nothing good to say about the King; Jehoiakim spent recklessly on luxurious new quarters for himself and him use of slave labour in this building Project offended everyone besides Jeremiah. Worst of all he was violent and dishonest, and cared nothing for justice or for helping the needy (22:13-17). Jeremiah could only Predict a shameful end for this King (22:18-19).

When, the city surrendered to Nebuchadnezzar in 597, Jeremiah was again active speaking the divine word and articulating as well the expressions of grief which were widespread (10:17-25; 13:15-27). His message to the departing exiles was hopeful yet bittersweet (31:21-22). Jehoiachim, he said, would not return home nor would any of his offspring sit on David's throne (22:24-30).

Nebuchadnezzar put Zedekiah on the throne before departing from Jerusalem, and, with this King, Jeremiah had to endure another round of hard times. It is not that Zedekiah disliked Jeremiah Particularly; the Problems seems rather to have been Zedekiah's non Principled behaviour during a time when the city lived continually on the brink of Chaos. Zedekiah seems to have been Powerless in the midst of this sorry state of affairs. Jeremiah was active during the first four years of Zedekiah's reign, 597-594/3, and then again when Jerusalem was under siege for the last time in 588-587. During Zedekiah's middle years we are not sure Jeremiah's activities. He was Perhaps addressing certain foreign nations with oracles (Chapters 48-51) in addition to writing more scrolls with Baruch. In 594/3 Jeremiah gave Seraiah, the brother of Baruch, a scroll of oracles written against Babylon (51:59-64).

Jeremiah's final decade of Prophetic ministry was controlled by a vision received about good and bad figs (chapter 24). The good figs were the exiles who had gone to Babylon, the bad figs were the people remaining in Jerusalem. This message Put Jeremiah at odds with the nation's leaders who at the time were talking revolt with their allies (27:3). Certain Prophets such as Hananiah lent them support by predicting a speedy return of Jehoiachim and the other exiles (28:1-4). A classic confrontation took place between Jeremiah and Hananiah which brought the question of true and false Prophecy into sharp focus (chap. 28).

We are well informed about Jeremiah's activity just Prior to Jerusalem's fall. He had now become the key figure in the tragic drama which was unfolding. Zedekiah continually sought him out, hoping against hope that Yahweh would save the nation as in times Past (21:12). Jeremiah informed him, however, that Yahweh was fighting against the city. Taking words almost verbatim from Deut 30:15, but giving them a new twist, he told the King: "I set before you (the way) of life and the way of death" (21:18), The way of life now was to surrender; to resist was the way of death. But Zedekiah did not listen. He seemed irreversibly bent on Plunging himself and the nation into ruinous defeat. Jeremiah told the King there was no way he could escape a face-to-face meeting with Nebuchadnezzar (3:1-7), which eventually took place.

When the city was under siege, Zedekiah made a covenant to grant liberty to all Hebrew slaves (34:8-22), something he should have done simply because the law required in (Deut 15:12). But when Egypt marched north and forced the Babylonian army to Pull back from Jerusalem, the king reneged. on the covenant, and took the slaves back. Jeremiah was swift with a word to him and his fellow schemers: "I Proclaim to your liberty to the sword, to pestilence, and to famine" (34:17). During the lifting of the siege, Jeremiah attempted to leave the city to take care of some personal business at Anathoth, but he was stopped at the Benjamin gate and accused of deserting to the Babylonians (chp. 37). Jeremiah dismissed the charge, but to no avail, Royal officials beat him and threw him into Prison, where he remained until the King summoned him to his residence - this time secretly and asked him for another oracle from Yahweh. One came, but there was no change. Jeremiah then pleaded not to be sent back to prison, and Zedekiah granted the request. He was placed instead under, the house arrest in the court of guard. There he remained until the city fell, receiving each day one loaf of bread as long as the supply held out (37:21). Jeremiah is also reported during these last days as having been abandoned in a cistern for Preaching surrender (chap. 38). There he would have led had not Ebed-melech the Ethiopian rescued him. Zedekiah in this situation is portrayed as powerless over against those who were forcing his hand (38:5).

While Jeremiah was in the court of the guard he received from Yahweh a new word of hope. On the other side of the doom would be deliverance and restoration: exiles would return; the land would be repossessed; Yahweh would replace the broken covenant with a new one Jeremiah accepted this word, but not without struggle. He bought a family plot at Anathoth to symbolize Yahweh's promise (32:1-4). Despite moments of deep despair, Jeremiah seems not to have lost faith completely in Yahweh's ability to save (23:5-8; 31:23-40; 33:1-13; 39:15-18). When they city was taken and large number of People were either killed or taken captive Jeremiah was given his own life "as a Prize of war", This fulfilled earlier Promises which Yahweh had made to him (1:8,19; 15:20-21), Nebuzaradan, acting on a direct order from Nebuchadnezzar freed Jeremiah and allowed him to go wherever he desired (39:11-14; 40:1-6).

With Jerusalem in ruins, the People who remained took up residence at Mizpah under Gedaliah whom Nebuchadnezzar had appointed governor. Jeremiah joined them. The reconstituted community was soon fractured, however, when Gedaliah was murdered along with others in a plot instigated by the King of Ammon (chap. 40-42). Once again the people turned to Jeremiah for a word from Yahweh (Chap. 42). Ten days later it came: They should stay in the land, not to go to Egypt which is what the current talk was. This word, however, like so many others spoken earlier, was disregarded. In fact, the people accused Jeremiah of treasonous collaboration with Baruch (43:2-7), A group consequently left for Egypt, taking Jeremiah and Baruch along, and settled at Tahpanhes (43:7).

Jeremiah was about 55 when he arrived in Egypt: once there, he reiterated Yahweh's judgment upon that nation (43:8-13). His message to expatriate Jews who were continuing their worship of the Queen of Heaven was essentially what it had been back in Jerusalem some years earlier (chap. 44). These People, however, had a different view of things. They said the destruction of Jerusalem came about because worship of the Queen of Heaven was discontinued. To this Jeremiah could only say ironically "Go ahead then and confirm your vows!" (44:25). Yahweh, Jeremiah assures, will have the last word. This remnant in Egypt will die though it came there to live.

We hear no more from Jeremiah and the Bible does not mention his death. Later sources contain conflicting reports about martyrdom and a natural death in Egypt.

***Jeremiah's Rhetoric (speech) and Preaching:*** While it is generally agreed that Jeremiah as one of the great thinkers in the OT, his language and style have not always won high acclaim. According to Jerome, "Jeremiah the Prophet…" is seem to be more rustic in language than Isaiah and Hosea and certain other Prophets among the Hebrews, but equal in thought... Moreover, the simplicity of his speech was the result of his birthplace. For he was a native of Anathoth, which even today, is a small: village 3 miles distant from Jerusalem." But this statement is not altogether true, because we see a skillful Poet in the sayings of Jeremiah (as argued by Holladay, Lundblom etc.). We shall briefly examine few speech forms used by Jeremiah in his Preaching.

***(c) Repetition: Jeremiah makes effective use of repetition, the most basic element of all in ancient Hebrew rhetoric, there are sub or minor types of repetition as follows:***

***Repetition of a word as a Paraphrases for the superlative:*** "Peace, Peace" in 6:14; 8:11. (ii) Repetition of a word for emphasis (germinato): "my bowels, my mowels" in 4:19; "land land, land" in 22:29; in Prose text: "the temple of Yahweh, the temple of Yahweh, the temple of Yahweh" in 7:4.

***Accumulation: It is heavy and stereotyped:*** Nouns heap up in twos, threes and fours, and longer Phrases balance rthymically in Parallelism. The Jeremiah Prose contains some of the same noun chains and balanced Phrases found in Deuteronomy and II Kings. Some examples of this type are: "Sword, famine, and Pestilence" (14:12; 12:9; 24:10; 27:8 etc.); "reproach, by word, taunt, and curse" (24:9); "cities of Judah and streets of Jerusalem" (7:17, 34; 11:6; 33:10; 44:6,17,21); "the voice of mirth and the voice of gladness, the voice of the bridegroom and the voice of the bride" (7:34; 16:9; 25:10; 33:11); other examples are found in: Jer. 7:33; 16:4;

19:7; 34:20; 1:18 etc., and in the Poetic text: 12:7 "1 have forsaken my house, I have abandoned my heritage, I have given the beloved of my soul into the hands of her enemies."

### *Metaphors and Related Things*

***(i) Metaphor:*** Jeremiah uses a variety of vivid metaphors, some are brief, i.e., only a word or two, while others expand into an entire verse of poetry (9:1). Jeremiah's metaphors describe Yahweh, the false God's, kings, the nation, the enemy, and even Jeremiah himself. Yahweh is "the fountain of living waters"; the false God's by contrast are but "broken cisterns" (2:13) Jeremiah speaks of the fractured covenant relationship when he says to the people, "You broke your Yoke and burst your bonds" (2:20). In 2:21 the nation which was once a "choice of red Vine" is now said to have degenerated into a "Wild vine."

The most disparaging metaphors, Jeremiah reserves for his own nation Israel. He calls the nation "a restive young Camel interlacing her tracks" or a "wild-ass... in her heat sniffing stallions" (5:8). Jeremiah seeks to evoke repentance from the People with a couple of agricultural metaphors: "Break up your follow ground, and sow not among thorns" (4:3).

In describing the enemy, Jeremiah uses the common metaphor the "lion" Earlier foes from Assyria were roaring lions (2:15); now the foe from the North is another lion (4;7; 5:6) or else a "wolf" or a "leopard" (5:6). In 8;17 Babylon is depicted as two different varieties of snakes. King Jehoiachim says, Jeremiah, has become in defeat a 'broken pot' (22:28). As for Jeremiah himself, in order that he may withstand the opposition sure to come from people in Jerusalem, Yahweh promises to make him into "a fortified city, an iron pillar, and bronze walls" (1:18).

***(ii) Simile:*** Jeremiah uses Simile extensively, covering with it much of the same ground he covers with the metaphor. The wayward individual is "like a horse plugging headlong into battle" (8; 6). Way word Israel waits on the road (for lovers) 'like an… Arab in the wilderness" (3:2), Yet she cries out rebelliously against Yahweh, "like a lion in the forest" (12:8), when judgment comes, however, she will cry "like a woman in labour" 1, (6:24; 13:21; 22:23 etc.) The besiegers of Jerusalem are "like keepers of a field against her round about" (4:17); their quiver is "like an open tomb" (5:16); and the soar of their coming is "like the sea" (6:23) Yahweh will scatter the People "like the east wind" (13:24).

***(iii) Euphemism:*** On some occasions Jeremiah substitutes more mild term or one with adjunct meaning in order to avoid saying something either too harsh or too explicit. This is euphemism. In 8:14 he says, "let us go into the fortified cities and be silent there, for Yahweh our God has silenced us."

"Be silent" (Heb, dmm) is a euphemism for "die" (RSV: "perish"). The same verb appears in 25:37: "the peaceful folds are made silent" (RSV: "devastated").

***(d) The Exaggerated Contrast:*** In this the first statement will negate an idea, but the speaker does not really mean to deny it for the idea, is otherwise valid and true. Jeremiah, for example, says that Yahweh did not command the fathers to make burnt offerings and sacrifices when the People left Egypt: he commanded them to obey his voice (7:22-23). Following Josiah's death and the deposition of Jehoahaz, he also says, "weep not for him who is dead, nor bemoan him, but weep bitterly for him who goes away" (22:10).

***(e) Drama:*** In the Jeremianic Preaching there is more than a little theatrics mixed in. For example, he will now and then turn to address imaginary audiences: the heavens in 2:12; Jerusalem in 4:14; the land in 22:29 and Yahweh's sword in 47:6. He imagines a ready in scribe as his side be says in 22:30, "Write this man down as childless...," referring to the deposed King Jehoiachim.

***(f) Prophetic symbolism:*** Act and Being: Jeremiah's Prophetic message is more than words, Jeremiah like many of his Predecessors went a step further and dramatized the spoken word with symbolic action. He buried a loin cloth and later recovered it ruined in order to symbolize the spoiled Pride awaiting a nation which abandons its covenant with Yahweh (l3:1-11). He broke an empty flask at the Potsherd gate to symbolize Yahweh's determination to make empty the plans of an ambitious People in Judah and Jerusalem (chap.19). When the Babylonians began asserting rule over Palestine, Jeremiah wore Thorns and Yoke bars around his neck to symbolize subservience which Judah must now offer to Nebuchadnezzar (chap. 27). Later in Egypt, Jeremiah buried stones in the Pavement before Pharaoh's Palace at Tahpanes. These were to symbolize the future erection of Nebuchadnezzar's throne on that site (43:8-13). But when Jerusalem was about to fall, Jeremiah bought Property at Anathoth from his cousin Hanamel to point People ahead to the day when Yahweh would restore them to the land (chap. 32).

These actions, like the spoken word in all its fullness, were powerful means of communication. Symbolic action, therefore, was a natural extension of Prophetic Preaching. At the same time Yahweh was behind all those expressions of Jeremiah. Jeremiah's entire being bad now become the message - a dual message about a suffering nation and a suffering God in whose service the Prophet steadfastly remained to the very end (For that matter, Jeremiah's celibacy had symbolic meaning (16:1-9).

***The Message of Jeremiah:*** One of the main. objective of Jeremiah's message was to utter an explanation of the catastrophe, which will fall on Judah in 587 BCE Because People have failed to comply with the law and the words of Yahweh mediated to them by the Prophets (cf. 3:12ff, 11:3ff). However, Yahweh will certainly restore the fortunes of the People and gave back their land to them (29:4).

Jeremiah's message on Babylon is very Positive. He warns People of Israel to subject to the Babylonian authority; (27:11). Moreover, Jeremiah sees the Babylonian authority as a legitimate monarchy on the earth established by Yahweh himself. In one of the remarkable passage i.e., 27:4-6, Jeremiah even gives the title 'ebed'. (servant) to the Babylonian King Nebuchadnezzar (Previously in other Places this word is applied only to Davidic dynasty). In the words of Klaus Koch, "Jeremiah gives the phrase (my servant) a universal connotation in a way that was unheard of for Israelite ears. It is true that Amos and Isaiah had viewed the Assyrian Kings as tools of destruction instigated by Yahweh; but they did not see the foreign power as a Positive ordering force". (The Prophets, vol. II 562), Every Kingdom that rebels against 'Nebuchadnezzar' will be visited by Yahweh through three active powers sword, famine and pestilence. Yahweh's Kingdom will extend as far as distant Elam, and will bring down evil on evil men through the agency of the Babylonian troops (44;34-39). At the same time Jeremiah points out the limitations of the Babylonian Power. After seventy years (i.e., from 605 to 538 BCE), even this Power will be shattered and the relief will come to Israel (27:21f, 51:59f).

Jeremiah proclaims in his message that exile is not purposed for mere punishment, even though it is intended to Punish the sins of Judah, it is more as an opportunity to turn to God (29:10-14). This message of hope is impressively presented by Jeremiah in his preaching on the new covenant (chp. 32), also through a symbolic action by purchasing a piece of land (32:17-44). Jeremiah's basis of new covenant will be made effective by Yahweh (cf. 31:31-34; 32:37-41).

Thus starting from the saying that people's sins are cause of the events occurred in 587 BCE. (21:5), then he moves on to say the words of assurance, hope and new creative action of God to restore his people from their misfortunes (36:3, 18:11-12; 24:6; 27:22) and in particular assures them the return to their home (31:17).

***ZEPHANIAH:*** A Prophet during the reign of Josiah (640-609 BCE) identified as son of Cushi, son of Gedaliah, son Amariah, son of Hezekiah (1:1). Zephaniah exercised his prophetic ministry in Jerusalem.

Zephaniah's Period and Person: According to Zeph 1:4, the period of the Prophet was stated to be a time of syncretism. Both in Judah and

Jerusalem People Practiced the Canaanite cult of Baal, Assyria's religion of Astral mythology (or star worship of the cult of god Moloch or Milcom) which originated among the Ammonites. The Prophetic critique aims at those cults that were undermining the pure monotheism of worship of Yahweh, had to the conclusion that Josiah's reform of the cult had not yet taken place. We are thus at a Period Preceding the Deuteronomistic reform of 622 BCE. According to 1:8, the "Phrase" "Kings sons" may means Josiah's childhood (II Kings 21:1). On the basis of 2:13-15, a reference to Nineveh indicates, perhaps we are at a date before 612 BCE. since the fall of Nineveh had yet taken place.

From these reference Points we are led to conclude finally that Zephaniah must have made his appearance after the Period of the dark reigns of Manasseh (687-642 BCE.) and Amon 642-641 BCE See II Kings 21 and II Chronicles chap.33). After almost a half century prophetic silence, among as a group of new witnesses we find Zephaniah in the last decades of the seventh century along the side of the Prophets Nahum, Jeremiah and Habakkuk, according to this calculation, Zephaniah came to the fore in 639 BCE in the first half of Josiah's reign in Judah, and served Primarily in Jerusalem.

The name Zephaniah means: "the lord has hidden" or "the lord has caused to be hidden." This name was, common in Israel (eg: Jer 29:29; Zech. 6:10,14). the authors intention in tracing the Prophets family three generations beyond his father remains a mystery; perhaps it is to show that the Prophet comes from royal family, therefore King Hezekiah was his great-grand father, but his father Cushi, a foreigner.

The circumstances of Prophet's life are completely unknown, he knows well about the capital city and its, leaders. He gives Precise topographical descriptions of Jerusalem, royal palace (1:8-9), a temple mounts and its neighboured (1:10-11), old city (1:12-13), new city (1:10-11) Zephaniah is a relentless critic of his age. He knows well the leading strata of society and castigates them severely: the royal court (1:8-9), the priesthood (1:4, 3:4) the judges and officials (3:3), the merchants and financiers (1:11).

Zephaniah is well acquainted with the works of 8th century Processors. eg: The Day of Yahweh (Zeph 1:7-13, 14-18, cf. Amos 5:18-20, Isa 2:4ff). Zephaniah contributes to Israel's rich literary heritage. The book, mainly Poetic, open with a dramatic judgment oracle on all creation (1:2-3) and on Judah (vv. 4-9) Zephaniah graphically develops the Day of the Lord in the imagery of War, theophany, and judgment (vv.14-18). He combines a universal message (vv. 2-3; 2:4-15; 3:6-8) and a Particularistic Judgment on Judah (1:4-6; 3:1-4). The prophets directs style employs Poetic device Parallelism, word Play, repetition, assonance and metaphor. The Prophetic Speech forms reflects a paucity of extended descriptions or a creative use of Prophetic heritage. Zephaniah communicates his message in a straight forward manner.

***The Theology of Zephaniah:*** Zephaniah's theology is placed right in the midst of his own historical situation. Following are the important concerns in his message.

***(a) A righteous God is offended by human sin:*** Zephaniah talks about the heterodox syncretism which Manasseh had imposed upon Judah and which was still a feature of life during Josiah's Youth comes in; Yet it is wrong to think that Zephaniah is only concerned about cultic matters. mishapt ("commands"), tsedheq ("righteousness") and 'anawah ("humility") are identified as the ideals by which the saved remnant is to be identified (2:3). This is in accord with the character of Yahweh who is righteous (tsadiq) and who each morning, "shows forth his mishpat" ("Justice", 3:5), In his description of ideal society which Yahweh will create beyond the Judgment, there will be a universal, acknowledgement of Yahweh's rule (3:9) and life will be characterized by humility, integrity, and truthfulness (3:12-13). It is the current absence of these qualities which angers and offends Yahweh.

***(b) Yahweh will destroy, all creation:*** Even though Zephaniah's primary concern is with Judah, Yahweh judgment will extend to all creation, Foreign nations will be destroyed because of their godlessness (2:5-15), all living creatures will cease to exist (1:2-3).

The phrase "the day of Yahweh" is frequently used by Zephaniah in his theology (1:7,10,12, 2:2; 3:8,9,11,16). In some Places, it seems, as with Amos, that the Day of Yahweh is near at hand (1:14), whereas at other times it seems to be somewhere in the distance (3:8).

The main emphasis of Zephaniah is that the total destruction of life upon earth has spoken forcefully to the people of God in times of great, disaster, such as during the middle ages when war, famine, and disease frequently wiped out entire populations. Similar thing is going to happen in Judah according to Zephaniah.

***(c) A remnant of the Jerusalem community will be restored to its land and will Preside over a renewed humankind:*** The idea of remnant who may be saved is suggested in 2:3 where those who are righteous and humble may Perhaps be hidden from Yahweh's wrath on the awful day. It is referred again in 2:7,9 where the remnant is depicted as inheriting the lands of Judah's evil neighbours after the Judgment has taken Place. In 3:9-20, it is stated that remnant will Preside over a humankind which acknowledges Yahweh (vss. 9-10). This remnant will dwell in safety and in a golden age will be admired by all the peoples of the earth (3:20).

***NAHUM:*** Absolutely nothing is known about Nahum the man other than the fact that he was a native of Elkosh (1:1). Even the location of that village is uncertain, although the most likely identification is somewhere in the Judean countryside. Like other prophets, neither Nahum's ancestry nor his occupation is disclosed. It does seem likely, however, that his words were Spoken just before the fall of Nineveh in 612 BCE. The word Nahum means "comfort", which fits well with the context of his work.

***Historical Background:*** There are two specific historical events mentioned in the book. The first (in chronological order) is the sack of the Egyptian city of Thebes, called No'amon in 3:8, by Esarhaddon, King of Assyria. He brought it under Assyrian control in 670 BCE but finally captured it in 661 BCE. The other is the fall of Nineveh in 612 BCE to Cyaxres, the Mede, in alliance with the Babylonians after a siege of three months. We might suppose from this that we are able to pinpoint Nahum somewhere in the period between 661 and 612, as it is done by many scholars: but two difficulties because of this: (i) it is by no means clear when a Prophet is referring to a past event and when he is predicting something yet to happen in the future. That is because of the rhetorical device known to Hebraists as the prophetic perfect (i.e., explaining a past event as though it happened at Present). This partly explains why commentators have been divided in their opinions as to whether Nahum is predicting the fall of Nineveh, or is describing something which had already taken place: (ii) the 'historical' references in the prophetic books is that they may have had at the time the original Prophet used them, or acquainted latter among those who passed on his words, a symbolic meaning (eg. Babylon in the first chapter of the book of Revelation as equal to Rome). It is quite possible that the book of Nahum uses 'Nineveh' in such a way and, if that were so, we could no, more 'date' it by the fall of historical city of Nineveh than we could date the author of 'Revelation' by the fall of the historical city of Babylon.

However, it is safe to assume that there was a prophet Nahum somewhere behind the present book, and that he lived in the time of Assyrian domination over Judah and much of the ANB, probably towards the time of the decline and fall of that empire. Micah lived in the shadow of cast by the rise of Assyrian power, Manasseh as the King of Judah (647-642 BCE) was a vassal of Assyria throughout his reign. The great Assyrian King Ashurbanipal (668-627 BCE) as the King who sacked Thebes in 661 (Nah. 3:8). But by the end of his reign Assyria was already being menaced by the combined threat of the Medes and the Babylonians. Soon after Ashurbanipal's death these inflicted a defeat on the Assyrians just outside Babylon in 626 BCE. In 614 the capital city of Asshur fell of Cyaxares the Mede, and two years later Cyaxates and Naboplassar of Babylon took

Nineveh. So if Micah may be said to have witnessed the dawn of the Assyrian empire, Nahum celebrated its sunset.

***The Poetic Style of Nahum:*** The Prophet expresses his ideas in vigorous, imaginative, lively poetry which makes it something of a literary masterpiece. The oppressor nation is a lion in its den (2:11ff) or again a prostitute (3:4), the shock of Yahweh's Judgment Produces the staggering and helplessness of drunkenness (3:11). Similes: God's victims are swept away like stubble before God's wrath which burns; like fire (1:12), the cries of the captive women sound like the moaning of doves (2:7,8). The city is like a pool of water evaporating in the sun (2:8) cf. 3:15, 3:16. The literary device of the rhetorical question sharpens the irony: 1:6; 2:11 et.al. In 1:6 "who can stand before his indignation?"; 2:11 "Where is the lion's den?"; 3:8: "Are you better than No-Amon?"

***The Message of Nahum:*** According to this Prophet, Yahweh is the Champion of the outraged and helpless and "will by no means Justify the guilty" (1:3). In the final analysis, the threat against Nineveh does not stem from Personal hatred of the human author or some historical event in the seventh century BCE., but from the nature of God who is jealous for the righteous, wrathful towards his enemies, and claims dominion over the world. The vision of Nahum renders intelligible this imminent sovereignty of Israel's God over the history of nations. In the words of B.S. Childs this idea is further captured strongly "What nation can withstand the God who overcame the primordial Chaos" (OT Introduction p. 444) The prophetic message is the defeat of Nineveh (Assyrians) is a sign of the victory of God and the basis for hope that his power and justice will ultimately conquer all evil.

***HABAKKUK:*** Habakkuk served Judah as God's prophet (1:1), the name Habakkuk means "to embrace" (cf. 3:1,1:1). Some relate the prophet to the son of the Shunamite woman in II Kings 4:16; others identify him with the watchman of Isaiah (Isa 21:6, see Hab. 2:1). According to one of the Apocryphal texts of Bel and Dragon, Habakkuk was the "the son of Jesus of the tribe of Levi." It is likely that Habakkuk was a Levite associated with the temple singers (3:1, 19; I Chr. 25:1-8), who lived in Judah during the last days of Josiah (640-609) and in the earlier Part of the regime of Jehoiakim.

***The Historical Context:*** Habakkuk's message fits historically in the context of the fall of Nineveh (612 BCE) and emergence of Babylon as the Neo-Babylonian Kingdom (605 BCE) mentioned in 1:6. Habakkuk witnessed significant shifts as the death of Josiah brought an end to the era of reform and Judah rapidly lost her independence. She would only dance to the piping of the international powers around her. Jehoiakim, a selfish, tyrannical, and godless King, took over following the brief reign of Jehoahaz (in 609 BCE).

Habakkuk cried out against the violence he witnessed (1:2), he spoke God's word in a crisis situation from an increased lawlessness and injustice in Judah (vv. 2-5). After Josiah's sudden death. (609 BCE) and the rise of Babylon in 605 BCE Assyria and Egypt had been defeated by Babylon at Carchemish, and Judah's days were numbered.

***Literary forms in Habakkuk:*** The book of Habakkuk has two Prophetic laments (1:2-4, 12-17) in which the Prophet questions Yahweh's righteousness. The Lord responds with oracles of Judgment (vv. 5-11; 2:1-4). The dialogue between God and the Prophet ends (2:5) only to be followed by a taunt, comprising five "woes" (vv. 6-20). The connection between the dialogues (1:2-2:5) and the taunt is left for the reader to apprehend, but this ambiguity and the terse Poetic style encourage the reader to listen closely to his speech, to God's speech to the Prophet, and to the Prophets speech against Babylon.

The third chapter is set apart with its own introduction, "A Prayer of Habakkuk the prophet" (3:1), and with its musical notation (see v. 1 on Shigionoth, v. 1 "For the director of Music. On my stringed instrument," v. 19). This chapter consists of several genres (hymn, lament, and thanksgiving).

***The Message of Habakkuk:*** Habakkuk deals with the moral questions of God's raising up the Babylonians. The Assyrians had been cruel, Nineveh had been destroyed in 612 BCE, just as Nahum had Prophesized, and the last vestiges of Assyrian Power were to come to an end at Carchemish (605 BCE). Assyria, "the rod of God's anger", had fallen prey to its own pride, but they wondered God could use Babylon to inflict Judgment on Judah when their cruelty and Pagan way further destroyed God's Kingdom? The questions of Habakkuk encouraged godly to develop an experiential faith (the righteous will live by his faith", Hab 2:4) and to submit to God's rule, who freely uses crooked instruments in the establishment of his Kingdom. To focus sharply on the message of Habakkuk, two important issues can be brought out here.

***God's Freedom and Righteousness in Judgment:*** Habakkuk charged the Lord with being unfair using the form of a Prophetic complaint (1:2-4). How could the Lord permit the country of Judah to continue breaking his covenant? Idolatry, immorality, and corruption were so prevalent that God's Kingdom was "Paralyzed" (v. 4). The wicked has overtaken the righteous in number. The days were so harsh that the godly were considered accused, whereas the wicked Prospered. The Lord's response (vv. 5-11) was not completely to Habakkuk's liking, but violence of the Babylonians. "Like" would be overcome by "like" but for Habakkuk, the Point is how can Babylon might accomplish God's purpose?

Habakkuk's second complaint (1:12-17) was twofold. *Firstly*, he charged Judah with destroying the foundations of God's Kingdom by reverting Justice and righteousness. *Second*, he lamented God's response, fearing that in his freedom, all his righteousness might be uprooted from the land and result in absolute anarchy (v. 17). "living by faith" is the key expression of Habakkuk, the lord revealed to the prophet that his righteous kingdom will be established in the end (2:2,14, 2:3 et.al.).

***The Final Triumph of God's Righteousness:*** The book of Habakkuk challenges the righteous to discern God's will in adverse times and calls for perseverance while awaiting the establishment of God's righteous Kingdom. The Last chapter is in the form of a liturgy with a prophetic prayer (3:1-19) to be sung. By means of a regular liturgical use, the people of God encourage one another meditate on God's Past acts and to hope for the glorious and victorious future to which Habakkuk has borne witness. Habakkuk's contribution to the Prophetic wisdom is seen here; Meditate on acts of God in the Past; pray in present crisis; live in fidelity to Yahweh; Rejoice in the future deliverance. These are perspectives for living with a vision according to the Prophet Habakkuk.

***Conclusion:*** Seventh century prophecy was once again influenced factors thatare moving fast due to changes in the international socio political and religious trends. Few concluding observations in this regard. First, during this period we can notice the peak in political activity both in Judah and in the international politics. Moreover, the Kingdom of Judah, after the fall of Samaria (Northern Kingdom), was moving towards the Babylonian exile. Second, prophets of Judah in the seventh century instruct the people that they should surrender themselves to the international powers as it is proper to do so within the plan of Yahweh. Third, consequently people of Judah should be ready to go to exile in Babylon and any disobedience to this is only to disobey Yahweh's will and purpose for the Kingdom of Judah.

Chapter 5

# Prophetic Ministry During the Exilic Period (Ezekiel and Deutero-Isaiah-Chaps. 40-55)

***Introduction:*** The Babylonian exile was one of the most decisive events in the history of Israel. It is also most traumatic, not only because of the fate of the people in exile, but more decisively because of the events that led to the destruction and deportation. The exilic age served as a turning point in the Jewish history, as it provided an opportunity for the new orientation of their faith, in the succeeding period. W. H. Schmidt observes that "the external losses of many kinds (in the exilic age) were spiritually profitable, because the period exile become one of uncommon literary productivity." The basic question posed by the people who were in exile was, Yahweh as God of Israel, was he still in control of the events in the history in the midst of the events that had occurred one after another, finally shattered the nation in this exilic age? Ralph W. Klein observes that all the institutions based on which the Israelite faith was rested (temple, covenant, monarchy etc.) had no longer functioned. What kind of future was possible for people which traced its unique election to God who had just lost? This as we have said repeatedly, was the assurance of Yahweh's external choice of Zion as his earthly seat, and his unconditional Promises of David of a dynasty that would never end. Sheltered by that dogma, the nation rested secure and, rejecting prophetic warnings, confidently awaited Yahweh's mighty intervention, and a future that would bring the ideal saviour of David's line-perhaps the next one-under Yahweh's righteous and magnificent rule would be triumphantly established and all dynastic promises made actual.

With these few preliminary remarks on the general theological climate of the exile, now let us move on the consider two great prophetic figures, who not only served as channels of communicating God's message, but also served as channels of comfort and hope to the people in exile.

***EZEKIEL:*** Prophet Ezekiel lived during the Babylonian exile and was active as a Prophet from 593 BCE to at least 571 BCE. He loved as an exile himself and, according to the label of the book that goes by his name, (1:1-2), did all his preaching in Babylonia, probably in the Jewish settlement of Tel-abib on the Kebar Canal near the ancient city of Nippur (3:15). The word Ezekiel (yéhezqél) means "God strengthens (this child)" or possibly "maygod strengthen (this person)."

***Personal Information of Ezekiel:*** Ezekiel and his family were undoubtedly among the 8000 (approx.) exiles taken to Babylon after the siege of Jerusalem in 598 BCE (II Kings 24:16) We are not sure of his age at the time of his call in 587 BCE., but may be 30 years (if date in 1:1 indicates Prophets age). Ezekiel was a son of priest namely Busi (1:10. His interest in the temple, his knowledge of sacral ordinances, as well as closeness of his language to that of the code of Holiness and Priestly document provide external support to the fact that Ezekiel was a member of an influential family in Jerusalem, deported in 597 BCE.

From the book we can make out very little of his personal information. According to 24:14ff he was married and lost his wife by her sudden death, roughly at the time in 587 BCE when Jerusalem fell to the armies besieging it and lost its existence and honour. The situation which is recorded on three occasions, that he was sitting in his house and received a visit from the elders of Judah (8:1), or Israel (14:1, 20:1), who expected to receive through him a word from God, giving the impression of being stereotyped as in the case of Elisha's disciples (cf. II Kings 4:38, 6:2ff). There are different opinions of the scholars who understood Ezekiel's prophecy as pathological phenomenon. We shall consider some such opinions.

(i) According to A. Klostermann, Ezek 3-24 chaps. we find Ezekiel as a diary of sick person over against which in chps. 33-48, the utterances of the Person, when recovered are to be found (cf. chp. 2; 3:22ff, 4:4) and in 33:21ff, form a turning point in the physical progress of the prophet, which in general is to be diagnosed as catalepsy; however, Kolterman comments that behind the sickness we must recognise an idea, implanted in his soul by God, as the effective cause.

(ii) B. Baentsch: sets out "Pathological features in Israel's prophecy" and concludes that, these actions, in all their details are so precisely calculated (as in the case of Ezekiel), and directed to their purpose, that we cannot speak here of a mutual disturbance.

(iii) E. C. Browne: referred the prophet directly to the sphere of psychological illness, these traits he understands in various traits of illness which appear in the symbolic actions by Freudian categories, hut also discern directly schizophrenic features.

But also to all these proposals, Walter Zimmerli makes an observation that, there are only a few passages, in which the prophet reveals his personal feelings, even for a moment: As a rule, his own feelings are forced into the background in the service of the high task which he fulfilled in the vigorous forms of his prophetic office.

***The Historical Background:*** Ezekiel was active during the years between 593-571 BCE, which fall in the period of the rule of Nebuchadnezzar II, the great King of Neo-Babylonian dynasty (605-562). Under Nebuchadnezzar, the contemporary Babylonian power had once again taken control of the area of the land routes from Africa to Asia, after an interval in which Egypt, the Power in the south, and sought to play a decisive role again, as it had once before in the Period of great Pharaohs of the middle and New Kingdoms.

The information given in the book of Ezekiel reflects the following important details:

It is clear that the internal strife in Jerusalem, with which King Zedekiah could not cope up with led finally to defection from Nebuchadnezzar and the withholding of tribute. On the 10th day of the 10th month of Zedekiah's ninth Year (II Kings 25:1; Eze. 24:1) Nebuchadnezzar stood at the gates of Jerusalem.

The wars surrounding the traumatic loss of Northern Kingdom under Assyria brought the Southern Kingdom of Judah into Assyrian orbit as well (cf. Isa. 6-8 chps). Its King Hezekiah had tried to revolt in 705-701, but failed; and although Judah was not wiped out completely, its next King Manasseh, remained a faithful servant of Assyria throughout his long reign.

In 605 BCE a victory over Egyptians brought the Babylonians to power over Judah. Jehoiakim pledged loyalty to Babylon but was soon attempting to rebel and work back Judah's independence. The prophet Jeremiah's message was lovingly carried out in opposition to this political opportunism of Jehoiakim. Jehoiakim died in the Babylonian siege, and captured, his young son Jehoiakinand in his place they named his uncle Zedekiah to rule as regent (II Kings 24:8:20). But later, when he rebelled, Nebuchadnezzar's army levelled the cities of Judah and finally burned Jerusalem to the ground, taking away whatever remained of value and exiling the rest of its leading citizens in the summer of 586 BCE (II Kings 25, Jer. 52). To this kind of situation, prophet Ezekiel brings out his message.

***Language and Speech forms of Ezekiel:*** The book of Ezekiel is distinguished from other books in that it is throughout composed in the

I-style, except in 1:3 and 111 24:24, Ezekiel is mentioned in the third person in a divine speech, which is introduced by the prophets in the first person (24;15,20). We shall now consider, few important speech forms used in Ezekiel:

- ***(a)*** ***The Visions: Four Elaborated visions are Found:*** (1:1-3:15; chps. 8-11; 37:1-14; chps. 40-48); added to these are: 3:16a, 22-5:17; 11:1-13. The visions are introduced by a quite stereotyped vocabulary. The experiences of ecstatic transportation are described in the visions of the Working of the spirit, his visions are guided by the spirit of God (3:12, 14; 11:24 etc.). The mention of "Seeing" is very much in the background. According to Von Rabenau, any idea of a visionary's secret knowledge and experience is removed in Ezekiel. This clearly distinguishes Ezekiel from the later apocalyptists, in which, according to Daniel 8:26, 12:4 (also 7:28), the visionary is commanded to keep secret what he has seen.
- ***(b)*** ***The Sign-actions:*** The purpose of prophet's sign actions is to set forth in a visible action the event announced by Yahweh as something already begun. These are not simple arbitrary meaningful didactic "pictorialization" by the prophet himself, but possesses its legitimacy solely from the fact that it is a part of the (coming) divine action. In this measure the divine command to perform the action becomes an integral part of it. eg: The three actions of siege symbolism, which are compiled into a three-sign composition in the basic text of chps. 4ff. 4:12-15, the exiles baggage in 12:1f; the action at the road junction in 21:23f and the joining of the two sticks in 37:15ff make a mention of prophetic deeds.
- ***(c)*** ***Metaphorical Discourses:*** (speeches using a figure: legal accusations, fables of animals, and plants. laments for the dead): eg: vine in the Ezek. 15 (vv. 2-5: the figure: vv.6-8: the interpretation): The figurative discourse in first opened up in the style of a discussion through a series of questions (vv. 23), to which the prophet himself, still within the figure, gives the answer which emerges with compelling force. chaps. 16: The figure of the ungrateful founding child, which Yahweh has brought up and taken in marriage. After the introduction in v. 2 it concerns an oracle to Jerusalem about a "revelation of abomination" i.e. an accusation. For, v. 35 the speech passes over into an announcement in Judgment, Prepared for by an accusation. For v. 44 we can see

a further formal peculiarity which is important for the history of the development of prophetic word in of Ezekiel. Here the theme of unfaithful wife is under the new perspective of a comparison with her mother and sisters (Samaria, Sodom); chp. 23 figurative discourse of two immoral sisters Oholah and Oholibah: the first part, accusation. From v. 22 the divine announcement of judgment follows in direct address to Oholibah; behind which is hidden the Judean remnant of Israel. chap. 17: The allegorical traits in the figurative discourse. The history of two eagles, the cedar, and the vine makes use of the features of wisdom fables of plants and animals. In chaps. 15 & 23, the whole is intended as an actual proclamation of judgment. Behind the figures of animal fables their lie hidden the kings of the two great rival powers, and behind those of plant fables the two Judean Kings Jehoiakim and Zedekiah. In particular Zedekiah's apostasy from Nebuchadnezzar is represented. Chap. 19: a figurative discourse, "a lament for the dead", here too an appendix of animal & plant world is given in vv. 10-14. It speaks of a lioness "and her two cubs and then of a vine. An elaborate lament in chap. 27 is given regarding Tye as a notable ship.

***(d)*** ***Legal Sayings:*** (eg: 22:1-16): which is introduced as an "accusation" holds up before the bloody city of Jerusalem and its crimes. Subsequently, in vv. 13-16, there has been added to it an announcement of judgment formulated as a proof saying. In chap. 20, the sin of defendant is not made evident here in the course of its earlier history. Rather there occur, as a declaration of this sin, throughout vv. 6-12 a series of apodictic clause which declare the rejection at each of these laws by the city of blood. In chap. 18: a series of sacred laws from the entrance-liturgy of the temple worship are given. The first part, which at its beginning is stylized as a disputation oracle, shows at once the division of the description into these phrases also found in Ezek. 20. cf. 22:6-12; 38:10-20.

***(e)*** ***Priestly Rituals:*** (43:18-19; 45:18-20a (also 46:2,12); 44:17-31) in part contains apodictic priestly laws, which have many counter parts in the Holiness Code. In 45:21-46:12, instructions for the temple worship of the prince and regulations for sacrifice in the style of P are incorporated. At no point can we see the recasting of the original legal from under the prophetic call for repentance. In all the legal material found in chaps. 40-48, we are dealing directly with borrowings from extra prophetic legal material, which is incorporated without formal change and which does not carry the signature of Ezekiel's hand (cf. 47:15-26).

*(f)* ***Disputation Oracle (Argument):*** This phenomenon makes it probable that the prophet spoke his prophecies outside the narrow circle of his disciples. His prophecy is formulated as an answer, or as a rule even more sharply, as our attack upon sayings voiced either by those around him, or more distantly, by the survivors of Israel in the old homeland. Eg: 25:3; 26:2; 36:2 Three specific things involved in this type.

(i) Quotations: (25:3) It is simply a bold exclamation of delight over the misfortunes, others which is put in the mouth of the enemy other examples, of this type are: 26;2; 36:2; 33:24.

(ii) oaths: (cf: 18:3; 20:33; 33:11; 35:11): Like any other prophetic sayings, these oath speeches found in the sayings of Ezekiel are very sharp and prominent sayings that describe the main concern and the message of the prophet.

(iii) Proof-of-Identity sayings: Based on the phrases "you will know, that, I am Yahweh", It consists of two parts: (a) The verbal element: "You will know that ....", in the profane sphere, belongs to the process of proving and demonstrating (b) the verbal assertion of recognition, the object clause.

***The Message of Ezekiel:*** Ezekiel's message rightly fits into his context. We shall briefly summaries the main concerns raised by him:

***(a) Yahweh and His Appearing:*** Yahweh and his action is also in substance the great, central theme of the prophetic preaching. In view of this description of the attributes of Yahweh is completely lacking except only in (42:12; 36:20-22; 20:39). Yahweh is never called great, the style of hymnic description, using the Participle (as in Deutero-Isaiah and Psalms) is not seen here. Where statements about Yahweh are made, the finite verb dominates. The expression as the recognition formula which as a rule sets the person Yahweh, as indicated by his name, in the center of what is known ("know that I am Yahweh") cf. 15:13; 6:10; 17:21; 37:14 etc.

***(b) Prophetic Announcement of Woe to Israel:*** The judgment speeches are expressed with a clear aim. Eg: 6:1-7, the threat of the day of Yahweh in direct address 6:1-7, threatens the mountains and valleys of Israel with, imminent devastation by war. In 6:11-14, the devastation is made clear and specific by the trial of sword, famine and pestilence (as in Jer. 28:8); the accusation is also very strong in the judgment speeches. In this, the very name, "house of Israel" can be immediately replaced by "house of rebellion", even their fathers are rebellions "upto this day" (2:3).

***(c) The Proclamation of Judgment Against the Nations:*** (Chaps. 25-32 and 35). Seven foreign nations are addressed in these oracles is also aimed at Egypt and its ruler (29-32). 29:1ff and 32:1ff speak of Pharaoh as the crocodile of the Nile which is destroyed. preaching against Tyre (26:1-28:19): on account of its selfish, calculating gloating over the fall of Jerusalem with its rival trade judgement is announced against Tyre.

***(d) The prophetic announcement of Salvation for Israel:*** Here Yahweh's faithfulness to the house of Israel comes most fully to expression in chaps. 34, 36-48. In 37:1ff, the creation's language is behind the thought, from death to life. For the sake of his faithfulness, Yahweh will bless the land and make it fruitful in a new way. In this land, Yahweh will also restore to the house of Israel its original unity. The sign-action of joining together two sticks, which carry the inscriptions, "Judah" and "Joseph" (37:15ff) makes this clear (Perhaps Josiah's reform in the background).

The new salvation, which the prophet has to proclaim, is especially illuminated by him is from two sides: (i) The Israel of the Period before judgment was shattered by its disobedience and (ii) The act of revival by Yahweh will consequently consist in his creating a people as an obedient and law-abiding people. The new situation; which Jer. 31:31-34 describes as a setting of the commandments on the hearts of the people, is set out in Ezek 11:9, and 36:26 as the gift of a new heart and a new spirit, the heat of stone replaced by heart of flesh (36:27; 37:14; 39:29). The salvation is that Yahweh will take up his abode in the midst of the house of Israel (48:30-35). This is explained in the light of the fact that Ezekiel saw that in a real way God's presence moved (1:1-3) form Jerusalem to be present among the exiles in Babylon, thus giving protection to the people who are in the exile. By this Ezekiel assigns significant role to Babylon and Nebuchadnezzar. It is in Babylon the word of God that laid the foundation to the history has to be heard, and it is here the prophet is appointed to speak. But when the people returned back to Jerusalem God's presence is once again found in Jerusalem, thus God brought new creative action among the people (36:23-28).

### *DEUTERO-ISAIAH (40-55 Chaps)*

The sixteen chapters (40-55) of the Book of Isaiah usually known as Deutero-Isaiah or Second Isaiah essentially contains the oracles of a single prophet, who belong to the time of Babylonian exile.

Traditionally it was taken for granted that the whole book of Isaiah consisted of the collected prophecies of one man, Isaiah, the son of Amoz, who lived in Jerusalem, the capital city of the Kingdom of Judah, in eighth century BCE (1:1). However, in the period before the rise of modern criticism at the end of the eighteenth century CE different views are expressed by the scholars which are universally accepted now.

In 1783 Eichhron and in 1789 Doderlein stated their View that Isa. 40-66 derives from an exilic prophet. In 1892 Duhm expounded this theory vigorously, through restricting to 40-55 and ascribing 56-66 to a later period. Duhm's view has largely won the day and may be considered almost universal. The conservative scholars like Allis, E. J. Young and R. Margalioth support the unity of the book by saying ("that all the 66 chapters are from a single author, but to do so flies in the face of statements actually made in 40-55, according to which Jerusalem and Temple are destroyed (44:26-28; 51:3; 52:9), the people languishing in exile in Babylonia (42:22,23; 43:14), Babylon (and not Assyria) is threatened with destruction (47; 48:14), and Cyrus has already embarked on his victorious campaign (41: 2-3, 25; 44: 28, 45:1-3). In addition, the different vocabulary, the exuberant style, and the unique theological milieu-all completely different from first Isaiah must be taken into account.

Since the prophet whose sayings are preserved in 40-55 is anonymous, he is referred to as Deutero-Isaiah (or Second Isaiah). He may have the same as his Predecessor Isaiah, which would account for the association of his book with the earlier one; there is no evidence to support this suggestion. The juxtaposition has sometimes been explained on the basis that the prophet's speaking in 40-55 and 56-66 were "disciples" of Isaiah, members of his "school". The existence of such a school, however, for more than two centuries is in itself unlikely.

Before Deutero-Isaiah could even expect to gain a hearing he had first to Present his credentials: he had to give a convincing account of how he had been called by Yahweh to be a Prophet. Deutero-Isaiah's call stands at the beginnings of the book, in 40; 18. It differs from the call narratives of earlier prophets in that the Prophets dialogue is not apparently with Yahweh himself but with a heavenly being or angel. But this in no way finds less and inferior place of Deutero-Isaiah'scall than other prophets. 40:1-8 is set in the heavenly realms where Yahweh holds court surrounded by his heavenly servants. Deutero-Isaiah's implicit claim to have been present at this 'heavenly council' was itself a claim to prophetical status. In 40:1-8 Deutero-Isaiah, like 'Micaiah ben Imlah, hears or overhears, what is being said there. Yahweh, apparently, is not present, or atleast does not Speak: "says" your God' in v.1 is part of a speech by heavenly being telling others, 'what God is saying'. The imperatives in vv.1-3 are in the plural, addressed not to the prophet, but by one angel to others, conveying to them Yahweh's instructions to make preparations for his return to Jerusalem accompanied by his exiled people. But in v. 6 "And I said, what shall I cry?", can be the voice of Deutero-Isaiah himself he asks what message he is to proclaim, and receives his commissions. In doing so he becomes a prophet of Yahweh.

***Historical Background:*** In 587 BCE the tiny Kingdom of Judah, the survivor of the two kingdoms into which the united kingdom of Israel had been split at the death of Solomon, succumbed to the military power of the neo-Babylonian empires despite its traditional confidence in its special relationship with its God Yahweh, but in accordance with the predictions of prophets such as Jeremiah and Ezekiel, its capital Jerusalem pillaged and burnt, the king and many high officials executed, and the whole apparatus of government brought to an end. Of those who survived, many including the former leaders of the nation, were deported to Babylonia. A substantial portion of the population, however, remained. The deportation of 587 BCE was only one of several. There had been a Previous one, following an earlier Babylonian campaign, in 597 BCE (2 Kings 24:10-17), and another was to follow in 582 BCE (Jer 52:28:30).

Deutero-Isaiah's prophetic ministry was exercised during the period following 587 BCE, which is generally known as the Babylonian Exile. That is during the half century between the fall of Jerusalem and the conquest of Babylonian scene establishes beyond reasonable doubt that he was one of the exiles in Babylon. His career, however, falls in the latter part of the Period. As has already been noted, he was familiar with the name of Cyrus, whom he regarded as the man destined by Yahweh to conquer Babylon and to release the Jewish exiles. Throughout his extant oracles he regarded these events as imminent. But in order to understand the situation in which he exercised his ministry it is necessary to survey the history of the preceding half century.

In 587 BCE the power of Nee-Babylonian Empire was at its peak. But it was not destined to be of long duration. Nebuchadnezzar, the conqueror of Jerusalem was its greatest king; and a decline began soon after his death in 562 BCE. In 556 BCE, after a period of confusion, the Babylonians placed on the throne one Nabuna'id (Nabonidus) a native of Harran Nabonidus caused divisions in the state by his antagonism towards the cult of Marduk, the patron on deity of the city of Babylon, and its powerful priesthood. He revived the cults of other God's whose worship had a special devotion to the god Sin, the god of his native city Harran.

For about eight years (552-545), Nabonidus, for some reason left the capital, Babylon, and set up his court in the oasis of Teima in the north Arabian desert. The absence of king in the capital not only caused confusion in the administration of the court in Babylon which is a serious problem in view of the Medes and the Persians posing a severe threat to the empire, but also, the absence of the king in the capital means, no celebration of the New

Year festival, which resulted in a terrible calamity to the Babylon (a view held strongly by the natives of Babylon).

The external menace to the empire had begun with the increasing power of the people known as Medes, in view of this, Nabonidus allied himself with Cyrus, King of Persia, against Medas, but in 550 BCE Cyrus, who was a vassal king within the Median empire, defeated the Median army without Babylonian assistance and found himself master of the Median empire.

Nabonidus now realized that it was the Persians who were the real enemy. Now he desperately made an alliance with the only two powers of consequence at that time, Egypt, then ruled by Amasis, and the Lydia, in the western Asia Minor, whose King was Croesus. But in 547 BCE Cyrus conquered Lydia. In 545 BCE Nabonidus returned to Babylon, and celebration of the New Year festival was resumed. In the years which followed Cyrus was absent from the scene, occupied with conquests elsewhere. But in 539 BCE, his army arrived at the gates of Babylon. Cyrus now claimed to be the deliverer of the Population from Nabonidus, and to be the true patron of their god Marduk whom Nabonidus had neglected. Cyrus had not miscalculated. The citizens of Babylon surrendered without a struggle and welcomed the conqueror, who took the titles of a Babylonian King and restored Marduk to his traditional position of honour. The neo-Babylonian Empire had come to an end swallowed up in the greater Persian Empire. The city of Babylon continued to flourish, but now as a mere Provincial city.

During this time the Jewish exiles in Babylon seem to have been well aware of the trend of political and military events. Most of the Jews in exile did not really took note of the developments with eagerness, because it matters nothing to them and they also thought that their condition will be same as before. But they may have been aware that the Cyrus, unlike the Assyrians and the Babylonians, did not make use of mass deportations as an instrument of Policy. Deutero-Isaiah, however, took note of all these developments seriously. the meteoric career of Cyrus made a profound impression on him, and he delivered a number of oracles in which he predicted that Cyrus would overthrow Babylon and release the Jewish exiles. (41:2-4; 41:25; 44:28; 45:1-6; 45:13; 46:11; 48:14-15). In a way contrary to Deutero-Isaiah's expectation, Cyrus did not destroy the city of Babylon (see especially chap.47), rather Cyrus made the city more splendid than ever. But Cyrus did allow the Jewish exiles to return home if they wished, though not in the triumphant manner which Deutero-Isaiah expected.

With all this information, now we may date the ministry of Deutero-Isaiah mainly in the years of 550-539 BCE and probably towards the end of that period. This again clearly indicates that Deutero-Isaiah is addressing to the Jewish exiles of second generation. The exiles in Babylonian become despondent and discouraged due to the un fulfilment of the words of Jeremiah and Ezekiel. There seems to be a tendency that they will no more be delivered from the clutches of the Babylonian oppression (through in a real sense it in not, like the Egyptian bondage). To such people, who were in a state of confusion and discouragement, Deutero-Isaiah brings out his message with a positive note of their future deliverance.

***Forms of Speech in Deutero-Isaiah:*** Based on the form-critical analysis following are the important types of speech used by the Deutero-Isaiah. We shall discuss on few of them:

***(a) The Oracle of Salvation:*** According to von Waldow (1953), some oracles of Deutero-Isaiah point to an actual cultic setting: their initial words like quotations of phrases, or even whole sections, taken from lamentations which had actually been recited by the exiles at their meetings for worship. In other words, Deutero-Isaiah had picked up these self-pitying epithets and appeals for help, and, speaking in the name of Yahweh, had assured the petitioners that their situation was now to be radically transformed. Thus 49:14 makes a specific reference to the recital of such a lamentation: "But Zion has said, "Yahweh has forsaken me, my Lord has forgotten me"! 51:9-10 similarly is quotation from such a lamentation. reminding Yahweh of his great deeds in the Past and appealing for a further display of his power now, In other examples, prophet, in addressing his audience, picked up phrases which they had evidently applied to themselves in describing their state of distress: 'You worm Jacob' (41:14): 'You whose heart fails, who are far from deliverance' (46:12); 'to one deeply despised' (49:7); 'You who have drunk from Yahweh's hand the cup of his wrath' (51:17); 'O barren one, who did not bear' (54:1). Much of this language is similar to the psalms of lament and the language of lamentations in the Book of Lamentations, which are themselves lamentations of the people from the exilic period (in Palestine, not Babylonia).

According to Claus Westermann the promises of salvation in Deutero-Isaiah are not numerous, and almost all occur within chapters 41-44. They comprise 41:8-13; 41:14-16; general, a strict pattern whose cultic origins are shown by their similarity to examples of Babylonian oracles addressed by priests to kings in answer to their prayers.

According to Westermann's analysis of 41:14-16, the following are the elements of structure found in it.

- *(i)* ***The address:*** 'You worm Jacob, you lose Israel' (14a) compare 41:8,9; 43:1a; 44:1. The address is missing in 43;5-7 and 54:4-6.
- *(ii)* ***The assurance of salvation:*** "Fear not!" (14a) this Phrase, which occurs in all the Promises of salvation (also in 41:10; 43:1; 43:5; 44:2b; 54:4) is in itself an assurance that the petitioner's

prayers will be answered, since it is spoken as Yahweh's own authoritative word; it may occur either at the beginning of the address or immediately after it.

***(iii)*** ***The basis of the assurance:*** (1) "I will help you" says Yahweh; (2) 'the Holy one of Israel is your Redeemer (14b), Here Yahweh substantiates his word of assurance, answering the appeals forhelp by affirming his presence, his intimate relationship with the petitioners, and the fact that he is already taking steps to help them. In four cases (here and in 43:1; 43:5; 54:4) this section is introduced by the explanatory particle Ki, 'for'. It may consist one or both of two elements: a statement about Yahweh's relationship to the petitioner (here 'the Holy one of Israel is your redeemer' elsewhere 'for your maker... is your redeemer', 54: 5) and a statement in the perfect tense (indicating certainty) that Yahweh is about to help and is already helping (here 'I will help you'; elsewhere 'I will strengthen you...,' 41:10b; 'I will redeem you...', 43:1b). This section is lacking in 44:1-5.

***(iv)*** ***The consequences of Yahweh's action:*** expressed more concretely and in greater detail, mainly in future (imperfect) tenses: vv. 15;16 a. Compare 41:11,12; 43:2; 43;5-6; 44:3-5; 54:4.

***(v)*** ***Yahweh's ultimate purpose:*** vs. 16b. This can be seen clearly only in two of the other oracles: 43;7, 44:5.

Even though these things suggested by Westermann are useful, some of them are still disputed by the scholars, i.e., the announcement of salvation. Westermann further clarifies that some more elements in it can be included:

(i) *Allusion to a previous lamentation;*

(ii) *Announcement of salvation: God's turning to his people; Go intervention;*

(iii) *God's ultimate purpose.*

***(b) The Hymn:*** One important feature of Israel's worship in the days when the Temple at Jerusalem was still in use was the Hymn or Psalm, of Praise in which the assembled People, at the major festivals of the year, offered their praise to Yahweh. Some of these hymns are quite elaborate; but (basically their structure was very simple, consisting of only two parts: first, a summons to praise, usually expressed in the imperative mood but sometimes in the cohortative ('Let us....'), and addressed to Israel' alone but sometimes to the peoples of the world, or even to the whole created universe; and secondly a statement about Yahweh's benevolence towards his people or about the consequences of that benevolence-his great deeds performed in the past in creation or in history. This section, the main section of the hymn, is often introduced by the word Ki, 'for' since it states the reason why Praise should be offered. This simple structure is well illustrated by Ps. 117:

"Praise Yahweh all nations! Extol him, all Peoples! For great is his steadfast love towards us; and the faithfulness of Yahweh endures forever".

The style of Deutero-Isaiah, was greatly influenced throughout by that of these liturgical hymns. There are complete hymns within this book; three examples are; 42:10-13; 44:23; 49:13. The last of these runs as follows: "Sing for joy, o heavens, and exalt, o earth; break forth, o mountains, in singing! For Yahweh has comforted his people, and has compassion for his afflicted" (49:13). Westermann calls these hymns as 'eschatological psalms of praise (he does not use the word hymn) on the grounds of their form as well as of their function: according to him it is only these psalms (of which a few are to be found in other prophetical books) that the summons to worship is followed by a statement Yahweh's actions rather than about his Personal qualities (as in Ps. 117).

In addition to this group of complete hymns, there are many phrases and stylistic devices of the hymn. The most striking examples of this are the Passages (eg. 42:5; 43:1; 43:16-17; 44:2; 45:18) in which he describes the nature and activity, especially the creative activity, of Yahweh in a series of Participial clauses (usually rendered in English translations by 'who…'). A good example of this is 42:5:

"Thus says God, Yahweh, who created the heavens and stretched them out, who spread forth and What grows from it, who gives breath to the people on it, and spirit to, those who walk on it..."

cf. other texts in Psalms: 103:3-5; 104:1-4; 136:4-7; 147:8-9, 14-17. Unlike psalms, however, in Deutero-Isaiah the messenger formula is used to proclaim the prophetic message by the phrase 'Thus says Yahweh'. Here also their function is to (like Psalms) evoke those sentiments of awe and dependence on Yahweh as the creator of the world and creator sustainer of Israel of which the cultic hymns had been the expression and which the exiles were in danger of losing, but which were indispensable if they were to be convinced by the promise of help which was to following in the ensuring oracle of salvation.

Sometimes such descriptions of Yahweh's nature and activity are placed in the mouth of Yahweh himself, so that he is represented as praising himself, as in 46:9-10.

" ........ For I am God, and there is no other, I am God, and there is none like me, declaring the end from the beginning and from ancient times things not yet done, saying, 'My counsel shall stand, and I will accomplish all my purpose..."

other passages in which Yahweh Praises himself include 41:4b; 42:8; 43:10-13; 44:24-28; 45:6-7; 48:12-13; 51:15.

***(c) The Trial Scene:*** Deutero-Isaiah had to deal with an audience which was reluctant to accept his message as authentic. Consequently, he was obliged to take on the role of Yahweh's advocate, attempting to substantiate his central message by means of argument. Such arguments are to be found in what A. Schoors calls 'the Polemical genres' in the book: forms of speech to which different scholars have given various names, of which Perhaps the most appropriate are the 'trial scene' (*Gerichtsszene*) and the 'disputation' (Disputations wort): Their Sitz im Leben (setting in life) is unlikely to have been that of Public worship.

The device of the trial scene had been used by earlier prophets (eg. Isa 3:13-15; Micah 6:1-5) to give additional effectiveness to their oracles of Judgment against Israel by planning them in the fictitious setting of a court of law. This procedure is probably based on the ordinary legal producers in use in pre-exilic Israel (cf. Jer. Chap. 26).

Deutero-Isaiah used the form of the trial scene mainly for the purpose: to demonstrate the worthlessness of the God's worshiped by the other nations. The 'trial' here seems not so much are the foreign nations and their God's; and the question at the issue is, 'who is the true God?', this is the of Deutero-Isaiah is most characteristic types of argument.

There are at least five clear examples of the kind of trial scene: 41:1-5; 41:21-29; 43:8-13; 44:6-8 -21-22; 45:20-25. 41:21-29 maybe taken as a model in which a number of the constitutive elements appear. The language vs. 21, which sets the scene, it clearly that of the law court. Yahweh is presiding Judge, though he is also one of the parties in dispute, the other side consists pagan God's. These are addressed and asked to present proofs of their activity and thus effectively of their existence vss. 22-23 state the nature of the matter in dispute and the kind of evidence to be admitted. But the God's are shown by their silence to be non-existent. Yahweh then presents, his own case, which is the main reason for the use of the device of the trial scene (vv. 25-28) and reaches his conclusion. The concluding judgement in v. 29 is that the other so-called God's have no existence.

A similar pattern but with slightly different features is followed in the other examples, 41:1 gives a fuller account of the setting. 43:9-12 mentions the witnesses: the nations on one side, Israel on the other. 44:6-8-21-22 ends somewhat differently from the others, with a divine promise to Israel (v. 22). But all these trial scenes are intended to leave the exiles with the impression that Yahweh is firmly in charge of events.

***(d) The Disputation:*** The disputation is a form of argument in which the speaker is usually not Yahweh but the prophet:

Westermann pointed out that Deutero-Isaiah had a predilection of one kind of argument in particular: the argument which proceeds by analogy. The speaker begins by stating a fact about which his audience would be in agreement a self-evident fact which either is a matter of common sense or forms part of the common religious tradition of Israel which no one would dispute; From this he proceeds, by means of analogy, to state a proposition which his audience had not previously been prepared to accept.

So in 40:12-17 and 40:18-26 the prophet argues from the Israelite belief that Yahweh is the creator of the world to the proposition that he must therefore be the one who controls historical persons and events. In 40:27-31 he argues from Yahweh's almightiness to the Proposition that he can make to the weary and the dispirited exiles all the strength which they need. In 45:9-13 he argues from the common sense proposition that it is absurd for a created absurd for a created abject like a pot to criticize the potter who made it, or for a foetus to question its Parents, to the Proposition that it is equally nonsensical for Israel to question Yahweh, their maker, about his plans. And in 55:8-11 he argues from the regularly and inevitability of the fertilizing power of the rain sent from heaven by Yahweh to the proposition that Yahweh's word spoken by the prophets equally cannot fail to achieve purpose for which it was sent. There are other passages in Deutero-Isaiah which take arguments, in different lines, passages, such as: 46:9-11, 48:1-11, 48:12-16.

The main theological message of Deutero-Isaiah: Before we consider the detailed study of several important theological themes in Deutero-Isaiah such as: the servant of Yahweh, Uniqueness of God, Sovereignty over the nations, understanding of history, election and covenant, comfort and hope, the word of God and other themes, let us briefly present the central message of the prophet.

The central message of Deutero-Isaiah is neatly summarized in the scene in the heavenly council (40;1-8). Its essential features are:

(i) The exiled people are to take heart because their sins now have been expiated and their term of punishment is over (vv. 1-2).

(ii) Yahweh is now about to come to the aid of his People in such a decisive fashion that the whole world will be astonished at this revelation of his glory (vv. 3-5).

(iii) The guarantee of this message of hope and restoration is the word of Yahweh spoken through the prophet, which is all-powerful and compared with which all human activity is ludicrously impotent (vv. 6-8).

Having state this, now let us move on to consider some of the important theological concerns of Deutero-Isaiah in which his message is still grasped in depth.

***(1) The Servant of Yahweh:*** is one of the special features of the oracles of Deutero-Isaiah that Israel as a nation is frequently referred to as Yahweh's 'servant' or 'slave' ('ebed). This epithet of Israel, though peculiar to Deutero-Isaiah, does not call for special remark. It is used in the Old Testament to God's children such as: Abraham, Moses, David etc. Deutero-Isaiah's designation of the nation Israel as Yahweh's servant is an example of his general tendency to personify the nation as a single individual. He used this term especially in the salvation oracles (eg: 41:8-10) to remind the exiles of their special relationship with Yahweh and so give them confidence in his good will towards them.

There are, however, a number of other passages which speak of a Servant of Yahweh but do not unmistakably identity him with Israel. The interpretation of these servant songs is a matter of debate and scholars continue to bring out new proposals on this matter. We shall briefly summarise some of the opinions:

In 1892 Bernhard Duhm put the interpretation of the Servant Songs in a new and precise way. He singled out four passages: 42;1-4; 49:1-6; 50:4-9; 52:13-53:12 in which a single individual "Servant of Yahweh" is to be seen, sharply distinguishing these from the reminder of the book, in which the Servant is Israel. These four passages he called 'Servant Songs' (Ebed-Lieder). The identity of the Servant with an 'individual' is questioned by other scholars, although the number of passages for the Servant Songs is not disputed much.

B. Duhm also found that the servant songs are different in their language and in their content. The difference with other songs in Deutero-Isaiah is also noted. Some poems picture Israel as the servant. But in the Servant songs except in 49:3, nowhere it has been mentioned that Israel is the servant. The servant of the other songs is different from that is mentioned in the servant songs. For example, the servant Israel become weary (40:27: 41;12). The servant of Yahweh was from the beginning dis-obedient (48:4). in the other songs the servant is pictured as the only person who receives salvation (49:5,6; 53:12). In the servant songs the foreigners were looked upon with compassion. But in other songs they were looked very unwantedly.

However, these arguments can be repudiated on the following grounds: though the content and style differ in Servant songs with other poems, the author is mentioning about two different servants; In 41:9; 48:2, Israelites were called as "God's witnesses" therefore we can say that the Israelites had a mission. To do so the task of Israel is not only to receive salvation, but as a chosen minority to serve as servants for a majority of people (47:5,6).

The main contention however, is the interpretation of the Servant, i.e., whom the writer of Deutero-Isaiah had in mind when he spoke of the Servant of the Lord. We shall briefly present the different interpretations on the Servant and his identity.

***(A) Collective Interpretations:*** the view that the Servant is a personification of the people of Israel is a very ancient interpretation. Apart from the explicit identification in 49:3, its main strength lies in the resemblance between the events of the Servants career-call, special status before Yahweh, suffering, imminent restoration and (according to one interpretation) mission to the world. But a number of objections are raised against the identification of the Servant with Israel.

(i) In 49:5-6 the Servant refers to a divine commission which he has received to restore Israel's fortunes. This is a difficult concept if the Servant and Israel are identical: Again in 53:1-6 the speakers ('we') refer to the things which the Servant ('he') has done for them. The view that they are the foreign nations and kings mentioned in 52:15 is difficult to reconcile with their confession in 53:46, which appears to imply that they are representatives, or at least members, of the people of Israel. But if this is so, the servant cannot himself he the embodiment of the nation.

(ii) in the songs the Servant is represented as completely devoted to the service of Yahweh as a wholly innocent sufferer. This Is in marked contrast with what Deutero-Isaiah says elsewhere about Israel, which according to him has thoroughly deserved its punishment. If the Servant of the songs were a personification of a nation, Deutero-Isaiah's whole message would appear inconsistent.

(iii) Apart from the occurrence of the word "Israel" in 49:3, the Servant is never named in the Songs. It appears to be taken for granted that his identity is known to those addressed. Such an absence of identification by name is extremely rare in Old Testament passages in which a corporate entity is personified. But particularly significant is the absence of such identification in the two songs (49:1-6 and 50:4-9) in which the Servant himself is the speaker. In the prophetical books it may be assumed that, speech in the first person singular other than that of Yahweh is that of the prophet himself, unless the contrary is specifically indicated by the naming of another speaker in an introductory phrase (eg. 'But

Zion said; 49:14) or in the body of the speech, or by the context that a personified Israel should be the speaker in these two songs without any such specific indication is therefore improbable.

The difficulties attending the simple identification of the Servant in the songs with Israel led some scholars (eg. S. R. Driver, Skinner, Blank) to suggest that he stands for a section of the nation: a righteous remnant 'ideal Israel', or something similar. Although this is a plausible theory, we can hardly accept it because no such distinction of'remnant' made with in the nation by Deutero-Isaiah.

An attempt was made by H. W. Robinson and O. Eissfeldt (1932-33), working separately, to reconcile the portrayal of the Servant as an individual with the corporate features observable both in the songs and outside, by means of the concept which Robinson called corporate personality. According to this theory the Prophets, 'Primitive Psychology' enabled him to speak now of himself and now of Israel as the servant of Yahweh: The servant can be both the prophet himself as representative of the nation and the nation whose Proper mission is actually being fulfilled only by the Prophet and that group of followers who may share his views. But this hypothesis is seriously questioned.

The most recent of the corporate theories is Proposed by Eaton, who, while pointing to certain supposed royal characteristics of the servant in the songs, believes that he stands, not for any individual king, but for the Davidic dynasty. His theory depends on the View that the Pre-exilic autumnal festival as celebrated in Judah had included a rite in which the Davidic king was ritually humiliated and then restored to his throne. This theme together with others drawn from the festival, was used in Deutero-Isaiah's oracles as a symbol of the fate of the whole Davidic dynasty: after a period of divine favour it had been humiliated by the exile, but was about to be restored by Yahweh. The main message of the book is the coming restoration of the nation, after humiliation, by a divine act of salvation; and the restoration of Davidic monarchy is an integral part and symbol of this restoration. Apart from its dependence on a particularly and disputed interpretation of the autumn festival, this theory makes two assumptions which need further substantiation: that the Servant of the songs is in fact primarily described in royal terms; and that the fate of the Davidic dynasty (explicitly referred to only in 55:3-5) played a significant role in the thought of Deutero-Isaiah as a whole.

***(B) Individual Interpretations:*** the wealth and variety of the imagery employed in the songs to describe the Servant's character and role have provided the basis for a wide range of interpretations of the figure as an individual. Different scholars have seen him as a new Moses, as a prophet, as a teacher of the law and as much else besides.

The studies of Gressmann, Engnell and Nyberg based on the AWA myths, especially the myth of the dying and rising God and its supposed re-enactment in fertility cults supposed that one version of this type of theory is applicable to the description in chapter 53 of the humiliation and subsequent restoration of the Servant is a prediction of a Messianic figure, whose career and functions are expressed in terms derived from the sequence of events in the cultic myth of Tammuz. This myth could have been familiar to Deutero-Isaiah either directly through Babylonian sources or through Canaanizing elements in the pre-exilic cult of Jerusalem. Theories of this kind have however lost support in recent years because the evidence both for the existence of a cult of a dying and rising God for influence of this kind on the Israelite cult of Yahweh now appears very fragile.

There remains the possibility that the Servant was a contemporary of Deutero-Isaiah, well known to him and to his audience. Duhm, Mowinckel (at one time) and more recently G. R. Driver believed that he was an anonymous contemporary of the author of the Songs of whom no mention is made elsewhere in the Old Testament. It would, however, be strange if a person so remarkable and so important to the author of the Songs had remained anonymous and had left no other memorial. However, if the servant was a member of Deutero-lsaiah's own generation, there is an alternative possibility: that he was none other than *the prophet himself*. But this is very old theory.

What evidence do the songs offer in support of this theory? The evidence that the Servant was a prophet is strong. In 42:1-4 the terms in which Yahweh affirms his choice of the Servant, promises to support him in his assigned task, and assures him of success despite opposition suggest the commissioning of a prophet and are strongly reminiscent of the calls of Jeremiah (1:8, 17:19) and of Ezekiel (2:3-7; 3:4-11). Again, like Jeremiah (1:5, 10) the Servant is to be Yahweh's instrument in the establishment of his sovereignty over the nations. This song, however is not the call-narrative (which is found in 40:1-8) but a subsequent oracle continuing the prophet's claim to speak with Yahweh's authority.

In 52:13-53:12, it may be inferred from the astonishment of the speakers (53:1) that an even later stage in the career of the servant has been reached. After passing through such intense suffering and humiliation that he was regarded by others as singled out by Yahweh for a special punishment (vv. 2-4), he has now in some unexpected way been rescued by the intervention of the 'arm of Yahweh', if the Servant in these lines is the prophet Deutero-Isaiah, then the prophecy may be regarding the release from a Babylonian prison, consequent on the fall of Babylon to Cyrus.

Not all the scholars who identify the servant with Deutero-Isaiah himself accept the above interpretation of the final song. The traditional view that the song was composed after his death by his followers still commands support 53:7-9 are held to refer to his death, while 53:10b-12 promise his future resurrection.

Against the identification of the Servant with Deutero-Isaiah or indeed with any merely human figure - it has been argued that the Servant's character and role especially as described in chapter 53, for transcend those conceivable of ordinary humanity. Some would answer this issue by saying that the servant transcends the suffering of an ordinary human being: in his supposed role 'vicarious sufferer', certain Christian exegetes interpret this as the suffering of the servant vicariously for others: that is, through his own unmerited suffering he enabled others to escape the divine punishment which they had deserved.

But to this view Orlinsky and Whybray expressed their doubts, by saying that people in exile had already suffered and Yahweh had now pronounced their forgiveness. No vicarious suffering, therefore, was required, apart horn this, the idea of vicarious suffering, as Orlinsky has shown, is totally alien to the Old Testament belief. For Yahweh to accept the punishment of the innocent and to acquit the guilty would be an unthinkable infringement of the principle, maintained consistently throughout the Old Testament, that "He who Justified the wicked and he who condemns the righteous are both alike an abomination to Yahweh" (Prov. 17:15).

The statements made from Isa 53:9b are to be seen in the context of the life and times of Deutero-Isaiah. It is clear that he was an exceptionally righteous man and that his exceptional suffering was understand. They were caused solely by the fact, that he had accepted the prpphetic office and so undertaken the proclamation of a politically dangerous message: the prophecy of the fall of Babylon. He thus bore the sins of many not in the sense of suffering instead of the many-as we have noted, was not the case, but of enduring additional and exceptional suffering. This suffering, as in the case of other prophets, was the consequence of the nation's sin, for it was the nation's plight which had made his prophetic activity necessary. At the same time, it could be said that his sufferings led to their restoration to 'wholeness' or their 'healing-that is, to 'their release from exile: for had he not preserved in his dangerous work at the risk of suffering and death, the divine word which, like a sharp sword in Yahweh's hand, brought about the fall of Babylon would not have been pronounced.

The portrait of the Servant of Yahweh which emerges from the songs on the basis of the above interpretation is not one of a person who transcends ordinary humanity, but of an exceptionally faithful prophet of Yahweh who, like his predecessor Jeremiah, endured great suffering in the course of his ministry but also experienced the intervention of Yahweh on his behalf to deliver him from danger. His ministry was entirely bound up with the life of his people, and it may well be that his rescue from death was regarded by those who composed chapter 53 as the turning-point in the fortunes of their community.

***(2) Uniqueness of God:*** In spite of their traditional belief, expressed in psalms and creation-narratives, that Yahweh was the creator of the world, the Jewish exiles in Babylon, surrounded by the grandiose worship of the Babylonian God's, to whom of course the Babylonians attributed their conquests, were easily tempted to wonder whether their own beliefs were mistaken: Whether their humiliation was due to Yahweh's having been defeated by God's more powerful than himself. These doubts would have been nourished by the celebration of the annual New Year festival at Babylon, a festival which commemorated the creation of the world by Marduk, his installation as king of God's, and the supremacy, of his city, Babylon. Although the actual rites of this festival were celebrated in Private, there were Public Processions along the great sacral way, and the festival was the occasion of Public rejoicing. Moreover, it is Probable that the Babylonian creation myths such as the 'Creation Epic' (Enuma Elish) which describes Marduk's exploits, were familiar to the ordinary citizens through public recitation. festivals and myths alike must have seemed to the Jewish exiles to correspond to the political reality of Babylon's supremacy.

***The question is:*** how could, Deutero-Isaiah combat the effects of this pro-Marduk propaganda? All that the prophet could do was to set the mythological tradition of Babylon against the soberer theological tradition of Israel, and to attempt to show in point after point that the latter was more credible (Yahweh) than the former (Marduk). In addition to rational argument, he also used his poetical skill to evoke the mood of joyful confidence in Yahweh's incomparable power and majesty which had been the Keynote of the Judean festival cult in the days when Yahweh's Kingship had been celebrated in Jerusalem. It was in this context, Deutero-Isaiah produced some of his finest poems.

In 40:12-31, he used the disputation form as a vehicle for his argument, In the first of these disputations (vv. 12-17) he restated the Israelite creation tradition in a series of rhetorical questions creation in order to make the point that if it is indeed Yahweh who created the world of nature with such skill (vv. 12-14) he must also possess absolute control over his human creatures, and so over the historical process. (vv. 15-17).

This disputation also puts forward an argument to show that the Israelite creation tradition itself is superior to that of Babylon. In vv. 13-14 the question is asked, rhetorically, Whether Yahweh had needed help to carry out his work of creation. This is an indirect allusion to the Babylonian polytheistic tradition such as is found in Enuma Elish, where Marduk, himself appointed as king by a 'committee' of 'God's', nevertheless received help in his creative work from the wise, Ea, his father, who is in fact alone credited in one Passage with the creation of humankind. None of the Babylonian God's therefore could be 'God' in an absolute sense as was Yahweh, to whom therefore Deutero-Isaiah can simply refer absolutely as 'God' (eg. in v. 18). The implication is clear: The Israelite tradition of sole creator is the one which has the ring of truth.

In 40:21 comes a series of further questions, which are in fact reproaches: Deutero-Isaiah asks his audience how they can Possibly be in any doubt Yahweh's incomparability. Surely they know their own tradition! In v. 22 he reminds them of that tradition, using the Participle style and vocabulary of the creation hymn (cf. Ps.136 and 104, esp. 104:2b).

The concluding Verse 40:26 about Yahweh and the heavenly bodies may at first seem to be an anti-climax; but in fact it is equally Polemical. In Enuma Elish (Tablet V) the heavenly bodies are not Marduk's creatures: they are the great God's themselves. Marduk established them in the heavens with their Prescribed, movements, but they were still God's. Against this polytheistic belief Deutero-Isaiah set the monotheistic Israelite tradition. The heavenly bodies are simply Yahweh's creatures He uses the special word 'bara''create', here, a word which is used only of the divine creation, and so makes an absolute distinction between creator and creatures. Having created the heavenly bodies Yahweh Put them, as it were, 'on Parade', bringing them out to shine 'by number! 'Not one is missing! Yahweh, then, really is incomparable: for him there are no divine rivals.

The polemic against Babylonian Polytheism is taken up again in 43:10-13, Part of a trial scene (vv. 8-13) in which Yahweh is the speaker. Yahweh's claim, which Israel's traditional belief, is that "Before me no God was formed, nor shall there be any after me" (v. 10). This is a clear allusion to Babylonian mythology, according to which Marduk belonged not to the first but to the fourth generation of God's (Enuma Elish, Tablet I), his father, Ea and his mother Damkina being mentioned by name. Marduk himself had children: so there were God's before Marduk was born, and God's after him. Deutero-Isaiah is, by implication, asking his audience which they would rather believe: the fairy-tale mythology of Babylon, or their own tradition of Yahweh who had existed since eternity and would always exist: the only God, without birth and without sexuality. The Phrase 'I am He' (v. 13 and repeated frequently in other Passages): means in effect 'I am the only one.' Deutero-Isaiah pursues the argument: the sole creator must also be the sole saviour: there is no other God to hinder him from saving his People. A similar point is made in 44:6-8; 44:24; 45:5; 46:9; 51:6.

The Israelite belief in Yahweh as creator is also made the basis of some of Deutero-Isaiah's other leading arguments. As has already be Pointed out, he used it in 45:9-13 (a disputation in which Yahweh is the speaker) to defend Yahweh's right as creator to do whatever he wishes with his creatures, as does a potter with his Pots or a father with his children. The Point here, as the final verse makes clear, is Yahweh's choice of the foreign King Cyrus as his instrument in the salvation and restoration of Israel, a choice which will certainly have needed some defense. Other passage which affirms Yahweh's supremacy as creator is 54:16-17.

Deutero-Isaiah also used the doctrine of creation to support his teaching about the efficacy of the prophetic word. In 45:18-19 he began from the Purpose fulness of Yahweh's act of creation of the world: he created it not to be chaos but to be inhabited-a different view of mankind from that of Babylonians, for whom man's sole duty was to act as slave to the God's.

Thus Deutero-Isaiah by using the Israelite creation traditions ina number of different ways is attempting to convince the exiles of the truth of his basic message of imminent salvation: he used them to expose the absurdity of Babylonian Polytheism, to show that it was Yahweh who possesses sole control over world history, and to stimulate trust in Yahweh and in the word of promise which he was Sneaking through his Prophet.

***(3) Deutero-Isaiah's Presentation of History:*** Israel's Pre-exilic narrative traditions, now incorporated in the biblical books from Genesis to Kings: comprised accounts of Yahweh's great deeds in the past: his creation of the world, guidance of the human race in its infancy, and finally his creation of Israel as his special People and his subsequent dealings with them. The Babylonian exile, because this story had now been brought to an abrupt end, was a time for reflecting on the meaning of this history, bringing together the various strands of tradition into comprehensive and theologically oriented literary works, and attempting to draw lessons, and perhaps hope, for the future from it all. Deutero-Isaiah, who was evidently familiar with the earlier traditions has used them in quite different way, he used the material as an appeal to history which forms an additional argument to support his main message.

Other prophets before Deutero-Isaiah used examples from past history to illustrate their teaching, especially as dreadful warnings (Eg. Jezreel: Hos. 1:4: Sodom and Gomorrah: Isa. 1:10; the fall of Shiloh: Jer 7:12-15; Parables of Israel's history in Ezekiel). Deutero-Isaiah used his examples in various ways, but above all to remind the exiles of incidents in which Yahweh had shown power not in anger but in love towards humankind or to his People, so that his hearers could take heart and be brought to a state of mind in which they could accept that Yahweh was both able to Perform such deeds once more.

To consider Deutero-Isaiah's usage of historical tradition, we shall look into few important ones as follows: In the use of the flood story (54:7-10), Yahweh is speaking. The question at issue is Yahweh's reliability. His aim is to Persuade the exiles, who believe that, despite his covenant with them, he has forsaken them, that it is now his intention to return to them and to behave towards them with a love which will never cease: "My steadfast love shall not depart from you, my covenant of Peace shall not be removed!" In order to convince them that he will keep the oath which he had sworn to them, he uses the analogy of the oath which he swore to Noah after the flood, that he would never again send a flood which would destroy humankind. That oath he has kept; he can therefore be relied on to keep the new one.

The next historical references are to Abraham (48:18-19) and in 51:1-3, the Prophet, addressing a dispirited audience convinced that there is no hope for them in their wretched and depleted state, used the traditions of the miraculous Parenthood of Abraham and Sarah and the marvelous gift to them of numerous and Prosperous descendants to support the new Promise and numerous Population. What Yahweh once did for their ancestors he can and will now do for them. The description of Abraham (41:8-13) as Yahweh's 'friend' (literally, 'the one whom I loved'), Which occurs again in II Chron. 20:7, reminds the exiles both of the intimacy and the constancy of Yahweh's love for them; which stretched back to their most remote ancestor.

The period of Israel's history from which Deutero-Isaiah most frequently drew lessons was that of Israel's beginnings: the release of the nation's ancestors from slavery in Egypt, their crossing of the Red Sea, and their journey, under Yahweh's guidance, through the wilderness. These events-often called as the 'Exodus events' - offered an obvious analogy to the Picture which the prophet was Presenting to the exiles of what was, about to happen to them. Deutero-Isaiah not only reminded the People of their Past events in which Yahweh's greatness is manifested, but, he taught that the 'New Exodus' would be even more spectacular and lasting in its effects than the first Exodus; so much so that he could claim that Yahweh was saying (43:18-19): "Remember not the former things, nor consider the thing of old" Behold, I am doing a new thing."

In 52:11-12 the Prophet. gives a form of command to his fellow-exiles to begin their home. This is a projection into the future: he speaks as if Babylon has already fallen, or is falling, to Cyrus. They are to leave the city, Preceded by the Ark on their wilderness Journeys (Numb. 10:33-35), The reference to the Exodus is even clearer in v. 12. The departure from Egypt had taken place secretly, by night, and in haste. (The word 'haste' or 'hurried flight' (hippazon) used here occurs elsewhere in the Old Testament only in connection with the Exodus Events-Exod. 12:11, Deut 16:3). The departure from Babylon, on the other hand, will be more like a ceremonial procession.

Another clear allusion to the Exodus is to be found in the announcement of salvation in 43: 14-21. In vv. 16-17, in a series of epithets attached to the messenger -formula, which refers in Plain terms, closely following the account in Exod. 14:21-29, to God's action at the Red Sea, when the Israelites were enabled to cross on dry ground while the Egyptians were drowned. This is a prelude to the admonition 'Remember not the former things. The 'new Exodus' will be far more glorious. The oracle ends with the Promise Proper (vv. 1ad-21), which speaks of a repetition of the feeding of the People of old in the wilderness during the Period after the crossing of the Red Sea, rendered even more marvelous by the motif of the homage of the animal world (vs. 20). Here the theme of Yahweh's glory and its effect on the beholders' is a major theme of Deutero-Isaiah's. For Deutero-Isaiah the salvation of Israel was not an end itself. The ultimate purpose was the manifestation of Yahweh's glory to the world. Deutero-Isaiah was clearly determined to turn the thoughts of the exiles away frown their Preoccupation with themselves to a deeper acknowledgement of the transcendent Saviour-God. It is significant that three of these Passages emphasize this theme: "And the glory of Yahweh shall be revealed" (40:5); "that men may see and know... that the hand of Yahweh has done it (41:20), "...they might declare my Praise" (43:21).

Deutero-Isaiah makes very few direct references to the Period of the monarchy. For him like other prophets this was essentially a time of apostasy leading to the disruption of the Kingdoms and to the exile, (52:3-6; 43:28). In 55:1-5, the reference to David is made. In this passage, Deutero-Isaiah speaks of an everlasting covenant which Yahweh will make with his people, and links this with God's 'steadfast, sure love for David', the great leader of the Past, whose greatness had been acknowledged by the surrounding nations. The mention of this 'golden age' of the time of David was intended to evoke the same feelings as were evoked by the references to Abraham: Confidence that Yahweh who in the Past had made Israel. Great and prosperous could and would now do so again. There is no Promise here of the restoration of the Davidic dynasty rather it is the whole People who will now be united with Yahweh, as David had been in v the past, in an everlasting covenant.

As one looks back on this survey of Deutero-Isaiah's references to past history, it is clear that he had a remarkably detailed knowledge of the nation's historical traditions, and he used them in a special and creative way. Deutero-Isaiah was very much aware that, despite the terrible interval of the Exile, there was a continuity in Yahweh's dealings with his People: it was not Yahweh who had ceased to love and care for his People but Israel which had ceased to love Yahweh. Yahweh is consistently Picture as always ready to demonstrate his love for Israel, and now even more abundantly than before.

***(4) Election and Covenant:*** Deutero-Isaiah's theological message is dominated by his presentation of election, the theology of election in Deutero-Isaiah takes a totally new and radical approach Deutero-Isaiah's message is Primarily directed to the Babylonian exiles, who confronted with the might of Babylonian Power. Therefore, the prophet wanted to assure them of a great comfort. Israel too was seeking God's abundant grace in this time of trouble. By combining two themes, i.e., creation and election, Deutero-Isaiah at this time addresses the discouraged people. By using certain selected vocabulary, the Prophet comforts the People: "Fear not", "I redeem", "I strengthen You", "I am with You", "You are mine" (Isa: 41:10,13; 43:1,5; 44:2ff). Deutero-Isaiah affirms the fact that Yahweh is on their side. For Deutero-Isaiah, it is the election that precedes creation in the sense that at the time of exile whom People pondered over their situation as "the elect" evokes them to reflect upon creation.

Some of the crucial Passages in which Deutero-Isaiah brings out the election tradition of Israel are: 41:9; 43:1,7,15,20-21; 44:1-5,21,24,28.

In 41:9, the verb bahar (to choose) is used with the shade of Deuteronomy. Here the idea of election refers to God's choice of Israel out of many other People, and that Israel is chosen with a future hope. Further the Prophet refers to the fact of election that was initiated with Patriarchs, but it is actively intensified in the creative action of Yahweh by his special intervention in the history.

In 43:20-21, the activity of God in creation and redemption are explained as inseparable formulas. The main setting here is deliverance (God's election) and Placed it in the wider setting of God's activity in creation. The language used for elected People (v. 21: "whom I fonned for myself", "they might declare my Praise") is reflected in the Purpose of God's creation that the elect People in the creation may glorify Him.

44:1-5 is Perhaps the most crucial Passage in Deutero-Isaiah's theology on election theme. In this passage the election is understood as something man a mere exodus event. It is in the election frame work Israel's act of deliverance took place in the course of history. This fact is further strengthened by the Prophet by referring to creation (as creative redemption of Yahweh). This being Primarily an oracle of salvation, it has special theme of election. In vv. l-2, the conspicuous note of electionis noted "Israel whom I have chosen." According to Stuhlmueller, the major stress of election of Particulars in the Past and it is the continuation of that choice in the Present.

In vv. 3-5, Yahweh's choice of Israel is explained by means of Powerful symbols. The words used here: water, spirit, blessing in the sense of recreation, Purification and renewal and God's creative power. Yahweh Provides a new dimension to the election or to the chosen ones even in the hopeless situation. These verses theologically affirm the fact that Yahweh's creative redemption in election, i.e., Yahweh controls, guides and Pervades in all the areas of Israel's life and existence.

Klaus Koch argues that Deutero-Isaiah's uniqueness to the elect and the world Yahweh does a new creative action of calling Cyrus to create the ground for the liberation of Israel from exile. Yahweh has also chosen the servant as the representative of the Israelites to the restorative action for the elect and to create a new world order for the nations. In the course of this he had been Put to death. The cultic community recognises this act as a vicarious suffering of atoning the sins of the elect. Yahweh makes an assurance that the Servant will be resurrected to life and glorified, this will enable the nations to be Partakers of this redemptive process.

Just as election is a central theme in Deutero-Isaiah's theology, covenant too finds a very important place in the oracles of the Prophet. Deutero-Isaiah uses the idea of Covenant (54:10,55:3) in order to link it with the Past, i.e., with the election of Abraham (41:8f; 51:2). The old covenant is totally overshadowed by the new covenant which Yahweh himself will initiate. However, this covenant is mediated through the Servant, who functions as mediator not only to Israel but to the entire world (all the nations; cf. 42:6 & 49:8). For Deutero-Isaiah the covenant is operative in the context of *misphat* (Justice) and *sedaka* (righteousness 45:22; 51:5). Furthermore, the Servant, i.e., Covenant of a people and light to the nations. It is obvious here that the task of the Servant is seen in the context of liberation (Light=mishphat; cf. Micah 7:8ff; Hosea 6:5; Zeph 3:5).

Thus Deutero-Isaiah the ideas of covenant and election are blended together. Just: as God elected and entered into covenant with Patriarchs (Abraham: 44:1-5, 24-28), same election-covenant act of God continues in the present.

***(5) Comfort and Hope to the Exiles:*** It was the sufferings and disappointments of the Present which made the People in exile reluctant to believe in the readiness of Yahweh to help them. Deutero-Isaiah had to interpret these sufferings; he had to account for them, and also to convince his audience that they were now coming to an end.

First of all, the prophet emphasized that it is Yahweh who had inflicted them: it was not the Babylonian kings, who were only Yahweh's instruments, and certainly not their seemingly all-powerful God's. Deutero-Isaiah makes his Point clear in 42:18-25 by saying that a nation so stupid that they had been unable to see that what was happening to them was the result of their sin.

But to tell the exiles that they deserved what they had got was to risk leaving them in despair, and also to leave them still with the feeling that Yahweh was unfair to them, since the generation felt (as we learn from other exilic writings such as Jer. 31:29; Ezek. 18:2-4; Lam. 5:7) that they were being punished for their Parents' sins. Precisely the new generation which was to be treated differently from that of their Parents. The sufferings of the Exile had never been intended by Yahweh to last forever. He had always intended that they should have a limit and that limit had been served and the exiles were therefore about to become freemen again (40:1-2). This is also the Point of the Passage about the supposed 'divorce; between Yahweh and his people (50:1). Hosea (2:2), Jeremiah (3:8), and Ezekiel (16) had all used the metaphor of divorce to stress that Yahweh had rejected his People and broken the relationship between him and them. They had, it is true, envisaged the Possibility of a reconciliation. Deutero-Isaiah however, seems in 50:1 to have denied that there had even been a real divorce: since there is no 'divorce-certificate' (see Deut. 24:1-4; Jer 3;8), these had only been a temporary separation.

In an answer to the question of People's repentance, Deutero-Isaiah stressed the grace of Yahweh which does not wait for repentance Isa 43:25, a declaration of free pardon is given in an oracle which begins as an oracle of Judgment. Deutero-Isaiah's theology is a theology of grace which outweighs all other considerations.

***(6) Cyrus:*** The Persian King is named twice in the book, probably in a single oracle, 44:24-45:7. But many other passages refer to him: 41:1-5; 41:21-29; 45:9-13; 46:9-11; 48:12-17 and Probably 42:5-7. Cyrus is directly addressed and given his commission to carryout Yahweh's purpose. In all these passages Yahweh is the speaker. Deutero-Isaiah's main Point was to say that the future lay in the hands of a great and irresistible conqueror who, however, was simply an instrument of Yahweh, created by him in order to carry out his good Purpose towards Israel.

Deutero-Isaiah went to great lengths to emphasize the complete dependence of Cyrus's achievements on the support given him by Yahweh. Yahweh not only calls him 'my shepherd' (44:28), a title used both in Israel and elsewhere in the AWA of Kings who ruled by divine appointment, but even his 'anointed one' (masiah, 45:1), a title which had Previously been reserved exclusively for the reigning Kings of the dynasty of David, God also states that he 'loves' him (48:14). The idea of Yahweh's making use of foreign Kings to carry out his purpose for Israel was not in itself new; but in the Past this had been in order to Punish Israel for its disloyalty to

Yahweh: Assyria had been 'the rod of Yahweh's anger' (Isa. 10:56), and Nebuchadnezzar, as Yahweh's instrument, but Yahweh's intentions towards his people were now wholly good, and it was Babylon which was to receive the divine chastisement (48:14). The use of the title 'anointed one' is astonishing, and was no doubt intended to administer? salutary shock to those who heard it: the exiles had no anointed King of their own who could save them; but Yahweh who could do all things (45:9-13) had created one out of the unlikely material of a foreign ruler, who was already poised to deliver the blow which would open the prison gates, set the captives free (42:7; 45:2,3; 48:14), rebuild Jerusalem and other cities of Judah, and even lay the foundations of a restored Temple (44:26-28). The fact that Cyrus was a pagan who 'did not know' Yahweh (45:4) and might be expected to attribute his successes to his own God's was of no consequence in any case, together with the world at large he would eventually come to acknowledge Yahweh as the God (45:3).

***Conclusion:*** The exilic prophets of Ezekiel and Deutero-Isaiah have immensely contributed to life and theology of exilic community. We may now summarize the discussion if the chapter in the following conclusions:

First, Ezekiel not only serves as the prophet of exilic context but he was one among the exiles who knew the mindset of the Babylonian exiles.

Second, when exiles are in a state of utter despondency, and also with the view that they lost the Jerusalem Temple, thus they are now in a foreign land and God's presence was also absent. In that crucial context Ezekiel assures the exiles that they are now safe in Babylon because Yahweh's presence also moved and is now present among the exiles even when they lost Jerusalem Temple.

Third, Deutero-Isaiah was afforesting the younger and second generation of exiles whose mindset was totally different about their present condition. This prophet took trouble to explain all that happened in the history of the nation and how Yahweh led the people thus far.

Fourth, when the exiles thought that the Babylonian gods are superior on account of their victory over Judah, D. Isaiah explains clearly how all the Babylonian pantheon of gods are totally inferior and are subjected to the authority of Yahweh. The prophet establishes with clear facts the uniqueness of Yahweh. Through his theological explanation Deutero Isaiah convincingly explains the universal plan and purpose of Yahweh.

Chapter 6

# Prophetic Ministry During the Post-Exilic Period (Trito-Isaiah, Haggai, Zechariah and Malachi)

***Introduction:*** A great deal of misunderstanding arose from the common assumption that for all practical purposes prophecy came to an end with the Babylonian exile. But this is not true at least four of the prophets whom we are going to consider belong to the Post-Exilic period (also Joel and Jonah beyond the scope of our discussion).

In order to understand how prophecy functioned and in what ways it was different from earlier forms we must first take stock of the quite different political situation in which the province of Judah found itself after the transition from Babylonian to Persian rule.

Jerusalem and the surrounding area of Judah (Yehud) formed one of several provinces, together with Syria, Samaria, Megiddo and others, under the jurisdiction of the local satrap, probably resident in Damascus. under Persian rule these provinces enjoyed a fair degree of autonomy, issuing their own coinage, policing their own territory, and collecting tribute and taxes. In keeping with the policy of the Persian rulers, in this respect much more enlightened than that of their predecessors, the juridical status of local political entities was generally respected. Judah's was one of several provinces the status of which was determined by its Temple and the cult carried on there. It was the policy of the central government to sponsor subsidize and, where necessary, restore such local cults. So, for example: the founder of the Achaemendid empire claimed to have restored the Marduk cult in Babylon after the neglect that it had suffered under the last Babylonian king, Nabonidus. Later Darius reproving the satrap Gadatas for imposing tribute on the shrine of Apollo in Magnesia. It is therefore possible that the same king should have subsidized the rebuilding of the Yahweh Temple in Jerusalem (Ezra 6:8).

In keeping with this policy, local law codes remained in force and were backed by the coercive power of the central government. Darius, mandated a codification of ancient Egyptian laws and enjoined their observance, and in the same spirit a later king commissioned Ezra to enforce 'the law of the God of heaven' among Jews in the Trans-Euphrates satrapy (Ezra 7:14, 25-26). Much of the legislation in the Pentateuch formed the civil constitution of the Jerusalemite temple community backed by the authority of the imperial governments. This too must have been extended to the Jewish community.

The province Judah therefore, can be described as a temple community not unlike others in the Persian Empire (for example, in some of the Greek cities along the Ionian seaboard) The Temples were not just places of sacrifices and prayer, they served as administrative centers with their own bureaucracies issued loans, controlled colleges of scholars and scribes, apart from butchers, bakers, keepers of sacrificial herds, and the like. Supreme authority over this organization was, of course, vested in the monarch. It is with in this capacity, Cyrus restored the Jerusalem, Temple, formerly a dynastic Temple. An important reminder of this status was the requirement that prayers for the well-being of the imperial family be incorporated into the daily liturgy (Ezra 6:10).

Royal authority was normally exercised through officials and commissioners appointed by the central government whose main concern was to oversee the financial management of this complex operation and ensure political stability. Expediency and good sense would occasionally dictate the appointment of local people to discharge these functions. Cyrus, for example, appointed a Lydian to oversee the sardis treasury, while under Darius a Davidite, Zerubbabel, was sent out as governor of Yehud. Under normal circumstances, however, the day-to-day task of administration develop on the priesthood.

This last point is particularly important for understanding the situation in Jerusalem and Judah after the return. The authority of the priesthood is not only confined to the Temple but even to the civic field. The priesthood, wielded enormous power not only in the religious sphere (the cult being the primary and indispensable means of salvation) but also economically and politically.

Right from the beginning of the period basic issue was that of qualification for membership in the Jerusalem temple community. This matter could not be decided purely on grounds of national identity in view of the changes in the political history of the country from time to time. Other factors entered into play including, for the first time, laws governing ritual purity (eg. Hag. 2:10-14). It is therefore no surprise to find disagreement on the status of specific categories of people, including those who had defiled themselves with idolatry, resident aliens (gerim) and eunuchs, with respect to this last category, for example, Isa. 56:3-5 expresses an inclusive attitude quite at variance with the Deuteronomic law (Deut 23:1). For the same reason, marriage with women outside the group became increasingly problematic and emerged as a major issue at the time of Ezra and Nehemiah.

One of the major issue of the post-exilic community was not the conflict confined to repatriates versus natives, but was going on in the golah group itself (theories who claim to be indirect line of succession to the old Israel). One of the major issues was control of the cult and the status of Temple personnel. Some of them who claimed priestly lineage but who could not substantiate their claim were excluded "until there should be a priest to consult Urim and Thummim" (Ezra 2:59-63). These were members of priestly groups that had settled in Babylon. More significant, however, are the indications of conflict within the ranks of the priesthood that led to the emergence of a second order of clergy. Such a distinction was unknown during the time of the monarchy and is attested only in the very latest editorial stratum of Deuteronomy (27:14).

The incidents that happen following this, we shall discuss on Particular events in relation to the prophecies of each prophet at relevant places. One thing seems to be clear from the foregoing discussion on the post-exilic historical situation, i.e., the context is so complex that we can see the concerns raised by the prophets of this period are very crucial and vital.

***TRITO-ISAIAH:*** The Theophany which Deutero-Isaiah had Painted in such glowing colours failed to materialize. Cyrus was not converted. And in Jerusalem restoration measures soon came to a halt because of an extremely uncertain Political and economic situation. Israel's fate had taken a new turn; but it certainly did not mean an eschatological revolution: Deutero-Isaiah had overcome the discouragement of the People for a time; but it can be no surprise to discover that this discouragement now made itself felt once more.

The last ten chapters of the Book of Isaiah (56-66) tell us about this. The language is so closely; reminiscent of Deutero-Isaiah that he had continually been taken to be their author. But the conditions underlying these writings are completely different, Pointing to the Palestinian homeland and not to the gola (the dispersed community).

***The Historical Context of the Prophet:*** Trito-lsaiah is of particular importance in dealing of the issue on the specific question of the nature and cause of the dissension which threatened to disrupt the life the community in the Period after the return from the exile. Isaiah 56-66 provides the main source of evidence of these internal divisions (esp. in 65-8-16, 66:5 and in chp. 57: vv-1-2 and 19-21). But to detect the nature and the depth of the Problems is not an easy task because either the information is not adequate or it is ambiguous. One commonly held opinion suggests that the roots of the Problem lay in a conflict of interests, together with a divergence in theological orientation, between those who, remained in the land during the period of exile and those who, having been deported to Babylon and come under Powerful foreign influences. Babylonian culture and religion undoubtedly had a Profound impact on those who experienced the exile, even where their response was one of rejection, not assimilation. It is generally supposed that fresh impetus to Israel's life and worship came from these returned exiles, whereas syncretistic and semi-Pagan cults such as those which the pre-exilic prophets had denounced continued to flourish among those who had stayed in the land. On this basis, 57:3-13 and 65:1-5, 11-12 have been understood as describing the debased religion of those left without adequate leadership when the elite of society were deported to Babylon.

P. D. Hanson (*The Dawn of Apocalyptic*) gives to certain extent the sociological and the nature and the causes of the dissension in the postexilic community during the time of Trito-Isaiah. Hanson seeks to elucidate the nature of the opposing factions, and the causes and subsequent development of their mutual hostility with the pervading polemical note he finds on indication of their historical setting. The roots of the conflict lay, he believes, in the opposition between-two parties the one eager to maintain the status quo by which they had control of the temple and of the official cult, the other motivated by a sense of rejection resulting from their exclusion from participation in worship, yet lacking the power and resources to wrest control of Zion from their opponents. The former Hanson terms the 'hierocratic Party' which consisted of a group of influential priests who had returned from Babylon and seized control of Zion; the latter Hanson describes as 'visionaries', a group composed of followers of Second Isaiah in association with the disenfranchised Levites who had been excluded by the Zadokites from participation in the service of the temple (cf. Ezek. 44:13). Hanson remarks that Trito-Isaiah is permeated deeply by priestly concepts. For example, a recurring emphasis on God's holy mountain, Zion (66:7, 21-22; 61:7; 63:17b-19; 57:13; 65:1-10), for one of the main issues at the heart of the inner-community struggle between visionaries and hierocrats, as Hanson sees it, was concern for the possession of Zion.

Hanson regards chs. 60-62 as the restoration program of the visionaries, and to this same general period he assigns 57:14-19 with its joyful message of comfort and healing for the whole nation.

The sudden change of tone in 57:20-21, a passage which according to Hanson's analysis is probably a secondary insertion, is explained as a later attempt, in the light of the developing rift within the community, to modify the initial promise of pardon and salvation which had been addressed to the whole nation. As optimism faded and bitterness grew it was necessary that the promises of Second Isaiah should be reinterpreted if hope was to be sustained in the face of disillusionment and despair. As Hanson puts it, 'disintegrating historical circumstances prompted new modes of conceptualizing that restoration hope.' Thus expectations for the future took on a different shape, increasingly detached from the real world of politics and history; and in this way apocalyptic was born.

Hanson regards the rivalry between the two factions as the motivation of chs. 56-66 throughout. Not only is the dissension interpretation consistently as a sectarian struggle; but even the formulation of the restoration program in 60-62 is to be understood as deliberate, opposition to the hierocratic program in Ezekiel 40-48. For this reason, Hanson rejects the widely held view that 63:7-64:12 is an early exilic lament by the community against the external enemies who desecrated the sanctuary when Jerusalem fell in 587, and sees it as further evidence of the bitter hostility between the hierocratic party and the visionaries. It is, he believes, a lament by Levites at their exclusion from the sanctuary by Ezekiel's program. Thus the enemies who have defiled the sanctuary (63:18) are not external ones but internal rivals'. In this context Hanson takes the threefold affirmation, 'You are our Father' (63:16, twice; 64:8), as evidence that his claim by the Levites and their associates has been rejected by the rival faction who claimed the names Abraham and Israel as their own exclusive right: (63:16), thus depriving the visionaries of their legitimate part in the covenant community. This circumstance is reflected also, he suggests, in the repeated emphasis on the new names which are bestowed on the faithful (62:4,12) who have reached the ultimate point of disowning the traditional designation Israel.

One of the main objections to this carefully constructed hypothesis is the unfortunate ambiguity of much of the evidence. Thus in the particular instance discussed here it can equally be argued that Abraham and Israel refer not to the community but to the Patriarchs, the human 'fathers' of the nation now unable to assist the Present Generation in their distress, unlike God who alone 'is a living and present father.'

Third Isaiah opens with a remarkably liberal statement on membership in the community, conferring secure status on non-Jewish adherents of the Yahweh cult and on eunuchs, permitting them to participate in the cult on condition of observing the community's covenant requirements, especially regarding the Sabbath (Isa. 56:1-8). The same broad perspective is apartment in the final section (66:18-23) dealing with proselytism, missionary preaching, the ingathering of the nations and dispersed Jews to participate in the Parousia in Jerusalem.

The nucleus of Trito-Isaianic passages, containing a compendium of the eschatological teaching of the group, is found in Isa 60-62. Like 57:14-21, they come from either the last years of the exile or the early years after the return and betray no signs of the opposition and conflict to which these teachings were to give rise with the passing of time. They begin with an apostrophe to Jerusalem: the glory of God will appear in Zion bringing salvation to an oppressed people, those scattered abroad will return, the nations will be subject to Israel, will bring tribute and help rebuild the city, the Temple will once again be glorious and shine at the center of the earth.

It is important to note that throughout Third Isaiah prophetic eschatological faith is focused on Temple and altar (eg. Isa 60:7,13; 61:6; 62:9). There is therefore no opposition in principle between the bearers of this faith and the Temple authorities and no evidence that the former were anti-cultic. The seer who speaks for them in fact goes on to expound a teaching not unlike the priesthood of all the faithful. The entire people will in the last days be relieved of servile labour, as are the priests, and will receive tithes from the nations. In this way the covenant to the house of Levi will be extended to all (cf. Numb. 25:10-13).

In the last two chapters of Trito-Isaiah (65-66), there are clear indications of internal conflict in the province of Judah involving the prophetic eschatological group within which Third Isaiah originated.

Literary Forms and Poetic Imagery in Trito-Isaiah: Not only it is true that Trito-Isaiah used several or variety of literary forms, but these traditional forms were forced into new directions to suit the requirements of a changing historical situation. The following are the important categories of speech forms and poetic imagery used in Trito-Isaiah.

***(1) Judgement Oracles***

***(i) Isa. 56:9-12:*** This passage is a masterly example of a prophetic oracle of judgment, comprising the two traditional elements, pronouncement of judgment and grounds of accusation. Its figurative language has certain reminiscences of Ezekiel's indictment of Israel's leaders (34:1-10), but its brevity is in marked contrast to Ezekiel's extended metaphor. The kaleidoscopic imagery in which the denunciation is couched reflects the multifarious sins of which the leaders are guilty. What kind of leadership is castigated is not entirely clear: both religious and political leaders may be included? 'Watchman' is a term which generally signifies a prophet (Jer. 6:17; Ezek. 3:17; 33:7) whereas 'shepherd' refers frequently to political leadership (Jer. 23:1-4; Ezek. 34:1-10, especially v. 4). The accusation is comprehensive. At first it is the ignorance of the watchman, their failure to realise the dangers of the situation and to alert the community to an appropriate response, which is at issue. They are quiet as sleeping dogs murmuring in their dreams (hozim, a word occurring only here which has the sense 'to talk confusedly.' But then the accusation changes. Dogs, all dogs, have ravenous, insatiable appetites, and so do the shepherds of Israel, intent on their own advantage with never a thought beyond the pleasure of the present moment as they sing their drinking songs, behaving arrogantly as if the future were at their disposal not the Lord's The pattern of the metaphors is deliberately chiastic (placed opposite to each other): the newly coined metaphors of dumb and ravenous dogs: the former useless, the latter dangerous, serve to illuminate the conventional expressions of "watchman' and 'shepherds', and to provide the transition between them.

***(ii) Isa 58:1-14:*** This passage is of particular interest both from the form-critical viewpoint and for the insight it gives into the problems and religious attitudes of the post-exilic community in Judah. Of the two traditional elements-accusation and pronouncement of judgment the former appears briefly in vv. 3b-4a; the latter is entirely absent. the rest of the passage consists of a series of exhortations followed by conditional promises of blessing. It is here, in this break down of the conventional form of the judgment oracle, that the contrast with earlier prophets is most apparent.

Westermann calls this as 'symptomatic of the coming together of prophetic and liturgical speech: Following immediately on the divine authorization of the prophet as a messenger of judgment there is a parenthetical description of the outward piety of the community (vv. 2-3a), a people who lament that their practice of fasting is ineffectual and secures no response from God. It is clear from this, as well as from the language in which the promises of blessing are couched, that the community, or the section of it addressed is conscious of some kind of distress and lack of well-being, probably attributable to the disappointment of hopes raised by the promises of Second Isaiah. The responsibility is laid firmly at the community's door. Despite their outward religious observances there is only apparent, not actual, commitment to righteous action and to obedience to God's commandments (v. 2).

Westemann points out some signs of wisdom influence in this passage, there is a hint of 'the ridicule of the rationalist' in the satirical expression 'to bow down one's head like a rush' (v. 5).

***(2) Laments:*** Isa. 59:1-15a; 63:7-64:12: These two laments differ considerably in their literary form, 63:7-64:12 has more traditional structure. Westermann describes it as probably the most powerful psalm of communal lamentation in the Bible. It follows the conventional pattern of such laments within the Psalter, consisting of the usual elements: recollection of God's past saving actions (63:7-14 cf. Ps.89); Plea for help, which includes a descriptions of the distress which was the immediate cause of the lament (63:15-64:5a), and confession of sin (64:5b-7). Finally the various elements in the lament are gathered up (64:8-12), culminating in the anguished questioning of God, characteristic of the lament form: "Wilt thou retrain thyself at those things, a LORD? Wilt thou keep silent, and afflict us sorely?" (64:12).

Chp. 59 is an interesting example of departure from traditional forms of lament. Many would even question whether it is appropriate to classify it as lament. The opening words introduced as they are by the particle 'behold', are to be understood as the prophet's response to an unrecorded lament by the people, perplexed by the failure of Yahweh to intervene and by his apparent disregard of their prayers. The problem, says the prophet, lies not in any limitation of Yahweh's power; It is the result of sin, their own sins that which have raised a barrier between themselves and God. The accusation in vv. 2-3 is as sharp as anything in the pre-exilic Prophets (cf. Isa. 1:15); but in place of the announcement of punishment which traditionally accompanied the accusation, the direct address to the hearers soon passes over into a description of their sin. its impact heightened by the striking poetic imagery (vv. 5-6). It is this descriptive aspect of the material which gives the passage something of a sermonic character since it constitutes an explanation to a despondent people rather than an accusation. The sins, referred to here are social injustices not cultic irregularities, the evils by which justice is perverted in the law courts.

Two strands seem to be inter twined, the community's lament and the prophetic voice, thus some would characterize, it as a prophetic liturgy. This chapter falls into three distinct sections: *First*, the prophet's response to a communal lament which vindicates Yahweh by way of accusing the people (vv. 1-8); *Secondly*, the ensuring lament, by or on behalf of the people, which includes confession of sin (V. 12: and unusual feature in the traditional form of judgment oracle) and admits the truth of the accusation (vv. 9-15a), *Thirdly*, the assurance of God's intervention to save those who repent (vv. 15b-20; for a similarity abrupt transition to words assurance compare Joel 2:18). Yahweh is portrayed here as the warrior God who avenges those who 'turn from transgression' (v. 20; cf. 42:13 52:10). A similar pattern of community lament followed by Yahweh's epiphany is to be found in Psalm 60. The two sections, lament (1-15a) and epiphany (15b-20) are linked together. Yahweh takes action precisely because he sees that there is no Justice (v. 15 cf. vv. 9 and 11). The salvation which was far from them (v. 11) is seen to be at hand when he intervenes.

***(3) Portrayal of the Divine Warrior: (Isa 59:15b-20; 63:1-6)***

There are interesting, and significant, contrasts between the portrayal of the divine warrior in these two passages. What originally concerned Yahweh's intervention against foreign enemies has now been directed against internal adversaries. In 63:1-6, the prophet makes use of secular form familiar to his hearers - the customary summons of a watchman to an approaching stranger to identify himself - but the contest is based on the motif of the divine warrior. Yahweh is not named but the identification clear (cf. 5:17-). Fresh from his victory he announces that 'right has won the day.'

***(4) Oracles of Both Judgment and Salvation:*** (Isa. 65:8-16). It is oracle both of Judgment and of salvation, addressed respectively to two opposing factions within the community. In this dual orientation it differs in a remarkable fashion from the traditional forms of Pre-exilic Prophecy in which the nation is treated as a corporate entity for judgment or for salvation. In its present form ch. 65 as a whole is symmetrical in structure: vv. l-7 consists entirely of accusation against idolaters; vv. 8-l6a set out the contrasting destiny of two disparate groups within the community, detailing the blessings in store for the one ('my servants' vv. l3-14, 'my chosen', v. 15) and the sorrows which await the other; vv. 16b-25 are purely a description of blessing. These diverse sections are held together by the theme of call and response which is reiterated in vv. 1,12 and 24. The central concern of Isa. ch. 65 is with the deep division within the community between those who, from this perspective at any rate, one regarded as faithful worshippers of Yahweh and their opponents who are considered by them to be apostate. It is to this latter group that the oracle is addressed from v. 11 onwards as a pronouncement of judgment.

***Theology of Trito-Isaiah:*** The majesty and omnipotence of Yahweh, the choice of Israel to be Yahweh's people, divine anger over human sin, and the deity's determination to work the divine will in the world, all are themes found in third Isaiah connect this prophet of the restoration with the older traditions of prophecy within Israel. Following are the three major concerns of the prophet in his theology.

(i) Yahweh's restoration of Jerusalem is still in the future and when it comes, it will be a day of great glory for the city and its people: Yahweh's glory will be present in the life of the city (60:1-2). The city will be a "crown of beauty" and a "royal diadem" to Yahweh (62:3) All people will respond to the magnificence of the new Jerusalem, both gentiles (62:2) and Jews still scattered abroad (60:4). Great wealth will belong to the city, which will be the place of worship for all people (60:5-7; 66:23). It will be a time of peace and concord (65:25) in which Yahweh's presence will provide all needed light (60:1a).

(ii) Although Yahweh's love is universal, two groups are singled out for special treatment: the gentiles and the wicked: The Gentiles are clearly to be participants in the glories of this new age, "foreigners" will join themselves to Yahweh (56:6). They and "aliens" will serve Yahweh in the age to come but their menial labour is contrasted with the work of the Jews who are to be "Priests of Yahweh" and "ministers of our God" (61:5-6). As for the wicked, they are responsible for deadly of the coming of the new age (59:1-2) - Yahweh, who judged this people of old will also act in judgment upon any present enemies (59:18). The prophet implores Yahweh not to allow these wicked people to delay any longer the fulfilment of the divine promises, but to institute the judgment swift and sure ways (chp. 64).

(iii) The Worship of Yahweh through sacrifice and joyful song characterizes the life of Yahweh's people: In this new age Jerusalem will "thrill and rejoice" (60:5). The prophet rejoices over what is to come pass (61:10) as does Yahweh also (62:5). This message is consistent with the views of other restoration prophets like Haggai and Zechariah. The words of prophet's jubilation are seen thus: "But be glad and rejoice forever in that which I create; for behold, I create Jerusalem a rejoicing, and her people a joy. I will rejoice in Jerusalem, and be glad in my people; no more shall be heard in it the sound of weeping and the cry of distress" (65:18-19).

***HAGGAI:*** Very little is known about Haggai, the individual. Since his name is related to the Hebrew word meaning "festival" some have suggested that he may have born on the occasion of one of the important Hebrew holy days. Nothing is known about his ancestry, nor of his vocation. He was probably a priest, for he was certainly interested in strengthening the cult. There is no direct evidence for this, however, and the fact that he seeks priestly guidance concerning a matter of ritual cleanliness (2:10-13) may indicate that he was not ordained. His reference to the splendor of Solomon's Temple (2:3) suggests that he may have been among the original generation of exiles. If so, he would have been a very old man at the time of his prophetic activity.

***The Historical Setting:*** During the years from 558 to 529 BCE, Cyrus, the King of Anshan, engaged in a series of conquests. The Babylonian empire: which had up to that time controlled the Tigris-Euphrates basin, often called Mesopotamia, was overthrown, and Babylon itself captured a new power was established, now generally known as the Persian Empire, whose western boundaries extended into modern Turkey and reached to the borders of Egypt. prophet Haggai, Zechariah l-8, come from this period when Persian rule was first being established in Syria-Palestine.

Persian rule was to last for some two hundred years, until the conquest of Alexander the Great about 330 BCE; Yet our knowledge both of the Persian Empire in general and its impact in Syria-Palestine in particular remains very limited. The Old Testament is one of the chief source of information. Yet in comparison with Babylonian and earlier periods the information is very scarce in this period. Nor is there from Persian sources anything comparable to the wealth of Assyrian and Babylonian inscriptional material (The most important exception to this is the 'Cyrus Cylinder', which relates to the conquest of Babylon).

From the various Old Testament sources a very different picture emerges. Cyrus himself is described in the book of Isaiah as 'the shepherd' and the 'anointed' of Yahweh the God Israel (Isa. 44:28; 45:1); much of the book of Ezra is given over to an account of the favourable treatment of the Jews be Persian rulers; both the story of Esther and the episode of Daniel in the lion's den (Dan. 6) picture Persian emperors in highly favourable terms. The books are dated by the Years of the reign of the Persian emperor Darius, as if his rule were part of the divine ordering of affairs. It is striking that in Haggai (1:1,15) Darius is simply called 'the King'.

The general historical setting of Haggai is established beyond doubt. He lived and proclaimed the word of Yahweh at time when Persian rule in Palestine was being established, and Haggai is in no way opposed to the establishment of Persian rule. When we come to look at the historical situation in greater detail, however, certain problems arise.

Cyrus, the founder of Persian empire, died in 529 BCE and was succeeded by his son Cambyses (529-522). Under his rule Persian Power was extended to the borders of Egypt. In 525 BCE in his attempt to invade Egypt died in 525 BCE, precipitated a series of riots which put the whole empire under pressure for more than a year. Eventually Darius I Hystaspes established himself as king (522-486) and as already pointed out, Haggai's activity is dated in this Period.

Some of the events that happened during this period are related to the prophet Haggai. For instance, the alleged 'disappearance' of Zerubbabel, during Darius' period, permission was available for the rebuilding of the temple in Jerusalem (cf. Ezra chps. 5-6). Haggai summoned the people to work on the temple reconstruction (1:1-2:9 and 2:15-19).

But an historical difficulty arises in the construction of the temple if we compare Haggai's account with that of Ezra's. According to Ezra. 3, a Start on the work of rebuilding had already been made in 538 BCE, immediately upon the first return of exiles from Babylon; yet Hag. 1:4,9 speak of 'the house', that is, the temple lying in ruins. Apparently, according to this, no work of rebuilding had Yet been done. It would obviously be possible to construct some kind of harmonization of the two accounts: One might argue that work done nearly twenty years before Haggai's time and then neglected would be in ruins. Whether or not some preliminary work on the temple had been done, there was still much to be achieved, and this was a major focus of Haggai's prophetic words.

***Haggai's Message in his Context:*** In Haggai's time the generation that had known of a living temple in which God's glory manifested had now effectively passed away (2:3), and they found it possible to survive without a temple (or at least without a properly restored temple). This attitude seems to Haggai to reflect a perverted sense of priorities. Now a more ambitions work of rebuilding could be embarked upon; that such a plan was possible seems to have been common ground between Haggai and his hearers (1:2). Haggai supposed that all other blessings would automatically follow upon proper attention to the temple. Just as current troubles were due to its neglect (2:15-17), so future blessings could be guaranteed if rebuilding was taken seriously in hand (2:18f). Haggai's intention is not simple rebuilding of the temple, as Ackroyd had rightly pointed out that 'the failure to rebuild is much more than a matter of reconstruction of a building. It is reordering of a Temple so that it is a fit place for worship. Rebuilding is therefore linked to the condition of the people for the service of God" (Exile and Restoration, p. 156).

Thus there is another wider concern here based on 2:1-9, that God is assuring the people of his lasting presence with them, a presence which is recalled in the past history of his dealings with them (of the promise that I made You when you came out of Egypt'), which is assured as present reality ('My spirit abides among you; fear not'), and which is promised as a sign of future glory ('I will shake all nations, so that the treasures of all nations shall come in').

A restored community would need effective leaders, both political and religious; and this supplies the context for the concern shown by Haggai for Zerubbabel and Joshua. There is no suggestion that Haggai simply had, in mind a return to pre-exilic days with the Davidic monarchy in controlof an independent nation-state. A dual leadership of the community's efforts was needed. The words which Haggai proclaims to Zerubbabel, the ruling governor, are just as high-flown as the expectation of the period of blessing which is to ensure immediately after the reopening of the Temple. He designates him as nothing less than the ruler over the whole world. Yahweh will soon shake the universe so that the thrones of the ruling Princes will topple and a struggle of each against all will break out on earth. Then Zerubbabel will be the signet ring on the hand of God, the ring which God will use to stamp his will to peace into the very earth itself (Hag. 2:20-23). However, Haggai does not usually confine what he says solely to the governor. He also addresses the high priest, Joshua (1:1-2:2).

***ZECHARIAH:*** Zechariah is regularly associated with Haggai. This association can be traced as far back as the book of Ezra, in which the two prophets are twice (5:1; 6:14) spoken of without differentiation as those whose ministry was decisive in bringing about the rebuilding of the Jerusalem temple.

According to Zech. 1:1,7b and Ezra 5:1, 6:14, Zechariah was the son of Berechiah and the grandson of Iddo. The priestly interests of the prophet are explained in the book. The date of his Prophetical activity is fixed at least to some extent by the three dates in 1:1, 7a; 7:1, which cover the period from the eighth month of the second Year of Darius (520) to the ninth month of his fourth Year (518 BCE). It is likely, however, that his appearances extended beyond the latter date, as the sayings in 3:8-9 suggests; it may have been pronounced at or following the dedication of the new Temple in 515 BCE. In any event, he is a younger contemporary of Haggai, who probably returned from the exile with Zerubbabel. He began his prophetical preaching somewhat later than Haggai, continued it alongside him for a time, and extended his ministry after close of Haggai's. He also backed the building of the Temple, but devoted most of his preaching to the themes of the irruption of the eschatological age and the organisation of the eschatological community, together with the practical problems of his period.

***Literary Form of Zechariah:*** The book of Zechariah is "the obscurest and longest of the twelve prophets", but its complexity is in proportion to the significance of the message. Baldwin comments that it is a mosaic written byan "artist adding colourful, windows with their symbolism, gaiety and light." The book is largely prosaic with poetic sections (chaps. 9-10). It contains a mosaic of hortatory oracles (1:2-6; 10:1-2), Visions (1:7-6:8), symbolism (6:9-15), prophetic judgment oracles (9:1-8; 12:2-8), liturgy (9:9-10), salvation oracles (vv. 11-13; 13:1-6,7-9) taunt song (11:1-3) narrative (vv. 4-17), and apocalyptic. The presence of visions, symbolism, and eschatological imagery classify Zechariah as a prophetic apocalyptic writing.

The first eight chapters are united by a dating formula (1:1-7; 7:1), common formula. The lack of dating, the variety of thematic content in the chapters 9-14, and the absence of the messenger formula have led scholars to posit that another prophet (Deutero-Zechariah), whose concern was, more with the restoration of the Davidic dynasty and the Kingdom of God than the temple; accepting the division between chapters 1-8 and 9-14, Childs argues in favour of a relationship between the two sections. According to him the second section expands, develops and sharpens the theological pattern of the "end time", which emerges from chapters 1-8. The book thus seeks to explain that notwithstanding the return from exile, the full experience of redemption still lies in the future.

Zechariah in all its diversity contributes to a vision of (1) The New Jerusalem (2:5; 9:8; 14:1): (2) The grandeur of fulfilment (1:17; 4:10; 8:6-15; 9:12); (3) The removal of evil and God's judgment on the nations (1:15,21; 6:1-8; 9:1-8; 12:1-9; 14:1-15); (4) The participation of Jews and Gentiles in the mercies of God (2:11; 8:7-8,22; 10:9-10; 14:16); (5) the cleansing, consecration and empowering by the spirit of restoration (4:6; 5:4; 12:10; 13:13); and (6) The humble and glorious messianic figure (3:8; 4:6; 9:9).

***The Message of Zechariah***

***(i) The Age of Responsibility:*** Zechariah's prophecy complements that of 'Haggai. He too, was concerned with the completion of the Temple and with the renewal of spiritual life. Haggai emphasized the responsibility of the 'people in view of the dawning of the new age. Zechariah urged the post-exilic community not to repeat the mistakes of their ancestors, but instead to devote themselves to God (1:1-6) and to trust him in Working out his promised deliverance. Like Haggai, he attached great importance to the future of the temple and Davidic dynasty. But he focused on the presence of God with his people, and in this regard comes closer to Ezekiel. So P. D. Hanson writes "Zechariah sees his nation at the point in history prophesied by Ezekiel when Yahweh would return to Zion to dwell in the midst his people"! (Dawn of the Apocalyptic, P. 249).

Zechariah provided a theological perspective on covenant life with its blessings and threats. He exhorted the people to remember that the prophecies of exile had become a reality (1:6; 7:7-14). Fearing the recurrence of God's judgment, Zechariah encouraged the new generation to reflect on the past. They must not repeat the mistakes of their forerunner who had been led into exile and alienation and had received the curse of God (1:5-6; 7:14). The lessons from the past explain that the former (pre-exilic) prophets had called in vain for repentance (1:4; 7:6-7), that their ancestors had failed to respond (1:4; 7:11-12), that they had angered the LORD (1:2; 7:12), that he had stopped listening to their prayers and appeals to his covenant love (7:13), and that he had unleashed his curse on them.

***(ii) The present Reality of Restoration:*** Zechariah went beyond the past to a reflection on the situation and opportunity at hand. He inspired the people of

God to see how the prophetic word regarding restoration was being fulfilled in their generation. Though the fulfilment seemed distant, God encouraged the new community with visions (1;7-6:8) that gave them a perspective on the progressive fulfilment of the prophetic oracles.

***The Eight Visions May be Organized Structurally as Four Parallel Visions***

A. Vision of the nations at rest, 1:7-17; B. Vision of judgment on the nations, 1:18-21; C. Vision of Zion; 2:1-13; D. Vision of the new age; forgiveness and peace, 3:1-10; D'. Vision of the new age; messianic ministry; 4:1-13; C'. Vision of the removal of evil; 5:1-4, B'. Vision of Judgment on Babylon: 5:5-11; A'. Vision of the spirit at rest, 6:1-8.

These eight night visions portray what God was doing for his people. Through the interpretation of the angelic intermediary, the prophet explains what he sees. The visions, are given for the purpose of comfort and the godly might know that the Lord was zealously working out all aspects of redemption. This redemption consists of the vengeance on God's enemies the vindication and glorification of his cleansed and holy people, and the consequent glorious established of his holy rule (1:13-15).

The night visions may be viewed as a set of a stained glass windows placed opposite each other: The first and the last, the second and the seventh, the third and the sixth, and finally the fourth and the fifth. The central visions (four and five) form the acute and the focus of the symmetry. All aspects of restoration are rooted in the hope of God's presence, and presence of God is at the same time the goal of restoration.

***(iii) The Era of Restoration: Fulfilment of the Promises:*** Zechariah confirmed the promises of concerning the people, the land, and the presence of the loan in blessing, protection, peace, the spiritual metamorphosis (forgiveness cleansing, and holiness), the inclusion of the nations, and renewal of creation.

The presence of Yahweh in blessing and protection is the present guarantee of the restoration as well as the hope of the transformation to come. The focus of the promise is the return of God's presence symbolized, by the temple people (1:16). His presence will assure the covenant relationship, symbolized in the names associated with the city of God. "Then Jerusalem will be called the city of truth, and the mountain of the LORD Almighty will be called the Holy Mountain" (8:3). Yahweh's presence was experienced in the postexilic community, as God affirmed: "Now I have determined to do good again to Jerusalem and Judah. Do not be afraid" (8:15). The LORD promised to remove their fear and to give them reasons to rejoice in his goodness (2:10-11).

The LORD was present in blessing (8:12-14), in protection, and keeping watch over his people (vv. 12-14; 9:8). Though they might suffer adversity, he is with them as their God, for they are his precious people (9:8-16; 14:3-7,9). The LORD is kind and the people make up his kingdom on earth. He gives them the peace that the pre-exilic prophets had proclaimed: "In that day each of You will invite his neighbour to sit under his vine and fig tree", declares the LORD Almighty" (3:10). His peace will be extended to all the nations, as envisioned in God's covenant with David (9:10; see P 8. 72:8-11).

The people of the LORD will increase in number as Jews and Gentiles together will seek shelter in Zion (3:10; 8:20-23). Zion, the city of God, denotes here, God's blessings and Protection that come from God's presence with his people (see. Ps. 46). Yahweh declares that he is zealous for his people, and his zeal comes to concrete expression in the restoration of the people to the land and cities (1:17), in the joy and prosperity of his people (8:4-6), and in the honor his children will enjoy instead of shame (9:16-17). No one will be permitted to hurt his people, without hurting himself (10:4-12). Yahweh reassures his people and the godly from the nations that he will be zealous in working out the restoration of his children (1:14; 8L12). They constitute the new community, composed of people who have been cleansed and forgiven by "the blood of my covenant" grace. but the LORD delights in children who are zealous for the LORD, his kingdom and his worship. They will enter into the fullness of the covenant privileges (8:20-23; 14:20-21).

The land is intimately connected with the restoration of the people of God. He will grant his blessing on the land by giving rain and increasing the crops (10:10). In the vision of new creation, the prophet affirms the hope of the cooperation of creation with the redeemed because of God's kingship, symbolized by light and water (14:6-11). He will establish his kingship "over the whole earth" (14:9).

The benefits of God's rule confirm the promises of all the covenants. Zechariah used promise and covenant language to assure them that the LORD is faithful in the progress of fulfilments. However, God also expects his people to be involved. Involvement in Zechariah's time Pertained to the temple of God, which was still not complete (8:9-10). This involvement also pertains to God's concern for the justice on earth. Wicked and selfish people (i.e., covenant breakers) have no place in the eschatological kingdom (13:2). Covenant keepers establish the Kingdom of God by living in accordance with the principles of God's rule of Justice, righteousness, and love (8:16-22; see 7:9) The LORD promises to bless his people in proportion to their commitment to his kingdom.

***(iv) The Humble and Glorious Messiah:*** In the visions of Zechariah portrayed the harmonious relationship between the high priest and the branch, the Davidic descendant. The branch will foster the worship of God and bring in an era of peace and prosperity. He appears both humble and glorious. He is humble in his entrance (9:9). The prophet also intimates that this Messiah is to suffer as the smitten shepherd (11:7-14; 13:7-9). But this humble Messiah is powerful enough to bring to his people full deliverance from suffering, to be God's means of grace and purification, and to bring the gift of the spirit of restoration to all who mourn over his being pierced (12:10-13:1). He is the priest King who serves "the LORD of all the earth" (14:14) and rules over all who believe on him, Jews and Gentiles (8:20-23), The presence of God will be evident: "The house of David will be like God, like the Angel of the LORD going before them" (12-8). In the end, the Messiah will vindicate the saints and judge the unbelieving nations: "On that day his feet will stand on the Mount of Olives...Then the LORD my God will come, and all the holy ones with him" (14:4-5). On that glorious day the LORD and Creator of humankind will transform everything (14:6-8) and grant his blessing on the new community, which may share in this transformed and holy world (14:20-21).

***MALACHI:*** According to the superscription (1:1) the prophecy is accredited to Malachi ("my messenger"), Very little is known about the prophet Malachi. Malachi prophesied during the Persian period, after the reconstruction and dedication of the temple in 515 BCE. His interaction with the priests at the temple suggests that he lived in or around Jerusalem.

In fact, the word Malachi is not a proper name, but the noun with possessive suffix (my) messenger (3:1) placed in 1:1, as the name of the author. It is possible, however, to infer something of the time and circumstances under which these oracles are composed, and what we discover in this regard offers important insights into the life of post-exilic Jerusalem.

Number of scholars feel that the material in the book of Malachi constituted "independent" prophetic oracles which circulated in the post-exilic Judah and that the Malachi material was placed in its present position in the Jewish Canon in order to: round out the so-called "Book of the Twelve" (the twelve "Minor prophets" of the English Bible, that is, the books of Hosea through Malachi). In most of the Christian Bibles, Malachi is placed at the very close of the Old Testament. The obvious reason for this arrangement may be that it allows Malachi's promise of the return of Elijah to appear just before the Gospel of Mathew that Gospel which places the most emphasis upon the Old Testament as a treasury of prophecies concerning the life and ministry of Jesus Christ.

***Date of the Prophet:*** There is generally agreed date emerged regarding Malachi. the first half of the fifth century BCE, after the establishment of the Second Temple in 515 and before the reforms of Nehemiah began about 445 (If the traditional dating of Ezra, 458, is accepted, this would make the conventional dating of Malachi is still more precise). The grounds for this judgment are mainly twofold: first the reference to the 'governor' (1:8) clearly implies that Peha (governor) appointed by the Persian authorities, rather than a native king is in a position of responsibility. and this implies the second rather than the first temple. The word Peha, governor, is that used of Zerubbabel in Haggai and also of Nehemiah (5:14, 12:26). Secondly, it is commonly held that a more precise identification within the Persian period can be made on the basis of the various abuses listed in Malachi: The implication is that the reforms of Ezra and Nehemiah had not Yet taken place. This is thought to point to period after the first enthusiasm for Temple building had worn off and before the reforms which led to a purification of the cults. sometimes the attempt is made to provide external support for this dating by reference to the history of Edom. (cf. Mal. 1:2-6). But two Points are supposed to be noted here:

***First:*** It is far from certain whether the references to Edom should be taken as historical or Whether Edom represents here the typical enemy. Edom is in fact portrayed as such in a great variety of material in the Old Testament, from the Jacob-Esau stories in Genesis through Amos, Jeremiah and Obadiah down to Malachi, but it would be Precarious indeed to attempt precise historical reconstruction of the underlying situations behind each of these prophetic condemnations. In other words, Mal: 1:2-6 may reflect a literary continuum as much as an historical comment.

***Secondly:*** We need to be aware of the gaps in our historical knowledge. In the second Temple period in particular these are far too great for detailed reconstruction to be legitimate. Book of Ezra and Nehemiah each claiming to made reforms in the returnees of the exile, but even their precise dates cannot be given accurately. Most of the dates are based on the superscriptions, as in the case of book of Malachi, which are considered to be later additions, therefore the living prophetic traditions cannot be pinned down to precise points in time. Our conclusion with regard to the date of the Prophet Malachi therefore be that he is to be placed within the Persian period, sometime between 515 and 330 BCE, but that greater precision than that is scarcely available.

Very often Malachi's words are linked with the theme of Deuteronomic writings. J. M. P. Smith, for instance in 1912 noted in particular that the reference to the priest as bound by the covenant with Levi (2:4,8) and use of such expressions as 'the law of my servant Moses', 'Horeb' and 'all Israel"

(4:4) all point to a links with Deuteronomy rather than with the priestly code. This may also have some bearing on date, in so far as reference to an Aaronic priesthood and to the holy mountain as Sinai increasingly became the norm; but a greater significance of this kind of usage lies in the fact that Malachi appears to have been attempting to apply the particular emphases of the Deuteronomists in the circumstances of his own day. R. L. Smith pointed out that Malachi uses the themes characteristic those of Deuteronomy. Smith refers in particular to 'Love' 'fear', and 'faithfulness' as being especially noteworthy in this regard.

***Form and Message of Malachi:*** Malachi seems to have been deliberately adapted to the substance of the message he has to give. The form, is unique in a prophetic book in that it consists of an exchange of a series of questions and answers between the prophet and his hearers. This form is found elsewhere as one element in a prophetic collection (eg, in Hag 1:4ff; 2:3ft) but nowhere else is it carried through as here so as to cover virtually the whole book, and nowhere else are the supposed answers of those accused set out in the detail given in Malachi, which is interspersed with phrases such as 'you say', introducing the answers to the prophetic accusations. Such a form probably has a legal background, with charges being made, answers being put forward, and these in their turn being dismissed as inadequate, Malachi has some elements in common with the rib Pattern, particularly in the accusatory material of 1:6-2:9, but it would be impossible to reconstruct anything like a complete' 'law suit' from Malachi.

Malachi is overwhelmingly concerned with religious matters, with the priesthood and the Temple, and with the proper way in which God should be worshipped. He also sees this responsibility laid on the religious leaders, on whom he is very much severe than on the community at large. The priests in particular are harshly condemned (1:6-2:9).

Malachi's words of judgment expressions bring out a strongly positive aspect of God's power. Thus in 1:5, The initial condemnation of Edom, which is in some respects very negative and harsh, reaches its climax in an assertion of Yahweh's supernatural power. 1:11, is most difficult verse to interpret. Some would interpret. It as (based on Christian liturgy), the 'pure offering to which it refers being interpreted as being in some way 'fulfilled by the Christian Eucharist. But this is hardly accepted as the intention of the author. Another possibility is that the reference here might be to the Jews living away from Jerusalem, in the Diaspora. This is the interpretation accepted by the most Jewish commentators, also by Blenkinsopp. But perhaps the most likely interpretation, is provided by the clue given by Mason, that the phrase 'from the rising of the sun to its setting' is virtually identical with Ps. 50:1b. In that psalm, as in this verse, the lord's universal power is proclaimed, and the efficacy of animal sacrifice rejected. In Malachi 1:11 to the sacrifices referred to are not those of animals. It seems therefore that we May legitimately see here a proclamation of the Lord's universal power, perhaps set over against excessive claims made on behalf of the sacrificial system of the Jerusalem temple as being the only assured way to divine favour. If so, Malachi would have anticipated some of the bitter disputes concerning the status of the Jerusalem cult which characterized post biblical Judaism and can still be traced in the New Testament.

The section 3:13-4:6, characteristic warning of judgement for the wicked, but the last part (4:1-4) stand somewhat apart. Some would regard it as a later addition, though the continued Deuteronomistic links (eg. The use of 'Horeb' in 4:4) certainly supply a measure of continuity with what has preceded. Some suggestions are worth considering in this regard:

(i) The reference in 4:4 to 'the law of my servant Moses, the statues and ordinances that I commanded him', is surely, intentionally reminiscent of Deuteronomy. Even in Deuteronomy the information is given as a looking back upon what God had done for his people at Horeb, with the intention of emphasizing the continued importance of the commands made there for a later generation. Here in Malachi at even later time than Deuteronomy we find it strongly emphasized that those laws are still operative despite all the changes that have taken place in the life of the community.

(ii) The form of this reference strongly suggests that the 'law' has now reached a fixed and effectively final shape; it can in effect be appealed to as 'Scripture'. The community, that is to 'remember' this law is now the community which is bound to God by a Holy book as well as by the sacrifice of the temple. And it is now 'Israel' in the sense of a religious grouping not of a nation-state.

(iii) The second appendix (4:5-6) has little connection with the first and may have come from another hand. It is in effect an explanatory note on 3:1, elaborating on the identity of the promised messenger, the link between the two passages perhaps being provided by the reference to 'Horeb', the name given to Sinai in Deuteronomy and the mountain to which Elijah fled according to I Kings 19. The first appendix (4:1-3) looked back this one (4:5-6) looks forward. It is the first example known to us of the Working out of a role for Elijah in God's future plans.

(iv) This section relates to the way in which it rounds off the whole prophetic collection.

In Malachi's time the Jews had been home from exile in Babylon about one hundred Years They were cured of their idolatry, but had returned to then former state of indifference and spiritual lethargy. The priests had been lax and degenerate, sacrifices were inferior tithes and offerings were neglected, divorce and mixed marriage were common (3:9-11).

Still chafing under a foreign yoke, the promises by the prophet concerning Israel's glorious future yet unrealised, many in the nation had begun to ask whether or not God loves Israel (1:2). What had become of divine Justice (2:17)? Was it profitable to serve God any longer (3:11-15)? They complained that as God's chosen people they were left in a low estate while the wicked heathen prospered. If God still loved them, when was the promise of the Messiah and His universal kingdom? And where was Justice? "Everyone that does evil is good in the sight of Yahweh, and he delights in them......where is the God of Justice?" they cried. Again others lamented, "It is vain to serve God; and what profit is it that we have kept his charge, and that we have walked mournfully before Yahweh of hosts? And now we call the proud happy; Yea, they that work wickedness are built up; Yea, they tempt God and escape", Many, therefore, in the face disappointments, the lack of prosperity, and unscrupulous nobles and priests, turned to sin, religious indifference and skepticism. Thus the Jews, impatiently awaited Messiah. Malachi assured them that God would surely come, but His sudden appearance would only issue, judgment for such as they except they repented and rendered faithful obedience (chaps. 34). In this regard we can see how the prophet Malachi places considerable emphasis on the "day of the Lord." Six times prophet announces its approach (1:11 (implied); 3:2,17; 4:1,3,5).

***Conclusion:*** The postexilic prophecy was filled with several new and complex problems since the time of restoration has brought in new issues with the community composed of returnees from the exile and other communities apart from the Judahites. Following observations can be made as concluding remarks

First, Trito-Isaiah had to deal with new issues within the Israelite community. Transgenders' issue was one such critical matter and the prophet takes an inclusive approach on this matter.

Second, Haggai and Malachi exclusively dealt with the people's lethargic and careless attitude towards cultic matters. These prophets warn the people that their careless attitude towards cultic matters when they are to be more serious about the cult.

Third, Zechariah, through his visions give cautions about the present reality but also predicts the future hope.

Chapter 7

# Prophecy in the Ancient West Asia

***Introduction:*** The authors of the books of Kings were cognizant of the existence of ecstatic prophets in the Semitic world outside Israel. The god of Carmel (perhaps fused with Baal Shamem, Baal of Heaven) had his prophets, so had Asherah and the Tyrian Melkart (I Kings 18, II Kings 10).

Now we are in possession of literary documents which give evidence of the existence of such prophets in different parts of the AWA. The story of Wen-Amon's journey to Phoenicia (about 1100 BCE) related to the famous Golenischeff papyrus, contains an episode that witnesses to the existence of prophetic phenomena in ancient Phoenicia. We shall now examine the details of the various types of prophecy in the AWA. The texts described in the AWA context involved predictions, or apparent predictions, eschatology or apocalyptic, social or religious criticism, and commissioned messages from deities.

### *1) Syria Palestine*

a) **North Syria:** Ebla and Emar: Ebla texts dated from 3rd millennium may have evidenced prophecy. From Emar (Meskene) on the middle Euphrates, texts from ca 1300 BCE indicate an office with the Akkadian designations *anabbiatu*and *munnabbiatu* associated with the goodness *Ishara*. The editor translates these titles of office "prophetesses", but nothing is indicated of the role.

b) **Ugarit:** There are announcements of future blessings that have been labelled "prophetic" in Ugaritic texts and reference to technical divination as "prophecy", but there is no evidence as yet for divinely commissioned messenger.

c) **Phoenicia:** As mentioned earlier, Bible has many references to prophets of the Phoenician god Baal (and even Asherah) using for them the same Hebrew term, *nabi*, as used for Israelite prophets. The Baal prophets share ecstatic behaviour with the Israelite prophets, but they are not identified as giving oracles. However, the Egyptian report of *Wen-Amun* states that while Wen-Amun was in Babylon (ca 1090 BCEE) one of Phoenician prince's young attendants became ecstatic and delivered an oracle authenticating Wen-Amun's mission from God Amun. Primarily because of these references it was at one time argued that biblical prophecy derived from Canaanite (Phoenician) prophecy.

(d) **Ammon:** The laster inscription from 700 BCE found at *Tell Deir 'Alla* in 1967 refers to Balaam, Son of Beor, a "visionary of the God's" (*hazoh' ilahin*) who saw a vision during the night and obtained a somewhat enigmatic revelation from a group of numinous beings (sdyn). This is reinforced by Numb. 24:4-5, in which Balaam, son of Beor hears the words of God has a vision of the Almighty (*mahazesaddae*).

***(2) Mesopotamia: A rich variety of texts come from Mesopotamia including Babylonia, Assyria, and the domain of the Mari texts***

(a) **Uruk (southern Babylonia):** A text from 1850 BCE distinct from "uruk prophecy" reports a visit to an unnamed person by a deity who speaks directly to him concerning the future of Uruk and its ruler, who the deity will appoint. The person responds to the deity and reports to the king "the words which Ishtar spoke to me."

(b) **Mari (middle Euphrates):** From several thousand texts now published from Mari and dating to the first half of the 18th cent. But, there are many references to prophetic activity, using a variety of titles over a dozen deities are involved: and some eighteen prophets are named, apart from many others who are unnamed. Both male and female prophets are cited. We shall discuss on few items in Mari prophecy.

***(i) Prophets with Titles:*** These persons are associated with particular deities.

1. **Apiilu/apiltu ("answerer"):** An ordinary Akkadian form, this title for both men and women seems restricted to the Mari texts and lexical compilations. The title implies that the person provides an answer to all explicit or implicit Inquiry, although texts do not exemplify the process eg: one of the most important letters, sent from Aleppo, concerns the answer of Addu, Lord of Kallassu who "reclaims the territory of Alahtum as property", the "answerer" 'is thus someone who"came and spoke" or "got up (in the temple) and spoke" addressing a court official with message for the king.

2. **Assinu, "cult functionary":** the two assinu attested are affiliated with annunitum, a form of Ishtar. One of these speaks in a state of ecstasy: Another assinu apparently resides in an abandoned and partly ruined sanctuary.
3. **Muhhu/muhhutu, "ecstatic":** deriving from the Akkadian root meaning "to become ecstatic." This is the most common prophetic title at "Mari". The range of behaviour may involve self-wandering, "ecstatics" are associated with the deities Nergal. Itur Mer, Niuhur-saga, Annunitum, and especially Dagan.
4. **Nabu, diviner (?):** This appears for the first time as a "prophetic" title in the Mari texts. A Mari functionary advises the king that he went to meet with a Hanaean leader. He then assembled the Nabu (plu) of the Hanaeans and had an omen taken on king's behalf, putting a binary question to them and obtaining apparently, a favourable answer.
5. (i) **Qam(m) a tum, unclear title:** The reading *Qabbatu* (?) "speakers" an attractive interpretation confidentially accepted by the major dictionaries in correction of the original editor reading: *Qamatum*, is no longer tenable.

   (ii) Prophets without titles: Those without titles include a slight majority of women, one of whom was a high official at Mari. Also, a majority of, the revelations derive from dreams a means not yet attested for those prophets with titles.

   (iii) The context of the oracles: A number of texts provide information about the context of the message. The typical locus of revelation is a temple, either in reality or by dream visit one correspondent advises the King that '(when) I offered a sacrifice to Dagan for the life of my lord the 'answer' (masc) of Dagan Tuttal got up and spoke as follows:' O Babylon... (here follows an oracle against Babylon).

   Another text referring to a female ecstatic. suggests a sequence of messages: "0 Zimri-lim, do not go on a campaign, stay in Mari and I will continue to answer."

   The message is usually communicated to a royal official, but of two cases a temple administrator (sangu), who is not a cultic priest, serves as intermediary with the royal official. The Sangu presumably had some jurisdiction over such temple activity: A number of oracles are public even in the presence of assembly of elders.

   (iv) The content of the oracles: Because of the nature of the Marl archives, the oracles deal almost exclusively with the king's affairs. Commonly the prophets communicate a message from, a deity speaking in the first person, often referring to being "sent" by the

deity. The message may begin with the formula such as "thus says (the deity)." The content is generally an assurance to the King or a warning to the king of dangers (and an assurance of divine assistance) but a number of messages deviate from this pattern.
A unique letter from an *apilu* contains a cultic request from several deities and promises support for the king. In other case the king is chided for not meeting the cultic expectations of the deity - failing to provide "pure water" or neglecting the funerary offering for a predecessor or ancestor.

(v) The status of the oracles: Several letters specify that a position of the prophet's hair and piece from the fringe of the prophet's garment are being sent on to the king. These items surely were intended for use in a confirmation process involving technical divination. Some texts show that prophets as rather assertive at times.

**(c) Assyria:** Especially characteristic of the reigns of Esarhaddon (680-669 BCE) and Ashurbanipal (688-627 BCE) is their special interest in a wide variety of modes of communication with the divine powers, including prophetic-type speakers. Esarohaddon used the word "a proclaimer" (raggimu), "ecstatic" (mahhu) or "a dream interpreter."

**(i) Prophets with Titles**

1. **Mahhu/mahhutu, "ecstatic":** This title is variant of Mari *mahhu/muhhutu* provides the only continuity with the older titles, predominantly male, character is unknown
2. **Raggimu/raggimtu, "proclaimer":** In the seventh century BCE the "proclaimed" deliver prophetic messages, also plays a role in connection with the substitute king ritual; presumably he had status in the cult.
3. **Sabru, "revealer":** derives from Akkadian title *ba ru*, "to see" The "revealer" has a message dream apparently through incubators from Ishtar and report it to Ashurbanipal.
4. **Selutu, "(female) votary":** literally means "someone sent up (for deity): this title identifies one of the speakers in long collection of individual oracles for Esarhaddon, a woman presumably devoted by the king to the deity. The title is known from contemporary contracts recording dedications to Ninlil/Mullissu. As a "votary" given by the queen, one contract notes, no creditor or legal adversary can seize her, though she is married.

**(ii) Prophets without titles:** Identified by Esarhaddon, absence of title may be due to the lack of official position in the cult, especially associated with Ishtar of Arbela.

**(iii) The context of the oracles:** All oracles fit fuller record of the context of an oracle. A crisis situation - minor or major prompts a complaint to or an inquiry of a deity, who responds with a message of reassurance. Communication of the oracle to the king (or queen mother) may be oral or written down, depositing in the temple, and presented to the king in connection with ritual acts; some oracles seems to concern the occasion of a treaty ceremony.

**(iv) The content of the oracles:** The oracles are typically oracles of assurance for the political and succession concerns of the king communicated directly as it were, from the deity. "Fear not" is a common phrase, as in other AWA oracles of assurance. The speakers rarely admonish the king, and if so, they use a mild form, such as saying that former utterances by the deity have been ignored. The principal association of the prophets is with Ishtar or Arbela (and allied deities), though a number of other deities provide oracles.

**(v) The status of the oracles:** The oracles are reported individually to the King, noted 1n the official annals, and collected into cumulative record.

**(d) Egypt eg: "The Admonitions of Ipu-Wer":** a critique of the socio-political order, is labelled as prophetic in biblical sense. Text as "The prophecy of Neferti" are cast as foretelling a future deliverance for a country in a time of trouble, though written ex event. But those texts are seen more in relation to wise man of the east" not a charismatic prophet, probably Amun in kanak prophet/priest: In actuality there is very little known from Egypt, that illustrates the prophet as an inspired speaker. Generally, however, Egyptian oracles result from a form of manipulate divination such as movements of a deity during a public procession.

***Conclusion:*** On the basis of our foregoing discussion on the prophecy in the ancient West Asian context we in most cases observe that they stand in parallel in terms of the context and the content. In most cases Israelite prophecy was dependent on the West Asian prophetic phenomena. However, Israelites modified the prophecy they derived from the ancient West Asian context in order to suit their own context. The prophets in ancient Israel are only the representatives of God and they solely interpreted and communicated God's message and predicted the future events as directed by God.

Chapter 8

# Formation of the Prophetic Books

***Introduction:*** As pointed out in our previous chapter, the ancient West Asian material has been discovered to show that prophetism as such was no more unique to Israel and the Old Testament. In ancient Israel we find both sociologically conditioned forms of prophetism: *the nabi* ("called one"), encountered in the form of the ecstatic prophet associated with the exciting fertility cults of settled areas: and the seer encountered among nomadic cultures. The seer, like all Israel's nomadic heritage, soon became insignificant; one of the last great representatives of this type was Nathan.

Under the influence of Yahwism, seers and *nebiim* together gave rise to Israelite prophetism proper, as I Sam: 9:9 suggests. The immediate result was various transitional forms. Besides the bands of prophets, who are mentioned repeatedly, we have individual figures like Ahijah of Shilo (I Kings 11:29ff); Zedekiah (I Kings 22:11) and Micaiah the son of Imlah (I Kings 22:13ff). The first figures of whom we can recover a relatively clear picture, however, are Elijah (I Kings 17-19) and Elisha (II Kings 2-13).

In the period of so-called literary prophecy, the earlier forms gradually gave rise to a comprehensive class of prophets, which though having its own complex structures can be referred to as a whole by the term "professional cultic prophecy." Besides the unorganized prophets who wandered through the countryside, this class included cult prophets and court prophets. Besides those professional prophets stand the great individual prophets of the pre-exilic period, a group small in number: Amos and Hosea, Isaiah and Micah, Zephaniah, Jeremiah, and Ezekiel. In them Old Testament prophecy reaches its apex. They do not exercise their ministry as professionals, but on the basis of a special call that has uprooted them from their chosen profession. They think of themselves exclusively as representatives and, messages of their God. In contrast to the professional prophets, they see human beings as being unrighteous before God. These prophets do not base their preaching on a dead ideology but on a personal life of faith. In the post exilic period, professional prophets were absorbed finally in the guilds of Temple singers, while the words of the great individual prophets were increasingly collected and considered sacred.

With Deutero-Isaiah, towards the end of the exile begins eschatological prophecy, which draws upon the traditions of both the great individual prophets and the optimistic professional prophets. Eschatological prophecy (besides Deutero-Isaiah, Joel, Haggai, Zechariah and Malachi) reinterprets the either/or of the great individual prophets as a temporal before/after.

After the eschatology and expectations of the late exilic and post-exilic period were shattered, because despite the promises of the prophets all remained as it had always been and extensive circles in the community had turned their backs on eschatology. Daniel becomes prominent writing of this period. This book inaugurates a series of apocalyptic writings that seek to unveil the mysteries of the end time and provide revelations concerning the coming and passing of the ages of the world, in order both to determine the time when all history will end and to fix the place of the present age. A sharp contrast is drawn between the whole of world history and the Kingdom of God, which will begin after the last judgment yet to come. Having looked into few important preliminary matters now to understand the formation of the prophetic coups/literature, we now turn to few important matters involved in it.

***(a) The function of the Prophets:*** The prophets begin their work after the experience of a call. This work may go on continuously despite rejection (Hos.9:76) or denials on the part of the people (Ezek. 12:21-28) it can be interrupted by external force (Amos 7:10-13) or discontinued temporarily by the prophet on account of its failure (Isa 8:16-18) or on account of his inward conversion to a new message (Ezek. 3:22-27, 24:25-27, 33:21-22). It is of the nature of prophetism that the message is preached directly to those that are to receive it. Therefore, for the most part the prophets proclaim their short or long discourses directly or orally. To this extent the expressiox1 "literary prophecy" is, strictly speaking, erroneous, and should only be applied with reservations to those prophets whose discourses, unlike those of other prophets, were written down at a specific stage of their transmission.

***(b) Development of the Prophetic Oracle:*** The development of the prophetic oracle - like the actions or experiences described in the biographical accounts of the prophets-normally consists of an extended process involving at least four stages as suggested by Hempel. We shall briefly look into these four stages.

***First Stage:*** Is a movement of personal experience of God, in which God's "spirit" or "word" comes to the prophet - the "spirit" being most in the case of the nabi and cult prophet, the "Word" in the case of the great individual prophets or in which he is transported to announces include like Isaiah 6, auditions like Jer. 4:5ff; sudden inspirations like Isa. 7:13-17, and miraculous knowledge like that in Jeremiah 4-6 concerning the foe from the north. The secret experience takes place in the full light of spiritual and intellectual consciousness but can be accompanied by an ecstatic experience. In short, the prophet is gripped by a power that he cannot escape. What he experiences or perceives he is constrained to put into words and to proclaim (Jer. 20:9; Amos 3:8). Therefore, immediately after his secret experience the prophet begins to ponder over it.

***Second Stage:*** During this stage comes the prophet's interpretation and exposition of his unique experience according to the faith by which he lives. The new experience is interpreted in such a way that the individual experience is incorporated into the prophet's previous total picture of God's nature and will, enlarging it and vitalizing it. This interpretation usually distinguishes between true and false prophecy.

***Third Stage:*** This stage is the process of intellectual revision. Since what has been experienced must be proclaimed, it cannot remain at the babbling level of glossolalia, but must be translated into comprehensible and rational words. This takes place so naturally that the prophet sometimes adds an appropriate motivation or appends an obvious conclusion to the word of Yahweh. This much can generally be said: the less meditation and rational revision a prophetical oracle betrays, the more tersely and unconditionally it proclaims God's will, the more clearly it preserves as its nucleus a primitive complex of sounds (eg. Isa. 8:1), the closer we are to its origin.

***Fourth Stage:*** In this stage there is an artistic development, to which belong the adaptation of the message to a specific, sometimes very ancient, rhetorical form and its clothing in metrical poetry. This development can draw upon an image or idea and elaborate it artistically. eg. the fire that goes forth from Yahweh (Amos. 1:3ff) or his hand (Isa. 9:8ff)

***(c) Style of the Prophetic Oracle:*** In the style of the prophetic oracle, one can still note the influence of prophet's experience, so that the images follow hand upon each other's, the language seems unreformed, and abrupt transitions occur. A good example of this agitated vitality. The use of concrete images and superlatives which surpasses even the usual Israelite idiom is seen. Characteristic of prophetical style, are the introductory and concluding formulas that characterize a prophetical discourse as Yahweh's word: "Thus says Yahweh..." introduces the discourse by employing the ordinary messenger formula and "...oracle of Yahweh" concludes it in most cases. These formulas are subject to various poetic transformations. In addition, we frequently find introductory formulas belonging to the prophet personally; these state the identity of the divine "I" that sends the prophet and the recipient of the message, or who else is called upon to give ear (Isa. 1:2). Likewise, the state of the prophet during his secret experience can be described (Isa. 8:11). The prophet can expand the beginning of a discourse by adding a motivation to explain the following declaration of God's will (Amos 4:1).

***(d) Literary Types:*** The literary types used by the prophets in their preaching can be classified into three great groups: prophetical sayings, prophetical reports, and imitations of rhetorical forms from other spheres of life. We have already pointed out different literary forms of speech used by individual prophets at their appropriate places, thus we will not repeat them again here.

***Compilation and Transmission:*** Having presented in brief the various elements involved in the prophetical preaching of ancient Israel from the point of view of their traditions let us now briefly examine the elements involved in the process of compilation and transmission.

***(a) The Development of the Traditions:*** In an earlier day the prophetical books were naturally assumed to be single units and esteemed as the unchanged word of God. We may assume that the prophetical sayings and reports were soon recorded and transmitted in writing: Most of them were written down while the prophets were still alive following their oral proclamation or the performance of the symbolic acts. In latter times they may even have been written down beforehand. Of course we have very little data about these written records, we shall attempt to venture few conclusions in this direction.

In Isa. 8:16, which describes the end of the prophet's activity in terms of binding up the testimony and sealing the teaching, "among my disciples"; it may be considered as a later addition. Isa. 30:8 does not describe the writing down of prophetical sayings, but rather the incising of an inscription, whose text is given in v. 9. This disproves the assumption that the sayings were written down for future ages in order to provide subsequent legitimation for the prophets that violently attacked their contemporaries. In the case of Jeremiah 36:39b, the King seeks to render the threats of disaster in effectual by destroying the scroll and trying to seize its authors, Jeremiah and Baruch, while the new scroll is intended to secure the validity of Jeremiah's pronouncements, their threat continues unabated.

The major reason why the prophetical sayings and reports were written down, collected and transmitted was therefore to preserve the efficacy of a word once it had been spoken, and perhaps even increase it, by preserving the word in writing. Each time the words were read or recited, their power was released once more and made efficacious. This implied that the prophetical sayings were written down very soon after they were proclaimed orally. The spoken word had to be recorded quickly so as to preserve its effectiveness. Even the collection of individual texts which took place at a later dates and their gradual assembly into books may largely have come about for reasons of efficacy. Gradually, of course, theological and cultic reasons for the continued Preservation and transmission of the Prophetical writings became increasingly dominant as these writings came to be considered holy scripture. Even under these circumstances, however, we have an echo of the conception that the Prophetical word comes to life when it is read in the context of worship.

***(b) The Development of Prophetic Writings:*** Minor collections of sayings and reports in written form grew into larger collections, and these grew into books. This holds true for most of the prophetical books; only few of them are essentially unified compositions. The basic principle can be seen clearly in the case the book of Isaiah, which consists of three independent groups of writings, and the Book of the Twelve, which consists of twelve separate books.

Often, though not invariably, the original, minor collections can still be recognized. These represent the first stage in the growth of the book. In some cases, they have their own superscriptions, like Jer. 23:9, "concerning the Prophets"; 30:1-4, with the command to write down certain words and the introduction "These are the words"; 46:1, "the word of Yahweh which came to Jeremiah the prophet concerning the nations", and 50:1, "The word which Yahweh spoke concerning Babylon." Sometimes catchwords furnish the organizing principle, like "idols" (Ezek. 6) and "sword" (Ezek. 21); sometimes the identity or the similarity of the subject matter, like Ezek. 12:21-12:23 concerning prophets and person's authority and 34 concerning shepherds and sheep, sometimes similar events, as in the collections of reports concerning symbolic actions (4-5; 12:1ff; 24); and sometimes the compilation of words deriving from the same period as in Isa. 7-8.

***Three Types of Prophetic Texts are in General Recognized*:** poetic sayings, either first-Person speeches of Yahweh or words of the prophet; first-person prose reports of the prophet; and third-person prose reports concerning the prophet. The "simple" "composite" books comprise several types. In the case of more extensive writings, the second minor collections to form larger collections, like Isaiah 1-12 and Ezekiel 1-24. The linking of these larger collections can then be termed the third stage.

***(c) Structure of the Collection and Books:*** Various Principles determination the structure of the collections and books. The earliest and most important was clearly the chronological principle, by which sayings or collections were juxtaposed or linked in the order in which they were produced. We see this principle at work in the priority of place given to call narratives such as Jer 1:4-10; Ezek 1:1-3:15; and the corresponding section Isa. 40:1-8, as well as in the order of the Isaiah collections in Isa. 5:10, the words of Jeremiah contained in 1:1-25:14, which derive from difficult periods, and the order in which the dated words of Ezekiel were included in his book. The order of Hosea 1-3 also, with two reports of his marriage, is probably intended to be chronological, the way in which the passages dealing with the Servant of Yahweh are inserted in Isaiah 40-55 may suggest the same principle for Deutero-Isaiah.

One may note a qualitative principle at work, which had led to a passage considered particularly important being placed at the beginning of prophetical book. (Eg. Isa.1; Hosea 1-3, Amos 1:3-2:16). In the course of time, arrangement according to an eschatological scheme became the most important principle. Such a minor collections of Isaiah 1-35, where almost invariably the major portion of collection has appended to it an eschatological promise, which transforms the either/or proclaimed by Isaiah (judgment and punishment or deliverance through 'conversion) into a before/after of transitory disaster and eternal deliverance. The same scheme accounts for the order of Isaiah 1-39 followed by 44-66, Amos 1:2-9:7 followed by 9:8-15, as well as Micah 1-3 followed by 4-5 and 6:1-7:7 followed by 7:8-20. The collection Hosea 1-3 by contrast, is pre-eschatological while the book as a whole concludes with the promise. 14:2-9.

The composition of the first part of the book of Israel, comprising the two section 1-12 and 13-23, still follows the two-part scheme, but the addition of the collections in 24-35 marks the first step towards a three-part scheme. The latter provides the basis for the books of Ezekiel and Zephaniah, as well as the earlier form of the book of Jeremiah preserved in the LXX. Here threats against foreign nations are perhaps interpolated between the threats against Israel and the promises to Israel (and perhaps to foreign nations) because judgment upon the foreign nations is considered a transitional 33-48; Zephaniah 1-2:3; 2:4-3:8; 3:9-20; Jeremiah 1-25: 14;25: 15ff and 46-51 26:35. This method of composition imposes upon the prophets' peaching the two-or-three-part eschatological scheme, transforming it from the literary point of view into eschatological writings, although this contradicts the message of the pre-exilic prophets.

***(d) Later Prophetic Apocalyptic Books:*** These are the books which did not become a part of the Old Testament include Ethiopic and Slavonic Enoch (collection of several apocalypses), the assumption of Moses (an apocalypse with framework sections), IV Esdras (accounts of seven visions), the Syriac and Greek Baruch apocalypse (accounts of visions), in part the Sibylline oracles (fictions Pagan, Jewish, and Christian prophecy), and finally fragments of many apocalyptic writings from Qumran.

***Conclusion:*** Our discussion on the prophecy in the ancient West Asia reveals that much of it has given or we can find common elements between West Asian and ancient Israelite prophecy. The latter has borrowed much from the earlier prophecy. At times the parallels are very close between them and often Israelite prophecy has adapted its phenomena with few or more modifications.

Chapter 9

# Exegetical Study on the Selected Texts of Isaiah 40-55

***Introduction:*** In our preceding Chapters we have considered the general description on each of the Prophets in their historical setting. In Chapter IV (B) we had considered in detail the background to the prophet Deutero-Isaiah. This chapter is therefore a continuation of that section. The reader is expected to go through IV (B) before reading this exegetical chapter on Isaiah 40-55. We shall divide the entire block of material in 40-55 of Isaiah into small and individual pericopes to treat them each in detail.

***(1) Isaiah 40:1-11: Comfort My People:*** Unlike the majority of prophetic books, Deutero-Isaiah 15 without any superscription or literary introduction. But 40:1-11 seems so much like a beginning, an overture, a prologue, as to suggest that they come from the Prophet himself, and were intended by him as the introduction to his message.

In the line with other books, which start with Prophet's call, most critics regard vv. 6-8 as the equivalent of this. Nevertheless, these verses form part of a larger unit whose subject is not the messenger, but the message. The really important thing is that the message should be introduced: the introduction of the messenger is peripheral and forms only a part of the larger whole, a part, moreover, couched in veiled terms. The two passages which form a framework for the Prophet's call: the one an order given to unspecified listeners to prepare a way in the wilderness (3ff), the other a summons to Zion to get up into a high mountain and proclaim to the cities of Judah, 'Behold, your God!' (9). all three sections are introduced by the cry, "Comfort my People" (1f). the whole makes up one cry, and the context is to be understood as an interlinked series, in which the first, 'comfort' has obvious priority not only of place but also of importance. 'Comfort my People' - this cry determines, and sets the pattern for all that is to follow: the starting-point of this series, it resembles the general's order that gets stationary troops on the move by being taken up and passed on in the form of 'operation orders', until finally every single man is on the move. What is pictured in 40:1-11 is the message of God's new act; and with its delivery the new event, the exiles' release and the new exodus, is already under way.

One would naturally expect these verses to depart from Babylon, move out from exile. This does in fact occur, but not at the end of the prologue; it comes only just before the final servant song, at 52:11: "Depart, depart, go out thence." Deutero-Isaiah's words in this section also presents the Exodus tradition. The first Exodus, too, began with a cry to depart from bondage; then, too, there was the voice of one crying, with the function of proclaiming the release on which God had resolved; then, too, the decisive move towards this was the making of the way through the wilderness, as was made clear in the cry, 'Comfort my People', is meant to lay down the lines of the whole prologue.

***Interpretation***

**vv. 1-2:** the word comfort also is elsewhere in the Old Testament. at different places, and also in Deutro-Isaiah itself (49:13; 51:3,12; 52:9). All these passages have the following features in common: (a) the one who comforts is God, and the one comforted is Israel; (b) comforting is spoken of in the Past tense (in 51:12 the participle is used). Here the question is 'who helps you and comforts you?' (Lam 2:13 and Isa 51:19) to the exultant cry, the anticipated answer of those delivered, 'for Yahweh has comforted his people' (Isa. 49:13). This word of comfort is spoken with authority, because the cry 'comfort' proceeds to the cry 'prepare'; the messenger's word that turns lamentation into joy has as its counterpart the intervention in history of the God who is lord of history, who exalts the humble and casts down the mighty.

The cry: "comfort, comfort my people" is an example of the stylistic feature in Deutro-Isaiah's preaching which expresses the urgency of situation. It occurs similarly with imperatives in 51:9; 'Awake, Awake', and 51:17; 'Rouse yourself, rouse yourself.' The urgent cry is uttered at a time when people of Israel were gradually turning away from God, gradually closing their minds to him, and gradually letting their faith grow cold. These are the circumstances which lent urgency to cry. Israel must be aroused.

v. 2b and c reflects the description of turning point, all else depends e upon it; the word 'service' in 2b (cf. Job 7:1, 10:17 RSV translates the word as 'hosts') refers to the situation that, Israel's time of service is ended; the echo of glad tidings that Israel's physical hardship is enforced exile are how at an end. But these tidings are not understood unless the parallel sentence in 2c, 'her iniquity is pardoned' is taken together. The change in Israel's fortunes is based on the divine forgiveness. this means then the fundamental activity of Israel's sin led them to their hardships in exile. This reveals two factors: first, it-shows that, over Deutro-Isaiah's entire proclamation, there is still no radical divorce of religion for politics; a non-religions understanding of history (history, that is not determined by God or God's) was quite impossible for him. For Deutero-Isaiah, God and history are linked inseparably, and due to this inequity and forgiveness is not only applied to the individual, but to the nation as well. Second, the message of Deutro-Isaiah is in line with prophets of doom in the pre-exilic prophets, who proclaimed that Israel's sin responsible for their hardships in the exile. The prophet says that, "now is enough, now it is over and done with." But his words make them once more aware that what is now over and done with was the consequence of Israel's iniquities. And only recognition of this fact made any continuance of her history possible.

**vv. 3-5:** Introduces a new factor: 'A voice cries', whose the voice is, is deliberately left unsaid. the prophet obviously intended to make the speaker hard to recognize, and this must be given due weight in exegesis. Volz calls this voice as 'the one who calls and those to whom he calls are invisible powers.' De Boer thinks that we may discover an allusion to the heavenly court. But these contentions are not so important, the person of the hearer is of no importance, and is to remain in the dark. The voice that cries the words of vv. 3ff introduces the fulfilment of the divine order by giving a new one, an operation order, prepare the way.

The manner in which vv. 3ff follow upon vv. 1f is the first instance of the truth expressed at the end of the book: 'My word shall not return me empty, but it shall accomplish...' once Yahweh cry, 'Comfort my people', something was bound to happen. The cry could not return to him empty. But the comfort is to start with the preparation of a way. In this sense the word 'comfort' means: a turning away of suffering, which means helping, and so, an active intervention to turn the suffering away. This is precisely the sense here. Israel's comforting begins with the preparation of a way, for the way spoken of is the one which bring her through the desert back home. In v-3, the phrase 'in the wilderness' is to be taken along with the verb "to prepare" and not with the preceding clause 'a voice cries' (although Luke and Matthew 3:3, John 1:23 takes it in this way). The implication here is way through the wilderness not to pick up a "voice in the wilderness".

Deutero-Isaiah's proclamation has signs of encounter with the world in which the prophet lived, the sphere of influence of the Babylonian empire and its capital city. The 'highway' has its own secular place in Babylonian hymns; the layout of the city of Babylon is itself proof of the importance of the great processional highway. Thus in Babylon, the ways prepared and made level for the triumphal entry of the god or the King. For exiled Israelites in Babylon, these imposing highways were symbols of Babylon's might, the might that had brought about Israel's own downfall. It is however, designated a highway 'for Yahweh our god.' Just as the magnificent highways of Babylon were strictly highways for her God's. Its designation as the highway for Yahweh shall be revealed'. This too, is to be read against the Babylonian background. There, the primary function of the processional highways was to allow the great processions to display the power and majesty of God's in visible form. But this very background highlights the difference in the being of Yahweh: his 'glory' his kabod, cannot possibly be manifested in the same way as that of the God's of Babylon; for what created the impressions of majesty in the Babylonian processions - the images of the God's-is absent here. What reveals Yahweh's glory is his action in history. In the way for leading his people home, Yahweh is giving proof to the highway made through the desert. This restoration demands a divine intervention in history, thus the language in 40:3ff about making straight the way in the desert is figurative rather than literal.

v. 5b reveals that, when the glory of Yahweh is revealed, it is for the whole world to see, not in a direct way, but in the history. The phrase, 'for the mouth of Yahweh has spoken it' is only refers back to v. 1 'says your God'. this justifies the purpose as 'operation order' of v. 1f. the order that Israel was now to be comforted had been issued by Yahweh. Since this Was what his mouth spoke, intervention in history followed in editable, and a v,3ff. this is represented as the preparation of a way. Yahweh's intervention is this grounded in his word.

**vv. 6-8:** A fresh cry, a fresh command rings out: A voice says, "cry!". The introduction is similar to that of vv,3ff. The speaker is again unspecified The important thing lies in what he says: the execution of what was commanded in vv. 1f is carried a further step forward. The voice in v.6 has the function as that in v. 3: the 'crying' command in v.6ff and the preparation of the way commanded in v. 3 ff serve the same end - the comforting of Israel.

When God commanded to 'preach' by means of imperatives originating from 'comfort', a human voice with question, 'What (shall I) Preach?, resists this mighty downward pouring of God's gracious will, and with its words, so brief and so charged with emotion, perfectly gathers up all the vanquished nation's lamentation and sheer despair. vv. 6b-7 looks like a quotation. Some of these words seem familiar with the Psalms: 39, 49 and 90, and similar passages in the book of Job. They represent a well-defined form often found in the Psalter. This cry is however is the [rophet's counter-cry due to a particular set of circumstances; and the question is how can the

Prophet substantiate it by means of such general sentiments? the answer is that the exiles' greatest temptation - and the prophet speaks as one of their number. The resignation and despair constitute the spiritual state of Israel to which the Prophet is called to Preach.

The expression: 'Surely the People is grass' is the comment of the reader who was deeply moved, and the prophet says 'Amen' to these words. this is one of the numerous examples of additions or glosses which constitute valuable witnesses as to what happened to the biblical text as it was read by or to the congregation of the faithful.

v. 8 contains the answer given to the Prophet when he objected. The first part (8a) takes up the substantiation of the objection word and thus admits its truth. The voice that now speaks does not therefore intended to deny that Israel's circumstances are what the Prophet, as 'one of the nation', takes them to be. In v. 8b, however, the sheer hopelessness of the situation is confronted with the reality of the word of God. The 'word of our God' spoken to Israel in her past history is not part and parcel of the inevitable decay: it stands, it persists, it abides.

The words 'But the word of our God stands forever' form the point of focus in the prologue. they express what is basic to, and crucial for, the proclamation of Deutro-Isaiah. This is also seen in the background of: Israel had lost not only her land and her statehood, but also her temple and its worship, the fountain - head of life for land and nation. But she was still left with the word of God committed to her keeping, which at once took on a significance never hither to seen or even dreamed of. This is the starting point of Deutero-Isaiah's proclamation.

**vv. 9-11:** In the third of the three cries which carry out the command 'to 'comfort a completely different, a new, note is heard. the cry is directed to Jerusalem, but is given no specific introduction; the voice which utters it may possibly be the same as that in v. 6. Here, too, a duty is assigned by means of an imperative which links on to the proceeding imperatives. Zion is called upon to bring to the (other) cities of Judah the glad tidings, 'Behold, here is (comes) Your God!'

vv. 9ff go along with vv. 3-8. the duty imposed upon the powers who are called on in vv. 3ff is clear: they are to prepare the way. The same is true of the duty laid on the Prophet in vv. 6ff. But how does the task to which Jerusalem is summoned fit in with these? But is it not Zion herself who is to be comforted?.

The Zion here spoken to is called 'herald of good tidings. The verb is used of the bringing of good news, e.g. I Sam. 31:9 (news of the victory of the Philistines), II Sam 18:19 (Ahimaaz wishes to bring David the good news), and Jer 20:15 (news of the birth of a child). In these passages, the event which the glad tidings announce has already taken place. Does this mean, then, that the order here given is not to be carried out until the first caravans have already made the Journey home and arrived in Jerusalem? Not at all. Rather, the "herald of good tidings, Zion, is to proclaim the advent of Yahweh now, and to proclaim 'without fear', even it still lies in the future. She is to call for Praise of the who comes to help his people, as if the help were already given. These verses of prologue (9-11) are the basis of the literary category of 'eschatological Psalm of Praise' peculiar Deutro-Isaiah. Here the call to praise is always substantiated by a verb in the perfect tense: God has already acted. For the comfort to become effective, Zion (that is, the People of Israel) must herself accept and assent to the message (vv. 6ff) of the coming of salvation (vv. 3ff). If now, while still in exile, she is bold enough to break into jubilation at it, then she has accepted it. In this respect the song of praise which Zion is summoned to raise in vv. 9f corresponds to that literary category which bulks largest in Deutero-Isaiah's proclamation, the oracle of salvation in which the deliverance promised to Israel is proclaimed in the perfect tense - that is which says that in the counsel of God the change in her fortunes has already taken place (40.1f). the connection of the two literary categories is also suggested by the word 'fear not' at the end of v. 9, they are taken form the oracle.

In v. 9 we find that just as the watchman who has to announce the coming of the King mounts the tower, Jerusalem is to 'get up to (the) high mountain', in order to see the exiles approaching while they still far off, so to be able to announce this to many and far- scattered cities Such a high degree of personification of Zion shows that the Prophet's way of speaking is extremely figurative and indirect: the thing would be fantastic as actual fact. Then vv. 9b-11, too, what is described is not properly and directly the return of the exiles. Rather, the one who comes is Yahweh himself; he 'just' brings Israel in his train. Perhaps Deutero-Isaiah here is talking about Israel's return as divine advent or epiphany in his way of implying that this is solely and entirely the work of Yahweh. At the same time, he links sup with the ancient tradition of the 'divine epiphany', the earliest 'form' in which Israel sung the praises of the God who made haste to help his people in their direst need. These old epiphanies always depict Yahweh's advent as a bi-polar event: he comes as the mighty, the majestic one, his advent convulsing the cosmos and overthrowing the foe; but also as he who condescends to his people in their need and graciously has compassion on them. Both motifs are taken up here: 'He comes with might, and his rules for him'; the nation's restoration needs his antecedent victorious intervention. The details given in v. 11b emphasize the fact that the shepherd does not lead an undifferentiated multitude, but individuals, each one receives the care he needs from him, all are to share in the joy of the return (cf. John 10:14); and the shepherd knows how to make the way easy for every single one.

***(2) Isaiah 40:12-31: The Creator is the Savior:*** This is a particular unit; the sections (vv. 12-17; 18-24; 25-26: 27-31) all fall into the one literary category of disputation. All these sections are closely connected to each other. Looking closely at the questions by which each is introduced, we find that in vv. 12 ('Who measures the waters... the heavens?), 13f,18 and 25, they are really rhetorical; only the final section, vv. 27-31, is introduced by a true disputation: v. 27, 'Why do you say, O Jacob... my right is disregarded by my God?'. Here the prophet quotes the assertion being made by Jacob-Israel, that God had abandoned his people, and in vv.28ff he challenges it. 'Do you not know? have you nor heard?' The background of vv. 12-26 is the unspoken question inevitable in view of the situation into which Isaiah's defeat had brought her - 'Can our God still really help us?' The answer given to this question depends on the answer to the other, 'Does our God still want to have anything more to do with us?' Both are then in fact gathered up what God said in vv. 12-26, the other comes in vv. 29-31. The correspondence between the two answers, 'he does not faint or grow weary' (v. 28c) and 'He gives power to the faint' (v. 29a), is perfectly deliberate.

To counter the challenges offered by the foreign nations in their might. the princes in their power, and the apparently victorious star-God's, Deutero-Isaiah proclaims to the weary and despondent the majesty of the creator and lord of history, who in his compassion towards the weary comes to meet his people. The passage taken together is modelled on the structure of his majesty and of his goodness. Praise of God's majesty is frequently developed along the two lines (e.g. Ps.33), that he is the creator and lord of his creation (so here vv. 12-17), and that he is the lord of history (so here vv. 18-24). The creator god is also the lord of stars, for he made them (vv. 25-26). Thus 40:12-31 not only contain features deriving from hymnody and display the style, proper to it; the model for the verses is manifestly the structure found in descriptive praise, which Deutero-Isaiah wants to revive for his people to counter their laments (for this reason it is associated with the disputation).

**vv. 12-17:** The questions introduced by the word 'who' lay down the lines of vv.12ff. The link between them is their subject matter: v. 12 'Who measures the waters with......?, vv. 13f. 'Who measures the spirit of Yahweh....?. They are quite rhetorical; the answer nobody is obvious.

The verbs in v. 12- measure, enclose, weigh-are all different ways of describing the same process, ascertaining the total amount of something by measuring or weighing it. The prophet ranges over the sea (or the waters), the heavens, the earth and the mountains. These stand, as in Job. 38, Ps. 90 and elsewhere, for the basic magnitudes of the created universe. The verbs in the rhetorical questions make the heavens, the earth, the sea and the mountains stand for that which is absolutely immeasurable (In a hymn,

Marduk is called 'the one who traverses the heavens, heaps up the earth, and measures the waters of the sea').

vv. 13f appear to continue in just the same styles to how much greater a degree does this immeasurability pertain to God! v. 13a, however, puts the question, who measures the spirit of Yahweh...?, while v. 13b takes the line, 'who is the counsellor who instructs him?' The 'spirit of Yahweh' does not mean either the all-encompassing and spiritual nature of Yahweh' or the 'organ of the divine intelligence', but the power of God which works miracles. The same thing is said in v. 14a and b. Because no one can measure God's knowledge, the divine incomparability and immeasurability consist in the fact that no body possesses the measures for pronouncing judgment on the divine planning and activity; as a result, nobody can give him advice, or say to him that in this or in that he ought to have acted rather differently (as in 45:9ff).

vv. 15-17 depicts the situation that when water is drawn, the drop that falls from the bucket does not matter, nor, when things are weighed does the dust on the scales. In the divine plan, whole nations may matter as little! (v.17): 'All the nations are as nothing before him.' Deutero-Isaiah is clear the successor of the pre-exilic Prophets in that they warned their fellow-country men against either placing too great reliance on one of the world empires or being, too greatly in fear of them. (cf. Isa 2:7ff; 31:1ff), Judah should know that the manifest expansion of foreign nations" power had meant the lessening or weakening of the power of God in history; and of his lordship over it. But Deutero-Isaiah goes one step forward, unlike other pre-exilic prophets, whose words were always to one specific nation, Deutero-Isaiah boldly sets foreign nations in total over against God, and says that, as compared with him, they are all nothing. Then word 'nothing' used here occurring only in Deutero-Isaiah (40:17,23; 41:11,12,24) and in later passages (Hag 2:3; Ps. 39:5,6; 73:2).

In vv. 18ff, the subject is the divine incomparability. v.18 is a rhetorical question line in vv.12ff. It also be compared. Here the description suggests the way in which the Prophet stresses the idols solidity and stability (that does not move) hints at a delicate indirect mockery. This impression is confirmed by the liturgy of the Babylonian New Year Festival, where we find as part of the sacred rite a similar description of the manufacture of statues of the God's; it, too, names, the materials and the various craftsmen (ANET, P. 33):

"When it is three hours after sunrise, (he shall call) a metal worker and give him precious stones and gold (from) the treasury of the god Marduk to make two images (for the ceremonies of) the sixth day (of Nisannu). He shall call a wood worker and give him (some) cedar and tamarisk (pieces). He shall call a goldsmith and give him (some) gold..."

It is very significant that, at the time when Israel's ancestors left the lands where God's were worshipped by means of images, she was given the command and forbidden not to make any images of Yahweh. It is equally significant that, when the Israelites again had to leave their own land for a foreign one in which they saw images and their manufacture, they understood the great consequences of the, fact that it was impossible to make an image of their God.

**vv. 21-24** These verses are to be read as the direct continuation of the questions in v. 18. The four questions in v. 21 exemplify a leading characteristic of Deutero-Isaiah's style, intensification by means of putting sentences with the same meaning one after the other, the first often being the shortest and the last the longest. The first two questions: 'Have you not known?, Have you not heard?' describe the one aspect, the third, 'has it not been told you from the beginning?, the other. the words which follow the questions in v. 21, '...who sits above the circle of the earth..... who stretches out the heavens as a curtain....', are obviously taken from a Psalm. similarly, in v. 27-31, the same questions are followed by other words also taken from Psalms: 'Yahweh is God everlasting, the creator of the ends of the earth....' Therefore, when Deutero-Isaiah put these questions, he was thinking of his people's liturgical traditions, of the Psalms in which the praises of the creator were handed on. In order to prepare the ground for his message of comfort, he revived among the remnant of his people a particular component of pre-exile worship.

v. 22 contains some very rare words. The word for circle occurs only once or twice and always in the context of the creator and creation (Prov. 8:27; Job 26: 10). the word for "curtain" (*doq*), and also for 'stretches out' (*mth*) are only found here. This suggests well-defined, distinctive traditions. Praise the Lord of history is added in v. 23: 'who brings princes to naught...' something closely resembling this is found in Job 34:19f (also Job 12:13-25). In the picture of the divine lordship over history, Israel recedes into the background, and the emphasis is laid on God's intervention against the mighty one of the earth. For e.g.: Ps. 33:10, 16f. In the connection the correspondence between the two sections is clear. (i.e; vv. 12-17 and 18-24). In vv. 12-17, reference after reference to the creator and lord shows the nothingness of the nations in Yahweh's sight, and in vv. 18-24. the nothingness of the Princes. Both passages deal with the challenge to which she was exposed. what, the hearers of the Prophets should know is that, Yahweh, who created the world, is absolute lord of the nations and powers.

vv. 25-26 The same question is raised as in vv. 18-24, then follows the earnest appeal, 'Lift up your eyes on high and see' (cf also v. 21). In both cases there is emotion in the references to the creator: 'who created these?' This statement refers to the astral bodies which were the chief God's in

Babylon, all dominant, and its virtual rulers. Marduk is the sun god, the King is his priest and representative on earth: the part played by astral cults were immense. To this, Deutero-Isaiah says that the astral bodies, who are lords in Babylon is being Principle deities there, are created things, and nothing more (the mere createdness of the astral bodies is expressed in similar terms in Gen. 1). They are all subject to Yahweh, the God of Israel, their creator and lord. Not a single one of them but must obey his commands. 'who created these?', asks Deutero-Isaiah, and in so doing rejects their claim to divinity and puts them where they belong, under the word of command of their creator and lord.

In vv. 27-31, the real feelings of the Prophet's hearers, feelings of despondency and doubt concerning Yahweh's action on their behalf, are brought out into the open. In these in a lament in v. 27, by proclamation of the God who condescends and stoops to help his people in their need. This confirms the fact that the whole poem is descriptive Praise. This so because, the Prophet discourages the nations weariness and despondency expressed in the four discourses.

In v. 27, Deutero-Isaiah quotes words of a community lament, using them to express Israel's complaint and protest against the way in which God acted. The question 'why' is introduced here (cf. Ps. 44:24,25). Here Deutero-Isaiah cites words from a lament in actual use by the exiles at the time. In v. 28, the Prophet once more refers to the majesty of the creator, and the language is clearly that of Psalms of Praise: "Yahweh is an everlasting God, he sees unto the ends of the earth." One of the creator's properties is his limitless extension in time (everlasting) and in space (the ends of the earth). The creators unrestrained vastness is set over against the narrow lot of Israel and the challenges which faced her. V.28c states the significance of this vastness for these who have Yahweh as their God: his understanding is illimitable, and therefore unsearchable; his designs infinitely outstrip those possibilities for the future which Israel herself can see.

In vv. 29-31, the passage reaches its goal, comfort for Israel. The stumbling blocks of Israel are all removed now. These verses resemble very much the words in Ps. 33. vv. 30-31 develop the two sides a of the paradox. the strong and stalwart fall exhausted; but the faint and 'spent' complete their journey. Here again we find clear echoes of a motif belonging to descriptive praise: the exalting of the humble in vv. 29-31 contrasts with the humbling of praised in the psalter: 'he casts the mighty from their seats and exalts the humble. This is the mode of action of him whose power is without limits and whose understanding is unsearchable.

In the section, 40:1-23, first three sections Deutero-Isaiah proclaims to the faint and the despondent the majesty of the creator and lord of history (vis-a-vis challenges offered by the nations in their greatness, the princes in their greatness, the princes in their might, and the seemingly victorious astral God's), in the fourth he proclaims the mercy of the God who, in his people 3 hour of need, condescends to them.

***(3) Isaiah 41:1-5: Who Performs and Does This?:*** The section 41:1-5, opens the series of trial speeches in which Yahweh, the God of Israel, calls the 'islands and nations', and along with the latter their God's, to appear in the court.

The point here at issue is the claim to divinity both by the God's of the foreign nations and by Yahweh, the God of Israel, a claim which of course could only be validly made by one of them. Deutero-Isaiah here avails himself of the form used in pleadings. This allows him to say two things: first that the foreign God's claim to divinity, and therefore to worship - as will appear later, he was thinking primarily of the God's of Babylon - can be declared invalid by judicial means, that is, by means of impartial arguments which both sides are bound to accept, and secondly, that it is perfectly possible for such a legal contest or lawsuit to be held, which means that Yahweh recognizes the foreign God's as a body of corporate, and that they can perfectly well be summoned and speak. Thus the background of this literary form is not a criminal case which has to do with an offense and its punishment, but the civil case which turns on a claim and its admission or dismissal. Thus Deutero-Isaiah uses a form that is peculiar to him in his context, in the midst of the exiles placed in Babylon. For their daily life, the Babylonian empire was an imposing and undeniable reality, and they knew that its nerve-centre was its cult, with its innovation of the God's, its sacrifices and processions. In such a situation the question of which claim to divinity was true and who was in fact God was inevitable.

In v. 1, foreign nations and certain parts of the world are summoned to appear in court and at the same time bidden to be silent (in Heb. 'Coming to me be silent'). These are the formalities necessary and customary at all times throughout the world when pleadings are opened, but here two, parties are summoned as they are that are very much more than preliminaries. There may be yet another background involved here, i.e, of the heavenly court as in the classical Babylonian epic Enuma Elish - which, under the presidency of the god-King, deliberated on the destinies of God's and men, and also served as a court of law. However, Deutero-Isaiah demythologized it, since the God's summoned by Yahweh are replaced by the nations and certain parts of the world, and the aim is the declaration that these God's' claim to divinity is baseless.

In vv. 2-3 as the one party in the suit, Yahweh puts the question who stirred (him) up from the east?' (in Heb, the sense of the word is: (him) whom victory meets at every step, a peculiar form of supplementation parallelism). Here the name Cyrus is not mentioned, but it is only mentioned in 44:28-45:7 there can be no doubt, however, that Cyrus is the person meant here, for the next verses manifestly describe his appearance on the scene They look back on it, and reflect the stir which it caused throughout the whole world at the time; it perhaps points out to Cyrus' first conquests The subject changes here: he (Yahweh) gave up nations before him he (Cyrus) pursues them, Deutero-Isaiah makes an assertion which his hearers found both increditable and highly obnoxious, namely that in the raise of the King of Persia, which had never before come with in the sphere of Yahweh's action, he saw the hand of the God of Israel. This passage merely lays down the base that such a course of action on God's part is possible.

In v. 4, the words 'I, Yahweh, the first and with the last, I, the same', is properly understood as 'divine self-prediction' (cf. Ps. 90, opening lines). The words: 'the first...the last', indicates the ground which makes possible on activity of his that embraces the totality of universal history. Because his activity proceeded all the movements of history, and will also terminate them all, he is the one 'who calls the generations from the beginning' (4a). What is expressed here is not the permanence of an always existent divine being, but the contrast between God and history in its totality ('and with the last I am still he'). It is the expression of a divine eternity related to history, and not of one philosophically contrasted with it. In the context of 41:1-5, v. 4 carries the meaning: Our God, who was there at the beginning and will be so at the end, is the one who calls the generations from the beginning.

v. 5 relates to the simple fact of the stirring up of Cyrus. The coming of Cyrus cause shuddering and dismay throughout continents, even to the ends of the earth. The context implies that men realize what the trial speeches are to prove: here God is present, here people may see the divine activity in all its grandeur.

***(4) Isaiah 41:8-13: Fear not!:*** This is an oracle of an assurance of salvation (also 41:14-16; 43:1-4,5-7; 44:1-5 and 54: 4-6 and other Passages); It is the most characteristic form and central to the message of Deutero-Isaiah. Begrich ground that in many of the Psalms in the category of individual laments there was a clearly marked sudden transition from lamentations to expressions of the suppliant's conviction that his prayer had been granted which indicated that someone else, a Priest (or a cult Prophet), 'speaking in the name of God, had given his assurance. To this assurance Begrich gave the name 'the Priestly oracle of salvation' and perhaps it is the same found in the case of Deutero-Isaiah, who reshaped the form for his use. Deutero-Isaiah primary idea in using this form is to tell Israel: because of the fate which had over taken the scattered remnant of Israel, the only thing left for them was to lift up their hands in supplication to God and wait for a word of grace and consolation. Two thing clearly show that an assurance and grant for the prayer is given. First, is the clear echo of a lament in numerous phrases and words in these passages in Deutero-Isaiah, Second, and more direct proof comes a few passages in Psalms of lamentation, which hint at an oracle of salvation. Deutero-Isaiah achieved a very significant combination of the Prophetic proclamation and the cultic declaration of salvation.

vv. 8-9: The words 'But you' with which the address to Israel begins, are explained by the form taken by the oracle of salvation. The word 'But' also introduces the word of consolation addressed to Israel as against the pronouncements of judgment on the nations who are dismayed at the evidence of God's power in history. God addresses Israel as 'you my servant.' this is the first occurrence of a word which is of tremendous significance in Deutero-Isaiah's proclamation. The Hebrew word used here for servant (*'ebed*) means trust, honour and protection (cf. Gen. 24). For Israel to be God's servant means primarily that she has a master with whom she feels secure, whom she can trust, and who cares for her.

The phrase 'You, Jacob, whom I have chosen' (41:8f; 43:10,20; 44:1f; 45:4) conveys the same idea as the appellation 'my servant'. The verb *bachar* (to choose) has the shade of meaning found in the book of Deuteronomy. The word signifies both here and in Deuteronomy, out of many other Peoples whom God might have chosen, he chose Israel. This Israel's election is carried back to patriarchs: 'the offspring of Abraham, my friend.' The words are proof positive that he historical traditions of his nation were the source of Deutero-Isaiah's inspiration (cf. Gen. 18:17, II Chron. 20:7).

In v. 10, central to the whole oracle is expressed: 'Fear not!' It is the cry which banishes the fear, rather than 'exhortation not to be afraid as many think. It is found in two different significances in each cases. First, it may be connected with a theophany, and spoken in this context. Here the fear on man's part is due to the manifestation of the deity as such) an the cry, 'Fear not!, takes this away. Second, distinct from this is the Individual lament, where the cry comes as the answer to the lament. In this case, what evokes the fear is the threat or danger that inspired the lament. The clear example of this kind is found in Dan 10:8ff (Judg 6:23; Exod. 20:18-21). With Deutero-Isaiah, the cry has very close affinities with those passages in which, in the context of Yahweh as the man of war (the holy war), the same cry is spoken to an Israel threatened by enemies (Josh. 8:1; 10:8; Numb 21:34; Deut. 1:21; Exod. 14:13f).

The cry's first substantiation is given in two noun clauses, 'I am with You', 'I am your God'. These two assurances either come into operation at the moment the pledge is made, or else the pledge gives them effect. The first 'I am with you' has long history outside Israel, as well as within it (cf. Deut. 20:1; 31:8; Jer. 42:11; 46:27). the second 'I am your God' is particularly talks to counter a god's self-prediction occurring in the same way in the Babylonian cult: 'I am Ishtar of Arbela... Fear me not, extol me' (Norden, *Agnostos Theos*, Leipzig, 1956, p. 208). This may be described as an explicit self-glorification on the God's' part which is given its point by the background of polytheism- the glorification of one god rises above that of others. Deutero-Isaiah therefore adopted the form deliberately for purposes of Polemic. By putting self-glorification into the mouth of the God who alone is God, he reduces the self-glorification found in the Babylonian pantheon to absurdity. Thus God's 'self-exaltation' serves only to exalt his being God for Israel: I am you God.

The phrase in v. 10 'I strengthen you' once again express the assurance of salvation which is effective the moment the comfort is given.

vv. 11-12 refer something to the future (imperfect tense in Hebrew). In contrast to the assurance of salvation proper, this part alone is proclamation of something that is to take place later on. The four half verses in v. 11f. have one single theme your foes shall be destroyed! These verses correspond to a particular part of a Psalm lamentation, the double wish or the one aspect of the 'wish.... that simultaneously is expressed it two directions', which is often to be found at the end of Psalm of lamentation (Ps. 35:26; 40:15f; 56:10; 58:7-10; 63:10f).

V. 13, repeats the assurance of salvation. By means of this verse Deutero-Isaiah executes the commission God gave him, of comforting his chosen people with the assurance, 'God has espoused Your concise.'

***(5) Isaiah 42:1-4: Behold, my Servant:*** This so called servant song is an important part of Deutero-Isaiah's proclamation. (other songs 42:1-4 and 5-9; 49:1-6 and 7-13; 50:4-9 and 10ff and 52:13-53:12). The structure of this song is my very clear and concise. The key-note of it all is given in the first two words, 'Behold, my servant' or 'this is my servant'. These in themselves epitomize the event described throughout- God points to someone and designates him as his servant. The song is thus the designation of God's servant. Even though the song is clear and concise, the interpretation is very difficult. On three matters we are left in the dark: Who is the servant here designated by God for a task? What is the nature of the task? And in what context is the designation made? The veiled manner of speaking is intentional, and much described here was meant to remain hidden even from their original hearers. While most commentators are controlled by the questions: Who is this servant of God?, it is better to be controlled by the question: What do the texts make known about what transpires, or is to transpire, between God, the servant, and those to whom his task pertains.

v.1 The first words plainly describe a designation. This means that someone with the right so to do designates or appoints someone else to perform a task or to hold an office. Israel knew of such designations during her early days of her charismatic leaders in the time of Judges (cf. Judg. 6) and (I Sam. 9:15-17 and other passages). Probably what is suggested in 42:1-4 indicates a royal designation.

'Whom I uphold': the one who upholds gives his own strength to the one upheld (cf. Exod. 17:12). 'My Chosen' have preserves its original meaning: out of many who have performed the task, this is the one whom God chooses for it, and the designation makes the choice public and known. The reason for the chose of this man and mother, rests with God alone. God has pleasure in him. someone is appointed and equipped by God for a task whose nature is no more than suggested on the description which follows. The servants designation is differentiated from the call of a prophet by the fact that the latter is invariably a transaction between God and the prophet alone. But the servants designation requires the presence of others who witness it and it also bears the stamp of an accrediting. These features link it with a royal designation, its importance and historical significance are the same. The Servants task:

v. 1c: he is to bring forth, Justice to the nations.
v. 3c: he brings forth Justice in truth
v. 4b: till he establishes justice in the earth.

These three sentences give three descriptions of the servants task. All three lines contain the word mis pat. But what is mispat? (Justice?) This is also used in the light of 49:6 'I will give you as a light to the Gentiles. The basic meaning of the word is 'justice' or 'judgement'. If we examine Deutero-Isaiah for instances of mispat with reference to the Gentiles, we shall at once find them in trial speeches (cf. 41:1-5, 21-29) which present a legal process between Yahweh and the gentile nations. They all turn upon justice, mispat, and result in the Gentiles' God's' claim to divinity being declared to nothing: Yahweh alone is God. This can perfectly well be the meaning of mispat in 42:1-4. It gives excellent sense. And the probability is increased by taking the final trial speech (45:20-25) into account as well. In it the 'survivors of the nations' are invited to participate in Yahweh's salvation (cf. 49:6). This being so, the servant's task, according to 42:1-4, would be to bring this judgement to the Gentiles. About his way of doing this, vv. 2-4 give only a veiled hint. However, there no idea that the servant was to go as a missionary to the Gentiles, but by bring out the message to his own people, the servant was to bring God's mispat to the Gentiles in an indirect way.

**V. 2:** As the servant promulgates judgement, he is not to follow custom and cry aloud in public. Here we may remember that in oriental law, when a new King succeeds to the throne, he re-enacts the laws and has them publicity proclaimed. The way in which the servant was to bring forth justice and establish it is to be. The opposite of this. So far, the actual method is not stated.

**V. 3a:** According to J. Begrich, the metaphors used here may be in an old legal usage as their background. But if so, their wording preserves no more than a faint echo of it. For those concerned, bringing forth the divine justice is not death for those already under sentence of death. The servant makes God's justice prevail in such a way that his action contradicts the harsh law of the world, which says that what is broken and burns dimly inevitably perishes.

**V. 4:** The lines allude to the verbs in v. 3a and promise the servant himself that he will not burn dim or to be broken before he has completed his task. This is the only place in the song which suggests that the servant's task is to involve him in grievous suffering-this is to be taken up in the other songs. (cf. Jer. 1:19). V. 4c the phrase 'And the isles wait for his teaching' compare 51:4, where the same thing is said not of the servant but of God: 'for teaching, will go forth from me, and my truth for a light to the Gentiles.' (cf. 51:52) The gentiles are already waiting and looking for the divine justice which the servant is to bring forth. This does not involve our idea of 'seeking after the one God, and Yearning for him'. the verb implies intent expectancy of deliverance or help. The sense is therefore that among the Gentiles the servant's gospel finds an expectancy similar to that which greeted Deutero-Isaiah's message to Israel, eg. in the exile.

All that can be said about 42:1-4 is that the echo of royal designation, as well as the proclamation of justice and the sparing of those already under sentence of death, point in the direction 'of a mediator who discharges his office by way of action, like the judges (charismatic leaders) and Kings in the past. On the other hand, the servant's task as set forth in vv. 2-4 points rather to one who mediates by word of mouth.

***(6) Isaiah 43:1-7: Fear not!:*** Words like these takes us to the very heart of Deutero-Isaiah's proclamation. Here we can most early feel the assurance with which he was able to proclaim to his fellow-captives that the decisive change in their lot had already taken place. This oracle is constructed in two parts, vv.1-4 and 5ff, which are parallels. V. 1 begins with the assurance of salvation, 'Fear not', which is substantiated in the perfect tense ('I have set you free') and be means of a noun clause ('You are mine', also v. 3a, 'I am'), and is carried on in the proclamation of imminent salvation couched in the future tense (vv. 2ff). The oracle is rounded off in v.4a by the repetition of substantiation in the perfect.

**v. 1:** The two individual verbs: 'I have redeemed you' (the Heb. word ga'al) signifies the redeeming, or liberating by payment, of a relative imprisoned for debt, and was originally a technical term of family law. In the same way, the words 'I have called you by name' can properly relate only to a transaction involving two persons, and has been transferred from this use-between two human beings - to the realm of the dealing of God with his chosen people. Deutero-Isaiah strikes a personal note to the people who are in exile, who needed a personal touch of God's redemption and salvation at this hour.

What made this personal note possible was the Prophet's boldness in adapting the oracle of salvation intended for an individual so as to makes relate to the nation and its fate. Just as it was once said to Abraham, 'Fear not, Abraham' (Gen 1.521), so now again, in the hour of her deepest humiliation, it can be said to Israel, 'Fear not, Jacob.' And the significance of the words, 'I have called you by name', is made perfectly clear in the story of the offering up of Isaac, in which, at its most terrible momenta Abraham hears a voice calling to him, 'Abraham, Abraham.' Referred strictly to Israel the nation, the words can only mean, 'who created you as a nation, that is, by delivering you from Egypt and leading you through the wilderness and bringing you into the promised land.' the creature of and forming would then refer to an actual historical act of God, the saving at by which he brought Israel into being'! Since we are told in this oracle the concern is for individual, the individual Israelite here addressed is told and reminded that he is God's creature (as in Ps.139).

**V. 3** The substantiation in the perfect which has just been discussed is accompanied by three others in the form of noun clauses, 'You are mine' (V. 1b), 'I Yahweh, am Your God' (v. 3a), and 'I am with you' (v. 5a). These are all time-hallowed formulae know to everyone in Israel. Between them and the substantiation in the perfect there is a difference. The latter refers to a single act ('I have redeemed You'). These, on the other hand, express something which continues, an intrinsic relationship between Yahweh and Israel. the declaration, 'You are mine', is originally a legal formula, the form in which a person declares himself to be the owner of something. The noun clause, 'I, Yahweh, Your God', is the same as that which introduces the first commandment (Exod. 20:2), the formula 'I am with you' dates back to Israel's very earliest days, and is even found in Sumerian texts. In these a god who is lord of a particular region uses the formula to declare that he will protect someone who intends to travel there.

**V. 2:** The assurance with its substantiation's in the perfect tense and in noun clause is now followed by the proclamation, which contains specific promises (vv. 2 and 36-46). In v. 2, the speaker is the creator and Lord of the elements, in vv. 3b-4b, the lord of history. V. 2 promises Israel safe conduct on her journey. No force of nature, no hostile element, is to be able to do her any harm as she travels. The whole oracle shows that Deutero-Isaiah here means the journey home from exile. Water and fire stand for dangers from any element, as in Ps. 66:12. Although quite clearly referring to Israel, this promise, too, has a personal note: It is the reminiscent of the personal assurance of the personal assurance of blessing is Ps. 91 and 121.

vv. 3b-4b: Israel's saviour is the lord of all nations. While v. 4 uses general terms, lands and peoples, v. 3b is specific as to those of them which God is to give in Israel's stead or as her ranson-egypt. Ethiopia and Sebia. What is most important here is, here it is taken for granted that God, the God of vanquished Israel is at cross in the great political changes afoot in the world of the day changes which revolved around the liberation of Israel. The middle part of the two verses is occupied by the substantiation, 'Because you are precious in my sight, and honoured, and I love you'. These words, placed as they are between the two descriptions of the way in which God was to intervene in world -history, are a very good illustration of the characters of Deutero-Isaiah's proclamation. Here we find most beautiful words of election of Israel. A tiny, miserable and insignificant band of uprooted men and women are assumed that they are the people to whom God has turned in love: they are dear and precious in his sight. These words are send. by the lord of all powers and authorities, of the Whole of history and of all creation! When time comes, she will positively be able to pass through rivers and walk through fire, and to discern this God at work in the mighty political movements which led to her return.

In vv. 5-7 the assurance of salvation, substantiated by means of a noun clause, is followed by a proclamation (vv. 5b-6), this time a perfectly clear promise of the return of the Diaspora from exile. The activity of the creator and that of the lord of history are here set together: just as the creator commands, the winds, since they are his servants (Ps. 104:4), so God commands four quarters of the heavens to give up and bring back, the quarters being the political powers which prevent the dispersed of Israel from returning home: thus the four quarters do not in any way refers to four quarters geographically or politically. When Israel is redeemed it ultimately means for God's glory. Israel had been reminded of her creator, and at the end, she is told the ultimate implication of her having been created: for my glory I created you' At the beginning of this poem, the assurance of salvation was substantiated with the words, 'I have called you by your name' now, at the end, comes a reminiscence of them, where the many exiles dispersed in all the far places of the earth are told that they are all without, exception embraced in God's saving work, for everyone is called by my name.'

***(7) Isaiah 44:1-15: Water on the Thirsty Land:*** This passage falls into the category of oracles of salvation (41:8-13, 14ff; 43:11-4, 5ff), its central point is the assurance of salvation, the cry 'fear not'. But unlike other oracles it differs in its presentation that the substantiation to the salvation is given in future tense of the cry, 'fear not', have as their subject not the event of the return or restoration, but the conditions is the new era of salvation, strictly speaking the news salvation is not promised to the recipients of this oracle, but to their descendants. These verses gave a summary of Israel's past, speaking of her forefathers; in the same way) 44:3ff, that of her future, the descendants of the generation them living.

v. 1 The assurance of salvation begins with the words, 'But Now' in contrast to what was said of Israel's past in 43:27-28, in the same way as 43:1ff. contrasts with 42:18-25. Israel is summoned into the new era to her the new word and, in substantiation of the summons is addressed by the parallel terms of God's servant and his chosen one. The two designations supplement each other in that election is more concerned with God's gracious will, and 'servant' refers rather to the end which he seeks to achieve by meant of Israel's election.

v. 2. The assurance of salvation is introduced by the messenger formula. Here, however, this no longer has its original purpose of accrediting a message through the messengers its function is the more general one of conforming the authority of a word of God on an utterance introduced in this way. Israel's election which took place in the act of deliverance that set her history on its course is given a still firmer basis by means of a reference to the creation. Muilenburg says: 'Second Isaiah is constantly seeking to ground Israel's unique character in something more ultimate than the Exodus'. The phrase who forms you from the womb', shows that the prophet is thinking of God's creative activity in the primary sense of the word, and in particular of the fact that every single member of the nation Israel them living was created by him.

The cry 'fear not' suggests that a new situation has come about. The relationship between God and Israel as described in 43:22-28 is at an end for God has blotted out her quilt (453:25). This is what makes it possible for Israel to have a future, and this is proclaimed in vv. 3 ff. The name used to designate Israel **yeshurun** (formed like **zebulun**) occurs only here and in Deut. 32:15; 33:5,26. It may be derived from **yasar**, the upright, but the meaning is uncertain. It may be intended as a title of honour for Israel.

In vv. 3-5, the future is made possible because God is to intervene (v. 3) and the consequences of this are described in vv.4ff. Commentators agree that this intervention in v. 3 does not refer to the new exodus, the journey home through the desert, but has a more general sense, the ever repeated miracle of growth. This proclamation of salvation, different from those hitherto considered of a new growth for the now dried-up Israel, demands special attention in any consideration of Deutero-Isaiah's preaching, but the effect is not immediate, but among the generations to come. This time to the Yahweh's activity of blessing is added to deliverance. From the very beginning of Israel's faith the God who delivers is also the God who blesses: both aspects have their own time and place, and neither is ever resolved into the other.

### *(8) Isaiah 44:9-20: A Satire on the Manufacture of Idols*

This taunt song differs from all the rest of Deutero-Isaiah in that is says nothing about Yahweh and his dealings with Israel. The main point of proclamation is to say that Yahweh is one God (44:8b) other passages in Deutero-Isaiah that deal are the polemic against idolatry are 40:19f; 41:6f; 42:17; 44:9-20; 45:16f; 46:1f;5ff. This song in 44:9-20 falls into two parts. vv. 9-12 are a general verdict passed on the manufactures (and worshippers) of idols amounting to the fact that those who make idols are to be put to shame The first part (vv. 9-12) is probably to be regarded as the matrix of the taunt-song.

v. 9 the song begins with a forceful statement which strikes the key note of all that is to follow: 'all who make idols are nothing (tohu) the original meaning of the word 'idol' was an image hewn out of stone. later it could also designate one carved for an image of a God or God's. The 'witnesses' are the worshippers of these idols. The 'see' nothing and 'know' nothing -both verbs here refer to the sense of 'experience' the worshippers have no experience of anything done by those homemade God's, and for this very reason they are to be put to shame.

The description of the manufacture of idols is structured as follows: 12; the work of ironsmith, 13: the work of the carpenter; 14, the procuring of the material; 15-16: the use made of it: for cooking and for making a God; 17: worship offered to the wood; 18: a marginal note on the absurdity of such an act; 19: he does not know what he does!, 20: the conclusion of the whole oracle: the makers of idols are to be put to shame. The series of pictures given in those verses is amazingly true to life: This section is a master piece of satirical writing or it can also be called a taunting song.

In the conclusion we can note that in this passage the idolaters are ridiculed, not the idol but the worshippers are the object of laughter. They are entimess, who see nothing and know nothing, they are shamed, less than a human, a more deceived.

### *(9) Isaiah 45:17: The Oracle Concerning Cyrus*

45:1-7 the royal oracle itself is contained in vv. 1-4. vv. 5 and 7 are part of the self-predication of Yahweh v. 6 is a note added to vv. 1-4. This royal oracle in vv. 1-4 closely follows the terms used at an enthronement and ritual enacted there. The same words are also found in Pss. 2 and 110. It has been noted by the scholars that the actions in rituals connected with the King of Israel were to a large extent taken over from her neighbours. In commenting on 45:1-7, editors all refers to the Cyrus cylinder, an inscription on a clay cylinder dating from about 538, which shows quite astonishingly close parallels with text before us. On it Cyrus describes how he captured Babylon without the striking of a single blow, and gives the credit to-of all the God's-the Babylonian god Marduk, the 'lord of the God's who was enraged at the misrule of the last of the Kings of Babylon, and then took action out of pity for the oppressed.

In this place too, a god (Marduk) chooses Cyrus as his agent, grants him success in his conquests, calls him to a world-dominion, takes pleasure in him, directs his way to Babylon and accompanies him on it. The words, also found in 45:1-7, to the effect that Marduk took Cyrus by the hand and called him by name, indicate an act of enthronement. This clay cylinder was obviously not made until after the capture of Babylon. Deutero-Isaiah cannot then be dependent on it. Both texts presuppose the riots connected with an enthronement and the royal oracle that accompanied them. The amazing thing is that the self-same historical event, Cyrus' capture of Babylon, is in both attributed to the intervention of a non-Persian god who chose Cyrus for this act and equipped him to perform it. This is what Deutero-Isaiah says about Yahweh's actions with Cyrus:

Cyrus is Yahweh anointed (v. 1); He holds him by right hand (v. 1); He calls him by name (vv. 3b and 4b); He gives him a name of honour (v. 4b), He girds him (v. 5b). All these indicate acts connected with the royal ritual; the most astonishing for Deutero-Isaiah's audience, the most astonishing is Yahweh's calling Cyrus his anointed. The title normally applied to Israel's high priest (Lev. 4 and 6) or to Israel's King (I Sam. 24,26; II Sam. 1 and repeated uses in the historical books and Psalms). It would become Judaism's term for its expected deliverer, the Messiah. It describes the one who is anointed with oil as a sign of being set apart for a special task. David is chosen to subdue nations within the territory assigned to Israel and thus to establish Yahweh's sovereignty over Canaan. Now that task is being assigned to Cyrus. As the Assyrian was summoned to destroy, so now the Persian is called to perform the military and political tasks necessary to rebuild Jerusalem.

Grasping the right hand indicates continuation in the royal office. The girding of the King is" an act of investiture. God's presence with Cyrus makes him successful in his march of conquest: nations are to be subdued (v. 1b), doors are to be opened (v. 1b); doors are to be broken in pieces and bars of iron cut asunder (v. 2b); treasures of darkness are to be bestowed (v. 3a).

vv. 4-5, while the Cyrus oracle is continued here, it is interspersed with clear indications that the commission given to Cyrus by Yahweh has limits set to it. The first bound set to Cyrus commission consist in the fact that it is given him for the sake of Israel (V. 4a). The latter is also called God's servant or chosen one, or God's chosen servant. In this connection it is to be noted that while Deutero-Isaiah calls Cyrus Yahweh's anointed, he never calls him his servant, and this simply because 'servant' implies a mutual relationship in which there is permanence. This does not apply in the case of Cyrus: for what god give him is a no-recurrent task in one particular set of. circumstances. This is. all that he is anointed to do. The following verses define the bound in even stronger terms, in v. 4b, 'I give you a name of honour, though you do not know me' and in 5b, '1 gird you, though you do not know me', this repetition of words though you do not know me, is important. Spoken to Cyrus, they imply a paradox. Yet, the Paradox is perfectly deliberate. The idea of permanence is not here, Deutero-Isaiah had no idea that Cyrus was to converted and become a servant of Yahweh. If Deutero-Isaiah's words are truly otherwise than we now stated, he himself would have proved a false prophet.

In v. 6, Deutero-Isaiah states that the View is not the conversion of Cyrus and the nation of Persia to Yahweh. It is something more, and indeed greater-over the whole world men are to know that Yahweh alone is god.

What is to inspire the outside world to seek such knowledge of the God of Israel in his commissioning of Cyrus? Deutero-Isaiah can declare a fore gin monarch to be God's anointed. What God once did though Israel's King he can now do through an alien King, the King of an alien power and a believer in an alien religion. The moment the Cyrus oracle was spoken, Israel as God's people ceased to be a people with political power. This break did not have to wait for the coming of Christ, but took place now.

In V. 7, a logical conclusion is drawn, each and everything created each and every event that happens, light and darkness, weal and woe, are attributable to him, and to him alone the question raised in this verse is that if God's action reaches so far beyond his chosen people, if he calls, equips, accompanies and bestows honour so far beyond itself, and if a worshipper of foreign god can be given the approved, help and guidance of the God of Israel where can it all end? The words I, Yahweh who do 'all' these things can be discussed in the light of Genesis 1 and 3 creation story. There it clearly shows that even though God is Lord over the darkness, he is certainly not its creator. He has it into creation and set bounds that, but he did not bring into being. Evil irrupts into God's creation, but it does so through a creature. And there it is left without explanation the limit has once more been reached in contrast this oracle of Deutero-Isaiah says, for the one and only time in the bible and in direct opposition to Gen. 1 and 3, that God created the darkness as he did the light. God brings about woe, just as he brings about salvation, this shuts the door firmly on any dualism if the creator of evil and woe is God, there is no room left for a devil. But what kind of God is this who created evil as well as good, woe as well as weal? In his action upon Cyrus and through him God does a thing which really goes far beyond what he had said to his chosen people about himself and his Workings. For this reason, the final words of the Cyrus oracle indicate that God's divinity transcends the limit imposed on human speech or thought about him-which means the limit imposed on all theology.

***(10) Is 47:1-15: Come Down into the Dust:*** This chapter is unique among Deutero-Isaiah's utterances, while there is no doubt that the prophet himself is the another of this section, its literary form occurs nowhere in the book. C. R. North comments that this chapter contains forty words not found elsewhere in Deutero-Isaiah. Duhm designates it as a triumph song, and Muilenburg as a Working song. But Westermann says that it falls into the category of oracles against foreign nations. Such oracles, spoken against foreign nations hostile to Israel, constitute a main form of prophecy of salvation, found even in the pre-exilic times, thus it is an oracle of salvation. This song is one among numerous oracles against Babylon (Isa. 13,14, Jer. 50-51), it might have delivered before the fall of Babylon. The use of imperatives such as: 'come down', sit in the dust, 'go into the darkness' etc. Presuppose that what is proclaimed has already been fulfilled, and they describe its consequences. Thus, from the first to the last verse the prophet speaks of an event which has still to come to pass: he proclaims the fall of the Babylonian empire.

The prophet's word of doom has its two usual parts, a substantiation (the charge and its elaboration) and a proclamation of doom (God's intervention and its consequences).

vv. 1-4 the poetic force displayed in the proclamation of Babylon's fall is quite extraordinary. This section begins with a series of imperatives which are spoken to a person, the virgin Babylon (Israel to often similarly personified in pre-exilic prophets of doom eg. Amos 5:1f). Babylon's coming down from her those into the dust is paralleled in the Ugaritic Baal and Anath: "Therefore God of Men, goes down from the throne, sets on the footstool, and from the footstool sets on the earth' (C. H. Gordon, Ugaritic Literature 1949, p. 42). Thus the opening words of the poem depict the humiliation of Babylon in terms of movements, a human figure moving directly before our eyes. Babylon is no longer tender, the delicate one, the terms conjure up the idea of luxury, the refinements of the court, the elegant life of care-free enjoyment: she is now a slave, forced to do most of menial tasks. Her humiliation extends even to her dress; she works with her clothes tucked up, like a servant girl. The addition of 'Yahweh of hosts' is deliberate; Deutero-Isaiah was thinking of the importance attaching to the heavenly bodies in Babylon (v. 13); but they are no more than the creatures of God, who obey his command (40:26).

**vv. 5-7:** The movement from the exalted throne down to the dust at the beginning of the first section is now followed by the other, Babylon's translation from the glory and blare of world-domination to silence and darkness come the words that substantiate her fate. The charge the God is making against Babylon, is not because of her treatment on Judah, for in general, the treatment meted out to the exiles in Babylon was not particularly cruel. But as v. 7 shows, the general attitude of Babylon is questioned. 'You said, "I am forever mistress, forever." It is Babylon's attitude of arrogant self-assurance that is the real object of the divine chastisement; for Israel, the God of Prophet any attempt to perpetuate power, or render it absolute, was blasphemy.

**vv. 8-9:** These words here condemns any power which regards itself as absolute. Now comes the proclamation of doom. The result of God's intervention (V 3) is childlessness and widow-hood. (cf. 54:1-6: the two great evils that can befall a woman', they signify unprotectedness and loneliness). They befall the one who had been quite certain that this could never happen to her. V. 9 adds the motif which becomes the detriment motif in the following sections: God's judgement Spells the complete breakdown of all Babylon's intellectual ascendency and her science.

**vv. 10-12:** Deutero-Isaiah saw here the connection between Babylon's absolute power and her intellectual eminence. The verses translated by Duhm are: "Your wisdom and your knowledge led you astray, so that you said in your heart, 'I, and no other'.

This is probably the first occasion in world history when the way of making power absolute was not conceived in material terms such as armies, armaments, and financial resources, but in terms of the intellectual substructures of power. The literature of the neo-Babylonian empire furnishes us with enough knowledge of the diversity and profusion of Mesopotamia's intellectual and religious life during the period to let us to understand this. Deutero-Isaiah mentions sorceries, enchantments, expiatory rites, and astrology. The simple cultic forms such as sacrifice, prayer, the giving of oracles, and proclamation, assumed exaggerated forms in which the entire emphasis was concentrated on such branches of knowledge and such practices as furthered or safeguarded existence. This is the way in which we should view the cultic magic and the traffic in prediction in the late forms of Babylonian religion and elsewhere.

**vv. 13-15:** Finally, Deutero-Isaiah mentions astrology, which was of course exceptionally important in Babylon. The word, 'You who divide the heavens' refer to the houses into which the heavens are divided by the constellation - in this matter our present day astrologer remains the heir of the Babylonian astronomers- some periods are favourable others as unfavourable.

The conclusion let us see very clearly how seriously the prophet took Babylon's intellectual and cultic methods of safeguarding her existence. There is no word of sarcasm or jeering. Instead, he indicates the tragic element in her complete breakdown: What fails in the hour of disaster is the wisdom and scientific knowledge elaborated in the course of a long and glorious history (from your youth). They do not deliver themselves Deutero-Isaiah uses similar terms of idols in 46:1ff and, without being able to help the empire in its collapse, 'they stagger into one another.'

***(11) Isaiah 48: 12-17, I Called You:*** the proclamation of 48:1: 'from this forth I make you hear new things', is explained at greater length in vv. 12-17. Here the affinity with the trial speeches is even more marked man it was in vv. 1-1 l, witness in particular the various summons in vv. l4 and 16a to assemble for a trail. God speaks to Israel as the one who is everlasting (v. 12b), and as the creator (v. 13). As creator, he is the Lord of history (vv. l4f). He is the only one of the God's (v. 14a) who proclaimed what Cyrus was to accomplish (v. 14b). He makes Cyrus perform his work (vv. 14f) and grants him success in it. But all this is done for the sake of Israel. Thus in the second part, what is said in the first part is supplemented in that God is being called the redeemer (v. 17a). From the beginning he had not Spoken in secret (v. 16b). And now the event attests that he had been present (v. 16b). And throughout he has acted in order to benefit Israel and prepare the way for her (v. 17b). On this way the conclusion of the whole section (vv. 20f) summons Israel to set out.

**vv. 12-13:** The terminology used here is same as in the trial speeches, its purpose is to exalt God in his chosen people's eyes, abased as Israel then was. He is the everlasting God, the creator of heaven and earth. His people has been overthrown, but he who now appeals to them is the one who at the beginning called heaven and earth into being.

**vv. 14-15:** Except for the address to Israel, and all four verses (12-15) could be part of a trial speech. Deutero-Isaiah's purpose here was to impress them with God's sovereign power that they would regain confidence. They are oppressed. They have been made insignificant. They are without prospects. Yet, this is the very moment at which God proves himself to be the everlasting one, and the creator and lord of the universe. The thing, however, to which they can hold fast is God's word. The drama now being enacted before their eyes on the stage of history had been proclaimed to them beforehand. The emphatic 'I' standing at the beginning of v. 15 and continuing throughout it (cf. vv. 12f) means this. It is I, the God who is known to you, of whom you have had experience, who am at work here, even if this fresh work does shatter an old concept of the old God.'

**V. 16f:** God speaks now as Israel's redeemer who has used his sovereign power on his people's behalf. Even though the terms used here are very general, the meaning probably is that in this fresh act Israel is experiencing an entirely new way in which God can help her. It is only the final words of the utterance, 'I am Your God… who makes for you the way in which you should go', that reveal its objective. God can prepare the way for his people by granting a foreign nation and a heathen King success.

***(12) Isaiah 49:1-6 - The Second Servant Song:*** the exposition of this song has reference to the nations. Its pattern (summons to hear the messenger formula, and Yahweh's word to the speaker) is of the nature of a Prophet's report about himself. The speaker here reports how there came to be the word which God now speaks to him, what went before it. Three stages of development are described. Vv. 16-3: The election, call and equipment of the Servant; v. 4. His despondency; vv. 5-6: His new task. These three stages are marked by conjunctions: v. 4 ('but I') and v. 5 ('But now"). The servant describes here in this section: God called me to be His servant to perform a work on behalf of His chosen People (vv. 1ff and 5b,6a), but I became despondent and regarded the work in vain (v. 4). But then-inspite of this-God extended the scope of my commission to include the Gentiles (v. 5f), in order that his salvation might reach to the ends of the earth.

**vv. 1-2:** It goes well with 42:1-4, both places the task of the servant is to embrace Gentiles. The Servant's discourse begins in v.1. He gives an account of his call (v. 1b), his equipment (v. 2), and his installation (v. 3). This verse reminds something like Prophets' call as in Jer. 1:5. V. 2 makes it clear that the servants work is a work with the word (so in 50:4). The two metaphors used in vv. 2a and 2b,c must mean that God has endowed the servant's word with the power to penetrate (a 'sharp sword') and to range far and wide ('a polished arrow' cf. Jer. 1:9f; Heb 4: 12). The words 'he hid me' refers to the Servant's equipment (cf. Jer. 1:19).

**V. 3.:** Only here the servant tells the purpose for which he was called by God. V.3 suggests something like in Ps. 2:7. This indicates the call of a Prophet combined in some measure with the designation of a King, as in 42:1-4. The appearance of the word 'Israel' in v.3b needs some discussion: most probably scholars argue that it is to be a later addition. The following are the reasons: (i) 'Israel' is absent in one of the Mss. of the Lxx, but it does not stand in the new Isaiah Ms, from the Dead sea. Thus the history of the text rather favours its retention; (ii) Form itself is quite important here. It has been noticed that, apart from 49:3, Deutero-Isaiah never uses 'Israel' except in parallelism to 'Jacob'; (iii) A feature in all other servant songs is that the servant is never given a name. (iv) The greatest difficulty, however, in that the Servant whom v. 3 calls Israel is in v. 5 given a mission to Israel. This is given an understanding that 'I' in vv.ff and v. 4 refer to a single person.

V. 4 the servant now contrasts his high calling (1b-3) with the result? of his efforts in its performance. When he was troubled. The words reflect here, however, are not concerned - servant himself, but troubles concerned with his office and task. V. 4b says that something did, however, remain over when the task proved unsuccessful, his 'right' and his 'reward' by which are meant that, although men throughout that his task had miscarried, God vindicated and accept it. This indicates the divine continuation of a work which had seemingly ended in failure. This failure has not broken the relationship between God and the servant.

In v. 5, a new word of God to the servant sets the new task afoot. It is a single person whom God calls from his mother's womb (v. 1b), to whose word God gives effect (v. 2) and whom he keeps safe (v. 2). It is a single person who had to regard his work as a failure (4a), while at the same time knowing that God had approved it (v. 4b). But the point at issue in connection with these various individuals is not they themselves, but their office, their ministry, their ministry, their being servants. The change in the ministry described in v. 6 allows the particular servants in a series of them to be spoken of as the servant, the servant who at this moment is given a new task, a new era in the Servant's life, in which he becomes a light to the Gentiles. Yet it must be said that the whole thing is put very cryptically. First, there is the proclamation of a change in the Servant's office. Its scope is extended to include the Gentile world. Secondly, this is preceded by a ministry to Israel aimed at bringing her back to God. In the servant's own view this part of the task is a complete failure. Nevertheless, God showed his approbation of his servant by giving him a new and greater task, even though the servant's task is unsuccessful earlier, through whom God intends to glorify himself, may bring God's salvation to the ends of the earth.

### *(13) Isaiah 49:14-26: I Have Gravan You on My Hands*

This passage is composed of three parts: v. 14-20,21ff and 24ff, each of them begins by disputing an assertion made by Israel v. 14: You maintain that God has forsaken you; You had thought, I am childless, left alone, V. 24: You thought, how can a strong man be robbed of his prey? But all three parts pass over into a proclamation of salvation. To counter Israel's despondency, she was given an assurance that God takes care of her and restore her. The three sub-sections in this passage are united in the sections of a lamentation the charges brought against God (v. 14), the lament in the first person (v. 21), and the lament because of enemies (v. 24).

vv. 14-20: the starting point of Deutero-Isaiah's entire proclamation is the despondency and despair of the remnant of Israel. The questions raised by the people here are: 'hast thou utterly, rejected us? Art thou so exceedingly angry with us? (cf. Isa 40:27). Deutero-Isaiah quotes in v. 14 a lament that was usually made. They are the words used in worship, and well-known to everyone who heard them. This lament he disputes. He opposes this religion that harked back to the past. For Deutero-Isaiah the creator and the redeemer were absolutely the same person. As vivid and ever-present tokens of the work of the creator the exiles still had these two things - the stars in heaven and a child in his mother's lap. Here the Prophet indicates that everything pertaining to the created, even the love of a mother, has limits beyond which it cannot go. He bases trust in the new thing Oil that faithfulness, which can never fail.

Vv. 16ff: God's absolute faithfulness, is now pictured in a different way. The summons to 'lift up your eyes round about and see' (v. 18) is characteristic of Deutero-Isaiah. Imagine it spoken to men and women in a village in Babylon. The Prophets makes a great demand of his hearers, even though there is nothing to be seen he invites the people to join with him in this vision. God takes an oath that those who return from many lands (49:12) are to be ornaments of the new Israel. Here the term 'ornament' is not really an aesthetic one. Adornment is 'what renders someone beautiful in the sight of others, splendour or dignity. It is not here conceived in terms of its objective value or beauty. The reason why Israel regains her honour and standing in the world's eye is the vast number of those who return.

In vv. 22ff what the Prophet really wants to do is answer Zion's lament and her question - she is given her children back. According to Volz in vv. 22b and 23a Deutero-Isaiah does not imply that the nations are to serve Zion in perpetuity. He gives metaphors for careful protection, and the deference and attention, to be accorded to those who return home.

Vv. 24-26: In vv21ff, it was a lament in the first person. Here the lament is because of enemies. They are the sources of the trial. 'We have become the prey of a mighty one.' It was inevitable for the exiled Israelites to think of it in this way. So there was nothing that could be done about it. All hope has gone. The people thought that this was the fate of countless other people and nations in the world, now it is our turn. To this despondent idea of Israel, God makes his answer. The answer is that this very thing that seems impossible is possible for God. Of course as one might-expect, Deutero-Isaiah here is not interested in the destruction and the castigation of the Babylonians, but more than that, all flesh is to know the work of

Yahweh. Deutero-Isaiah corelates two aspects of the divinity of Yahweh? God is the one who wields sovereign power (the very ancient designation found in the Patriarchal stories. Gen. 49:24, Isa. 1:24) is at the same time the saviour of Israel. Yahweh's act in redeeming Israel speaks a language that attracts among the Gentiles, too.

***(14) Isaiah 50:49: The Third Servant Song:*** Of all Detuero-Isaiah's servant songs this is probably the easiest to understand, because it is possible to ascertain the provenance of all its component parts. According to Begrich, it is the individual lament. But Westmann refutes this form on the basis of the fact that except vv. 5 and 6 we don't find any lament here. Moreover, he suggests based on the confidence motifs in Jeremiah's laments (11:20; 15:15,16; 17:14; 20:11.12; 18:23), he calls this passage of containing the protestation of innocence combined with confidence motif along with the 'certainty of being answered motif. All these three motifs are combined in this passage.

V.14 the whole of this verse is the utterance of a man whose being governed by hearing and speaking. In both aspects he is 'like a disciple' which means that in both his hearing and his speaking he is concentrated on God, and that those have God as their source. He could hear nothing if God did not open his ear and this morning by morning and he could say nothing of what he was to say were not told him. The servant has to be awakened, aroused, in order to hear the prostrate. As such Israel is not in a position to hear the word, thus, like the servant, she, too, must be aroused before she can hear the word that applies to her case. In fact, the word 'servant' does not appear in 50:4-9, instead, here the servant is the **limmud** i.e; 'God's servant is God's disciple', but the servant is more than a disciple of God.

Vv. 5-6 these verses presuppose that the speaker had experienced hostility, attacks on his person, even blows and abuse, the word 'but' indicates: in spite of it all, I was not disobedient nor did I shrink back. If the lament says nothing about the attacks it resembles somewhat Psalm of confidence, and there, while the lament is still there in the background, it is no longer uttered because what it complains of has been allayed. Another motif of the protestation of innocence found in a lament, which is in the background of vv. 5-6, has been changed into an assertion. The servant avers that in spite of all attacks and abuse, he has been true to his task V.5b indicates that in spite of the attacks and abuse, the servant has not labelled against receiving the word from God, he has not been deterred into ceasing to hear and to speak. V. 6 the servant regards his attacks, blows and insults as justified, and so concedes that god IS on the side of his opponents.

V. 7 it stands in sharp contrast to v. 6 at the beginning. The words say something that is strictly impossible- the servant is certain that God is on his side, although his conduct in v. 6 indicates the opposite. This the start of the new factor - his conviction that God himself wills his Servant's suffering and its acceptance. As the sufferer, the servant knows that 'I shall not be made ashamed. Therefore 'he makes his face like flint' (cf. Jer. 1:18; Ezek. 3:8f). But unlike earlier prophets, the servant wilfully accepts the hard things on him.

Vv. 8-9: the certainty that God is on his side (corresponding to the 'certainty of being answered' in the Psalms) is now expressed in a different, and very forceful way, by means of terms taken from a legal process. V. 8 is a challenge to take part in a legal contest. The servant summons those who oppose him - the same people as smite him and shame him and spit upon him to come into court, for he is convinced that god justifies him and that no one can condemn him. In the opponents view the Servant is already defeated, but the servant once again comes out boldly in v. 9a, 'the lord Yahweh helps me.' How this is to happen? The last line (v. 9b) expresses the servant's conviction that his opponents who can now mock and smite him with impurity will perish, is after all no real answer to the question. Therefore, the question is left open and points forward to the final servant song.

***(15) Isaiah 52:13-53:12: The Fourth Servant Song:*** This is the last of the four servant songs and it is also the lengthy one among all other songs.

The early church saw in this passage a prophecy of the sufferings of Christ and of the salvation he brought to all peop1e. That is how Philip, one of the first Evangelists, explained this passage to the Ethiopian official who he heard reading these very verses in Acts 8:35 (esp. vv. 32,33). It would be of a great deal of discussion on the identity of the servant even in this passage. The idea of this section is not to bring out all those interpretations, but to give a fair treatment to the text and its relevance to the mission and ministry of the church.

If we read this passage carefully we will recognize that it has three clear divisions: (i) an introduction: 52:13-15; (ii) the main section: 53:1-10a; and (iii) a conclusion: 53:10b-12. Both in the introduction and in the conclusion, it is God who speaks and He is referred to in the first person at 'I', God tells what will happen to the servant in the future. See 52:13: "my servant shall prosper"; and 53:11: "my servant shall vindicate many", However in 53:1-10a there is change in the speaker. The speaker changes to "we" and it is a narration about what happened to the servant in the past. "Who believed the report that reached us? (53:1), "he had neither beauty or charm so that we should look at him" (53:2) etc. This central section about the future exaltation of the servant. Any exposition of the text should take this point into consideration.

52;1.3-15 speaks about the sharp contrast between the condition of the servant now and what people will experience about him later. They are shocked at him. He is so disfigured that he can hardly be recognized as a human being. But there will leap in amazement and their Kings will have no words to explain their surprise.'

Concerning the interpretation of this section, even though the servant is depicted as a person and possibly taken for individual interpretation, it is possible to regard him also as a symbol for the people of Israel in captivity. In several other Deutero-Isaianic passages, the people of Israel are described as God's servant (cf. 41:8-13; 4421-5). The reaction of the nations: 'so shall many nations leap in amazement; Kings shall shut their mouth' (52:15) will be more appropriate if the change in the condition of the servant refers to that of a people than that of a single person. In his message, the prophet exhorts the nations to assemble together to see the transformation in the condition of Israel (43:9). The nations had rejoiced over the fall of Jerusalem. There was no sorrow (Lam1:12). But now, "the LORD has bared his holy arm before the eyes of all the nations; and the ends of the earth shall see the salvation of God" (52:10). No one ever imagined that the small community of Judah once captured by the mighty Babylonian empire, would ever become free again and return to their homeland. "Deutero-Isaiah tells the people and they are challenged to shake off their pessimism and look for the signs of God's hand at work. If the servant is understood in a corporate way, then the introduction speaks of the miraculous transformation in the condition of the people in exile.

In the main part of the song, 53:1-10a, the sufferings which the servant had to endure in the past as described in some detail. It is no longer God who is speaking as in 52:14-15, but a group of people, or a community, referred to as 'we'. This group has received a report about the servant and they now pass it on, as if they themselves are eye-witnesses of the sufferings of the servant had to endure. This community or group could be the faithful remnant in the exile or the disciples of the prophet in the exile, who is the author of Isaiah 40-55. By using the metaphors of a feeble plant in the arid desert and of a sick person, the prophet depicts vividly the plight of the servant and shows how repulsive the servant is to others (vv. 2,3). This description of the sickness is somewhat similar to Job's words (19:16,17). Like the friends of Job, the people had thought that the servant was being punished by the sickness because of his sins, those who give the testimony about the servant have come to the realisation that he was suffering on their behalf (v. 4). What the people were saying about the servant and the actual truth about him were two different things. The thought is developed further in vv. 6 and 7. The suffering of the servant has been caused by 'our' guilt, and thereby he has brought peace and salvation to us. The servant is not guilty, but the people are! The suffering the servant endured has a healing and restoring effect on the people. The early church saw in the figure of the suffering servant a shadow of Christ's saving work: "He himself bore our sins in his body on the tree, that we might die to sin and live in righteousness. By his wounds you have been healed" (I Peter. 2:24). Further, the servant endures the suffering on him without protesting against his oppressors (v. 7).

The words in V. 8 'fate' means in this context 'condition' and not 'generation'. It is also emphasised in vv. 8-9 that the servant's death was not a natural death, but due to a criminal act done by others. Ancient Israel distinguished between death in honour and death in disgrace, between honourable burial and a disgraceful burial. (cf. The lament of David at the news of Abner's death in II Sam. 3:33,34) and also Prophet Jeremiah's announcement of the death of King Jehoiakim and without receiving a burial in honour appropriate to royalty: Jer. 22:19). The point in v. 9 is that even in burial, the servant was marked out as an evildoer, even though he had committed no act of violence or broken any of the commandments. And yet God permitted all this to happen and in fact his death was an expiatory sacrifice.

We have already noted that in 52:13-15 the servant symbolically represents for the People of Israel, in captivity. However, this is not the case in 53:1-10a. For instance, the sufferings of the people cannot be taken as an expiatory sacrifice. In fact, the message of comfort with which Isaiah 40-55 begins recognizes that Israel's suffering was caused by her own sins: 'She has received from the hand of the LORD, double for all her sins" (40:2). Further, the details about the life of the servant narrated in this central section are such that the most natural explanation would be to regard the servant as an individual. The use of the past tense in this section over against the future tense in the introduction and conclusion, point to the servant as one who lived in the past.

53:10b-12 is the final section of the song which speaks as in 52:13-15 about the future glorification of the servant. In contrast to his past experience which has been one of humiliation and suffering. As in 52:13-15 it is God who speaks in these concluding verses. The servant will have the joy of seeing children, he will enjoy long life and will have the satisfaction that the purpose of God prospers through his ministry. The poem closes by restating the expiatory character of his suffering and death.

As pointed in the beginning of our discussion, the servant and his identity is one of the major problem in this song. On the one hand, the servant of the song has been identified as an individual: Moses, Uzziah, Jeremiah, Cyrus the Persian emperor, a leprous Rabbi in exile, the Prophet who is the author of Isaiah 40-55, and the Messiah to come. On the other hand, scholars who agree for the servant not as an individual but a community such as: the people of Israel in exile, the ideal Israel, the faithful remnant: Christian tradition has seen in Jesus Christ the fulfilment of the servant of the Lord of Isaiah.

Whatever be the concrete figure behind the servant of the LORD, it is certain that the author was inspired by the vocation of the Prophetic ministry when he described the servant in this song and in the other songs. He has reflected on the experiences of the different Prophets, especially on the measuring of the persecution and suffering which the true prophets had to endure in carrying out their prophetic mission.

The Prophets were convinced that God had called them and the divine mission brought with it ill-treatment, ridicule, rejection, suffering and death, because it involved exposing the evil and influence of those who were in power and speaking a message which was unpalatable to them. Out of this accumulated experience of suffering for God which many a prophet in ancient Israel had to undergo, a servant concept emerged. It is amazing how close this servant song is to suffering and exaltation of our Lord Jesus Christ.

***(16) Isaiah 54:1-10: Sing, O Barren One!:*** This poem is an exceptionally impressive example of Deutero-Isaiah's poetic art. A whole range of motifs is fused here into something quite new: a hymn of Praise ('Sing O barren one'); a promise of salvation ('Fear not') and a proclamation of salvation ('my grace shall not depart from you'). We should note that the double imperative 'Sing…cry aloud is answered by the double imperative in v. 4: 'fear not... be not confounded". The situation of change from wrath is due to God himself and this fresh compassion is due to God is permanent and everlasting, as shown by a new act of deliverance by God himself (v. 9ff). The three-part structure vv. 1ff; 4ff and 7-10 is deliberately constructed, and they are based on three component parts of a lament: the charge brought against God (vv. 7-10, 'why hast thou forsaken us?', Why does thou hide thy face from us?' why does thine anger boil up against us?'). The lament is the first person lament made by Jerusalem in lamentations), and the lament over the shame of the suffering as in many community laments, vv.4ff, in this final proclamation, Israel's lamentation is turned into a short of joy.

Vv. 1-3: The various summons 'Sing...break forth into singing and cry aloud', correspond to the hymns of praise as in 44:23; 49:13 and 52:9, these cries are paralleled with the cry for salvation. Here the age old lament of the childless woman (e.g. Rebekah's lament) is transformed as a corporate body. The expression 'Sing O barren one' may sound like extreme paradoxical. The word for barren in Hebrews (*'aqara*) suggests expiry beyond recall. How could a barren woman be summoned to sing? This was both meaningless and pitiless, but exactly the similar situation God wants to change. God who makes the barren and childless one the joyous mother of children' (Ps. 113), Here Deutero-Isaiah makes use of motifs from the hymns of praise.

The series of imperatives in v. 2, 'enlarge.....stretch out......lengthen' is a style of Deutero-Isaiah's preaching. Through these words, the prophet wants convince Israel of the reality of the glorious future. Deutro-Isaiah by using the tent metaphor in an age when Israel had for long had houses as her dwelling places, recalls the days of old when the promise of increase mattered so much.

Vv. 4-6, Along with the removal of Israel's suffering goes the removal of shame of it. Earlier Israel's defeat costs its honour in the eyes of the rest of the nations. By using 'Fear not' formula the prophet proclaims of the removal of shame on Israel. In v. 5f, God takes the woman forsaken and, grieved in spirit back again, and she once more has a husband. The state of forsakenness, loneliness and shame is past, and she who was solitary is given back, the happiness and honour of the married state and status.

In vv. 7-8. Deutero -Isaiah speaks about the challenge without any metaphor. As in the case of Psalms of praise the exaltation of person who has been delivered may be expressed as the follows: as he looks back at the distress, this now seems to have lasted but a little, while the life resorted to him by the deliverance seems to stretch far on in a future free from trouble (Ps. 30:5-6). In the similar way Deutero-Isaiah states, for a brief moment I forsook you, but with everlasting love I have compassion upon you. The message of the prophet as very clear: with God himself and in God himself the change has already taken place, and therefore everything must alter. A small band of people whose destiny is bound up with the immense complexities of world - history has no reserve in regarding that destiny as absolutely, and absolutely simply, dependent on the action of God.

Vv. 9-10 According to Muilenburg V. 9 and this passage should be understood: the imminent events are of essentially the same order as the promise to Noah after the universal flood. The story used by the prophet as an illustration is to proclaim that Israel's redeemer is the creator. The two verbs in v.10 'not depart' and 'not remove' correspond to this, that is, they are reinforcements of the element of continuance in the news salvation. The word 'covenant' occurred here is also in the sense of God's salvation as a condition occurred here is something permanent. What the covenant does is confirm the new relationship established between God and the chosen people. Deutro-Isaiah's promise of an interrupted condition of salvation points far beyond history, or far beyond the path by God's people on their journey through history.

***(17) Isaiah 55:6-11: The Word that Goes Forth from My Mouth:*** This section is often called as an epilogue due to its connection with the prologue especially with 40:6ff.

**Vv. 6-7:** The summons in the final section of the book Deutero-Isaiah to seek Yahweh means essentially the same as do its fellows in the earliest writing prophets (Amos 5:6, Jer. 29:12f). Basically these are cultic Summons, but they also have wider meaning, they are continuation of 55:1-3a.

**Vv. 8-9:** Here the word 'thoughts' does not have the meaning of 'reflections', a plan or design. The subject is, what God purposes and how he carries it out. These words also are very apt to bring parallel between God and Man. The main point of the prophet is this: God's design at this very time to procure Israel's salvation, and, as against this, Israel's lassitude and acquiescence because of the situation in which she found herself. Here Deutero-Isaiah extols God and magnifies him as creator and lord of history. By pointing to the boundless horizons of God's designs and ways, immeasurably greater than people can think them to be, he gives his confidence. Though they are no longer able to believe it, all things are possible with God.

**Vv. 10-11:** In these verses the subject is something different but a continuous thought is present. God's word can be depended upon. God's words of salvation are now begin to appear and in which Israel now can depend what God wills with it, it accomplishes. The words here perhaps reflect the sphere of blessing. Two process are set side by side: The word expressing spoken to the needs of a particular salvation and meeting with faith or lack of faith in it, understanding or lack of understanding, is an entirely a different matter from rain or snow in the world of nature. Nevertheless (just as with the parables of Jesus) it is precisely this difference in kind that makes the comparison possible, and both have something in common. With both something is effected and achieves its purpose. For the prophet the word is not primarily something with a content, but the instrument by means of which something is affected. God's word is a word that does things. When God speaks, something comes about. This View of the word domination the whole prophecy even before Deutero-Isaiah (Jeremiah).

But we should be careful not to interpret it by saying that: God's word does not magically call a new state of salvation into being. The only way by which it effects what God designs it to do is the hearkening to, and acceptance of, the message of salvation. The conclusion of the words here needs our attention: A great deal of what was said by Deutero-Isaiah which means a great deal of what he proclaimed as the word of God, was not fulfilled in the way in which he said it would be. Israel's return home was no triumphal procession through a desert transformed into a garden. But ever and always God's thoughts and ways are higher than those of Israel. This holds true also of the fulfilment of his promises. When ascertainment of it is possible, the fulfilment may well be different, very different even, from what the prophet led people to expect. The only thing that is absolutely certain is that prophecy inevitably results in fulfilment. The word never returns void. Even though the exact nature of fulfilment is not stated, it is God who fulfils and his ways are immeasurably greater than those of the people of Israel. It is true to say in the final analysis (as in 55:13b), whatever comes about comes about for God's honor, just all creation exists in order to render him praise.

Chapter 10

# Prophecy in India

A brief survey of the prophetic phenomena found in the various religious traditions of India and identifying the distinctiveness of Israelite prophecy from Indian phenomena:

In general, we can say that the prophet in all the religious tradition is credited with spiritual vision, active worship, persuasive eloquence and pantie faith. Close analysis of the powers and perfections of a prophet will show that they all can be summed up in one word, namely, the triumph of the spiritual over the material. The prophets are credited with the gift of foretelling the future. In moments of ecstasy the prophet transcends the temporal plane and views all things from the standpoint of eternity things remote in space and time stand revealed to his gaze. The past no less than the future Buddha could see at a glance, he remembered all his previous incarnations, human and sub-human and he also foretold the future greatness of Pataligama (Pataliputra) and the hastened decay of his church when nuns were admitted into his order. The Jewish prophets foretell the fall of Jerusalem and the doom of many other cities as also the fates and fortunes of many nations and individuals. Sometimes they are informed in dreams and sometimes in waking moments; sometimes they profess to communicate divine utterances (Thus says the Lord) and sometimes they transmit their vision as directed by God ('I saw' or 'Thus says the lord').

It is curious to note, however, that while prophetic knowledge of the future is regarded as a sign of spiritual insight, the attempt made by others to know the future is condemned in most of the scriptures. Sooth sayings and divination were almost universal in the ancient world. Oracle were delivered and signs of the future interpreted in Greece, Rome, Egypt, Babylon, Assyria, the Jewish states, China and India long before the rise of monotheism proper, and various methods were adopted to know the will of the God's or to ascertain the future. Buddha warned his disciples against dabbling in foretelling; Mohammed prohibited the casting of lots; and in Judaism false and pagan prophets were warned against. The psychology underlying this prohibition seems to be that in the case of the true prophet foreknowledge implies special communication by God to his chosen of what is eternally known to himself, whereas in other cases, e.g. astrology and divination, it implies that the course of the world is predetermined and can therefore be calculated to a nicety, leaving divine will and providence entirely out of account.

The magnitude of a prophet's task can be seen from the fact that he has to rouse a whole social group into consciousness of its religious and moral imperfections and of abandoning its old beliefs and practices. Very often his love figure stands out clear against a background of sordidness and social iniquity and makes the surrounding gloom all the more visible by contrast. A society that tolerates corruption at the top and has not the courage to condemn its leaders badly needs the service of one who is not afraid to champion the cause of righteousness and truth even at grave personal risks prophets have very often found themselves in opposition both to civil power and to religious aristocracy- to princes as well as priests, the one standing for unethical conduct and other for soulless religious formality. They have served as unconscious mouth pieces of the inarticulate protests of the dissatisfied and the oppressed sections of the community, and when they have thus voiced the general sentiments of the social group their success has been immense and abiding. But often they have had to set to work against the whole social group, and only faith in their mission and infinite patience have enabled them to persist in their preaching. Under such conditions their faith has spread very slowly; for e.g. it took Mohammed nearly ten years to get a following of fifty persons and that Zarathustra could get only one follower 1n the same period of time.

If we compare the Hebrew prophets with the mediaeval saints of India, we shall have some idea of the secret success in Israel. There were, first of all certain advantages. The field of activity was small and any prophetic achievements was quickly reported all over the country. The population Was more or less homogeneous, and in spite of the rivalry between north Israel and Judah, all prophets spoke in the name of the same national God. There was, again, no such difficulty as caste prejudice against a prophet - a farmer, a citizen, a priest and a follower of an older prophet who could get an equal hearing if they had any message to preach. No prophet allowed the greatness of Israel to depart from popular thought; even her chastisement was divinely ordained to bring her ultimate triumph and exaltation. To a nation, ambitions to rise but temporarily in distress, a political message supposed to be divinely delivered, could not fail to be attractive as a matter of fact, Jeremiah had to pay the penalty of his prophecy because of its defeatist attitude towards national ambition and pride.

In India, for full nine hundred years' seers, mythologists and theologians were simultaneously at work. During the period from the 7th to the 16th century when the latter puranas were being written and the philosophical systems were being expanded there was a regular stream of devoted man in both North and South India who failed to find satisfaction in the ritualistic practices of Hindu religion and in the rigidity of its caste distinctions. The Tamil saints, the Mahratta mystics, the Vaisnavite poets of North India and those who, like Kabir and Nanak, came under Muhammadan influence all preached against a system of worship in which birth and not religious merit was the qualification for religious ministration and in which materials and mantras usurped the rightful place of devotion and social service.

While tolerant in many cases of the misting polytheism and even of idolatry among the masses, the religious leaders themselves were mostly imbued with a deep monotheistic spirit, even though different saints called God by different names like Rama, Krishna, Hari, Shiva, etc. They preached their message in songs, hymns and verses through the vernaculars of India and could therefore make a direct appeal to the hearts of the masses to who Sanskrit mantras were an unmeaning jargon. Those movements in most cases did much to expose the shortcomings of Hindu religion as then practiced, and planted in the land, especially in North India, small hands of devout men alienated to a greater or a lesser extent from the caste-system and the religious practices of orthodox Hinduism.

However, all those mentioned above failed to leaven the entire community like the Hebrew prophets is due to a number of causes. They could not all preach in the name of one and the same God -- polytheism was then as now the prevailing form of faith and although the saints intended to preach monotheism the names they used for God were bound to rouse sectarian jealously, while a strange name for God could not have made no popular appeal. Even Moses and Mohammed had to use an already familiar name for designating God in their revelations - they did not coin the words 'Yahweh' and 'Allah' themselves. It so happens therefore that while the Tamil saints poured forth their lyrics in praise of Shiva the Alvars and the North Indian saints used Vaisnavite names, with the effect that as there was no national God like the Yahweh of the Hebrews the reformed movements made no universal appeal. When we remember that even the Brahma Sutra of Badarayana was twisted like a nose of wax by learned philosophers in the interests of sectarianism We can easily understand how deep was the sectarian feeling in India and what prospect there was of any reformer being able to reconcile conflicting faiths under the banner of a single God.

One other fact prevented the wide diffusion of any reformed cult. The Indian saints were mostly imbued with the sense of personal weakness and what they generally sought to achieve through their devotion was not so much regeneration of the masses as personal salvation, the most notable exception being Caitanya, who attempted a mass-movement through his Sankirtana. But their personal influence and their preaching to a small circle bore fruit and at least one great religion – Sikhism - owes its origin to one such teacher, viz. Nanak. Here again, as in Judaism, political circumstances favoured cohesion and growth: it is not unlikely that but for imperial oppression the Sikhs would have remained in the same insignificant position of a minor sect as the followers of Ramanada, Kabir, Dabu, Charan Das and other mediaeval reformers. What gave these minor sects their lease of life is the necessity of a less costly and more direct faith than what the ritualistic and impersonal religious organization of Hinduism afforded. (Rhys David thinks that costly sacrifice was one of the causes of the rise of Buddhism). The rapidity and case with which each religions genius become a god in India, and stories of miracles gather round his personality, prevent the spread of the reform to the community as a whole which, though often ready to admit reasonable evolution and purification in faith, is not always willing to accord that pre-eminence to the reformer which is demanded by him personally or by his followers. The Hebrew prophets too had disciples and schools, but they were never accorded divine honors.

The message of Christianity was regarded [as well as the message of prophets] as being ultimately meant for humanity at large. But even with in the Christian community the question of Gentile conversion was quite acute, and only the forceful personality of Paul could triumph over the opposition of Peter and other Apostles who were enforcing all the Jewish rites in the case of the Gentiles also. Some of the mediaeval saints of India had the similar problem of observing Muhammadeans within the Church, and it is these that had to recede most from orthodoxy and to found a separate sect: for Hinduism, well tolerant of religious experiments and even of atheism, had always insisted on conformity to its social organization as a precondition of recognition and it is the defiance of their organization that made rapprochement impossible. Even the intellectuals, who on philosophic grounds had at this time been preaching a purer intellectual faith, were devoid of that Semitic urge to force a reform on the masses and preferred to follow instead the divine advice. For example, in Bhagavad Gita 3:26 it is stated: "A wise man should not shake the convictions of the ignorant who are attached to action, but, acting with devotion himself, he should make them apply themselves to all actions-." What happen, on the contrary, was that to the God's of the community were added deified teachers and preachers, and new rituals were added to old, the evolution of purity in faith and conduct in local areas and small sects was counterbalanced by the extravagant and event fancies of later Vaisnava writers. A large-scale absorption within Hinduism of Buddhists, seeking shelter from Muhammadan oppression, not only introduced the questionable practices of a decaying cult but also social complications in North India, as the caste system insisted on imposing disabilities on, and assigning lower social position to, the new converts. The old bottle refused to admit the new wine for fear of going to pieces.

Let us return now to the secret of prophetic success. While philosophers, theologians and ethicists have been able to influence and modify religious beliefs with the help of a slow process of filtration along with the diffusion of culture and the development of general intelligence, prophets have succeeded in spreading a contagion of faith, because, while the former are regarded as talking the language of man, the latter are looked upon as speaking the voice of God. Not only are their utterance supposed to be divinely inspire but the prophets themselves are possessed with "an irresistible sense of vocation." The gopis (cowherdesses) of Vrndavana (Brindavan) according to vaisnava accounts, used to leave everything precipitously behind when Krishna's flute sounded on the banks of the yamuna: So did the prophets when the divine call came to them. Buddha and Caitaniya leave their young wives behind, Amos has herd and sycamore trees, from an inner implies to obey the call of religion; even the child Jeremiah felt the irresistible call to prophecy in lisping numbers just as Dhurva and Prahlada are said to have sung the praises of Hari in their infancy. The sway that the prophets have held on men's minds in due to the fact that their messages were regarded as coming from God and they spoke with an authority not their own.

Broadly speaking prophetic inspiration can be divided into four classes. (i) Message by incarnation, (ii) message communicated direct by God to a prophet, (iii) Message communicated to a prophet through angelic or some other agency and (iv) Message found by the prophet in his own heart.

Hinduism affords the best illustration of the first kind of prophetic inspiration, although couple with it there is the wide spread theological belief that God does not create the truths. He is supposed to reveal yet later time ask the believe grew up that truth and morality were preached by God himself either by his own incarnated life or by direct instruction. Thus Manu only lays down the laws of spiritual life as heard from Vivasvan (Surya), who had them from Godhimself and communicated them to Iksaku from whom through a succession of royal sages, world received its spiritual wisdom. The three major God's, Brahma, Vishnu (or Surya) and Shiva were eradicated with having taught the human race through minor God's or sages not only the truths of religion and morality but also consume happenings, names of things, arts and crafts, and social and political events of bygone ages: hence God is significantly defined ask the first preceptor, the teacher of teachers, in the Nay treatise *kusumanjali*.

The exact prophetic function of each incarnation is difficult to establish and the number of incarnation also did not remain uniform in different accounts Ten incarnations of Vishnu are noted the fish, the tortoise, the Boar, the Man-Lion, the dwarf, Parasurama, Ramachandra, Balarama (or Vasudeva), Buddha, Kalki. In the Bhagavata purana such incarnations are regarded as innumerable. The other God's Brahma, Shiva and Sakti generally teach without incarnations the spiritual truths necessary for human knowledge and guidance.

But when the Visnava theory triumphed in the end, most of the prominent religious teacher of later times was supported to be God's reborn for the instructions of the world. Sankara is shiva himself and Ramanuja is Sesa, the Serpent-King reborn. Chaitaniya is an incarnation of Krishan and Radha together, and many of the mediaeval saints were likewise incarnation of this or that god. Even Buddhism caught the infections and Buddha was regarded as not having been born but as having voluntarily left heaven and assumed a human shape on earth to relieve suffering and, teach mankind. He had come again and again in the past as occasions demanded and will do so again in future. Jainism did not, it is true, regarded its prophets as incarnations, but it deified them when dead end also believed that Mahavira was not the first to teach the law of life although, unlike Buddha he was the last of the twenty-four Tirthankaras of the present age of the world.

It is quite conceivable that different prophets should fix their gaze upon different aspects of the mysteries of spiritual life, although to be founders of faiths they must all possess intellectual insight, abiding love and moral earnestness of a greater or lesser degree the nature of their message is very often conditioned by the needs of their time and the comprehension of their contemporaries. We may believe that to Buddha the spiritual message come into the form of an intellectual solution of the riddles of suffering, old age and death when at the foot of the Bo-tree he attained enlightenment. Not that he was not moved by the suffering of the innocent victims of the vedic culture of the sacrifice or the hardship caused by the inflexibility of a rigid caste organization, but tradition ascribes to him the primary enlightenment about the causes that lead to suffering and embodiment and an insistence upon earnest contemplation as the condition of freeing the mind from evil-sensuality, individuality, delusion and ignorance. To Zarathustra, the message from the sacred fire causes in the form of a moral problem as to how falsehood and evil are to be practically tackled. The moral position of Zoroastrianism had been indicated by one of the high priest of the creed thus: "Zoroastrianism" will leave by its external variation of the belief in the personality of Ormazd, an abiding faith in the triad of good thoughts, good words, good deeds, the inexorable laws of righteousness, the regard and retribution in the life hereafter, the progress of the world towards perfection, and the ultimate triumph of the good over Evil through the coming of the Kingdom of Ormazd with the co-operation of man. Not that Zoroastrianism or Zarathustra did not have his severe indictment of the worship of God's (daeva) or his commendation of a life based on the principle of family love and social charity; but the major burden of his religious theme is that, not by ecstasy and meditation, but by struggle and suffering must one redeem the world from the grip of falsehood and wickedness, and great is the reward of those who fight the battle of Truth and righteousness.

Now let us briefly consider the parallelism between Rishis o Hinduismand the Hebrew Prophets and most often there is a contrast between them: In ancient India several Rishis were popular, some of the prominent ones among them are: Kashyapa, Athri, Bharadwaja, Gowthama, Viswamitra, Jamadagni and Vasista. Hindus respected them even worshipped them. It was believed that these are the authors of Vedas and perhaps lived even before the Vedas came into existence. It was also believed that these Rishis are always in praise of God's and angels. Some among them were very intelligent poets. The character of those Rishis is very generous in nature; whoever approaches them for help they provide in abundance They possessed some extra powers and always used to transcend human and natural realm due to the possession of such powers. Like God's, they possessed eternal life, fertility, victory, property, all kinds of physical and material blessings. By virtue of their drinking of *Soma Pana*, they uttered wonderful and life-giving words possessed with extraordinary powers. The Rishis always maintained a good relationship with the kings and their court. Usually they live in ashrams with a bunch of disciples around them. Whenever there is a problem or a matter to be resolved in the king's court, Rishis visited them and gave advice. For certain wars with other nations or as the peacemakers between two enemy Kingdoms in case war breaks between them. When they met public they used devotional methods to inspire them with devotional messages. When they found undesirable way of walking in the people, they exhorted them with divine injunctions. They claimed certain privileges of food shelter and other provisions required for their daily bread. In spite of all these seemingly parallel characters between the Hebrew prophets and Hindu sages [Rishis] there remains still a major difference between them.

In the case of the Hebrew prophets, they receive a definite call from God and in obedience to such a can they dedicate their entire life to the service of God. But we do not see such a definite divine call in the Rishis. Moreover, Hebrew prophets are ordinary persons: in virtue of their calling from God, God endowed with best gifts in them and filled them with his

Spirit. Also the prophets are effective in communicating the message of God. Whereas the Rishis, most often due to their own and self-effort, especially through rigorous mediation and concentration [Tapas] are endowed with special gifts [varas] to the deity to which they worship did their Tapas. The Hebrew prophets proclaimed the message of doom and judgment without any fear. They even faced the rulers boldly and courageously. They too preached about God's salvific acts that followed after the punishment. However, the Rishis were always anxious and eager to declare their glory and power which resulted in terror and destruction even among the Deva loka. The prophets also predicted the future Messianic hope and the new age that will bring comfort among the people. Whereas the Rishis hardly mention anything about the future apocalyptic message.

A brief study of the New Testament understanding of prophecy, contemporary views regarding prophecy among Christians and the prophetic role of the church in the present context of India.

[a] New Testament understanding of Prophecy: In the New Testament even though we do not have full-pledged prophets like the Old Testament times, we still have some reminiscent ideas of prophecy.

***John the Baptist:*** The first prophet described in the New Testament is John the Baptist, whose career was contemporary with Jesus. He was a popular charismatic figure who created eschatological excitement, was alienated from conventional culture, was critical of the established authorities and suffered death of their hands [cf. Matt. 3:1-2; Mk. 1:4-8; Lk. 3:2-18]. Luke in particular is interested in describing John the Baptist as belonging to the prophets of Israel described in the Hebrew Bible [Lk. 3:10-14]. John's baptism could well be understood in the category of the symbolic actions of the prophets.

***Jesus:*** All four gospels picture Jesus as a prophet. In the eyes of the people he is regarded as prophet [Matt. 16:14; 21:11; Mk. 6:15,8:28; Lk. 7:16,9:8; Jn. 4:19;9:17] and Jesus Himself applies the proverb of a prophet rejected in his native land [Matt. 13:57; Mk. 6:4; Lk. 4:24;13:33; Jn. 4:44]. Moreover, Jesus is pictured as receiving a vision at the beginning of his ministry corresponding to a prophets call [Matt. 3:13-17; cf. Isa. 6:1-10; Mk. 4:10-12; Matt. 13:10-11; Lk. 8:10]. The Spirit that he received in baptism would be understood in a Jewish context as the spirit that made one a prophet. For Luke, Jesus is indeed the eschatological prophet promised in Scripture [Lk. 24:19; Acts 3:22-23;7:37; cf. Deu. 18:15-18], who specifically identities the spirit of Isa. 61:1-2 [Lk. 4:16-21]. Jesus authority is not the derived authority of the scribe, but the immediate authority of the inspired prophet [Matt. 7:29]. New Testament pictures Jesus as prophet is historical bed rock. Jesus as a prophet [Jeremiah: conservative scholar]; liberal scholars think Jesus as the prophet of social justice [Rauschenbusch].

***Paul:*** The first reflection of Christian prophecy in Christian literature is found in I Thes. 5:19-20, in which Paul appears as the advocate of the prophetic gift over against its detractors; When some problem arose in resulting the misunderstanding of the prophecy, Paul asserts that it is a gift of the spirit, but not without critical evaluation. The most extensive discussion of Christian prophecy in the New Testament is found inI Cor. 12-14. As in I Thes., the discussion has a polemical tone, again revealing Paul as an advocate of prophecy, this time over against an inappropriately high valuation of glossolalia, here Paul asserts its value to be for the edification of the Church rather than responses to the private inquiries of individuals. Prophecy, in fact, is the only constant in Paul's "lists" of charismata. (I Cor. 12:8-11, 28-30; 13:1-2; Rom 12:6-8). When Paul "ranks" spiritual gifts, prophecy appeared second only to the apostolic office or, from another perspective love. Paul insists so adamantly on his apostleship, there seems to be a less emphasis given to prophecy by him (I Cor. 13:2; 14:6,37; I Cor. 12:1-10).

The term "spiritual" in Col 1:9 and 3:16 suggest the fact that Colossians seems very reserved with reference to the Pauline enthusiasm for prophecy, and may already express a reaction. Ephesians on the other hand, look back upon the first generation and considers prophets, along with apostles, to be a constituent element in the foundation of the church (Eph. 2:20; 3:5; 4:11). In pastoral epistles, not as charismata but "regular" ordination at the hands of authorized officials designates people for leadership in the church. There may still be some stirrings of the prophetic spirit manifest in the references in I Tim 1:18; 4:14 and II Tim 1:14.

***John and Johannine Tradition:*** Only Jesus is called the prophet in the gospel of John (4:19,44; 9:17) and only Caiphas is said to "prophesy" (11:51). In the book of revelation number of points have contact between apocalypse and Christian Prophecy 14:15-17, 25-26; 15:26-27; 16:8-11,12-15. The functions of Christian Prophets are described here.

***Didache:*** The manual of church order (Didache 6-15) comes from a Christian community that both honours prophecy and has come to experience it as a problem prophet is the one who speaks "in the spirit" (11:12). The criterion of true is a false prophet who teaches according to the truth is a false Prophet "if he does not practice what he teaches" (11:10).

***Hermas:*** The shepherd of Hermas from first half of second century never refers to himself as a prophet, but there are some qualities like prophet that it repeatedly presents itself as the revelation of the Holy Spirit or Son of god to his church in latter days (e.g. Vis. IV. 1:3; Sim. IX: 1:1). The prophetic phenomenon seems still to be present in the authors church, where both "true" and "false" prophets can be observed and must be tested (Man. XI).

The above survey indicates that prophecy was not rare, episodic or isolated, but was widespread phenomenon in the early Christianity that has left its traces in a variety of early Christian literature. In fact, prophets and prophecy form a primary common denominator and line of continuity between the Hebrew Bible and the Christian scripture.

The context of prophecy is the worshipping congregation, to which prophets belong as constituent members. Although prophets, like others on occasion travel from place to place it is overdrawn to impose a doubtful interpretation of Prophecy in the Didache on all our other sources, and picture: itinerary as of the essence of Christian Prophetism.

Prophecy in the early church was not an amorphous, potentiality diffused throughout Christian community. There was usually an identifiable group that functioned as Prophets, who were recognized as such by the church. The Church as a whole, which also possessed the spirit, was charged with critically evaluating the utterances of the Prophets (Rev 2:2,6,14,15,20; I Cor. 14). The prophets spoke with authority as they announced the unqualified word of the Lord; but it is also clear that they should expect a deliberate engaged response from the community. The burden of their message was the edification of the community, not the satisfaction of private curiosity. Prophets could express their revelations in words of the historical Jesus1 which they sometimes took up and represented in a modified form more relevant to the new situation. In this way they served as the continuing voice of Jesus in the early church and Christianity.

### *Prophetic Role of the Church in the Present Context Especially in India*

The prophetic ministry in India is very much needed at a time when it is not given any importance in many circles of the Christian church and ministry. While we see on the one hand that the church and the Christians are more concerned about "individualistic Piety" or the "soul" of human beings, there is hardly any address that relates to the evil of the social system that leads to the fragmentation of in and around the individuals. In this essay we shall briefly capture few important concerns of the prophets and the prophetic ministry and role in Indian, situation.

Sometimes we should not equate the prophetic demand for righteousness in human life with a mere morality. No nation or society, least of all one which is seeking to reform and rebuild itself, can exist or survive without a commonly accepted moral code. The absence of, or defection from, such a code brings ruin. Yet morality in this sense is essentially legalistic. It prescribes a standard of behaviour and therefore has to maintain it by a system of rewards and punishments, and this is not the righteousness has a bias towards the "poor", the outcast and underprivileged, the widow or orphan, those who have no help or refuge but in God. (cf. Matt. 25, Jesus concern). The righteousness is a gift of prophets brought to fullness of expression in Jesus answer to the question, 'who is my neighbour', by this the implication of the prophets as well as Jesus is, 'whoever is in need he is my neighbour.' So the monotheism of the Hebrew prophets rescues people from the multiple demands of many God's, it sets clear standards of human behaviour, it requires love between humans as neighbours.

All people are God's people, those who are in need are particularly placed in God's care and concern. Human nature is fallen and corrupt. The birds in the heaven knows the times and seasons-obedience is their nature. But humans are willfully blind and obstinate - disobedience is their nature. They are rebellions against their creator and father. The prophets were the first to proclaim this view of sin, not as a moral fault, nor as a neglect of ritual demands, but as a matter of human heart, a taint or disease in human nature. It is they who lead us to the idea of sin rather than of sins, to the cause rather than to the symptoms of the human malady. Throughout the prophetic proclamation there is growing sense of the seriousness of sin and of the need for salvation. Prophets proclaimed that the world and the human life is good: a good marred by human sin, but a good which can be realized when beings are saved from their sin and guilt is removed, and themselves restored to the fellowship with God. So the church believes that in Christ sin is dealt with, forgiveness offered, human beings are reconciled to God and are made a new creation.

There is another aspect of prophetic message that gives us direction. Israel was aware of herself as a society. She was a people, a nation. So strong was this sense of individuality and of individual responsibility. Israel is God's people, called into being by Him to be his agent in his redemptive purpose. The Christian Church in India too, inherits this sense of communal vocation. Christian worship, witness and service are all communal.

Thus through the prophets the church inherits a message and a vision which combines the two essential facts about human beings that they are individuals and that they live and need to live in fellowship with others. Extreme individualism ends in anarchy. Extreme ideas of race and state lead to totalitarian dictatorships. Either denies a part of man's highest nature. But the church in India today, inheriting the prophetic tradition, meets not only human beings' need to know themselves persons, but their need to know themselves members with others in a community, and so offer them a way of life which fulfils their deepest needs.

Several prophetic messages talk about the gross injustice done to the human beings in their community life. Even when a citizen's rights are denied or undermined (cf. I Kings 21:1-19) the prophets responded immediately. In Naboth's story we notice that the authority and norm for conduct, were divorced from any consideration of the basic rights of a person and instead determined entirely by the self-interest of the powerful. People may react to such a situation with a feeling of helplessness, resignation or cynicism. Based on Elijah's ministry here, the church has often assumed the role of the prophetic voice and has been from time to time a corrective influence in society. But at times, the church has also tended to adopt the way of the world in perpetuating gross injustices both inside and outside. the church has also all too often ignored the cry of the oppressed. To cultivate a profound sensitiveness to the Prophetic message, and to discern the voice of the living God in all areas of our personal and social conduct have become more urgent today than ever.

In another familiar passage in the book of Amos (7:10-15), the prophet is speaking of the situation where there is a possibility of a threats from the so called rulers of the church or the "Statuesquo supporters." The message of Amos when spoken clearly and straight forward, that disturbed the royal priest, was not accepted for repentance, rather Amos' message was twisted wrongly at the king's court and Amos was asked to return to Judah. But we know that both the King and the High Priest, the state and the 'church' came under God's judgment thirty Years later at the time of the Assyrian invasion and the downfall of Israel. Both in churches and in public life in our context, people who represent points of view unpalatable to us are eased out or silenced. Many well-meaning Christians adopt a passive attitude and keep silent for the sake of 'peace'. There is often a refusal on our part to identify what is wrong and to take sides for the right cause because we do not want to get into 'trouble.' Can the church will muzzle or brand the messengers of God under one or another name so that they are made to appear as 'trouble makers.' The bible tells very clearly: 'See that you do not refuse him who is speaking' (Heb.12:25).

In yet another passage in the book of Hosea (6:124) we find God's chastisement of His people and warning of the prophet about their hypocritic spiritual life devoid of a concrete action. Here the prophets clearly show that the penitence of the people is only a show and their loyalty to God lacks any depth. It is merely a passing feeling. We might have expected the prophet to be very pleased with the people when they showed signs of grief over their plight. But the man of God has the perception and insight to see through the superficiality of the grief and to identify a deep-seated spiritual malaise. Today the church also suffers from that familiarity which takes God for granted without any regard for demands which he makes on her. The prophets' message seems to point in anticipation to the fallacy of the cheap grace of which Dietrich Bonhoeffer has warned un in our own times.

In a messianic passage of Ezekiel Chapter 34, the prophet attacks the rulers for not caring for the sheep, rather manipulating them for selfish ends, and we also see there the prophetic attack on the fat sheep (rich and powerful of the people) for abusing the rights of the thinner, weaker sheep. Same thing can be found in Jer. 23:1-7 where the prophet indicates that executing justice and righteousness has priority over defending Israel from its enemies. We can note few important points of the prophetic concerns here.

(a) There is conflict between the rulers and ruled; between powerful and powerless in the church. That is always the situation where power is not used for caring or sharing. Then it can only be used for establishing, enhancing, preserving the particular interests of the powerful, however much those interests may be identified with the national interests. When this needs changed them also a result of conflict and struggle.

(b) The image of the shepherd is of a ruler. It is the rulers of Israel who are to be denounced (v.1) (same is the situation today!). They have ruled with force and, harshness (v-4). Thus the concept of leadership is one of leading out and bringing in caring, protecting, providing, restoring (Ezek. 34:4-6,8) which is the need of the hour in India today.

(c) What provided these prophets with a point of entry which made possible a clear focus on the transformation of people and societies was their understanding of the spirit of God. As the societal concept of Messiahship is related to a releasing and restoring justice, so spirit is related to a releasing and restoring justice, so spirit is related to transforming human beings and -s societies As the prophets struggled with the nationalism injustice and oppression of their century, which destroyed awareness, sensitivity and openers, it became necessary to enunciate, not only their own experience, but the work of the spirit in Israel in the terms of their experience (cf. Isa 32:15-17). It is the same task with which the church in India is called for like the Hebrew prophets.

In Isaiah 5:8ff there is a reflection of the growth of large estates or "Latifundialization." It means in social scientific literature is generally defined as the process of land accumulation (large estates, hence latifundia) in the hands of a few wealthy land owners to the deprivation of the peasantry. Here the prophet is speaking against the crimes or the rich landowners in accumulating large estates by joining the small lots of land which were the inheritance of the peasants was a violation of sacred ordinance, the principle of distribution of land under Yahweh's ultimate ownership. prophet also talks against the avaricious motives of the landed elite to gain maximum economic advantage through the cultivation of cash crops. Therefore, Yahweh will respond with a total failure of the harvest. Two major items mentioned in Isa 8:10, that are exported from Palestine are wine and grain. These items were exported in exchange for luxury and military items. The primary Producers were in no way benefited by the fruits of their own labour. The judgment speaks of depriving the rich of the very things of which they had deprived the peasants.

The similar situation mentioned above is also found in the Indian context today. We find that only minority of the rich and elite in the upper social strata control the economic system and the rich resources of the land. Many landlords own several hundreds of property and they keep on accumulate large estates of property. Whereas the vast majority of people do not own any piece of land. To such a context, the Prophetic message of Isa. 5:8-10 is quite relevant. The new economic order is only a benefit to some people, the globalization concept is not at all beneficial to the millions of under-privileged masses in India. In this situation, certainly the church has the task of prophetic proclamation in order to restore the lost values of humanity.

***Conclusion:*** It is now clear that prophecy in India and in the New Testament has significant religious and theological insights.

First, we can notice the archaic nature of Indian prophecy with the full background of religious and social milieu. India being the multi-religious and multi-cultural country, prophecy shares similar views with variety of innovative insights from different religious and social contexts. Such a variety of prophetic insights enlighten and enriches all those who read and understand the available prophetic oracles and injunctions.

Second, the prophecy in the New Testament continues similar features as in the Old Testament and in addition it became more visible in the context of the church. Similar features.

Chapter 11

# Hebrew Prophets and Dalit Prophets A Comparative Analysis

***Introduction:*** The biblical prophets in the Old Testament are also called as ancient Hebrew Prophets have not simply revolutionized the society in which they lived without any basic commitment. In fact, they are deeply rooted in the genuine traditions of Israel and what they did therefore was to offer a constructive critique to improve upon the very society in which they lived. They took the faith of the people very seriously and thus articulated that faith in the form of certain ethical and moral demands. Thus their faith is seen in the sense of dynamism that addressed to their very life situation. Their vision was always bifocal. They were concerned with the vertical and horizontal dimensions of the faith of the people. The affirmed that one's relationship with the neighbor is as important as ones' relationship with God. They also addressed multivalent issues that concerning injustice and social oppression, crises of military invasions and the barbarities of war, creation of political alliances, religious apostasy, monarchical pretensions and tyranny, people lamenting their exile or directionless in trying to start a new life.[12] It is their intimate relationship with Yahweh that made them effective channels of communication between Yahweh and Israel. Whenever they communicated their message it is not their own but on behalf of Yahweh. The prophets spoke becausc there is some inexplicable force that compelled and summoned them to take it as messengers of Yahweh. Barton calls them

12 Patrick D. Miller, Jr. "The World and Message of the Prophets: Biblical Prophecy in its Context," in James Luther Mays, David L. Petersen & Kent Harold Richards (eds.) *Old Testament Interpretation: Past, Present, and Future – Essays in Honor of Gene M. Tucker* (Nashville: Abingdon Press, 1995), pp. 97-112.

as non-establishment figures that will not be silenced.[13] They mean business whenever they had opportunities to deal with the royal establishments. They proclaimed Yahweh's presence that is directly present in the midst of the concreteness of the life of people.[14] As stated above they did not live sociopolitical vacuum, but seem to have been emerged from the very concrete theological and sociopolitical traditions. Their communications reveal that over the period of time their interpretation took a very unfolding of their rooted traditions and at the same time they have surpassed thee given traditions in order to break the boundaries that are created by the royal establishment. For this purpose, they risked their very lives.

The message and voices of the Hebrew prophets certainly inspire any community seeking emancipation and liberation from the clutches of different kinds of social evils that keep them as slaves. Dalit community in India suffering from the heinous system of caste for more than three thousand years certainly find the message of the prophets not only relevant but also appropriate to fight against the oppressive system but also to see the converging points of contacts of certain prophetic figures among Dalits themselves. In this light the task of this presentation is to first of all talk about the import of the message of the Hebrew prophets in ancient Israel in their articulation of how they addressed the concerns of "Dalits" of their society in relation to justice and related issues and secondly to see how the message of those biblical Hebrew prophets would in some ways converge with that of the contemporary Dalit prophets' message and passion for the Dalit cause and liberation of Dalits from the castiest oppression.

***Hebrew Prophecy as a Domain for Articulation of Justice and Righteousness:*** Hebrew prophets of ancient Israel articulated with passion their concerns of justice and righteousness. In fact, it is their justice and righteousness accent that made the minds of hearts of their listeners' alert. They reiterated Mosaic practice of justice an irreplaceable social and ethical entity in all walks of life of the community. But this prophetic accent comes with particular strings attached to it. Walter Brueggemann points out such a situation:

> I take the core of this prophetic accent (as cited in the verses of the prophets like Ezek 18:5-9; Zech 7:5-9; Isa 56:1) to be that of all members of the community, rich and poor, urban and rural, wise and foolish, powerful and marginated, are bound to each other in a common historical and social enterprise. Every member, by virtue

13 John Barton, *Oracles of God: Perception of Ancient Prophecy in Israel after Exile* (London: Darton, Longman, and Todd, 1986), p. 112.

14 Walter Brueggemann, *Theology of the Old Testament: Testimony, Dispute, Advocacy* (Minneapolis: Fortress Press, 1997), p. 623.

> of membership in the community, has entitlement that cannot be abrogated. Thus "widow, orphan, alien" are ciphers for those most vulnerable and powerless and marginated in a patriarchal society, who are without legal recourse or economic leverage. They are entitled and must be given their share.[15]

With this particular punch of emphasis, the prophetic ethic works to seek to build an alternate society of justice and righteousness in which Yahweh's rule will be established. This particular emphasis is also deeply rooted in their politics of articulating divine government by means of not only talking about divine assembly, but the very involvement of prophets in the human political scene. As agents of the divine rule, they also called kings to account for their failure to carry out righteousness and justice in the community they ruled—as for instance in the case of Nathan's judgment speech against David for his acts of adultery and murder (1 Samuel 12), Elijah's condemnation of Ahab and Jezebel for their judicial murder of Naboth (1 Kings 21), and Jeremiah's condemnation of Jehoiakim for his unjust exploitation of his people for the sake of his extravagant and luxurious style of life (Jer 22:13-19).[16] Both the concepts of *mishphat* and *tsedekah* are the powerful concepts of actualizing God's rule and justice on earth right here. They are like powerful aspects of rhythmic flow of everyday life in concrete terms. If any disruption to one of these entities the entire society is said to have collapsed and its fundamental survival is in question. Thus it can even be compared to the Egyptian concept of *ma'at* which is a primordial principle of order that is bestowed by the benevolent gods of creation. As long as *ma'at* is present in the society there will be order and the society is protected, but once it is disrupted then they will be a collapse in the created order resulting in the breakdown of the society.[17]

The concepts of *mišpāṭ* and *ṣ ᵉ dāqā* used in the prophetic literature are something important we need a brief discussion at this point. Both these terms represent the highest value of human behavior and human condition.[18] Both these appear as spheres of power which already exist in advance of human actions. In Amos 6:12 they are compared with draught animals, productive powers which a person needs in order to live. Once they are misused they become poisons with a sinister effect. They also resemble like a fluid. They are expected like the ever flowing stream and river over the people (Amos 5:24). But once they are misused they turn into a bitter

15 *Ibid*, p. 645.

16 Patrick D. Miller, Jr. "The World and Message of the Prophets." pp. 104-105.

17 For more details on the discussion of *ma'at* and related issues see,

18 Klaus Koch, *The Prophets: Volume one – The Assyrian Period* (Philadelphia: Fortress Press, 1983), p. 57.

liquid. This river comes from above as the source of it is Yahweh who makes it rain *ṣ ᵉdāqā* (Hos. 10:12; Joel 2:23).[19] Moreover these concepts not only are related to the individual spheres of life but also radiate out to the whole land, creating harmony between *society and nature* (Ps. 72:1-3; Joel 2:21-23). The reversal which turns *mišpāṭ* into the bitterness of wormwood destroys environment, making fields unfruitful (Hos 10:4). Thus both these concepts are not abstract principles but they are spheres of powerful activity and interaction between God and humans and between humans and humans. These concepts are also supported by linguistic parallels from the Canaanite background. In Canaanite religion the words *ṣedeq* and *mišōr* (also used for *mišpāṭ* in Isa. 11:4) were gods. But they were not self-contained, individual figures. They were active forces which a person adopted and made his own, and in which he realizes himself. When Israel took over this language from Canaan, it rejected the ritual veneration of forces of nature and other elements but gave them a new function as Yahweh's active powers. For a Hebrew what is more sensible and valuable is to express his or her solidarity with his or her brother even at the time when a festive celebration is carried out. This sense of solidarity created an awareness and consciousness of community, not only between God and humans but also humans and nature. Thus both *mišpāṭ* and *ṣ ᵉdāqā* are like active forces power that are permeating the entire realm of individual and community life in ancient Israel and to these prophets became the guiding light of the people.[20] In other words the Hebrew prophets envisaged a kind of created and established order in which a particular course of God's salvation history is established in the realm of society, particularly to those *dallīm* who are marginalized in the society. This created order alone provides the conditions and possibilities for a successful and harmonious life in the society. If any this counters this established order it is the reversal of *mišpāṭ* and *ṣ ᵉ dāqā* and that condition is expressed in the term *Pesa'* which is a violent rebellion against Yahweh. It is at the same time a stupid demolition of the foundation of one's own life.[21] Thus in very clear terms and conditions the Hebrew prophets communicated their uncompromising message of justice and righteousness to the people of ancient Israelite community.

The term *mišpāṭ* is often a breach of justice suffered by Israelites at the hands of their corrupt leaders (Isa 1:17, 21; 5:7; 10:2; 59:8-9; Hab 1:4). Due to this, Yahweh himself enters into judgment with his own people. The

19 *Ibid*, p. 58.

20 *Ibid*, pp. 59-60.

21 *Ibid*, p. 62.

Lord's judgment is not only directed against corrupt leaders but towards the people for their sin (Isa 4:4; Jer 5:1; Ezek 5:6-7; 20:11; Hos 5:1; Mal 3:5).[22]

Concerning *ṣ ᵉdāqā* and its dynamism James L. Mays states:

> *ṣ ᵉ dāqā* is the quality of life displayed by those who live up to the norms inherent in a given relationship and thereby do right by the other person or persons involved. The two most important spheres for righteousness were the relationship between Yahweh and Israel defined in the covenant and expressed in the cult, and the relationship of man in the social order of the folk … In Amos *ṣ ᵉ dāqā* applies to the relational life of the social partners in the people of Israel. Of course Yahweh is regarded as the patron and enforcer of the social order, but what is in view is the righteousness of Israelites in relation to each other.[23]

Amos and other prophets in the Hebrew Bible often relate the concept of *ṣ ᵉdāqā* to the issues of social justice and it is talked in terms of maintenance of relationship between God and people.[24] There can be no future if the reversal of *mišpāṭ* and *ṣ ᵉ dāqā* takes place in the community of Israel. The well-being of the community very much depends on these two aspects and how they become operative on a day to day basis. There is no place for any individualism in this quest to establish justice and righteousness. On a similar concern Brueggemann writes:

> There can be no viable future of well-being for the Jerusalem establishment, except on the condition of the well-being of the entire community. This conviction is characteristically stated in the negative, as in the prophetic lawsuit speech. It is not, however, difficult to transpose the threat into a possibility. When strong and powerful mobilize their resources and energy for the weak and vulnerable, peace and prosperity are generated for all … Prophetic mediation of Yahweh, rooted in deep covenantalism, strikes a profound blow against all individualism that assumes that private gifts from Yahweh can be had at the expense of the community. The community to which Yahweh attends is grounded in nothing less than Yahweh's summons to membership, a summons that cannot

22 Peter Enns, "(*mišpāṭ*)" in Willem A. VanGemeren (ed) *New International Dictionary of Old Testament Theology & Exegesis* Vol. 2 (UK: Patennoster Press, 1996), 1144.

23 James Luther Mays, *Amos: A Commentary* (London: SCM Press, 1969), pp. 92-93.

24 David J. Reimer, "qdx (*ṣdq*) in Willem A. VanGemeren (ed) *New International Dictionary of Old Testament Theology & Exegesis* Vol. 3 (UK: Patennoster Press, 1996), p. 763.

> be evaded. For this reason the prophets stand against kings who characteristically imagined they were exceptional.[25]

The justice and righteousness thus talk about just dealing in the social sphere, particularly as they are related to jrd, "way" of life as found in Gen. 18;19 "So that they keep the way (jrd) of Yahweh by dealing with righteousness and justice." In Isa 59:8-9 we find similar words: "They do not care for the *way* of integrity, there is no justice in their course (Mtlgfmb). They make their *paths* crooked, no one who walks in them cares for integrity. That is why justice (Fpwm) is far from us, and righteousness (hqdc) does not reach us."[26]

***Hebrew Prophecy as a Domain for Symbolism and Evocative Poetic Expressions:*** Hebrew prophets of ancient Israel presents many literary accents and interesting points for us to see how these prophets used various poetic expressions and other literary devises to communicate their message effectively. These devices demonstrate the poets' craft and it also talks about the prophetic utterance—the words and worlds they create. We shall summarize and comment on some of the important devices that made the prophetic message all the effective and dynamic.

***Parallelism:*** Just as we see in the Hebrew poetic devices used in the poetic and wisdom literature of the Old Testament, the prophetic literature used parallelism throughout their speeches. External antithetic parallelism[27] is employed by prophet Isaiah at several points as follows:

> 1:19-20: "If you are willing and obedient, you shall eat the good of the land *but* if you refuse and rebel, you shall be devoured by the sword; for the mouth of the LORD has spoken."

In the above verses we can find that the first bicolon in v. 19 and the second in v. 20ab express opposing sentiments. This turn of situation between the first and second line is expressed by the word but.

In another example, we can notice the combination of synonymous and synthetic parallelism.[28]

---

25 Walter Brueggemann, *Theology of the Old Testament*, pp. 645-46.

26 Moshe Weinfeld, *Social Justice in Ancient Israel and in the Ancient Near East* (Jerusalem: The Magnes Press, 1995), pp. 30-31. In the Code of Hammurabi and in the Mesopotamian account of *kittum u mīšarum* similar statements can be noticed: "He led the people in the way of truth." "The road/way of truth and equity."

27 This term used by Norman K. Gottwald in "Poetry, Hebrew." *The Interpreter's Dictionary of the Bible* Vol. 3 (Nashville: Abingdon, 1962), p. 833.

28 For a detailed discussion on this issue see, Katheryn Pfisterer Darr, "Literary Perspectives on prophetic literature," in James Luther Mays, David L. Petersen & Kent Harold

> 1:8a-b: "For Jerusalem has stumbled and Judah had fallen; *because* their speech and their deeds are against the LORD, defying his glorious presence."

In another example from Isa. 1:3 we can note a mixture of several poetic forms and parallelisms:

> "The ox knows (*yāda'*) its owner, and the donkey its master's crib; (v. 3a) but Israel does not know (*yāda'*), my people do not understand" (v. 3b).

On surface level reading we may find simple synonymous parallelism. But scholars have observed certain subtle differences in this verse. James Kugel notes:

> The ox was hardly considered the most praiseworthy of beasts: nevertheless "ox" is in several significant respects considered superior to its frequent pair, "ass": More important, parallel to the "owner" of the first is "master's trough" in the second. The cumulative effect of these differences is the establishment of a climactic descent: "An ox knows its owner, and *even* an ass"—who may not be very obedient or attentive—at least knows where to stand to be fed, i.e., "knows his masters' trough" ; but "Israel does not know,"—or obey, even this much; in fact—"my people do not understand at all."[29]

Adele Berlin further observes the effect of verb "gapping," or ellipsis in this verse: the verb "to know" (*yāda'* ), present in the first colon, is missing( i.e., gapped) in the second, and reappears in the third without an object, "hinting that its object is nothing—'Israel doesn't know (anything).'"[30] W. G. E. Watson[31] translates Isa. 1:27 highlighting the additional "balance" between synonymous cola created by reversed gender parallelism:

> Zion [fem.] by justice [masc.] shall be redeemed and those [masc.] in her who repent, by right [fem.].

Commenting on this overall poetic variations on Isaianic passages K. P. Darr concludes: "We see, then, that examining correspondences between

---

Richards (eds.) *Old Testament Interpretation: Past, Present, and Future – Essays in Honor of Gene M. Tucker* (Nashville: Abingdon Press, 1995), pp. 127-143.

29 James Kugel, *The idea of Biblical Poetry: Parallelism and its History* (New Haven and London: Yale University Press, 1981), pp. 9, 102.

30 Adele Berlin, *The Dynamics of Biblical Parallelism* (Bloomington: Indiana University, 1985), pp. 97-98.

31 W. G. E. Watson, *Classical Hebrew Poetry: A Guide to its Techniques.* JSOT Sup. 26 (Sheffield: JSOT Press, 1984).

elements in parallel cola—nuances of words (e.g., "ox"/ "ass") and grammatical variations (e.g., the presence or ellipsis of certain words like "to know" in Isa. 1:3; the balancing of gender), enhances our awareness of the ancient poet's skill and creativity."[32]

***Prophetic use of Metaphors:*** Hebrew prophets skillfully used interesting metaphors to communicate their powerful message. In fact, their metaphorical way of communicating the message of Yahweh has come out so powerfully which is evident all through their oracles. Each prophetic voice became so powerful in that it has certain prophetic speech forms distinctly worked out.

***Prophetic Overarching theme of Justice:*** The prophets by and large do not want to make any compromise on the concerns of socio-economic justice. Their uncompromising fight against the injustices meted out to the marginalized sections of the society even went to the extent of risking their own lives. We shall make few observations in this regard in relation to each individual prophet. The three prophets from eighth century BCE are briefly discussed below in order to explain our point of view with further clarification.

***Amos*** knew about the murderous oppression of the poor. Amos not only stood against that situation but he also firmly proclaimed that it is diametrically opposed to the will of Yahweh. Amos knew the situation from the older tribal traditions where all the people are protected by the discharge of justice in the local courts. Amos was aware that these traditional laws are faithfully practiced in the small villages like Tekoa, the birth place of Amos. Amos vehemently attacks and systematically analyzes the situation of injustice prevailed during his day by comparing it on the basis of traditional Yahwism practiced at least in some parts of his country.[33]

***Hosea*** was mainly addressing to the generation of leaders who bent on protecting their own narrow interests by seizing every opportunity at the expense of others. In the opinion of these leaders Yahweh had become an awarder of their personal advantages. By means of working out with number of metaphors and similes the prophet communicates his message in a powerful manner.[34]

***Micah*** knows by his firsthand experience that the poor farmers and small landholders are expelled from their traditional livelihood by the dishonest

---

32 Katheryn Pfisterer Darr, "Literary Perspectives on Prophetic Literature," p. 134.

33 Norman K. Gottwald, *The Hebrew Bible: A Socio-literary Introduction* (Philadelphia: Fortress Press, 1985), p. 357.

34 *Ibid*, pp. 357-58.

business practices of the rich and landowning ruling minority. Additionally, the royal regime also is noted that it connives in the oppression of the poor. Micah is furious that the political and religious leaders of his day are responsible for the deterioration of the old tribal order of communal equity. He is merciless in attacking the rich and powerful who violate the rights of the poor peasants. Moreover the rich bureaucrats manipulate the legal procedures at the expense of their vulnerable fellow citizens.[35]

In all these the consequences of the prophetic speeches is severe. The city and its temple will be flattened, never to build again. The fate of the rich oppressors is such that there is no positive future for them.

***Dalit Prophetic Discourse in Poetic and Narrative Expressions:*** Dalit literature has emerged over the years as a conscious effort to fight against the evils of caste system and other oppressive elements related to it and it is also envisaged that it created a mind of revolution on the mindset of the dejected Dalits and to work for their emancipation to build a casteless society. It is built into the Dalit literature and its goal may be seen as follows:

> [Dalit literature] envisions art that speaks directly to the needs and aspirations of Dalits in India. In order to perform this task, the Dalit Literary movement proposes a radical re-ordering of the Hindu upper caste cultural aesthetic. It proposes a separate symbolism, mythology, critique, and iconology. Dalit literature exposes Brahminism, praises Dalits and supports the lower caste revolution … Dalit Literature protests against the oppressive Brahminical cultural system which tells lower caste people where they may go and what they may do, where they can live and whom they can marry. What it means to be a dalit in a society which treats people on the basis of inferior or superior birth and what are the real solutions for the emancipation of Dalit world are the major themes of Dalit literature.[36]

Viewed in the above light Dalit literature aims at providing a prophetic to the millions of Dalits who are oppressed on the basis of the caste and also to give a stern warning to the oppressors that they no longer accept the social constructs of caste and other derogatory labels. Before we venture into different areas of Dalit revolutionary prophetic sayings let us see the general tone such voices of resistance when others made Dalits vulnerable and marginalized.

---

35 *Ibid*, p. 375.

36 G. Lakshmi Narasaiah, *The Essence of Dalit Poetry: A Socio-philosophic Study of Telugu Dalit Poetry* (Hyderabad: Dalit Sana Publications, 1999), p. 6.

A Dalit talk to Brahmin about his economic inequality in the following words:

> I carry the dead body to the cemetery. I burn myself attending on it till it gets burnt. You come on the day of death ceremony respected by everyone. And like an eagle grab all things and run away with them.[37]

Dalits always expressed their uneasiness and discomfort for the ill treatment given to them based on caste. The following words affirm the same:

> I am still a prohibited human being. Mine is an expelled breath. Tying a brab tree leaf to my waist. And a tiny spittoon to my mouth. Manu made me a wretched human animal among others. The moment he left a mark of prohibition on my face, My race was gradually murdered.[38]

Dalits through their prophetic poetry talk about the history of atrocities forced by upper caste on them in the following words:

> When poured lead into my ears that heard vedas ,When chopped my tongue for speaking that some language, When lacerated my head for the thirst quenched by my sperm, Then itself I became a corpse.[39]

Yet in the midst of such distressing situations Dalits voice out strong protest against the oppressors and send a clear signal that they will not tolerate any unwanted imposition on them. This comes out in the following words:

> I am an erupting volcano. No one can blow me off. Mine are feet of fire. No ropes can fasten upon my eyes. My head is a proud flag. No one can destroy me. Today mine is a burning face. My hands are thunderbolts. I am walking sward the now. Nobody can touch me. I am awakened tiger.[40]

Dalits portray and protest the situation of slavery and bonded labourness imposed on them by the landlords. The words of revolt and revolution are as follows:

---

37 Elliah Vemula: *Bahu Vachanam* (Several Voices) ed. S. K. Reddy (Neelagiri Sahiti – Nallagonda, 1996) p. 21 Translated and cited by G. Lakshmi Narasaiah in *The Essence of Dalit Poetry*, p. 11.

38 Sudhakar K. Endluri, *Varthamanam* (The present) (Manasa Publications: Rajahmundry, 1992), p. 53. Translated and cited by G. Lakshmi Narasaiah in *The Essence of Dalit Poetry*, p. 14.

39 *Ibid*, pp. 53-54.

40 *Ibid*, p. 77.

> We live as home servants for twelve months. Most of these twelve months we go starving. Both husband and wife have to undertake this task. My son takes care of the cattle of the landlord. Day and night I toiled in vain only lacking sufficient food and adequate clothing. When get into sickness no cure for it. My debts are eternal. I can't stand on this fire and pull my life any more.[41]

Dalit poets vividly employ several daily life metaphors in order to make their messages of revolt and protest easily understandable to their listeners. This is done for the purpose of evoking a spirit of revolt and protest in the minds of the people. If only the words are heard and listened with open heart, then they will spontaneously respond to the crisis. For instance, a popular poet like Gaddar stirs up the spirit of revolt in the minds of his maala and maadiga comrades through his words:

> When the dominant oppressor shoots your blood relatives in the very day light as a hunter shoots the birds and eats their meat why are you simply shedding your tears without any reaction? When the oppressor surrounds your huts and drags your sisters, mothers and your elderly people by trampling them with their feet, and slaughters them with knife and bullets from their guns, why are you crying rather than raising like a sharpened axe?[42]

In another moving description a Dalit poet describes the in depth nature of Dalit struggle comparable to that of chicken fight that is traditionally conducted in the villages during festival occasions as competitions. His words are as follows:

> In our fight for justice we pierced each other by our own swords. We are hanging on the cross with the nails. Let our blood flow like a stream up to your wine glasses. Even then you don't take note of it We fight losing our feathers, shedding our blood until we die like the cocks fight their battle. Even when the skull is broken because of it self-pride the battle is fought by the he goat and in a similar way we continue our fight … our blood is like a cool water stream for you.[43]

---

41 Sikhamani, *Smaantara Aadhunika Kavithva Vyasalu*, (Hyderabad: Nandini Publications, 2006), p. 73.

42 Gaddar, " Rajyadhikaaraniki Maadiganna," in K. Lakshminarayana (ed) *Dalta Kavithvam* – 2 (Anantapur: Ramaa Publications, 2003), p. 42.

43 Saginaala Prakash, "Vivakshala Chhekati," in K. Lakshminarayana (ed) *Dalta Kavithvam* – 2 (Anantapur: Ramaa Publications, 2003), p. 151.

Among the Dalits women Dalits have a special story to tell that is in their own and unique way. It is common to see Dalit women work hard to support their family and they are subjected to eat some food that is available to them. Often they have to be satisfied with the stale available to them. Karra Vijayakumari presents the case of a woman who does cobbling getting some stale food for the work:

> Skinning the bull applying lime all over it till my hands become sore filling the mossy tank with potful of water drying the skin till it becomes tough. Saying I would make him a pair of tiny slippers. I've taken my little one along in the sun to watch over the skin. I've been ordered to make three pairs for the master mistress and the brother in the remaining skin if at all I see the pitiful face of my young one. Hoping they may give at least some *sombuvva* straining my back beating with an iron pestle till my hands ache collecting all my drained strength to make holes with an awl and stitch the slippers. When I carry the slippers in a pewter vessel apply castor oil on your soles and put the slippers on the master says throw her some food. For my hardship the mistress brings and throws into my pewter vessel some stale *sombuvva.*[44]

This story illustrates in a moving way how Dalit women lake slippers and the irony is that their own children are not provided with a pair of tiny slippers. While the dominant caste children enjoy the outcome of Dalit women's labor, Dalit children have to remain with 'pitiful' faces. However, the Dalit women do not silently suffer their fate, rather they question and at times demand their rights. Two things are clearly known to them: first, dominant caste women never hesitate to look down on them. Gender solidarity, in this connection, cannot exert influence on hem; second, Dalit men exercise their authority on their women irrespective of their caste consciousness. Thus they warn the dominant caste women for being part of their oppression. The following words reveal the same:

> You have done nothing to me. Even may man has never treated me as human I know. Your man too has never stood for you. At last the one that is fully damaged is me.[45]

Dalit women are very vociferous in arguing against the caste system and untouchability and they express it with anger in powerful words like the words of Teresa Devadanam:

---

44 Karra Vijayakumari, 'Sombuvva' from Mogi (Nalgonda: Gosangi, 1998), p. 23.

45 Darsie Sasi Nirmala, Note 38 cited in G. Lakshmi Narasaiah, *The Essence of Dalit Poetry*, p. 58.

At the same time Dalits are very optimistic about their future hope and this is once again symbolically expressed in the heart and soul of Dalit poetry in the following words:

> These clouds must be vanished. These walls must be ruined. This silence must be bursted. This gum must be dried up. O man, I want real citizenship, will you give? What do I want, I want you, I want a place in yur heart? I must wash my hands at your home. You must come to my hut and ask our girl for marriage. We must become relatives friend! This country become ours as we walk hand in hand this uneven earth become smooth will you come?[46]

The following words of Namdev Dhasal will tell the future aspirations of Dalits in a metaphorical way as follows:

> Our blood was spilled for this glorious city and what we got was the right to eat stones. Now, now, we must explode the building which kisses the sky. After a thousand years we were blessed with a sunflower. Now, now we must, like sunflowers, turn our faces to the sun.[47]

***Conclusion:*** In the light of our elaborate discussion on various aspects of prophets in ancient Israel and modern Dalits it is clear that in any community both in the ancient times and in our contemporary context, prophecy is a major nerve center for any community to with equality and justice at all levels including the whole cosmos.

## Select Bibliography

J. Lindblom — **Prophecy in Ancient Israel**, Basic Black well, 1963.

T. H. Robinson — **Prophecy and Prophets in Ancient Israel**, Duckworth, London, 1980.

G. Fohrer, — **Introduction to the Old Testament**, SPCK, London, 1976.

H. H. Rowley, — **The OT and the Modern Study**, Clarendon Press, Oxford, 1951.

______(ed) — **Studies in O.T. Prophecy,** T&T Clark, Edinburgh, 1950.

46 Madduri Nagesh Babu, "What is Your Caste," in *What is Your Caste* (Narsarao Peta: Sreeja Publications, 1998), pp. 60-61.

47 Namdev Dhasal, *An Anthology of Dalit Literature* ed. Mulkraj Anand and Eleanor Zelliot 9New Delhi: Gyan Publishing House, 1992), p. 60.

| | |
|---|---|
| ______(ed) | "The nature of Prophecy" in **The Servant of the lord and other Essays** Lutterworth. |
| E, J. Young | **My Servants, the Prophets,** Eerdmans, 1952. |
| G. Von Bad | **OT Theology,** Vol. I & II (SCM, London, 1975) |
| D. H. Mason | **Thus Saith the Lord** (CLS, Madras, 1962) |
| R. E. Clements | **Prophecy and Covenant** (SCM, London, 1965) |
| _________ | **Prophecy and Tradition** (Blackwell, 1975) |
| A. R. Johnson | **The Cultic Prophet in Ancient Israel** (University of Wales Press, Cardiff, (1962) |
| H. L. Ellison | **Men Spoke from God** (Paternoster, UK, 1973) |
| Westermann C | **Basic Forms of Prophetic Speech** (1967) |
| R. Coggins, | **Israel's Prophetic Tradition; Essays in honour or Peter** |
| A. Phillips | **Ackroyd** (Cambridge University Press, Cambridge, 1981) |
| E. V. Davies | **Prophecy and Ethics: Isaiah and the Ethical Traditions of Israel** (JSDT Supplement 16, Sheffield, 1981) |
| A. G. Auld | **Amos** (OT Guide, JSOT, Sheffield, 1986) |
| R. J. Coggins | **Haggai. Zechariah, Malachi,** (UT Guides JSDT, Sheffield, 1987) |
| H. H. Rowley | **Reading the OT Prophets Today** (John Knox Press, Atlanta 1979) |
| D. E. Aune | **Prophecy in Early Christianity and the Ancient Mediterranean World** (Eerdmans, Grand Rapids, 1985) |
| K. Koch | **The Prophets: The Assyrian Period** (Vol. I) (Fortress Press, Philadelphia, 1982) |
| ______ | **The Prophets: The Babylonian and Persian Periods** (Vol.II) (SCM, London,1983) |
| J. F. A. Sawyer | Prophecy and the Prophets of the OT, (0UP, Oxford 1987) |
| J. Goldingay | **God's Prophets God's Servant: A Study of Jeremiah and Isaiah 40-55** (Patenoster Press, 84) |
| E. W. Heaton | **The OT Prophets** (DLT, London, 1977) |

R. R. Wilson — **Prophecy and Society and Ancient Israel** (Fortress Press 1980)

C. R. North — **The Second Isaiah** (Clarendon Press, Oxford 12977)

——— — **The Suffering Servant in Deutero-Isaiah**, (OUP Oxford, 1956)

J. Skinner — **Isaiah, 40-66** (Cambridge Bible)

D. J. A. Clines — **He, We and They A Literary Approach to Isaiah 53** (JSOT. Supplement Series 1, Sheffield 83)

R. N. Whybray — **Isaiah 40-66** (NCB Eerdmans 1981)

——— — **The Second Isaiah** (OT Guides, JSOT, Sheffield, 83)

S. H. Blank — **Prophetic Faith in Isaiah** (Adam & Charles Black, London 1958)

G. A. F. Knight — **Deutero-Isaiah: A Theological Commentary on Isaiah 40-55** (Abingdon, Nashville, 1985)

H. M. Orlinsky & — **Studies on the Second Part of the Book of Isaiah** (SVT 14 EJ Brill, N.H. Snaith Leiden, 1977).

R. F. Melugin — **The Formation of Isaiah 40-55** (w de Gruyter, Berlin, 1976).

C. Westermann — **Isaiah 40-66** (OTL London, 1978).

# Part-II

# An Introduction to Poetic and Wisdom Literature of the Old Testament

Chapter 1

# Extent and Characteristics of Hebrew Poetry

***Introduction:*** The term "poetry" presents great difficulty to exclusively ascribe this to certain specific books. In general, several books in the Old Testament are poetic in character. But using certain exclusive features like high style or symbolic language as indicators makes us to limit it to certain books. While we make a general survey of different poetic sections in the following section, for our consideration we limit ourselves to three canonical books when we consider the section on poetic books viz: the book of Psalms, Lamentations and the Songs of Songs. We will also make brief mention of the poetic sections in the Apocryphal and deuterocanonical books.

The poetry is defined as evocative compositions that communicate more by connotation then denotation. Songs, Prayers, Proverbs, speeches and other lofty pronouncements in the Hebrew bible are usually written in a particular style, one that has traditionally been equated with the "poetry" of the bible. In other words, in simple terms poetry is the work of imagination, feeling and reflection. The Greek word poeties suggests, the poet is the maker, he plays his invective and creative power in order words in varied forms and patterns, to associate sounds in such a way as to produce a desired effect, and to stimulate the mind to range and explore beyond the barriers of literal fact.

### *1. A Survey of Main Poetic Sections in The Bible*

The presence of the poetry in the Bible has long been recognized. In an early and beautifully written fragment of Deut. 32 among Dead Sea Scrolls each stitches and colon appears in a separate line. Comment on the metrical forms of biblical poetry and their views are perpetuated for the most part among the fathers: Origin in a scholion on Ps. 118:1 (LXX), writers of the two stichoi in a vertical and of the measurement of enter by the number of accented syllabus.

It was Bishop Richard Lowth in an epoch-making word de sacra Poesi Hebraeorum Praclectionis academic, that the true character of the Hebrew Poetry was correctly grasped, and his work was followed in 1778 by a more detailed and discriminating treatment of the subject in his translation and notes on Isaiah.

In the early chapters of Genesis, all speeches appear poetic, though at some places it is a narrative text. In the creation account of Genesis 1, the measured style description indicates Poetry though the passage reveals little of the character of poetry Adam's pronouncement in Gen 2:23 "this is at last bone of my bones and flesh of my flesh; this one shall be called woman, for out of man this one was taken", provides better sample of the type and use of poetic lines throughout Genesis. Similar way then the birth announcement of Ishmael carries deep emotional overtones (Gen 16:11-12)

Genesis describes its only lengthy unit of poetry as a blessing when Jacob describes the fortunes of his sons (49:25-26,28). So also in the earlier case, the blessing of Isaac (27:24-29; 39-40).

In the book of Exodus, the full-blown poetic piece appears in Moses' speech in the song of the sea (Exod. 15:1-18). This song displays remarkable action such as three -line unit. (Exod. 15:8). This song also exhibits synonymous parallelism; the repetition lends weight to the wonder of divine deliverance.

In Numbers 6:24-27, a beautiful poetic piece appears entitled as the Aaron's blessing of the congregation. Here the name Yahweh ("the Lord") guaranteed the people the real experience of blessing. In another instance of Numb 10:35-36, Moses involves the presence of God both before and after the ark was taken up and set down. The taunt song in Numb 21:27-30 opens up with mention of "ballad singers" who perform it; The four oracles of Balaam (Numb 23:7-10,18-19; 24:3-9,15-24) is a reminiscence of its distinct poetry. Here in this section, when Israel describes its divine identity, poetry serves as the medium. The message of the poetry allows instruction of humor or skepticism.

The book of Deuteronomy contains many poetic sections. The little historical creed in, Deut. 26:5-10, the poetry follows overall theme of (i) looking back what the people have gained and (ii) contemplating what they have to lose by disobedience or neglect. A dialectic of blessing and curse pervades some sections of the Deuteronomy like: 27:15-26, 28:1-6,16-19. Deut. 32:1-43 contains a more polished composition which recounts the history of God's intervention for his people, see especially vv. 22-25 and 39-42. In all these passages of the book, the poetry serves a more philosophical or aesthetic role.

In the book of Judges, the song of Deborah (5:2-31) is a beautiful and most well poetically constructed section. In Judges 9:8-15, a rough fable which Jotham satirically chants from atop mount Gerizim is a beautiful poetic piece.

The song of Hannah (I Samuel 2:4-9) in its special theme makes antithetical parallelism the expression of choice. A poetic unit seemingly based on a proverb of the "better than" variety appears in I Sam 17:22-23, the story of David's encounter with Goliath, even though appears to be a narrative exhibits little parallelism, but contains a steady predictable rhythm, as though the character speaks (the narrator) in verse (I Sam 17:24-27).

The lament by David in II Samuel 1:17-27 for Saul's death do not conform to the psalmic variety evident in the book of Psalms and Lamentations. It contains three interwoven themes. *First* it expresses geographic interest. *Second* it voices love for the dead heroes (vv. 23,26). *Third* it describes the loss in terms of the warrior's weapons. The final summary of David's life prior to the death account (II Sam 23:1-7) also gives a good poetic piece.

Prophetic literature contains several pieces of well-developed and organized poetry. In Isaiah chapter 1 for instance, the poem opens with a prophetic lawsuit (1:2-3) which resembles the song of Moses in Deut. 32:1. Prophet Jeremiah's poetic oracles serve as medium for his special language of sorrow. His Personal complaints (11:18 12:4. 15:10-21; 17-14-18; 18:19-23; 20:7-13, 14-18) reflect the prophet's unique ministry of suffering. Ezekiel's oracles contain several beautiful poetic pieces. The oracles against the nations take the form of lamentations (15:1-15). All the three major prophets employed poetry to communicate God's judgment. Isaiah used older poetic forms and concepts. His oracles mostly appear psalmic, at times hymn types; the books of Jeremiah and Ezekiel uses several poetic devices in their future hope proclamation.

The Minor prophet's display a variety of poetic pieces in their discourses. Hosea's poetry consists of images using the language of family and divorce (Hosea 2:1-3). All the poetry of Joel shows connection with psalmic poetry (Joel 2:3-5). The poetic units of Amos possess an entirely different tone than Hosea. (Amos 3:3-8). The prophet's words (God's Words) compare to roar of a lion. Similar images of threat include the lion, bear and poisonous snake of 5:18-20. Amos offers some of the most interesting poetic forms of the bible. Two of the three visions in 7:1-9 present a stereotyped response. "O Lord God, cease, I beg you! How can Jacob stand? He is so small." The book of Amos also contains a good deal of word play, especially in 8:1-3, The word for "basket of summer fruit" (Q a y i s) and the word for "end" (Q e s) sound very much alike in Hebrew. The only poetic unit in Jonah appears to be the song of thanksgiving (2:1-9). Micah announces the appearance of God in language similar to the theophanies of the psalms (Micah 1:3-4) and (4:1-4). The book of Nahum also contains a vivid and beautiful pieces of poetry constructed in the form of prophetic oracles (Nah 3:1-3). The book of Habakkuk too contains variety of poetic expressions (1:2-4), series of taunt songs (2:6-17) and the depiction of divine warrior imagery (3:3-6). The book of Zephaniah takes up the concept of "the day of the Lord" in poetic piece (for e.g. 1:2-3, 14-16, 2:1-3) Haggai contains only brief portions of poetry (1:3-11). Zechariah chapters 1-7 contain brief units in the form of oracles. However, chapters 9-14 are entirely poetic which depicts the mastery of the poetic devices used by the narrator/prophet. Malachi's poetry reveals less careful measuring but possesses a captivating, rational style (1:16).

Prophets provide expression of emotional human experience. The pronounced passion of selected psalms appears endemic to the speech of the prophets. The prophets in general employed vivid forms and style of the communication in their poetic discourses.

Wisdom books do contain a variety of poetic elements. The truisms of Proverbs assume a loose poetic form. Hymns to wisdom (for example, Prov. 8:1-36) and similar units comprise the book's most "poetic" sections. The book of Job contains an elaborate poetic dialogues, towers high among the great literary achievements of the AWA.

We East, and its certain sections. as in the divine discourse (38:1-42:5) from the whirl wind, rise to the height of the sublimity. The content of the book also fits the designation, "Poetry of oration", in that it appears more dramatic than melodic. The book of Ecclesiastes shows that least poetic connections in its overall form. Longer poetic passages include the "time to" poem of 3:1-9 and collections of Proverbs in chapters 7,10 and 11.

In the Apocrypha and Pseudepigraph contains good amount of poetic literature with the display of several poetic forms. Ecclesiasticus or Ben Sirach belongs to the wisdom literature. This book has proverbs and wise sayings often expanded into innovative "essays" full of keen observation, shrewd insight, and fervent piety, wisdom of Solomon reflects the influence of Greek Philosophy, especially Stoicism. The historical book of I Maccabees includes several laments (2:8-12, 3:45) and eulogies (3:3-9:14, 6-15). The didactic romance of Tobit concludes with prayer of adoration (13:1-18) and that of Judith with a hymn of thanksgiving (16:2-17).

In Pseudepigraphical literature, the narrative of Jubilees is broken here and there by poetic sections. (eg 12:3-5,18-20,20:6-10;22:11-23) most of it belonging to the literature of blessing, similarly the Testaments of the twelve patriarchs (Testament of Simeon 2:1-4: Levi 4:1-6, Joseph 1:2-2:7) where, the poetic portions appear at the beginning of the Patriarchs. The Apocalypse of Enoch contains large sections of poetry, as in the opening and closing chapters, much of the parables (chaps. 36-71) and the miscellaneous materials of 92:1-100:9 IV Ezra, Syriac and Apocalypse of Baruch has poetic material of high order. The Psalms of Solomon of thanksgiving (Hodayoth) and in the manual of discipline, the poetry is moving.

### 2. Main Characteristics of the Hebrew Poetry

According to Fitzgerald poetry is "speech organized in measured lines". Poetry plays a very significant role in the Hebrew thought and world, because the Hebrews are music loving people. Several terms are used for the poetic compositions such as Sir (song) Mizmor (Psalm), mashal (Proverb) etc. In the early stages, there was a type of Hebrew poetry perhaps is told by the professional story tellers. For example, the story of Ruth could have been told in the country side (cf. also II Samuel 14:1-20 & 20:16-22). But in general it is very difficult to trace back the traditions of oral Hebrew poetry. But oral poetry may have some: (i) *themes* Judg. 5:1f mustering an army, (ii) *formula*: Isa 42:10 "sing unto the Lord new song," (iii) *adding style*: (Parataxis), here the poet feature of Hebrew oral poetry is sound pattern, archaisms, repetitions, word pair etc.

Along with the main characteristic feature of the Hebrew poetry, we will consider the related matters like parallelism, literary and poetic devices and types of Hebrew poetry.

### (A) Characteristics of Hebrew Poetry

1. Vocabulary: Some words occur exclusively for poetry:
   (a) Verbs: e.g.: man (enos in poetry) and (is in prose); way (oram in poetry) and (derek in prose); see (haza in poetry) and (ra'a in prose).
   (b) Prepositions: eg 'to' (in poetry) and (el in prose); upon (ale in poetry) and (al in prose); from (min in poetry) and (min in prose).
2. Grammar: In poetry definite article, waw consecutive, relative pronoun, the accusative sign (of definite object) are omitted for the sake of rhythm.
3. Sound: In the poetic forms the pronunciation is very important.

. Accordingly, we can see several categories:

   (a) Assonance: Means vowel repetition e.g.: Jer. 49:1 here "A" class vowel is repeated (and his people love in its cities) other references are Jer. 49:8 (E), Ps. 113:8 (I) Lam. 4:15 (u) also a complex vowel a-a-I pattern occurs twice in Job 9:16.
   (b) Alliteration: This means consonant repetition e.g.: Ps 147:13b (bless you people (sons) within you. We cf. in Isa 24:6; Hosea 5:14b-15a and (i) (S) in Ps. 122:5,6; 127:1; 137:3,8 etc. the function

of alliteration is to bind together the components of line, strophe, stanza and poem. It helps memorization in Hebrew oral poetry.

(c) Rhyme: Here two words sound like same. e.g. Isa 33:22 (Yahweh shapatanu and Yahweh malaknu).

(d) Word Play (Pun): Words have double meaning are used two kinds of word play.

i) Homonymy identical in sound but different in meaning e.g.: Amos 8:2 (Qayis: "basket of summer fruit" and Qes end).

ii) Polysemy: Same word is used with several meanings (sh) means: to do, to make, to produce etc.

(e) Meter: a form of rhythm, cannot be measured scientifically but can be distinguished linguistically. There are three theories in this regard. (i) the stress (accentual) theory: 3 stress (Ps 142:2a), 2 stresses or accents (Isa. 21:5) there are also combinations of 3 + 4 (Deut. 32:7a), 4 +3 (Job 3:20), 3+2 (Qinah meter inter used in Lamentations) (iv) Syllable counting and (iii) letter counting.

***(B) Parallelism:*** This nomenclature was first applied to Hebrew poetry by Bishop Lowth. It is so pervasive as to reflect virtually a mode of thought, borrowed from the AWA literary culture but elaborated with consummate artistry. In this technique the biblical line consists of two balanced colas. The balances between them can be material, syntactic, morphological, Phonic, semantic etc. e.g.: Prov. 15:32. Each colon here has four words, the lines have syntactic balance with each sentence following the pattern: participial subject + object + Participial Predicate + object. This being the general description, there are different kinds of Parallelism.

(a) Synonymous Parallelism: is one where the second line is the restatement of the first line e.g.: Ps 36:5 "thy loving kindness reaches the heavens; thy faithfulness reaches to the clouds"

(b) Antithetical Parallelism: The second line contrasts the first line e.g.: Prov: 10:1; A wise son gladdens his father but a foolish son grieves his mother".

(c) Synthetic Parallelism: The second line complements first or second line amplifies the first e.g.: Ps 19:8ff. "the precepts of Yahweh are right rejoicing the heart; the commandments of Yahweh are pure enlightening the eyes."

(d) Inverted Parallelism: (introverted Parallelism). In this the hemi-stichs (half lines) of the Parallel members are chaistically arranged e.g.: Prov, 13:24 "He who spares the rod hates his son; But he who loves him careful (diligent) to discipline him.

Spares Rod — Hates Son
Loves Him — Disciplines Him

(e) Climactic Parallelism: the heightening of the effect in the second or third line is noticed. e.g.: Ps. 55:12,13. (i) "If an enemy were insulting me, I could endure it: (ii) If a foe were raising himself against me, I could hide from him: (iii) But it is you, a man like myself, my companion..."

(f) Gender - Matched Parallelism: Here noun and verb are seen matching. e.g.: Jer. 46:12: "The Nations (Masc.) have heard your cry (Masc.) and the earth (fem.) is filled by your shout (fem.)."

(g) Inverted Gender - Matched Parallelism: e.g.: Isa 6:21 (Mas - Fem and Masc-Fem).

(h) Chaistic Gender- Matched Parallelism: Ps: 37:30 Mas-Mas; Fem-Fem.

(i) Number Parallelism: Since no number has synonym, the corresponding component is provided by increasing the value by one. e.g.: Job 5:19 from six calamities he will rescue you, in seven no harm will befall you" (other e.g.: Amos 1:3).

(j) Staircase Parallelism: (or step parallelism), that which proceeds in steps e.g.: Judg. 4:18: "Turn aside o Sir; turn aside towards me" (can also be termed as inclusion a formula to be used to open and close a sentence- e.g.: Eccl: 1:2, 12:8.

### *(C) Literary and Poetic Devices*

(a) Repetition:
  (i) initial repetition: "who has ascended to heaven" (Prov. 30:4)
  (ii) End repetition: "sun raises and sun goes down" (Eccl. 1:5a)
  (iii) Immediate repetition: "Away, Away, Away…" (Lam 4:15)

(b) Envelope figure: (lnclusio): that which encloses beginning and ending. e.g.: Ps.103: Bless the Lord my soul...Bless the Lord my soul.

(c) Ellipsis - The omission of the particle, word or word groups. For e.g.: Hosea 5:8 "Blow the trumpet in Gilead, the horn in Ramah."

(d) Oxymoron: It is yoking together of two expressions which are semantically incompatible e.g.: Jer. 22:19. "they will give him a (Jehoiakim) a donkeys funeral" (but donkey will never have a funeral).

(e) Merismus: The expression of totality in abbreviated forms. e.g.: Body and soul; heaven and earth; alpha and omega (Isa 10:8, Gen. 1:2 Tohu wa bohu - formless and void.

(f) Hendiadys: An expression of one single (complex) concept by using two separate words. e.g., Gen 1:2 “formless and viod” (Jer. 3:2).

(g) Double - duty modifier: This is also called “two - way middle” and one of the most subtle and skilled literary devices used. The device creates an interpreting and fluid entity in which phrases will go both with the sentence before and after with no break in the movement of thought, e.g.: Ps. 86:12: “I will thank you, my lord, my God, with all my heart: I will indeed glorify your name of eternal,”

***(D) Types of Hebrew Poetry:*** The categories of Hebrew Poetry are based on themes and literary contexts. We shall define and deal with them later in appropriate places. However, there are certain types of Hebrew Poetry fall under the broad categories follows:

***(i) Cultic Poetry:*** The division named “cultic Poetry:” encompasses so many forms and contests. me mostly find the material under following categories viz: early cultic use, Solomonic temple period, second temple period and later use not connected with temple liturgy. The early cultic uses include materials developed during the tribal period, with simplistic rituals involving individuals and groups within the extended family. This accounts for the etiology, vengeance songs, curses and blessings, various naming rituals, some legal material, explanations of the divine name, battle crisis, pronouncements of tribal status, and perhaps early songs of thanks, lament and salvation history. The monarchy produced earlier material of the Psalter with new emphases on temple ritual kingship and more liturgical and legal forms. The second temple are produced and final form of most cultic poetry as it appears in the Hebrew Bible. Legal materials, cultic disputations, salvation history hymns, laments, wisdom Psalms, Zion songs and Torah hymns were preserved or developed during or shortly after the Babylonian exile (587-539 BCE). Later non-liturgical use refers to a few forms, e.g., individual laments, naming ceremonies, and songs of trust in connection with the priestly office and the festival calendar.

***(ii) Prophetic Poetry:*** Prophetic poetry displays a broad range of settings and styles as well. All those settings and styles relate to the urgent divine message charged to the prophets. Prophetic poetry like cultic poetry, presents different faces at different stages in oracles to condemn or command the leadership of key figures. These oracles appear as shorter forms of the standard types later prophetic oracles. These display interests common to the kingship psalms. The bulk, of prophetic poetry originates in Israel’s monarchical history. Historical situations forged oracles which fit those situations for e.g., oracles of hope or lament). A small amount of prophetic poetry approaches history from a radically different perspective: apocalyptic materials places judgement and salvation on the fringe of history. These oracles offer a hope for final resolution merging from times of absolute national frustration and disillusionment. All oracles of hope bear similarities to later apocalyptic themes, but without the special apocalyptic view of history. Poetics. such as allegories of Ezekiel furnishes the fodder for apocalyptic prophets, who employ strongly symbolic images.

***(iii) Love Poetry:*** The Songs of Songs represents the only pure love poetry of the Hebrew Bible. Single units related to love poetry occur in Isaiah 5:1-7 and Jeremiah 2:1-3, Psalms 45, a wedding song, shares a few of the features of the Song of Songs.

***(iv) Wisdom Poetry:*** The Proverbial form dominates the wisdom materials in terms of its frequency. Furthermore, it occurs in all books of the wisdom canon and in many non-wisdom books. In contrast, the poetic dialogues of Job present a relatively unique category within the canon. Each of the speeches in Job forms a composition in its own right. The debate style appears more dramatic than did act ZAPHON canoes the need of the wisdom proponents to address theological questions with lengthily discussions. By comparison the diatribes of Qoheleth form briefer units, show more prosaic style and present settled conclusions rather than live questions.

***Conclusion:*** We noted in this chapter that Hebrew poetry is an interesting phenomena and by and large most sections in the Hebrew Bible are poetic sections with variety of poetic devices employed. Moreover, we noted marked difference between the poetic and prosaic sections in terms of their stylistic features. It is clear that wider types of cultic, love, wisdom and prophetic poetry in the Hebrew poetry is influenced from the ancient West Asian poetic categories although Israelites maintained their distinct marks.

Chapter 2

# Extent and Characteristics of Hebrew Wisdom

### *A Survey of Main Wisdom Sections in the Bible*

The principal collections of wisdom literaturc are found in the books of Job, Proverbs and Ecclesiastes and several other wisdom passages scattered in the both Hebrew canon and outside of canon. The three basic wisdom books (we shall study on them in detail at a later point in our course) express concern for wisdom as the exercise of mind as a religious pursuit. They each describe as wisdom as:

(a) the ability to live well, (b) Vocational or practical skill and (c) Ultimate concepts.

Wisdom themes, vocabulary and concerns are not only limited to the above mentioned three books, rather they appear scattered throughout the bible. In the Pentateuch wisdom concerns predominate only in the story of Joseph (Gen. 37-50) and in the book of Deuteronomy. Joseph's wisdom is considered as pure gift from god (see Gen. 41:38-39). His sojourn in Egypt, his ability to interpret dreams, and his ability to save Egypt from the famine are all attributed to divine intervention. Joseph possessed the "spirit of God" (Gen. 41:38) and introduced himself to his brothers as one who feared God (Gen. 42:18). Later "Fear of the Lord" serves as important theological principle of the wisdom tradition, especially stamped clearly in the book of Proverbs. Deuteronomy blends wisdom forms and terminology with prophetic forms and terminology to support the view that prosperity is linked to obedience. The Shema (6:4-5) carries the force of blessing or curse dependent upon the response of the laws it assumes. Passages such as 11:8-17 threaten disaster or blessing dependent on behavior. Proverbs promises similar threat or blessing to the wicked or righteous, as illustrated in Prov. 2:31-33.

In the former prophets we do come across several pieces of wisdom texts. Joshua reviews Israel's history in 23:14-16 in terms of punishment or reward based on obedience. Solomon gained his unrivaled wisdom in response to God's offer to grant one request (I Kings 3:5-14: II Chron. 1:7-12). Solomon's wisdom includes three specific aspects.

(a) Skill to rule with distinction.
(b) Skill to perform as a judge in deciding right and wrong;
(c) Preconscious depth and depth of intelligence, particularly associated with the natural order.

The later prophets also contribute to the understanding of wisdom to a certain extent. Isaiah (especially 1-39 chapters) seems most actually aware of wisdom traditions. Wisdom serves as the subject of several direct statements (e.g., Isa 19:11-15; 28:23-29; 40:13-14), the same is true of Jeremiah (8:8-9; 9:12 & 23). Ezekiel employs wisdom forms to convey the prophetic message (Ezek 16:44 & 18:2, open with introductions as mesalim, Proverbs). Prophet Amos presents series of historical questions in 3:3-8, similar to those occurring in Prov. 6:27-28 and elsewhere. Habakkuk deals with the theodicy questions at length. Theodicy explains apparent injustices in a world controlled by God.

Psalms associate wisdom with fidelity to the Torah (19 & 119). Depictions of the righteous and the wicked abound (Ps. 1, for instance). Like Deuteronomy, Psalms make use of wisdom themes to support a retributive theology. This viewpoint consistently defends God's just compensation for the goodness or wickedness practiced by each individual. Psalm 73 raises the theodicy issue, a view of divine compensation setting issue; "Those who are far from you Perish" (v. 27). Job and Ecclesiastes contain challenges to this view.

The two books of Deutero-Canon viz: Sirach and Wisdom of Solomon contain several Wisdom genres. Sirach innovates by linking wisdom with Torah and with cultic ritual in a way unparalleled in the Hebrew canon. In Deuteronomy, where obedience shows wisdom, the focus centers upon the response to God's election: Wisdom grew out of relationship with the deity. Sirach goes well beyond this by practically equating Torah and wisdom. A hymn praises wisdom: "All this (wisdom) is the book of the convenient of the highest God, the law which Moses commanded us" (24:23). Sirach places emphases on the Torah as an end itself.

The Wisdom of Solomon presents further departure from Israel's oldest wisdom tradition, 6:1-11 is addressed to rulers, though it is meant for larger audience. The book stresses the sovereignty of God (Yahweh) in contrast to Greek rational religion. The book at times equates wisdom with god's personnel transcendence. His work in (a) creation (b) the history of Israel and (c) the future of the world serve as illustrations of his transcendence. This book acts as vehicle for a larger theological message to the believing community, one of hope and encouragement grounded in the nature of god. Wisdom becomes a tool beneficial for the defense of faith in Israel's God, rather than for guidance in daily affairs.

### *Characteristic Features of the Hebrew Wisdom in General*

Interpreters almost agree on the general characteristics of biblical / Hebrew wisdom, based on the following themes: (a) the doctrine of divine reward for good or evil conduct (b) the choice of living responsibly or recklessly, (c) creation and (d) citizenship. The consensus also involves the use of the form known as "Proverb" in all wisdom books. In style as well as content, wisdom focuses on the ins and outs of daily living - business, love and marriage, morals, child rearing and so forth. Wide agreement exists on such basic concerns.

As the definition grows narrower, however each specialist limits the field of wisdom because each scholar assigns priority to different materials in the canon. A preference for Ecclesiastes leads to a more speculative Quasi - philosophical description. An opposing perspective based on Proverbs highlights a practical focus including a utilitarianism consistent with the theology of the Deuteronomist.

Segments of Hosea, Amos, Isaiah and Jeremiah exhibit numerous wisdom themes and forms. The narratives relating to Joseph and the court history of David also shows traits common to Israel's wisdom. All these texts support the definition and discussion of wisdom but are not "wisdom literature" in the full sense.

Israel's wisdom presented in Proverbs, Job and Ecclesiastes concerns informed observations regarding life and its challenges, rather than formal instruction by scribes or others. Hebrew wisdom encourages readers not to study, but to practice discretion. This leads to equating wisdom with righteousness and with religiosity. In distinction from its neighbors Israel's religious literature: (a) granted less priority to the privileged class, (b) remembered familial obligations in connection with its tribal roots, and (c) understood itself in terms of Yahweh's demands.

The question, for what audience was wisdom intended? cannot be answered exclusively, but wisdom is for the following groups; wisdom was preserved for the upper class (a general audience), royalty and governmental leaders, judges, business professionals, wisdom professionals, and children in a family setting.

### *Definition and Historical Sketch of Wisdom*

The word wisdom comes from Greek word Sophia and hokma in Hebrew, used to mean various skills of human beings. These root words mean several things in specific:

- (i) Skill in war (Isa: 10:13); skill in the technical work (Exod. 20:3, 31:6);
- (ii) Wisdom in administration (Deut. 34:9; Isa 29:14).
- (iii) It also means shrewdness (II Sam; 20:22, Isa 47:10, Dan I:4,17,20), and.
- (iv) Wisdom is essential and religious: wisdom as a divine attribute, god's wisdom is in the skies (Job 38:36), by wisdom god formed the earth (Prov. 3:19) wisdom is with god, but a secret (Job 12:13). God alone knows it (Job 28:23); god gives it (Prov.2:6), God shows its secrets (Job 11:6). wisdom can be defined very broadly as follows:

Wisdom is the ability to "cope" with everyday life; wisdom is quest for understanding (self-understanding) and for the mastery of the world. Wisdom asks for what is good for the people, believes that all the essential; answers can be learned in experience pregnant with signs about reality itself. Wisdom is that one God embedded truth within all reality. The human responsibility is to search for that insight and then to learn to live in harmony with the cosmos.

Israel's wisdom teachers were first and foremost students of the universe. They studied Yahweh's creation to determine order and command human conduct which would sustain that order socially and cosmologically. Based on the overall frame work of wisdom the following are the principle goals of the wisdom thinker:

- (a) to reduce broad truth to a simple statement or image.
- (b) to establish priorities that distinguish the wise, and so, to define wisdom.
- (c) to identify and discuss key philosophical questions or Problematic issues.
- (d) to persuade the foolish and the ignorant to search for life's truths and in other ways pursue conscientious living:
- (e) to mark the impasses (God's sovereignty, mysteries of nature, etc.).
- (f) to share proven insights on practical matters.
- (g) to warn against, excesses and foster temperance (e.g. alcohol, food, sexual, conduct, anger)
- (h) to define virtue and vice.

(i) to teach joje de vivre (French for "joy in living")

(j) to extol wisdom as the greatest good.

One overreaching concern is wisdom is its close association with the phrase "the fear of the Lord" (Prov. 1:7; 9:10.15:33; Job 28:28 et.al.). Typically, the statement assumes the form "the fear of the Lord is beginning of wisdom." This means three things in particular in the context of wisdom: *First* this statement expresses the positive claim: one who has reverence of God already possess a chief part of wisdom, one who recognizes the obligation owed to God displays a recognizable advantage over those who wish to be wise and have not made the same recognition. It represents an extremely significant head start. *Second* the phrase probably addresses the hearer's life style. One who lives honestly, justly, and relevantly exercise the fear of the Lord. This effectively identifies the fear of the lord with wisdom. After all, to live in such way not only shows regard for God, but also shows the ability to make good choices. Such a discretion serves as the basic component of wisdom. *Third* the phrase reminds the reader that wisdom's field of interest was showed in mystery like the name and character of Yahweh himself. If wisdom resides in the fear of Yahweh (translated "Lord"); then it remains in some exercise wisdom, but its origins lie with the creator.

Wisdom is most often explained in terms of personified wisdom. In this regard two things are to be stated. *First*, Wisdom is hypostasis, wisdom as the product of Yahweh's inspiration alone. Later in Israel's history, wisdom finds its definition in the personality of the deity. This view, known as hypostasis occurs in fully-developed form only in the wisdom of Solomon (see chaps 69). *Second*, Wisdom is an attribute of God. (Prov. 8 & Sirach 1& 24 chaps). The chief features of personified wisdom, are as follows: Wisdom is:

(a) installed and appointed by God (Prov. 8:23).

(b) begotten by God before the world was created (Prov. 8:22).

(c) Master of works whose plan for creation studied and approved by Yahweh as Creator (Prov. 8:27).

(d) Wisdom reveals the way of life and righteousness to human (Prov. 8:34).

(e) contrast with folly (Prov. 9:13-18).

(f) It is creature not creator (wisdom is equated with Torah: Deut. 4:4-7).

In form, wisdom is proverbial sentence, instruction, debate etc. in theme, wisdom instructs about mastering of human life, gropings after life's secrets with regard to innocent suffering, grappling with finitude and quest concealed in the created order and magnified in the dame/lady wisdom. When marriage between form and content exists the result is wisdom literature. Wisdom is the reasoned search for specific ways to assure wellbeing and implementation of these discoveries in daily living.

Origin of Wisdom: Judaism considered wisdom as a divine origin (Job 32:8). Wisdom is neither with the great nor with the old but from God (Ps. 105:22) (Isa 11:2 "and the spirit of the Lord shall rest upon him, the spirit of wisdom and understanding"), wisdom is divine. It derives from, God whose gift it is and at the same time the essence lies in the knowledge of his ways. (Hosea 4:6 and in obedience to his Torah Deut. 4:6). In Jewish view all wisdom comes from God (Sirach 1:10) and he will not bestow it on a malicious soul (wisdom of Solomon, 1:4). True wisdom then is high morality and wise living in right living.

N. K. Gottwald gives three proposals about the identity and setting of wisdom and wise.

***First*:** The wise were parents in families or elders and counsellors in clans and tribes.

***Second*:** They were government officials, scribes and possibly priests who kept the record of the state counselled kings and trained future political leaders.

***Third*:** They were non priestly authorities in the collected and venerated law of Moses who interpreted its meaning and present application and who passed on their skills in legal scribal schools.

According to an older view, the origin of wisdom literature is seen in terms of the activities of the wise at the Jerusalem court. But the recent studies pushed the questions of origin further back into a period when law and wisdom were still undifferentiated (R. E. Murphy, "Wisdom theme & Hypotheses" in Israel's Wisdom 1978, P.378f). Obviously Israel did not wait until Solomon to have its share of experiential wisdom.

Hebrew Wisdom: Historical sketch: Based on the analysis of Norman K. Gottwa1d the following are the brief comments and observations made on the historical sketch on Hebrew Wisdom.

***(a) Folk Wisdom:*** *(Pre-Monarchy)* Folk sayings were brief and pointed comments on human behavior and recurrent situations, to show absurdity and impossibility. In it the use of metaphors and comparisons and sometimes historical questions were made. Evidence for folk wisdom can be traced back to pre-monarchial times. e.g. Gen. 10:9 "As the saying is...", II Sam 20:18, Riddle and fable (Judges 14:10-18) and also Judges 9:7-15 etc. Even during monarchy Solomon's solving problems as in the case of riddles, put forth by the Queen Sheba is a type of folk wisdom. The use of proverbs of consequence, and proverbs of analogy by the classical prophets presupposes the popularity of folk wisdom common among the hearers (Amos 3:3-6, 8; Isa 10:15; Hosea 4:9; Jer. 13:23).

***(b) Monarchy:*** The reign of David and Solomon of about eighty years in the most natural explanation of the beginnings of a consecutive literary narratives of Israel's past. The wisdom writing coming from this period clearly reflects an overtone and flavor of Egyptian wisdom. For instance, Proverbs chapters 10-29 are found more similar to Egyptian instruction. The court scribes under David and Solomon (II Sam 8:17; 20:25) had Egyptian names. After court of Solomon under his patronage a court - wisdom school developed, which shows a clear orientation towards Egyptian wisdom. Solomon's wisdom and interest on nature wisdom reflects Egyptian Onomastica.

A renewed movement of wisdom during the period of monarchy took place under the reign of Hezekiah (715-687 BCE) who bought together the historical and religious writings of North and South, including wisdom materials. For e.g. in II Chronicles chapters 29-32, there is a starting of national revival with Solomon as his model. Isaiah witness to the fact that: the ruling circles of Jerusalem were under strong influence of Egyptians both politically and culturally. Isaiah condemns these self-styled "wiseman" of the court (Isa. 19:1-15; 20:1-6, 30:17, 31:1-3), Isaiah himself acts as wisdom prophet (Isa 28:23-29). Amos question and answer formula (chps 1 & 2 and 7:1-6, 8:2) also Hosea (2:21-23) are few examples of the wisdom influence at this point of time.

***(c) Judean Exile in Babylon:*** During the Babylonian exilic time, the concerns of didactic teachings of wisdom is shifted to scribal concerns. Sufferings and hopeless situations in the book of Job seeks to question the traditional Deuteronomistic view of wisdom movements of retribution. Jeremiah also spoke and raised questions like Job on several occasions (Jer. 20:14-18; Job 3:3; Jer. 12:1-2; Job 21:7ff; Jer. 20-7f; Job 19:1-12 etc.). However, Jeremiah did not enclose Job's doubt on the essential justice of God. The basic doctrine of Job as developed from this period is as follows: The almighty creator God has his mysterious wisdom as in the creation and on the contrast the man's impotency and frailty are depicted.

***(d) Persian Period:*** After 586 BCE intellectual and literary activities began to flourish in Palestine. The books of Ezra-Nehemiah had several points of proof for growing literary and intellectual activities in the post-exilic community (Neh. 8:7-9, Reading of the Law). Groups of scribes began to be developed who began to appear as professional students and authority on the law of Moses. They played a vital role in the further development of wisdom movement.

The production of wisdom work during this period was free from the concerns of the cultic elements of the Mosaic Law. Now a new emphasis began regarding the incorporation of religious aspect in the wisdom teachings. For instance, Proverbs 10:1-22:16 is concerned with the teachings of how to win favor from god and human beings. The first principle of knowledge is to hold the Lord in awe. The fools despise wisdom and instruction (Prov. 1:7). At this time theological cosmology and anthropology emerged very clearly as found in two poems in the book of Proverbs (1:20-23, 8:1-36). Here in these poems the personified wisdom affirms her nature of creative power coming from God and serving as a link between God and human beings. Other instances of the wisdom thought developed during this period are as follows; In the book of Job, Ultimate wisdom is divine secret (Job 11:5-9, 12:13, 28:12, 20, 23, etc). Sirach 23-27 chapters, Psalms 119:7-14 etc. Ecclesiastes, the book is associated to wisdom school (12:9). In this book we find a battle between revelation theology and rationalism within wisdom movement itself.

***(e) Hellenistic Age:*** Greek influence on Hebrew wisdom was at its peak during this time. Greek translations and compositions began to appear during this period. The book of Sirach, originally composed in Aramaic & Hebrew was later translated into Greek. Supplementary material was added to Esdars, Esther and Daniel. The book of Sirach for instance gave a particular emphasis on prayerful life, study of the law, experience of life concerning good and evil. Romantic fictions were composed about Judith, Tobit, Baruch, the letter of Jeremiah, Prayer of Manasseh, Esther and Daniel-in the form of "religious instructions" addressed to the wider public. The Hellenistic influence was seen tremendously in all these literatures mentioned above in Sirach 11:26-27 for e.g., the Jewish idea of immortality and offspring is influenced by Hellenistic thought i.e. No life after death is the dominant idea here in this passage.

The following chart (adapted from N. K. Gottwald, The Hebrew Bible P. 569) clearly gives an indication of the Institutional settings of Israelite wisdom during various periods of her history.

Time Dimension

| Intuitional Dimension | Pre-monarchy | United Monarchy | Divided Monarchy | Exile Restoration |
|---|---|---|---|---|
| Family & tribe; Parents, elders | | "Clan Wisdom" | | |
| State: Governmental Scribes | None | | Royal Wisdom | Colonial government Scribes |
| Torah (Law) interpretation, application leagal scribes | None Low treated Tribal elders and by Stater appointed Judges (?) | | Deuteronomic Scribes | Completed Torah Scribes |

The sociological setting of wisdom: Understanding Hebrew wisdom requires placing its themes and vocabulary in a plausible social setting. The basic problem is however that the wisdom books themselves do not give us sample evidences confirm this fact. We shall explain few things in this regard.

***(a) Connections with Solomon:*** Scant evidence exists in Proverbs connecting only a few of the sayings within the court. Ecclesiastes includes more significant biographical statements (for e.g. 1:12 & 2:9) and mentions for kingship and royal settings (for eg. 4:13 & 9:13-15). The book of Proverbs begins "The Proverbs of Solomon son of David, king of Israel." Ecclesiastes opens with "The words of the teacher, the son of David, King in Jerusalem" I Kings 4:29-34 note that Solomon authored proverbs and songs, but mentions no book. The lack of evidence allows for a wide range of suggestions from the claim that Solomon's connection with wisdom was "Royal Propaganda" (Glendon E. Bryce, The Legacy of wisdom: Lewisburg: Bucknell University Press, 1979, p. 170) to the assertion that "it is sociologically probable that Solomon was a patron of wisdom.

***(b) International Influences:*** Wisdom forms may have entered Israel by the way of Canaanite culture at large. The nation and its professionals then accepted them as part of the common heritage shared with neighboring groups. More clearly wisdom in the Hebrew society is certainly influenced by the Egyptian wisdom. This is seen in particular in new ways. ***First*:** the theme of God as creator of heaven and earth had to be traced pf before 6th cent BCE It appears primarily in Job and in Deutero-Isaiah. Its influence is the form of "admonition" and Hymn to Aton (1350 BCE cf. Ps. 104). ***Second*:** A philosophical pessimism seems throughout the writings of the Egyptian sages, a sense of fragility and fertility of human beings is seen (life), a brief span of life is filled with misery followed by the darkness of death- especially clearly depicted in the books of Job and Ecclesiastics. ***Third*:** Ethical teachings of Egyptian Proverbs came to the book of Proverbs in the Old Testament.

***(c) Relation of Wisdom to Hebrew Society:*** Leo Perdue finds two paradigms on the relation of wisdom to Hebrew society at large. ***First*:** Order and conflict. The book of Ecclesiastics, with its encouragements to submit to God and king, followed the model of order, as did Proverbs, with its emphasis on righteousness and discipline. By contrast, the book of Job presented God's creative forces in struggle with nihilistic forces. Proverbs, Psalms, Sirach and the wisdom of Solomon endorse ideas of prosperity for the righteous and the punishment for the wicked. This represents the orthodox view of wisdom. Both of Job and Ecclesiastes during such common assumptions regarding the basis of divine reward and punishment and so question human capability to predict or induce God's favor. The critical question thus arises: Does wisdom teachings primarily enforce or challenge prevailing cultural - religious attitudes? Interpreters remain divided on the issue. Central to the question is the interpreters' choice of Proverbs or Job/Ecclesiastics as normative wisdom. The direct opposition of the claims (the righteous do/do not suffer: the wicked do/do not prosper) makes such divisions inevitable.

***Second*:** The perspective on the social setting of wisdom is analyzed in terms of ethics. Ecclesiastes shows little concern for the poor presented in Job. Rather than emerging compassion, Ecclesiastes suggests a few relatively rigid patterns for behavior in what approximates a "least resistance" philosophy. The book advises the reader to find the measure of enjoyment amid life's confusion, proverbs mixes concern for following rules and showing humane concern. Wisdom serves as a tool which could be used either to reinforce or challenge the consensus; depending on the perspective of the thinker and the situation of community.

R. N. Whybray in his article shows that no one has succeed in positioning the sages in any distinct social group except some general observations made on the social setting of wisdom as done above. Scholars used several phrases to refer to sages like "elite class", "intellectuals, "urban owners of landed estates", "countries" and "professional counselors or teachers". In addition, interpreters usually acknowledge an early period when wisdom's origin and transmission occurred within family units (see historical sketch on Hebrew wisdom) and a late epoch during which teachers administered their own private schools, with a possible intermediate stage associated with the royal court. Andre Lemaire, analyses the complex system of education during the monarchy embracing most cities in Israel and extending to many remote villages.

***Conclusion:*** The discussion in this chapter reveals that Hebrew wisdom has international character and many parallels can be found between ancient Israelite wisdom and Egyptian and Mesopotamian and Canaanite wisdom traditions. Moreover, wisdom in Israel has complex and long history with multiple strands within its social and theological settings.

Chapter 3

# Poetry in Ancient West Asia

***Introduction:*** The poetic forms of the Hebrew Bible come from the wider milleu of the Ancient West Asia. The review below on the ancient West Asian poetic texts and forms reveal the fact that none of Israel's poetry existed without parallels in companion cultures. In most cases Israel employed existing forms. In many cases, the Hebrews added unique styles and interests stemming from the unique theology and traditions.

***(1) Mesopotamia:*** In Mesopotamia, the Sumerian and old Babylonian type of poetry begins about the middle of the third millennium at the latest and continues until around 1600 BCE. The texts identified are almost exclusively sacral or religious, these are mostly hymns, penitential poems and laments.

The hymns can be assigned to four groups: Praise of Gods (including hymns in the first person, especially common from the mouth of goddess Ishtar); Praise of the king (mostly extravagant self-glorification) songs of praise to the god's with interpolated blessings and prayers for the kings; poems mad glorifying Sumerian temples. The penitential poems and laments-apart from the lament over the destruction of Sumerian cities and city-states represent for the most part of the public penitential liturgies connected with ceremonies of propitiation. They comprise a lament over sickness and suffering, at times a confession of sins, and then a request for healing and deliverance from the sins. In a wider sense, this category includes royal prayers as well as liturgical charms embodying individual requests, which begins with an address to the duty and a passage in praise of him, followed by the complaint, the request and words of thanksgiving or blessing. Furthermore, the cultic love song developed as literary type; only fragments of such songs are preserved; most of which are different or impossible to interpret. They seem to refer to love between gods or sacral marriage, praising the beauty and allure of the beloved or mourning his loss.

The Sumerians were the first to classify their songs, sometimes according to the instruments for which they are composed ("songs for the Lyre" i.e., songs of Praise; "songs for the Drum", i.e. "songs concerning the gods) as well as into such categories as "Long songs" and "Hero songs." The later period mentions several additional types such as songs sung with lifted hands", with conjuration's and prayers for deliverance from sickness and misfortune, and "songs of Appeasement" intended to placate angry deities.

There was also political poetry, including a poem probably commissioned by the Sumerian king Tukulti - Ninurta Concerning the relations between Assyria and Kassite Babylon during 14th & 13th cent. BCE a poem in the form of a hunting song glorifying the battle fought by an Assyrian king (perhaps Tiglath - Pileser I) against Murattash, and also a poem belittling Nabondius, the last king of Babylon.

Few examples are cited as follows: One Akkadian Psalm appeared in both the Akkadian and Sumerian languages. The psalm of penance dates to sometime before 1000 BCE, Perhaps as early as 1500. It compares to Ps. 6, 32, 38, 51, 102 and 143.

"Who is there who has not sinned against his god - who has constantly obeyed the commandments? Every man who lives is sinful. I, your, servant, have committed every kind of sin, indeed I served you, but untruthfulness, I spoke lies and thought little of my sins... I raised my hand and defiled what was untouchable, I went into the temple in a state of uncleanness...... I constantly committed shameful acts, aware and unaware, acted completely as I pleased, slipped back into wickedness....... though my transgressions are many - free me of my guilt! Though my misdeeds are seven let your heart be still! Though my sins are countless show me mercy and heal (me)! (My God), I am exhausted, hold my hand."

A Hymn to Bel (also known as Marduk) from Babylon appears much like the descriptive Praise of the psalms:

"Powerful master of the Igigi gods, exalted among the great Gods. Lord of the world, Kings of Gods, divine Marduk, who establishes the plan... who is in heaven, heaps up earth, who measures the water of the sea, cultivates the fields, who dwells in the temple Eudul; Lord of Babylon, exalted Marduk" (Translated by A Sachs, Temple program for the new year's festivals at Babylon", A N E T, pp. 331 - 38, quotation from p. 332 cited in Donald K. Berry.

***(2) Egypt*:** Not much of earlier poetry of Egypt has been preserved. Its character is for the most part in accessible to us, because its Phonetic pattern and rhythm were not recorded, although the poetry depended upon the internal structure and the precise modulation of the words employed. Originally, the Egyptian poets sought for each object of their experience a form of expression that would define its intrinsic nature and that this poetry gradually came to include the expression of ideas, emotions, and moods.

The most important literary type is the hymnal addressed to a deity or a king. The hymn addressed to a good device from the cult. The earliest examples of the hymns are in the form of litanies assigning to a particular deity at certain places, sacred precedents and cult objects, these consist therefore merely of lists. Gradually as in Mesopotamia, the poetry is adorned by a plethora of epithets. The invocations of the royal crowns are also connected with the cult and above all the morning song, with which the deity was greeted by morning worshipers in his temple, as was the king upon awakening in his palace. Certain hymns began to emerge which contain mythological narratives or passages of deep emotion These include the Hymns to Amon, which depicts the god as the creator of the world and all the animals, describing his glorious appearance and great mythological deeds. The hymns to the sun, especially the hymn of Amenhotep IV, should be counted among the most valuable poetic texts in Egyptian literature.

The royal hymn is closely related in form and context to the hymn to a god, because court wisdom demanded that the king be addressed with the hymn. Even the many decorative epithets are taken from the hymns to gods. During Ramesside period the hymns are addressed in glorifying the victories and deeds of the rulers, we also find glorification of the royal power in the form of self-Praise and dialogue between deity and king.

There were also laments and dirges; the lament prescribed for the mourning ritual of the Osiris cult provided a further opportunity for mythological narrative. In addition, there was poetry chanted or recited on the occasion of the banquets in the tomb. There were also series of work songs pertaining to various professions found. From the new kingdom there are numerous love songs, mostly forming parts of collections. These songs use in them in the description the numbers, names of flowers to introduce plays on words, pretend to be the speech of trees in a garden, or take as their leitmotif the birds and their capture in the reeds. The poet wants the description of outward circumstances to characterize the mood of the person experiencing the event.

We shall give certain examples as to see how the Egyptian poetic forms appear. Official Egyptian accounts of the defeats of enemies' bear relationships to the poetry of Nahum, Habakkuk and Obadiah. The "stela of Amenhotep III" (about 1350 BCE) includes these lines:

"Woe to the Libyans, they have eased to live in the good manner of roaming the field; In a single day their stand was halted, in a single year were the Tjehemu burned."

In another example of Egyptian love poetry, the hymns have its fine description, sometimes resembling the poetry in the Song of Songs as cited in Miriam Lichtheim:

"Beginning of the sayings of the great happiness. The one, the sister without peer, the handsomest of all! She looks like the rising morning star, At the start of the happy year. Shining bright, fair of skin, lovely the look of her eyes, sweet the speech of her lips, she has not a word too much. Upright neck', shining breast, Hair true lapis lazuli; Arms surpassing gold, Fingers like lotus buds. Heavy thighs narrow waist, her legs parade her beauty; with graceful step she treads the ground captures the heart by her movements. She causes all men's necks to turn about to see her; joy has he whom, He is like the first of men...seven days since I saw my sister, and sickness invaded me; I am a heavy in all my limbs, my body has forsaken me. When the physicians come to me. my heart rejects their remedies; the magicians are quite helpless; my sickness is not discerned. To tell me "she is here" would revive me! Her name would make me rise, her messenger's coming and going. That would revive my heart! my sister is better than all prescriptions, she does more for me than all medicines. Her coming to me is my amulet, "the sight of her make me well! when she opens her eyes my body is young, her speaking makes me strong; Embracing her expels my malady – seven-days since she went from me!"

***(3) Canaan*:** In Ugaritic texts the frequent occurrence of word pairs indicates an awareness of parallelism. Many of these pairs of words appear in Akkadian texts as well. The most important categories of Canaanite poetry are hymns, laments and songs to accompany sacrifice. The use of such songs is illustrated by the ritual for a day of propitiatory sacrifice occasioned by a political disaster; the ritual contains the complete text of the laments composed for the occasion.

Few Ugaritic love songs exist; one such text is quoted below which is parallel to the Songs of Songs 5:10-16.

"His head is wonderful. Dew is between his eyes of hostility speaks his leg (even I (his) horns which are upon (him). His head is descending from the heaven (s), (From the tent) of the bull. There is his mouth like two cloud(s)."

In another context of the Hittite popular poetry the so called soldiers song from an old Hittite text has been cited. We do have hymns and prayers, some of which may count as literary compositions; they are often distinguished for the sincerity and profundity of their thought. In one hymn to the sun-god a Babylonian can be clearly recognized.

***Conclusion:*** the poetic features in the ancient West Asian context reveals number of similar and parallel features with that of ancient Israelite prophecy, owing to the fact the latter has borrowed much from the former despite maintaining its distinct features. The basic forms of poetic devices are employed in both the contexts for the effective communication.

Chapter 4

# Wisdom in Ancient West Asia

***Introduction:*** Israel's wisdom did not develop in isolation from their ancient West Asian neighbors, nor did it originate within the nation Israel itself. The inclusion of major portions of the Instruction of Amenemopet in Proverbs 22:17, 24:34 demonstrates that Israel borrowed a portion of its proverbial Wisdom from Egypt. Mesopotamia also provides examples of the pattern for wisdom in the royal court. From the semi-nomadic and patriarchal groupings of Canaan and Mesopotamia came the familial instruction which plays such a prominent role in Proverbs and Ecclesiastes. From the later Greek culture, the deuterocanonical wisdom books, Sirach and especially the Wisdom of Solomon, gain Hellenistic viewpoints. We shall trace briefly the importance of ancient West Asian wisdom literature on the basis of certain important documents.

***(1) Mesopotamia*:** In Mesopotamia there is no expression analogous to the Hebrew, there came into being, however an extensive wisdom literature, which-although for the most part preserved in Akkadian recession goes back in large measure to Sumerian traditions. Most of the extent Sumerian literature consists of a large number of Proverb? Collections, for the part arranged as school texts and commonly arranged according to the sign with which each Proverb begins. Later texts discuss ethical questions and furnish practical suggestions for how to live in harmony with the universe and therefore successfully (these include the texts cited in chapter 4-5 of W. G. Lambert, Babylonian Wisdom Literature 1960. The teachings of Shuruppak, the counsels of wisdom. The counsels of a pessimists, Advice or a prince, Hymn to Ninurta, Shamash Hymn) or else examine the problems arising from this order of the universe, (these include the texts cited in W. G. Lambert, chapters 2-3: The poem of righteous suffer, The Babylonian

Theodicy, and perhaps also the Dialogue concerning pessimism) so that some have at times been looked upon as forerunners of the book of Job. In addition, the Mesopotamian fables, disputations, debates and other texts whose literary type is often difficult to determine are traditionally placed with wisdom literature.

In the Mesopotamian instructions, the counsels of wisdom text are preserved which contains instructions of a father to his son. It reads as follows:

"Do not talk with a tale bearer, do not consent with some ideal, let you lose your own work, let blasphemy be away from you Do not loiter where there is a dispute and they will involve you in it... Do not speak ill, speak only good..."

In the case of Proverbs in Mesopotamia, Proverbs with cause and effect with catch-word are expressed as follows:

"Yield not badly with nature then you will not face...... Do good and you will receive good."

In a category called scribal literature, Sumerian texts copied by school boys identified as pieces of wisdom taught scribal schools, contains comprehensive lists on animals, places, minerals etc., like Onomasticon.

In another Mesopotamian instruction called "The instruction of Shuruppak", the Akkadian version is given follows:

"Shuruppak (son of Uburtutu give instructions), To Utnapushtu (his son he gave instructions, saying), "My son, (I will give you instructions, take my instructions), Utnapushtu, (I will give you instructions) (Do not neglect) my instructions. (Do not disobey) the words [I have spoken to you]. (One should not buy an) ass who (brays [too much]) (One should not locate a cultivated land on road [Way]. [Do not...] your field. In your cultivated field [do not...) Do not harm the daughter of a free man, for the Courtyard will find out about it."

Around 1000 BCE, a document known as "Theodicy" Presented alternating speeches of a sufferer and his friend. The suffer maintains the gods are Punishing him for nothing, while the friend cautions that he is angering the deity and should be Patient and wait for ultimate rewards. The Text on the Babylonian Theodicy, few lines from it reads as follows:

"Suffer I O sage ...... come, let me tell you ...... May God who has abandoned me give help, ....

Obviously this literature on Theodicy resembles the book of Job. (So also "the Poem of Righteous suffer" – 1500-1200 BCE shows some affinities and with source differences from Job. Like Job, the sufferer embodies complete righteousness, endures extensive suffering, and describes his bodily suffering using common terms including loss of, appetite, dreams, and other features explicitly given in Job. Unlike Job, his suffering is more directly attributed to the wrath of the deity, with the less overt theodicy).

In Pessimistic literature, "the dialogue of pessimism between the master and servant" resembles similar to the ideas found in the book of Ecclesiastes i.e. all in vanity is the focal idea of this literature.

In several fables from Old Babylonian, Sumerian and Akkadian wisdom thought and insight is clearly identified. Animals, Plants, Minerals, Trees are the participants in this dialogue claiming their superiority, God comes and then decides the dispute (cf also Judges 9:7-12).

In Old Babylonian context perhaps the wise are the ones who expelled demons, spill in the cults. The technical word for this is Manticism (means the divine future).

This is of two kinds: (a) Induced Manticism: Usually referred to divination. Sometimes Omens occur naturally (earth quakes) uninduced Omens (like stones, flight birds, abnormal creatures). The most common inducement is however whisper a question in the ear of the goat and cut it, then its liver is examined and the interpretation begins. This Process is called Hepatoscopy. The person who has skill in this called b a r u. A person who wanted to learn this is expected to go to school to learn lots (In Israel; Urim & Thummim; epode. e.g. I Sam 23:6. Question and answer is Yes or No?) (b) Immediate Manticism: A Person getting a revelation from God without any means; thus it is termed just immediate. e.g.: Dreams. But, if one sleeps in the temple, then it is induced, it is incubating (to slept in a cube room in the temple).

***(2) Egypt:*** In Egypt the norm of conduct, which wisdom instruction is intended to secure, is described by the word m a' a t, which is best translated "Justice", rightness, Primal order, order of the universe." The goal of wisdom instruction is to prepare the way for this order, which derives from the deity and is valid for the entire world, by preserving knowledge of it, transmitting this knowledge, and applying it in a new situation. Without neglecting Personnel experience which also plays an important role in wisdom instruction, the wise of Egypt think of themselves as faithful transmitters of a righteousness that has held throughout the ages (cf. Isa 19:11- "a student of wise man and kings of by gone ages"). Since m a' a t is a changeless quantity and applies to every member of the social group in question equality and without alternation, human beings' deity is to accommodate and subject themselves to it. The ideal of a such person is the "silent person" or the "correctly silent person", who acts according to m a' a t, restrain themselves under all circumstances, holds back, and avoids all excitement in contrast to the "hot person", who are unrestrained and subject to their appetites. The outcome follows directly from human conduct: at times the success of an activity and its "inner truth" are viewed as unity; at times the rules of conduct are justified by reference to advantage or detriment; at times these rules are presented as expressions of divine will, with consequent reward or punishment.

Since the concept of m a' a t comprehends both the order of the cosmos and the order of human life, realms that are distinct in modem thought, we find two literary types of primary importance in wisdom literature; the scholarly lists of onomastica, which are probably influenced by the Sumerian lists, and the "teachings" or "instructions" of fixed form, (The Egyptian word also means "education", "instruction", and theological doctrine. The title regularly reads: "The beginning of the teaching that A composed for his son (pupil) B, seven of which are preserved whole or almost whole, five fragmentarily, and six or seven others only through mention of their titles (They include the following: Teaching of Imhotep, Teaching of Prince Djedefhor, teaching for Kagemni, Teaching for Ptahhotep, Teaching for King Merikare, Teaching for king Amenemhet, Teaching Cheti, son of Duauf, Teaching of Anii, Teaching of Amenemope, Teaching of Papyrus Insinger). In addition, there are few. documents, that may be termed meditations or disputations. (E. Otto),

"Weltans Chauliche and politische Tendenzschriften", in Handbuch der Orientalistik, I, 2 (1952), PP. 111-119, includes also the Admonitions of a sage, the Dialogue of one Tired of life with his soul, the Teaching for king Merikare, the Prophecies of king Merikare, the Prophecies of Nefer-rehu, the Laments of Cha - cheper - Re-seneb, the Laments of the peasant. The teaching for king Amenehet, Papyrus Harris I, and the, so called Demotic Chronicles).

We shall cite few examples from some of the texts mentioned above: "The opening lines of teaching for Kagemni" offer the following Proverb:

"The respectful man prospers, praised is the modest one, the tent is open to the silent, the seat of the Quiet is spacious. Do not chatter."

In the instruction of Amen-em-opet, first ten chapters are equal to Proverbs 22:7-23: 14 some of the lines are found as follows:

> "Guard thyself against robbing the oppressed and against over bearing of the disabled. Stretch not forth thy hand against the approach of an old man, Nor steal away the speech of the aged.... Do not carry off the land mark at the boundaries of the arable land, nor disturb the portion of the measuring cord: Be not greedy after a cubit of land, nor encroach upon the boundaries of a widow... Better is a measure that the God gives thee than Five Thousand (taken) illegally. They do not spend a day (in) the granary or barn; they make no Provisions for the beer - jar.... Be sincere in the presence

> of the common people, for one is safe in the hand of the God. God hates him who falsifies words; his great abomination is the contentions of belly."

In another Egyptian wisdom instruction of "Ptahhotep" several lines are similar to Proverbs both in form and content. Some of the lines are read as follows.

> "Do not be greedy in the division, do not covet more than you share; Do not be greedy toward your kin; The mild has a greater share than the harsh...Then he said to his son...justice is great, its appropriateness is lasting...speak when you are spoken to...laugh after your heart laughs... Do not remind a rich person of his past......"

In one scribal literature, the familiar one is called 'The Saltire on the trade' the lines read as follows:

"Behold there is nothing that surpasses writing...... writing is greater than any other office... even if you are young scribe you are respected...." (compare these lines with Sirach 38:24-39:1).

***(3) Canaanite Documents*:** Excavations at Ugarit (in ancient Syria) from 1929-1976 discovered numerous documents, including several didactic texts. Ugaritic Poetic texts employed parallel word pairs, some of which are identical to the parallel terms of Hebrew Poetry, at times, these parallels appear in the form of the biblical masal (Proverb). Ugaritic texts also contain challenges to traditional, orthodox teaching regarding suffering such as those present in the book of Job. Though the date of its origins can only be questioned, the tablets contain a story of a righteous suffer who survived the destruction of Ugaritic just after 1200 BCE Later Version exists with Babylonian, "The Poem of the Righteous Suffer", other Ugaritic wisdom texts present proverbed or pessimistic content.

Evidence for Wisdom among Israel's immediate neighbors comes from biblical references to wisdom in Edom, which bordered Israel on the south west; Perhaps Job's home land UZ (1:1) was Edom. But Obadiah and Jeremiah 49:7 indicate an important emphasis on wisdom in Edom, but no Edomite wisdom texts exist to confirm such an emphasis.

***(4) Greek Documents*:** Vocabulary also provides an example of the corollaries between Hebrew and Greek wisdom. Direct influence of Greek ideology on Hebrew wisdom material can only be maintained for two latest wisdom books; Sirach and the Wisdom of Solomon. Israel's wisdom, however, exercised strong influence on Greek wisdom documents, as indicated by the nearby identical semantic ranges of metis (Gk. Wisdom).

Greek literature contains numerous examples of philosophical reflections on good and evil like those formed in Job. Greek Stoicism and skepticism provided even more examples of pessimistic literature like Ecclesiastes. In Greek wisdom, however, the element of Personnel theology (the sovereign direction of the creator God) is replaced by specific systems of rational speculation. This makes comparisons difficult to draw. The wise among the Greeks did not engage in the production of sentences and completes like those found in Proverbs. At least such activity did not comprise a major portion of their activity. The books of Sirach and the Wisdom of Solomon are greater part influenced by Greek wisdom thought.

In other places there are some wisdom texts found, in ancient Wear Asia, for instance, the "Peoples of the east' in the reign of Safa in the northern part Transjordan (I kings 5:10).

Ezek 28:3,17 speaks in general terms of the Phoenicians, Ezek 27:8 of semer, referring probably to Sumra (north of Tripolis, not far from Arvad) and Zech. 9:2 of Sidon.

***Conclusion:*** On the basis of our foregoing discussion on the issues related to the wisdom in the ancient West Asia we now make the following concluding observations:

First, wisdom in general is international and universal in its character. Many parallels can be noted between ancient Israelite and other West Asian religions and at times the parallels are either exact or very close both in form and content.

Second, while in ancient West Asia, wisdom can be part of human effort along with its divine embodiment, in ancient Israel wisdom only emanates from God and God created it and thus no divine status is ascribed to it.

Third, as noted above in both the ancient Israelite context and in the Ancient West Asian context wisdom can bring order and justice in the lives of the community and in the nature.

## Chapter 5

# Literary Types of Psalms and their Traditions

***Introduction:*** The form critical study of Psalms and their tradition is most crucial study in order to understand the book of Psalms on the one hand and also poetic forms in a general sense. Before making an attempt to trace out different literary types of psalms and their traditions, we shall briefly trace out the contribution of some vital scholars in this regard.

***HISTORY OF RESEARCH:*** There are two approaches to the formation of the Hebrew Psalter. The first is considering the final form of the text and studying the work as a whole. The second, is treating the book as a collection of disparate elements and considering each unit individually. The second method has been emphasized especially during this century by Herman Gunkel, Sigmund Mowinckel, Hans Joachim Kraus and others, who focus on individual Psalms loosed from their moorings in the Psalter and rearranged according to criteria other than canonical order.

***(A) GUNKEL:*** Gunkel was skeptical of inherent canonical order in the Psalter. For him, the Psalter was a product of a long history of development, not the scheme of an editor. Thus he identified Gattungsforschung (different forms or literary types) in the psalms. In this way he was able to treat the individual Psalms as independent units, divorced from their immediate or larger context, and to find unity (and therefore meaning) in the definition of psalm genres and the relation of each genre to its proper cultural matrix. According to Gunkel a literary work must be Formgeschichtlich, i.e. according to the history of the literary forms to which it belongs. Hence the study of the Gattungen (literary forms) must come first, these consist of literary units which draw a common stock of words, formulas and images to express concepts and sentiments associated with one same situation in life (Sitz-im-Leben). Because religious experience is couched in conventional phaseology, content and form belong together.

The literary work had its origin in a particular setting, which was that of the community rather than the individual. For Gunkel, each Psalm had a specific function which was related to certain ceremonies in the temple cult. e.g. a Psalm of thanksgiving would accompany a sacrifice of thanksgiving. Since it was written to meet the needs of many, it reflected that which was typical of the many situations in which thanksgiving was offered.

However, Gunkel's method has imperfections and a certain arbitrariness especially in his attempt to trace the history of the types. Moreover, Gunkel's textual criticism of the Psalms has been questioned especially the arbitrariness of his emendations. According to A. Robert, Gunkel exaggerates the importance of extra biblical sources and neglects the comparative material of the Bible itself. A. Weiser advocates a partial revision as lament and thanks giving are closely related in the setting of the cult community. Despite all these pointed problems, the attempt made by Gunkel was an important starting point for others to pursue on it.

***(B) MOWINCKEL:*** Follows the process of fragmenting the Psalter like Gunkel, while delineating major collections within the Psalter he speculates on how, in what order and for what purpose they were written and brought together. Mowinckel's primary concern is to recognize the individual psalms within the frame work of his hypothetical. "Enthronement Festival", which be afford as the true and matrix of the Psalter. He does not search for the significance of an order as he thought that this was 'superfluous and even accidental!

Further, according to Mowinckel, "the great majority of the psalms do not simply derive, as matter of form history or literary history, from ancient cult poetry" 'they are' "real cult Psalms composed for and used in the actual service of the temple. private and more personal Psalm poetry first occurs in the late Jewish period. In the Psalter such psalms constitute a minority" (S. Mowinckel, The Psalms in Israel's Worship, vol. 1, 1961, P. 23). The non - cultic psalms according to Mowinckel were mostly the sapiential and historical psalms. Mowinckel believed that Gunkel, by his form - critical and type - critical methods, had proved beyond doubt that in Israel also the origin of psalm poetry is to be found in the public cult.

Mowinckel criticized Gunkel for failing to admit it is not always that form and context are intertwined. He felt that even an alien form could have been used as an effective means of expressing that context. Further, a psalm may consist of parts belonging to different form types. Hence the form-historical method has to be complemented by the cult-functional method and seen in the right cultic situation. However, Mowinckel's theory has flaws as it is usually very difficult to get a clear picture of the original liturgical set up. According to Sabourin, Mowinckel concludes too easily from vague allusions or hypothetical connections.

***(C) ARTHUR WEISER:*** Criticizes Mowinckel for depending too much on ancient West Asian parallels. Weiser took the task to reconstruct the Sitz im Leben (situation in life) from the Psalms itself. For his focal point is not on the new year festival (enthronement festival) as proposed by Mowinckel, rather it is the festival of "renewal and the Sinai covenant" as the focal point to unfold the literary traditions of psalms. For instance, Weiser examined Psalms 50 as an example for the covenant renewal festival.

***(D) HANS-JOACHIM KRAUS:*** Like Weiser, Kraus also supported the setting for the psalms as renewal festival but adds that it is the celebration on seventh year is crucial rather than every year. Kraus says that southern kingdom in the period of Judges has "festival of covenant renewal" but it was replaced by the "royal Zion festival" in the monarchical period, with God's choice of Zion and the Davidic line.

***(E) CLAUS WESTERMANN:*** Lament is the basic form of expression in the psalms and most of these psalms are derived responses to the lament. Lament psalm expresses the basic moves of faith in God, ranging from deep alienation to profound trust, confidence and gratitude. For Westermann, literary dynamism in the movement of the psalms that corresponds to and gives rise to the dynamic of faith that we know in the experience with God.

***(F) WALTER BRUEGGEMANN:*** Brueggemann in his ground breaking contribution and explanation on the Sitz-im-Leben of the psalms in terms of their performative and practical application. He proposes three categories of psalms of orientation, disorientation and new orientation—based on the flow of human life character—basically located either in the external experience of one of these sufferings or is movement from one to another—to correlate between the gains of critical study (especially Gunkel and Westermann) and the realities of human life (those who use the psalms in a life of prayer).

(i) Psalms of Orientation: Human life consists of in satisfied seasons of well-being that evoke gratitude for the constancy of blessing. These psalms in a variety of ways articulate the joy, delight, goodness, coherence, and reliability of God, God's creation, God's governing law. These psalms are created, transmitted, valued, and relied upon a community of faithful people. These psalms express a confident, serene settlement of faith issues. Some things are settled and beyond doubt, so that one does not live and believe in the midst of overwhelming anxiety. Such a happy settlement of life's issues occurs because God is known to be reliable and trustworthy. For instance, it is understood as the mind-set and worleview of those who enjoy a serene location of their lives characterized a sense of orderliness, goodness, and reliability of life. Creation psalms represent the same themes as pointed above. Psalm 104:27-28" "these all look to you, to give them food in due season. When you give to them, they gather it up; when you open your hand, they are filled with good things." Psalm 145: it affirms God's providential care, Psalms of ascent (127, 128, 131, 133) belong to similar category of psalms of orientation, reflecting domestic life that is in good order. They are the voice of a genuine gratitude and piety for rich blessings.

Psalms 1 and 40: teach clearly reliable retribution, in which evil is punished and good is rewarded Psalm 37 offers imperatives and prohibitions about how to maintain and enhance this order (undistributed, uncritical equilibrium). Songs of creation, wisdom, retribution, and blessing all function in this same context (reaffirmation and reconstruction of this good world), of good order and well-being.

(ii) Psalms of disorientation: the psalms of lament (individual and community) are always of entering linguistically into a new distressful situation in which the old orientation has collapsed. There are various shapes and nuances of distress in different psalms, suggesting that different ones are appropriate for use depending on how fully the subject has accepted and embraced dislocation and how much resistance or denial remain. Thus some psalms remember better times (Ps 42:4) back in period of orientation. There is a wish to return to that situation. The mood here is that loss of orientation is reversible and old orientation is retrievable. However, life consists of anguished reasons of hurt, alienation, suffering and death. These evoke rage, resentment, self-pity, and hatred. This has the following structure:

1. Plea: A complaint that God should correct a skewed situation.
   a) Address to God—speak about Yahweh, one who has a long history of trustful interaction.
   b) Complaint: to explain how desperate the situation is—may be sickness, isolation, imprisonment, or destruction, about death (imagery)—to invite Yahweh for an intervention, formative act, to turn the petitioner's problem into Yahweh's.
   c) Petition: on the basis of complaint the speaker makes a petition that makes God to act decisively.
   d) Motivations: the speaker is innocent so is entitled for help. The speaker is guilty but repent, and seeks forgiveness and restoration; calls God's goodness in earlier generation, which serves as a precedent for God's goodness now; speaker is valued by God as the one who praises if the speaker is permitted to die, the speaker will cease to praise, Yahweh will be at loss;

finally, speaker goes beyond self, and appeals to Yahweh to consider God's own power, prestige, and reputation.

e) Imprecation: this is the voice of resentment and vengeance that will not be satisfied until God works retaliation on those who have the wrong (Ps 109).

2. Praise: something has changed as a result of psalmist's plea thus a movement from plea to praise has occurred. Three features can be found in the praise:
   a) Assurance of being heard: Yahweh has heard the petition.
   b) Payment of vows
   c) Doxology and praise

For the above pattern the following psalms can be cited as examples: 13, 74, 79, 86, 137.

(iv) Psalms of Reorientation: these psalms reflect a quite new circumstances that speaks of newness (it is not the old revived); surprise (there was no ground in the disorientation to anticipate it), and gift (this is not done by the lamenter). For these reasons, this new circumstance evokes and requires a celebration, for reversals must be celebrated. Human life consists in terms of surprise when we are overwhelmed with the new gifts of God, when joy breaks through the despair. When there has been only darkness, there is light. These psalms affirm a spvereign God who puts humankind in a new situation. For example, Psal 30 where the following elements can be noted:

a) Praise (vv. 1-3)
b) General invitation to community yo join in the praise (vv 4-5)
c) Disorientation to new orientation (vv 6-10). Old orientation (v 6), disorientation (v. 7) and in vv. 8-9 the psalm narrates the whole career of of the relation to Yahweh from well-being (prosperity) to new life.
d) Conclusion (vv. 11-12) affirm in vv. 1-3 acknowledging and celebrating the decisive transforming actions of Yahweh: "you have turned, you have loosed, you have girded. Other examples belonging to reorientation psalms include 34, 40 and 138. 65, 66, 124,114, 29, 06, 47, 93, 99.

***(1) LITERARY TYPES OF PSALMS:*** In classifying the psalms into various literary types, the primary criteria are formal questions of literary style; the content of the psalm is utilized only when absolutely necessary. Some scholars speak of major categories such as Zion songs or songs of Yahweh's enthronement, but this approach wrongly places major emphasis on questions of content; both categories actually belong to the literary type of the hymn song. Basically these are The Praises of God (the hymns songs and songs of thanksgiving included comprehensively), Laments and Royal Psalms. In addition to these major types there are several other categories which we treat them under minor types. This classification is based on the proposals made by Gunkel and other form-critics on the Psalms, comprehensively put forward by A, Anderson in his two volume work on Psalms.

***(A) THE PRAISES OF GOD:*** These are, basically response of the worshippers or the cultic community to what God has done. There are three further sub types in this broad category:

***(a) Hymns of Descriptive Praise:*** These are basically the Praises of Yahweh for what Yahweh has done in nature and history. In these Hymns, Yahweh (God) is spoken to third person. It has three parts structure: Introduction (exhortation to Praise), main section (grounds for exhortation, often begins with the particle ki. means because/for), conclusion (re-echoes introductory formula, occasionally ends with prayer or wish). This category again has three distinct types:

(i) Praise of God in General e.g. Ps. 114, 136.

(ii) Praises celebrating kingship of Yahweh (also traditionally called enthronement Psalms, but recently disputed by the scholars). For e.g. Ps. 47, 93, 96-99. According to Sigmund Mowinckel, Ps. 95 & 100 are also put under this category, but not accepted by several other scholars.

(iii) Songs of Zion: (also called indirect praises of God) e.g. Ps. 48, 76, 84, 87, 122 (possibly Ps. 46 & 132). These are basically praises of God for temple or the Zion, the holy city of God. Here there is lack of hymnic introduction.

***(b) Declarative Praises of the Individual.*** (also termed as individual songs of thanksgiving) e.g. 9,10, 18, 32, 34, 92, 116, 118, 138.

It has three-part structure as follows:

(i) Introduction: Invocation of Yahweh's name with hymnic additions and declaration of intent is given at some places.

(ii) Main Section: It talks about the distress experienced (Ps. 9:3f) and the Proclamation of divine deliverance.

(iii) Concluding Section: (e.g. Ps. 9:19-20) contains very often an invitation to praise. On the whole in this category the cultic occasion way has been the sacrifice of thanksgiving.

***(c) Declarative Praises of the People:*** (also termed as national songs of thanksgiving). Classical example for this type is Psalm 124. Hermann

Gunkel includes the following Psalms in this category: 66:8-12; 67; 124; 129. These Psalms basically declare God's doing either for self or for nation.

***(B) LAMENTS:*** Almost one third of the Psalms belong to this category. These are responses of human beings in affliction. It has two parts:

(i) Introduction: invocation of Yahweh's name and call for help.

(ii) Main Section: It has number of elements, but the order varies.
- Description of distress (Ps. 5) or misfortune.
- Prayer and cry for help and deliverance.
- Motivation for appealing to Yahweh.
- Confession of sin or protestation of innocence (this type is found in the book of Job)
- Wishes and curses (Ps. 137)
- A vow to praise God.

It is to be noted that often lamentation changes from supplication to thanksgiving due to priestly oracle promising deliverance. J. Begrich gives the following order in the Psalms of lament i.e.

Supplication-Assurance-Thanksgiving.

(a) Laments of individual: Large portions of Psalms are found in this category. Most of these Psalms are distinguishable based on the content rather than on the basis of type, The Psalms in this category include: 3, 5, 6, 7, 17, 22, 25, 26, 27, 28, 35, 39, 41-43, 51, 54-57, 59, 61, 63, 64, 69, 71, 86, 88, 102, 109, 130, 140, 141, 143, Two further subtypes are recognized in this laments of individual on the basis of content;

(i) Prayers of unjustly accused person: e.g. 7, 17, 26, 35, 57, 69. These Psalms are probably recited by/for the accused person in the sanctuaries in order to obtain a favorable divine judgment.

(ii) Psalms of Penitence: Ps. 6, 32, 38, 51, 102, 130, 143.

(b) Laments of the Nation: These Psalms has the background of national disaster affecting the entire people or nation. A day of fasting prayer would then be held. Moreover, these Psalms may have been used on fixed days of prayers and penitence or as part of annual rituals cf. Zech. 7 (5$^{th}$ or 9$^{th}$ month celebration). Psalms belonging to this category are 60, 74, 79, 80, 85, 90, 124, 126, 137, (?), 144(?).

(c) Psalms of confidence: These are individual Psalms which emphasize certain aspects of lamentation. Though the context is confidence, still there contains a motif of lamentation, thus classified under the Psalms of laments. Ps: 125 is taken as an important example of this category which is a collective song of Trust.

***(C) Royal Psalms:*** Ps. 2, 18, 20, 21, 45, 72, 101, 110, 132 (sometimes 28, 61, 63 & 89 are also included). The royal Psalms that have been preserved are religious and cultic in nature and can be assigned to the various literary types already mention. They deserve separate discussion, however because they exhibit characteristic OT features. One portion of these songs, some of which probably belong originally to the ritual to the king's enthronement, takes as its point of departure hymnic praise of Yahweh's power, from which the subordinate power of the king derives. The oracle form plays a significant role here. Psalm 2, for example, spoken by a king at his enthronement, refers to an oracle received from Yahweh. Psalm 110 mentions an oracle (or three oracles) delivered by a cult prophet for the king. Psalm 45 is an oracle of blessing on the occasion of a royal marriage. In Psalm 101, the king outlines the Principles, by which he will rule; Psalm 72 contains a petition for a blessing upon the king, Psalm 21 may have been sung at an annual commemorative festival, Ps. 132 on the anniversary of the founding of the royal sanctuary at Jerusalem, emphasizing the close ties between the ruling dynasty and the temple. Another portion of the royal songs are laments or Thanksgivings, Psalm 44 prays for divine aid in a coming war; Psalm 20 and 144 contain similar prayers. Psalm 89:8 reproaches God for military defeat; Psalm 18 B gives thanks for a Victory.

Despite the dependence of the royal songs on the oriental court style» with its emphasis on world dominion (adoption. election, legitimation, and guidance of the king by the deity; Proclamation of a period of blessing and prosperity; permanence, righteousness and victory), they remain securely Yahwism. Not the king, but God, stands in the foreground. There were apparently no songs glorifying the king, not did the king boast of his own renown. By the same token, the royal Psalms in the cult speak less of the kings might and his accomplishments than of God's promises to him, the petitions he addresses to God, the things for which he gives thanks to God. The relationship between God and King is emphasized in these Psalms. They talk about the theology of kingship, i.e., king as God's adopted son, vicegerent of God king represents people before God. Kings as Yahweh' s anointed is the key emphasis in these Psalm. Most of the royal Psalms are pre-exilic (coming from the monarchic period), however, some Psalms are possibly from post exilic messianic following the pattern of royal Psalms.

***(D) Minor Types:*** The Psalms belonging to this category have no clear structure like the ones described earlier. but they are linked by common content or aim. The following are the important ones in this category.

(a) Entrance liturgies: Used by the pilgrims wishing to enter the temple. Ps. 15, 24 (like Jer. chap 7, priest at the entrance of the temple).

(b) Wisdom Psalms: These Psalms do exhibit the character of reminiscent of wisdom literature in subject matter, style and language. Ps. 1, 37, 49, 73, 112, 127, 128, 133. The key phrase found in these Psalms is "Blessed is the man."

(c) Prophetic Psalms or liturgies: (sometimes also termed as oracular Psalms), in some cases only a small/average part of the Psalm is involved. e.g. Ps. 2, 12, 50, 60, 75, 81, 82, 91, 95, 110.

(d) Sacred legends: These are the Psalms that recapture the sacred salvation history of Israel in the past. God's mighty deeds in the community is recalled and praised, in order to set them as examples for people in the present generation, to know God's greatness. The didactic character and value is mostly attached to these Psalms. Ps. 78, 105, 106 (Ps. 40: concerning Exodus).

(e) Pilgrimage songs: The Psalms are basically to offer Praise to the city of God, Zion and the holy temple at Jerusalem. They may have been recited at the time of annual pilgrimage to the holy temple and city. Ps. 84, 122 (also called as Zion Psalms; other instances are Ps. 76.4 (cf. Isa 2 and Micah 4), Ps. 48.

(f) Mixed Poems: E.g. Ps. 119 (also sometimes classified under wisdom Psalms). In this Psalm every reference (verse) is to do with Torah (God's word). (cf. II Sam 22; Ps. 18 and II Sam 23; 119 Ps.) These are also mixed types and the construction of liturgies found. The mixed types occur when a poetic type is expanded by the addition of elements drawn from a different type. For example, the introduction of a lament may have hymnic character or the element of the vow may already incorporate the thanksgiving. A liturgy, by contrast, results from the thinking of several literary types to form larger composition, probably recited by several speakers or singers in a specific cultic situation. Each literary type is used in a fashion appropriate to its sitz-im-Leben. Examples include entrance liturgies (Ps. 15 and 24 already mentioned above) and thanksgiving songs (Ps. 66 and 107). Cult prophets also appear to have liturgies, to be recited in the cult by themselves by others. Examples of this include Isa. 24-27 chapters, 33; Micah 7:8-20; Habakkuk and Joel; also other prophets used liturgies for their own purposes (Jer. 14:2, 15:2, Hosea 5:15-6:6,14:2-9). The litany, common in Babylonian

Psalms, with frequent repetition of the same response by the congregation is Ps. 136.

***Conclusion:*** Our study on various literary forms found in the book of Psalms show that the variety of forms are employed by the psalmists in order to address different situations and the moods of the speaker and the needs that each section of the psalmst's they are freely circulated. When looked at each section of the psalms in the light of various literary category, the psalms carry a great significance for which it was composed.

Chapter 6

# Literary Types of Wisdom and their Traditions

***Introduction:*** The analysis of the literary types and forms of wisdom, rooted in their respective traditions is very important aspect in order to understand the context and the message of the wisdom books both in particular and in a larger context. Just as we pointed out few literary forms in the poetry based on the books of Psalms, the wisdom forms (literary types) are briefly discussed in this chapter.

***(1) Proverb (Mashal):*** The precise sense of mashal is not known, although it is translated as "similitude" and "ruling word" which covers a broad spectrum, still it is not a sufficient translation. But both meanings are possible etymologically. The former focuses on the sense of likeness, representatives, hence similitude, while the latter takes its departure from the root meaning, "to rule, have dominion, reign" thus a word spoken by a rule; or word bearing special power. According to William McKane, mashal is to be translated as "Paradigm, model, exemplar."

Based on such a diversity of the meanings, the word not only refers to similitude (Ezek. 16:44; Gen 10:9; I Sam 10:11), but also to popular sayings (Jer. 23; 28; 31:29, I Sam 24:13, Isa. 32:6; I Kings 20:11), literary aphorisms (Prov. 10:1, Micah 2:4; Hab. 2:6-8; Ezek. 12:22-23; 18:2-3), by words (Duet 28:37; I Kings 9:7; Jer. 24:9; Ezek. 14:8), allegories (Ezek. 17;1-10, 20:45-49, 24:3-14) and discourses (Numb. 23:7,18; 24:3-24; Job 27:11-29; Pss.49:4, 78:2).

At least five types of meanings are given to this terms (Proverbs) based on the book of Proverb They are: sentence, instruction, exhortation or admission, numerical saying and comparison.

The basic category to Proverbs is the popular Proverb, a number of which have been preserved in the narrative literature of the Old Testament. While most of these sayings are in prose. sometimes they are clothed in metrical grab (Jer. 31:29; Ezek. 18:2, "The fathers have eaten sour grapes, and the children's teeth are set on edge") and make use of consonantal and vocalic assonance (Proverbs 11:2; 13:3). Some other familiar passages containing no popular Proverbs are as follows, Gen. 10:9 - "Like Nimrod a mighty hunter before the Lord:'; I Sam 10:12 - "is Saul also among the prophets?" II Sam 5:8 - "The blind and the lame shall not come into the house", Prov. 10:6,11- "the mouth of the wicked conceals violence to which should be compared I Sam 24:13 out at the wicked comes forth wickedness", Jer. 13:23- "Can the Ethiopian change his skin, or the leper his spots?" By nature, secular and non-didactic, these popular Proverbs were occasionally enlisted in the service of morality and consequently by assumed a religious tenor.

The Proverb is bilinear and registers conclusion based on experience, such as it must be self-confirming, commending itself to empirical validation or to disconfirmation. Since the saying is a result of the collective experience of human kind, it has a retrospective character, and because of its nature as an observation of how things are, it lacks the imperative. Hence any didactic intent is secondary to the Proverb, and the style is succinct, epigrammatic and highly metaphorical.

In content, utilization by Yahwism marks a great advance. A Proverb may acquire religious overtones and illuminate religious situations (Prov. 10:6,11), and can refer specifically to Yahweh (I Sam 16:7) of course those who rejected Yahwism could also use the Proverb form to express their ideas (Zeph. 1:12).

***(2) Riddle and Numerical Sayings:*** Strictly speaking the riddle is rare in the Old Testament, occurring in pure form only in Judge. 14:10-18. However, there are some instances of it present and often, paralleled with Prov. 1:6, Ps. 78:2, Wis 8:8, Sirach 39:3 and Hab. 2:6. Sir 47:17. Besides this linguistic evidence, there is also a historical tradition of Solomon's mastery of the art of riddle solving (I Kings 10:1-5 and II Chron. 9:14) a tradition elaborated upon in Joseph's (Antiquities 8.5.3), who mentions riddle contest between Solomon and envoys sent by Hiram, king of Tyre.

On the one hand, the riddle (Hebrew hida) is connected with the popular Proverb; on the other, it was borrowed by wisdom instruction Prov. 1:6 practically equates riddle with the aphorisms of the wise. In many cases riddles originally expressed the mystery of an association and its watch word, the secret of a super human being (e.g. the Sphinx) or quite generally. a hidden power that becomes available to the person alto solves them. We therefore find riddle contests as kind of mortal combat or as an exhibition of power the latter being appropriate to initiation ceremonies, courtship, and marriage. According to Judges 14:14. Samson asked such a riddle in the course of a wedding celebration. The ancient significance of riddles explain why the queen of Sheba came to test Solomon with "hard questions" (1 Kings 10:11, later the solving of riddles became merely a form of entertainment. (cf. III Esdras 3-4; letter of Aristeas paragraphs 178-300). The ability to solve riddles, however, is still considered a special power in the case of Daniel (Dan 5:12); it enables him even to discover the content of a dream the king had forgotten.

The close relationship between riddle and divination, together with the fact that oracular utterance had an enigmatic character raises a question about the narrow definition of riddle functioning above. According Mueller's study and analysis on riddles in the Old Testament, four types of riddles are identified broadly: *First*: the popular riddle, namely Judg. 14:10-18; *Second*: the symbolic dream and enigmatic oracle, as found in Gen 37:40-41, Dan 2,4 chap (the dream), Dan 5, Ezek. 17:1-10; Dan 12:7-10 (the dream unveils a special reality which the peculiar language unfolds in the dream narrative for the first time) *Third*: royal contests allied to in I Kings 10, the intention of which is to drain the opponent of all strength (it is said of queen of Sheba - 10:5), and in Dan 8:23. *Fourth*: Court - school wisdom.

A note on post biblical riddle is in order particularly since they make extensive of the bible. In rabbinic literature there is considerable speculation about the nature of the riddles put to Solomon by the queen of Sheba, the subjects of these riddles placed in the mouth of the royal visitor include, among others, pregnancy and nursing, the unique relationship between Lot's daughters and their father and sons, male and female characteristics, antimony (used for cosmetic purposes), flax and naphtha. There is also an account of a riddle context between the children of Jerusalem and men of Athens, where the answer is obtained from a rabbi familiar with Jewish practice in regard to circumcision and with the number of months required for pregnancy, nursing and weening. The reply of the children indicates the relevance of this riddle to our discussion; "If you have not plowed with my heifer, you would not have found out my riddle" (Echa Rabbati 1:1). The contest literature gave rise to catechetical texts, both in Jewish and Christian settings; worthy of mention are the Pesachta haggadah, where a refrain is used to lead up to number thirteen ("one, who knows it? one, I know it. One is our Lord in heaven and earth. Two, who knows it? Two, I know it. Two are the covenants of the law. One is.....Thirteen are the qualities of divine compassion…") and the Jocha Monachorum, which makes use of the Adam/ Eve, Noah, Lot, and Jonah narratives for catechetical purposes.

The numerical saying is a form related to the riddle. It may be of Canaanite origin. (cf. Ugaritic text 51 iii . 17-21). If so, it was borrowed and developed by Israel. In it the first member of a verse mentions a number and the second member the next higher number, followed by a list of objects corresponding in member to the latter. It seems reasonable to suppose that the numerical saying, grow out of the riddle and that both the original question in the form of riddle and the present numerical saying served first as numeric aids for educational wisdom. Later practical wisdom made use of this form, which combines riddle and instruction. In the Old Testament we find such numerical sa ings in Prov 6:16-19; chap 30; Ps.62:1f, Job 5:19-22; expressions are similar to numerical sayings occur in Amos l:3-2:8 and Job 33. 14-15 (see also Sirach 23:16; 25:7-11; 26:5;28; 50:25-26; and in the Mishna,-Prike Aboth 5:1. 15).

***(3) Aphorism:*** The aphorism or artificial wisdom saying, although it draws upon popular proverbial material and has rhythmical structure, is no longer a popular form of expression; it is an artistic and sometimes an artificial creation. It always has metrical form, as befits the original significance of the Mashal as an expression of power; this form also made it easier for students to memorize. Such aphorisms were composed at least from the time of Solomon. The existence of Proverbs mentioning the king (Proverb 16:10; 22:29, 25:2) and the collection of proverbs made at the direction of Hezekiah (Prov. 25:1) Point to the period of Israelite monarchy. At that time the "wise man" was, so to speak, the state officials with an academic education, later, a class of wisdom teachers came into being the priests and prophets (Jer. 18:18). They are the bearers of the practical wisdom expressed in aphorism. As one might expect, this type of wisdom absorbed much. foreign material, much of which was Contributed by the foreigners in the king's service and the Israelites that had returned home to Israel after service in other lands.

An aphorism can take a form of a statement (Prov. 10:1ff), an account of a personal (Prov. 24:30-34), an exhortation (Prov. 3:9) or a question (Prov. 6.27). In contrast to the Proverb, which comprises only one line, the aphorism came to employ the long verse comprising two numbers as its dominant form, most of the parallelism is antithetical (Prov. 10:2) in case of synonymous parallelism, the second member frequently resolves the image used in the first (Prov. 10:26). Sometimes the second member is so vague and appropriate that its presence seems due solely to stylistic reasons. (Prov. 12:11). In addition, an aphorism can be expanded by means of a motivation clause (Prov. 25:21-22) or even a series of similar statements that contribute little or nothing by way of new contest (Prov. 6:20-21, 23) Qoheleth developed his own special form of aphorism (Eccl. 12:9-14; 1:12-15, 16-18; 5:1-7, 8-9). Aphorism make use of various literary devices, including synonymy (Prov. 17:21), listing (24:25), repetition (3:11), Paronomasia and assonance (11:2), alliteration (8:27), Puns (6:25), examples (24:30-34), comparison (15:11), and rhyme (11:2; 12:25).

***(4) Wisdom and didactic Poetry:*** In Ps. 49:4 and 78:2, the author refers to his Psalm as a Mashal. We have yet another literary type, that of wisdom poetry or didactic poetry, used by wisdom teachers to express their reflections and exhortations. For the history of the form, comparison with the two poems, Job 18:5-21 and 20:4-9; both of which discuss the fate of the wicked, is instructive.

The former is a single unified composition, but the latter poem clearly originated through juxtaposition of individual sayings or group of sayings and does not give an impression of unity. In many cases independent aphorisms have been borrowed but not integrated into their contest (Job 20:10,16,24-25). In Psalm 37:16, too is a saying of this sort within the context of a poem; here and in Ps. 112 the alphabetic form facilitates such stringing together of material.

Besides Job 18, there are other wisdom poems that were composed as single units, e.g. Proverbs 8 (wisdom's description of herself as the ideal teacher), Proverbs 9 (Dame wisdom and Dame foolishness invite men to dine with them), and Job 28 (a poem on the inaccessibility of wisdom). In all these instances, we are dealing with late texts from the Post exilic period.

There are also a few Psalms that represent wisdom didactic poetry. Psalms 37,49,73 and 91 share a common theme, based on the doctrine of retribution that supports practical wisdom; concern over the prosperity of the godless and the affliction of the devout. The doubt cast on the doctrine of retribution is answered by the reference to God's ultimate destruction of the wicked and deliverance of the devout or by a confident "nevertheless" based on fellowship with God, which transcends all distress. In Psalm 78, the poet interprets Israel's, history in such a way as to provide a guide by which his readers may conduct their lives. (cf. Ps. 105, 106). In Psalms 1 and 128, the introductory word, asre "Happy is…, blessed is…," also found in Ps. 127:5, is typical of wisdom literature, the only place this expression is found, where it corresponds to the cultic formula b a r u k, "blessed..." Poems such as these are an outgrowth of the approbation formula of wisdom instruction (e.g. Job 5:17). The introduction to Psalm 133, "Behold, how good and pleasant..." is likewise typical of wisdom literature. The alphabetic Psalm 34, 111 and 112 are at least influenced by wisdom and may perhaps be counted among the wisdom poems. Psalms devoted the theme of the law, like 19:7-14 and 119, show the influence of later wisdom theology.

Another form of didactic poetry is the problem poetry (Ps. 37, 49, 73, 139). This literature concerns itself with the fate of the wicked in light of their apparent prosperity, urging the just man to bide his time and trust in Yahweh's ability to enforce ultimate justice. Often the theme of the all seeing eye of God is appealed to in contexts dealing with the fate of the wicked (37:13,18, cf. Ps 73:11, which questions God's vision- 1 39:1-18). It is even said that God knows human beings before they are born and writes down the life span allotted to each creature (139:14-16). Related to the autobiographical narrative (confession) discussed earlier is the didactic narrative (Prov. 7:6-23). In this instance the narrator describes a typical happening, giving the minutest details and livening the account with superb dialogue. The event is a common seduction scene, which the narrator had viewed from his window and which the adulterous wife whose husband had gone on a long journey played with perfection. The metaphors descriptive of the obedient compliance of the foolish young man are intended to suggest that his conduct is animalic:

"With much seductive speech she persuades him; with her smooth talk she compels him. All at once he follows her, as an ox goes to the slaughterer, as a stag is caught fast till an arrow pierces its entrails; as bird rushes into a snare; he does not know that it will cost him his life" (Prov. 7:21-23, RSV).

Another type of didactic narrative is the historical summary (or historical retrospect). Sir 44-50 and wisdom of Solomon 10-19 fall into this category.

***(5) Parable, Fable, Allegory:*** The parable is a prose type, an outgrowth of the metaphors and similar frequently found in aphorisms. The best illustration is the parable of the poor man's lamb told by Nathan to David after David's transgression with Bathsheba (II Samuel 12). It is also not uncommon in the discourses of the prophets (e.g. Isa. 28:4b).

The fable is a didactic poem or narrative that takes its material from the world of animals or plants. In place of open controversy, it expresses a topical truth or criticism in veiled terms, it may even inveigh against unpopular persons, classes, and institutions in this fashion. Ancient West Asian fables abound, particularly in Mesopotamian wisdom literature (cf. "Dispute between the Tamarisk and the Date Palm" ANET, 592-93), in sharp contrast to the Israelite wisdom corpus. It is possible that the reference in I kings 4:32-34 to Solomon's three thousand Proverbs and one thousand and five songs, the context of which "trees, from the cedar that is in Lebanon to the hyssop that grows out of the wall" and "also of beasts, and of birds, and of reptiles, and of fish", should be taken to mean that the son of David was remembered as master of coming fables.

The fable is characterized by "dramatic personae" which are animals or plants; hence it bears an element of the comic. However, it is often used to underscore the horror of a situation, even when half comical (Numb.

22:21-35; Gen 3. 37:5-11; 41). Originally the fable was amoral, but it soon came to function in didactic contexts; it is particularly useful for an ability to call attention to the obvious, which because of its everyday character is often overlooked. Essentially, however the fable was at home in political settings, and found ready acceptance by those with appreciation for the satirical. In time it disintegrated into pure allegory, particularly in prophetic hands. (Ezek. 17:1-10: 19:1-14; von Rad, Weisheit in Israel, 65 "Here the form of the fable is completely dismantled by the prophet for his purposes").

The popularity of the fable is shown by its influence upon on other literary types: the parable, in which human beings and other creatures appear together (Isa. 5:1-7; 10:15; 29:16, 45:9; Jer. 18.1-11) the legend (Jonah 1:17; 2:10; 4:5-11) and allegory (Ezek.17:1-10; 19:1-9; 31:1-18).

Allegory consists of series of metaphors, each of which is significant and must be interpreted; inanimate objects or abstract ideas are often personified, e.g. wisdom and folly. A more extended allegory description of old are is found in Eccles. 11:9-12:8. Ezekiel was particularly fond of this rhetorical form, albeit is highly schematic shape; in this respect he exhibits the influence of wisdom instruction (Ezek. 15:16 and 23 chapters).

Two allegories have been of particular importance and significant in Wisdom literature. Prov. 5:15-23 and Ecclesiastes 12:1-6. Each of these texts may originally have been a riddle; nevertheless, the present form is that of an admonition with an allegorical key. In Prov. 5:15-23 the metaphorical significance of "cistern" is explained, so that none can read the text without recognizing the allusion to one's wife. Furthermore, the common reference to woman as fountain from which every man drinks becomes an occasion for warning against foul water, specifically, the loose woman. The allegory of Eccl. 12:1-6 takes up the metaphor of a wife as a fountain or cistern, and juxtaposes it against an exquisite description of old age. Although some of the metaphors are difficult, the following appear to be self-evident: the keepers of the house are the arms, the strong man are the legs, the grinders are the teeth, those that look through the windows are the eyes, the door on the street are ears, the daughters of song are the voice, the almond tree is the grey hairs, the grasshopper is the creaking bone or sluggish movement, the snapped silver cord, broken golden bowl, sheltered pitcher and broken wheel are death.

***(6) Lists (Onomastica):*** Israel was familiar with the construction of scholarly lists typical of educational wisdom. Only remnants of such lists have been preserved, and those segments themselves have been used in other compositions. Encyclopedic lists of this type were used numerical sayings, Gen 1, Ps. 104,148 are in order to discuss natural phenomena, which are all of different sort but nevertheless have a rational order. The book of Job contains many poems dependent upon lists: 24:5-8, 14-16a; 28; 30:2-8; 27-37:13; 40:15-24; 41:1-34; 38:4-39:30. Especially noteworthy is God's answer to Job, which mentions a series of examples draw from both animate and inanimate nature, quite possibly selected from an onomasticon (or) some would talk about its form as Nature Weisheit (Nature Wisdom). The lists of natural phenomena do not follow the Egyptian pattern, but depends instead on the cosmology and the geographical, climatic, and Zoological conditions of Palestine; this suggests the existence of a native onomastica.

While it might be argued that anyone wishing to enumerate the marvels of nature would have just so many phenomena to work with-hence the remarkable similarity between Amenemope, Sir. 43, Ps. 148, the "Song of the Three Hebrews", and Job 38 could be accidental it seems more plausible to follow Von Rad in postulating geographical, cosmological, and metrological "Catechisms" with in the repertoire of the sages of Israel. That being the case, a number of passages in Job, Sirach and wisdom of Solomon become more comprehensible: (Job 28; 36 - et-al as citied above). In Wisdom of Solomon 7:17-20 the author alludes to the entire curriculum of the wise man: (RSV).

> "For it is he who gave me unerring knowledge of that exists, to know the structure of the world and the activity of the elements; the beginning and end and the middle of times, the alternations of the solstices and the changes of the seasons, the cycles of the year and the constellations of the stars, the nature of animals and the tempers of wild beasts, the Powers of spirits and the reasoning of man, the varieties of plants and the varieties of root..."

There is a reference in this passage to philosophy, cosmology, chronology. astronomy, zoology, botany, and medicine. The other examples from this author consists of a list of virtues and vices, the Greek style of which is quite pronounced.

Sirach 43, likewise 7:17-20 uses the Nature Weisheit for the glory of God; the majestic hymn describes the wonders of nature as those especially fashioned to assure the prosperity of the righteous and to make certain the downfall of the wicked.

Another passage from Sirach may be viewed from the perspective of Onomastica, namely 38:24-39:11 (although "character portrayal" has been suggested as better description of the text). Here the wise man describes various trades, as with the Egyptian "The instruction of Duauf" and contrasts of leisurely life of the sage. However, Sirach has a genuine appreciation for the former, craftsman, smith, and Potter: The quotation is 38:32,34 (RSV):

> "Without them a city cannot be established,
> and men can neither sojourn not live there...
> But they keep stable the fabric of the world,
> and their prayer is in the practice of their trade."

***(7) Dialogue:*** The book of Job in the wisdom literature makes use of the form Streitgespraech (dialogue). The book employs this form as weapon of warfare. when Job's own vindication being at stake. The key to Job, according to this interpretation, is 13:16 (This will be my salvation. that a Godless man will not come before him).

A variant of the Streitgespraech, namely, the "Imagined Speech" appears in Wisdom of Solomon 2:1-20 and 5:3-13. Here again the similarity to prophetic text is noteworthy. In each case the musings of wicked man are brought to light, together with the warning that such reasoning leads to destruction. The subject of the imagined speech is usually the contraction between promise and fulfilment, expectation and reality, as intensified by the transitoriness of life. In 2:1-20 the pessimism of Qoheleth has left its mark, he similarly of language being rather noticeable (chance feelingness, finality of death, man's portion) - "come, therefore, let us enjoy the good things that exist, and make use of the creation to the full as in Youth" (v. 6) reads like a restatement of Qoh. 12:1, 9:7.

The "imagined speech" is found frequently in Proverbs, for example in 1:11-14, 22-33; 3-28; 5:12-14; 7:14-20; 8:4-36; 9:4a-6, 16a-17; 20:9, l4a, 22a, 25a, 22:13; 23:7b, 35; 24:12a, 24a, 29; 25:7, 26:13, 1ab; 28:24b; 30:9b, 20c, 31:29. It functions both as stimulus for correct thinking (31:29) and as a critique of false reasoning (30:20), which it holds up to ridicule. Often the malicious words prompt a strong admonition or even a pronouncement of judgement upon those who so think cf. 1:19, "such are the ways of all who get gain by violence; it takes away the life of its possessors"; see also 7:21-27; 24:12,24). On occasion the whole imagined speech is given over to a castigation of those who stubbornly stick to their own way. (1:22-23).

***(8) Confession (Autobiographical Narratives):*** Wisdom's rootedness in experience led to a confessional style in which the aged sage gave his pupils the advantages of his varied experience when the wise man was at the same time a king the authority of such retrospection was increased, as in the "Instruction for MeriKare" and the "Instruction of Amenemhat" (ANET, 418-19) as well as the fiction of Solomonic authorship of Ecclesiastes, The Egyptian origin of autobiographical style is generally acknowledged. In the Egyptian context not only kings and prominent officials left their confessions for the benefit of progeny, however, for the tomb inscriptions describe the experiences of ordinary individuals and land their exemplary lives. The formula for the autobiographical narrative is generally - “I saw ............ and I have seen”, together with the verb “pass by”, while the moral of the story usually is spelled out at the end.

From Proverbs two examples of autobiographical narrative are instructive: 4:3-9; 14:30-34, the first of these appears to be modeled on Egyptian Prototypes; in any case it includes the Egyptian motif of a garland to be placed around the wise man’s neck. In Prov. 24:30-34 the observation (vv. 30-31) Prompts reflection (vv. 32), the result of which is a moral lesson (vv. 33-34). To this may be compared Ps. 37:25, 35-36, a wisdom Psalm. In v. 25, what may be called hypothetically, “the creed, of the blind man” appears: “I have been young, and now am old; Yet I have not seen the righteous forsaken or his children begging bread”.

The confession is used in Eccl. 1:12-2:26 with great impact; here the affinity with the royal confession of Egypt is undeniable. Emphasis is placed on the fact that the author has been “king over Israel in Jerusalem” (v. 12). Here again the words “and behold” (v. 14) points to the ground of Qoheleth’s conclusions: he has seen with his own eyes everything under the Sun, thus arriving at the conclusion that all is vanity and a striving after wind. Qoheleth has tried every possible avenue to purpose in life, in each instance despairing of any meaning wisdom (note: “I know” rather than “I saw” in v. 17), pleasure, madness and folly, despair, all lead to the same conclusion and force upon Qoholeth a hatred of life, the opposite of everything wisdom literature stands for. The same style occurs in Eccl. 3:10; 4:8; 5:18; 8:9-9:1, 11, 13, 16; 10:5,7.

Sirach 33:16-18 makes use of confessional language to invite people to the “house of instruction”, the author comparing himself to the last watchman and grape gleaner who has excelled despite the obstacles to knowledge. Sirach cannot resist the temptation to call attention to his altruism: “consider that I have labored for myself alone, but for all who seek instruction” - v. 17. Similarly, Sir. 51:13-22, employs autobiographical narrative, although set within a thanksgiving song, where there is an invitation to the house of learning (51:23-30). In this passage emphasis is placed on wisdom as the answer to fervent prayer, and the heartfelt gratitude to God for answering the request for knowledge.

The two invitations to the school in Sirach suggest a probable Sitz im Leben for the confession; the autobiographical narrative serves as a certificate of credentials for the head of a school. The principle prompted these accounts is the value of recording for posterity the lessons learned from life itself by one who is trained to reflect on experience and to sift its teachings for the benefit of those less gifted.

***Conclusion:*** In the light of above discussion we notice that the richness of various literary forms used by the wisdom writers and as it was in the case of psalms, wisdom sayings too have different variety of literary genres used on different contexts as per the need and the content of the wisdom saying. This variety of literary types enrich our understanding of the purpose of wisdom sayings not only in ancient Israel but also in other West Asian context.

Chapter 7

# Survery of the Content and Theology in Poetic and Wisdom Books of the Old Testament

***Introduction:*** Thus far in our discussion, we have been concentrating on several preliminary issues related to poetic and wisdom context of the Old Testament. The consideration of all those primary matters, concepts and terms have revealed to us the fact that the poetic and wisdom material of the Old Testament is not a unique Phenomenon, rather it was an international scenario. Much of the basic underlying ideas in the Old Testament Poetic and wisdom corpus do share with the wisdom and Poetic corpus of the ancient West Asia. However, the Hebrew wisdom and Poetic corpus having utilized the ancient West Asian categories do radically differ at certain places, and in this sense becomes unique in their presentation to suit their own context and milieu. In this chapter we will mainly focus on the actual literature of the Hebrew canon in both poetic and wisdom material. Several uncovered issues in the earlier sections will be dealt with in appropriate places of the treatment on individual books.

## *PART I: POETIC BOOKS IN THE OLD TESTAMENT*

***(I) The Book of Psalms:*** Thematically, Psalms presents no beginning, middle, and end. It contains one hundred fifty (more in some collections) individual units. Some depict the psalms as the hymn book of the second temple - referring to the temple rebuilt and rededicated between 520 and 515 BCE. Only by analogy can the word Hymns describe Psalms. More properly, the Psalms served as temple liturgies which through prayer, penitence, or requests for deliverance offered praise to Yahweh. The Hebrew title of the book tehillim, most literally means, “praise”. The word for praise, hallal, occurs almost exclusively in the intensive forms hillel and hillal. The plural tehillim from the singular word tehillia introduces the entire collection as "Praises". The Greek title Psalmois originally indicated songs accompanied by the harp. The content of Psalm 150 and to a lesser degree the content of P83. 146-149 reveals the importance of; the conception of Psalms as "Praise".

The term Mizmor more Specifically designates a song. It typically introduces and describes individual Psalms. It commonly occurs in Psalm titles as in the description "a song of David" (for Eg. Ps. 4). The term Sir, also translated "song", does not carry the connotation of hymnic music. The term most often designates songs outside the book of Psalms, for instance, in prophecy, in the work of the Chronicles, and in the Song of the Songs. The term applies to Psalms as well but not as frequently as Mizmor.

The book of Psalms is called collection of collections because several smaller collections are put together and the Psalter having achieved its final process through a long and complicated process. Examples are as follows to this evidence:

(i) Doublets: Ps.14 is equal to Ps.53 and Psalm 40:13-17 is equal to 70:1-5
(ii) Triplets: Ps.108 is equal to 57:1-11 plus 60:5-12
(iii) In Ps. 72 at its end prayers of David are ended, but Psalm 86 again has a title as prayer of David.
(iv) The titles (superscriptions) given to the Psalms are not uniformly divided. Ps. 1-89 most of the Psalms have titles, Whereas Psalms 90-150 only a few Psalms given titles.

In the following pages we shall treat the book of Psalms based on some sub-topics, except the theme of literary types which was already dealt earlier.

***(A) Main Divisions and Doxologies:*** The Psalms may be divided into smaller or larger collections on the basis chiefly of the superscriptions and secondarily of shared key words (like the literary types: enthronement (royal) Psalms, the hallelujah Psalms and so on). Four times always at the end / conclusion of a sub collection (at the end of Ps.41, 72, 89,106) there is a doxology, "Blessed be the Lord...............". These make it possible, at least in retrospect to regard the Psalter as like the Pentateuch in as much as it comprises five books. Psalm 150 may be regarded as a concluding hymn for the entire Psalter. Conversely the invitatory call to salvation in Ps.1 and Ps.2, a royal Psalm that it probably interpreted eschatologically, is prefixed to the first book of the Psalter, which contains the extensive and relatively ancient Davidic Psalter (Ps. 3-14). Before we move on to discuss the possible process of compilation of the entire Psalter in five major steps, we shall present the picture of the use of divine name in different sub-sections of the Psalter:

| Psalms | God (Elohim) | The LORD (Yahweh) |
|---|---|---|
| 1-41 | 15 | 278 (Yahwistic Psalter) |
| 42-83 | 201 (Elohistic Psalter) | 44 |
| 84-89 | 7 | 31 |
| 90-150 | 9 | 339 (prefers to use the name Yahweh) |

The process of compilation presented below is only a hypothetical picture, which may be subjected to several modifications.

*First Stage:* Small collection of Psalms was initiated at individual sanctuaries as follows:

(i) First Davidic Psalter: 3-41
(ii) Korahite Psalter: 42-49, 84-85, 87-88
(iii) Asaphite Psalter: 73-83 plus 50
(iv) Second Davidic Psalter: 51-7l plus 72

*Second Stage:* During this stage, smaller collections are combined to make larger ones. During this stage, the major Elohistic Psalter was formed by combining

(i) The Korahite Psalter: 42-49
(ii) The Asaphite Psalter: 73-83 plus 50
(iii) The second Davidic Psalter: 51-71 and 72, thus make a collection of Ps. 42-83. In this stage, the divine name Yahweh is changed into Elohim. The first Davidic Psalter was untouched during this stage rather it existed separately.

*Third Stage:* In this step, the combined Elohistic Psalter in the previous stage has now been taken into it: The First Davidic Psalter i.e; 3-41 to make it as one block Ps. 3-89 and with addition at the introduction of Psalm 2 plus Ps. 84-89 added at the end, thus we now have a collection of Ps. 2-89 completed in this stage.

*Forth Stage:* The Compilation of Ps. 2-89 happened in the previous stage has now been further enlarged by the addition of other blocks of Psalms of different origin coming from different dates. They include the following:

(i) Songs of Ascents: 120-134
(ii) Hallelujah Psalms: 146-150

Those collections were added along with other minor gaps being filled with the addition of Psalm 1 at some point of time and it served as introduction to the entire Psalter.

*Fifth Stage:* In this final stage, the entire collection occurred in all the previous four stages have now been divided into the five books as we have in the final form. They are as follows: 1-41; 42-72; 73-89; 90-106; 107-150. Moreover, during this stage, doxologies were added to the each of 4 major divisions at their end. They include the following: 41:13; 72:18-19; 89:52; 106:48 and Psalm 150 is considered as doxology to the fifth division and also as a concluding doxology to the entire Psalter.

Closure and Compilation: Even after the above mentioned hypothetical five stage process of compilation, the entire collection was not closed all of a sudden. For instance, LXX has Psalm 151 (probably this is because of counting one Psalm into two). Psalm 151 is also found, in Qumran Cave 11 as 11 Q Heb Ps. 151. Many scholars would argue that the Psalter was closed in third century CE. Moreover, this scroll contains only 41 biblical Psalms. Based on all these observations scholars like J. A. Sanders argue that, there was an open-ended Psalter in the first century CE. But there are some scholars who argue that, the Psalm scroll discovered in cave IV of Qumran is not to be identified with Psalm scroll proper! Another compounded problem along with this is, we can hardly date any Psalm with precision. Psalm 137 may be dated during the time of Babylonian exile in 587 BC and several other Psalms are generally dated as Post-exile and there are few Pre-Exile Psalms as well, but on the whole they can't be accurately dated since most of them are meant for liturgical usage.

***(B) Canonization of the Book of Psalms:*** The position of the Psalter in the Hebrew Canon presents a perplexing picture in the various areas of text tradition. The familiar printed edition in most cases place the Psalter at the head of the Kethubim thus follow the tradition of the Jews of central Europe. The order varies between Psalms – Job – Proverbs and Psalms – Proverbs – Job. But we go back to the earliest time in the canon tradition that is still recognizable today, we find that the order is extraordinarily various. In the Palestinian text tradition, Chronicles seem to have stood at the head of Kethubim. Witnesses are Codex L, Michael Ben Uzziel, and the manuscripts of the Masora of Palestine. The Spanish "Jews follow this tradition, that is, in which the Psalter appears in the second place in the Kethubim. Still other principles of arrangement are operative among the Jews of Eastern dispersion. From Talmud (Baba Bathra 14b) we learn that, also the book of Ruth, among others, was w place directly before the Psalter. Obviously the ancestry of the Psalmist David was especially to be emphasized.

In the canon of the Masoretic Text (MT), the book of the Psalms, Job and Proverbs form a characteristic group within Kethubim. A Peculiar accent system is used exclusively in these books The special characteristic of this system is that in addition to the 'atnah. We also find the 'oleh we yored. While the 'atnah appears as the divider between verses only in shorter sentences, the 'oleh we yored serves as the chief divider in longer sentence structure. The 150 Psalms of the Psalter have different numbers in Greek (LXX) and in the Hebrew text (called Masoretic Text - MT). The following chart displays this point clearly:

| **MT** | **GREEK** | **MT** | **GREEK** |
|---|---|---|---|
| Ps. 1-8 | 1-8 | 116:10-19 | 115 |
| Ps. 9-10 | 9 | 117-146 | 116-145 |
| Ps. 11-113 | 10-112 | 147:1-11 | 146 |
| Ps. 114-115 | 113 | 147:12-20 | 147 |
| Ps. 116-1-9 | 114 | 148-150 | 148-150 |

According to this chart, Greek contrasts Ps. 9 and 10, and latter also Ps. 114 and 115, into one Psalm each. In addition, at the end Greek also preserves an additional Psalm 151, in which I Samuel 16:1-14 and I Samuel chapter 17 are freely used. But already in the oldest tradition this additional product is consistently labeled as "Supernumerary". Psalm 151 is an example of the later offshoots of Psalm writing as we see it in the non-canonical collections of the thanksgiving humans from Qumran such as the "Psalms of Solomon" and the "Odes of Solomon." As mentioned earlier, the open-ended nature of Psalter is highly probably, only at the late date, the compilation has been concluded.

***(C) Superscription's and Titles to the Individual Psalms:*** Before we go into the consideration of individual titles and superscriptions we shall note the types of titles or categories of superscriptions as proposed by Sigmund Mowinckel. There are four categories as follows:

(a) Titles that comprise technical designations of Psalms, including mizmor, mikhtam, maskil, tephillah and Shir hamma alath.

(b) Titles pointing to the purpose of the Psalms such as thanksgiving etc., hazkir, yedhuthun and leannoth.

(c) Titles of cultic origin, which, according to Mowinckel, include the bulk of Psalms such as the "Choirmaster" collection, these titles mentioning melodies and perhaps the obscure title muthlabben (Ps. 9)

(d) Titles containing specific musical references such as neghinoth, selah, haggayon, nehilogh etc…

The presence of superscriptions falls all except thirty-four Psalms (Ps. 1-2, 10, 33, 43, 71, 91, 93-97, 89, 104-107, 111-119, 135-137 and 146-150) poses certain difficulties of historicity and interpretation. Some of the allusions purporting to relate to King David, for example, follow a tradition that is at variance with Samuel. Thus in Ps. 34, the king before whom David simulated madness was named Abimelech, where as in I Sam. 21:10ff, he was named Achish. Again the title of Psalm 56 seems to imply that David was captured by the Philistines and brought to Gath where as in I Sam. 21:10, David is indicated to have to fled there on his own initiative.

It seems probable that in at least some instances the titles were the result of editorial activity that may well have been intended to preserve some historical tradition with respect to specific compositions, or to perpetuate a certain familiar usage, whether in connection with origin, character, music, or liturgical function of the psalm.

The superscriptions of thirteen Psalms support to preserve the historical traditions relating to the life of David, in terms of which the particular psalms were composed.

(a) Ps. 3 cf. II Sam. 15:1-18:33; (b) Ps. 7: Cush of Benjamin is nowhere mentioned in the OT accounts of the life of David; (c) Ps. 18 cf. I Sam. 19:1ff, 24:1f, 26; II Sam. 5:17f, 8:1f, 10:1f, 15:1-18:33; 21:15f; (d) Ps. 34 cf. I Sam. 21:10f, but perhaps this Psalm refers to another occasion of simulated madness than that which occurred in the presence of Achish and which is not recorded in the OT; (e) Ps. 51 cf. II Sam. 11:1f; (f) Ps. 52 cf. I Sam. 22:6f; (g) Ps. 54 cf. I Sam. 23:14f; (h) Ps. 56- This may preserved in different traditions from that in I Sam. 21:10ff, 22:1, 27:1ff, regarding the reasons why David went to Gath. (i) Ps. 57 cf. I Sam. 22:1f, 24:1f; (i) Ps. 59 cf. I Sam. 19:8f; (k) Ps. 60 cf. II Sam. 8:3f, 10:15f; (l) Ps. 63 cf. I Sam 24:1f, II Sam 15:1f; (m) Ps.142 cf. I Sam. 22:1 (24:1). It may well be that in at least some of the foregoing instances the titles were added by an editor who was aware of circumstances under which "the particular compositions of the Psalm in Question. Some specific terms related to superscription are as follows:

(i) Alanioth - is rare occurring only in Ps. 46, I Chronicles 15:20 and as a final word of Ps. 48. It's association with the Hebrew noun almah might indicate that it was meant of designate a tune for female voices.

(ii) Names of melodies appear to be reflected by several titles: "Do not destroy" - "Altaschith" - Ps. 57-59, 75, cf. Isa. 65:8; "The hind of the Dawn" (Ps. 22); "Lilies", "Shoshannim" (Ps. 45, 69, 80). "The lily of the Testimony", "Shushan-eduth" (Ps. 60); Uncertain in this regard are: Gittith" (Ps. 8, 81, 84), which may be (following LXX) a vintage-tune associated with the word git meaning "wine press" (cf. Joel 4:13) or may refer to Philistine (Gath) musical instrument.

(iii) Mahalath: (Ps. 53, 88), which may have been a tune named after a woman (cf. Gen. 28:9, II Chro. 11:18).

(iv) Mahalath Leannoth: (Ps. 88) - which also may have been dedicated to some female, although leannoth may mean "for affection" or for singing.

(v) Muth-labben: means "die for the son"? may be an obscure expression in the title of Ps. 9, may be a corruption of almot or alternatively, the name of a tune.

(vi) Musical instruments may be referred to under the named Nehiloth (Ps. 5) which occurs only here in the Old Testament, consequently obscure meaning and Sheminith (Ps. 6,12) - but "Sheminith" seems to refer to an "octave" and its only other occurrence is I Chro. 15:21, it is of doubtful meaning.

(vii) Stringed instrument: (in Ps. 4, 6, 54, 55, 67, and 76), 4 of these contain the term "mizmor", pointing clearly to instrumental accompaniment of singers.

(viii) Choirmaster: (in vulgate: "in finem", "to the chief musician"), appears to be reasonably assured in the light of the evidence furnished by I Chro. 15:21 (The verb seems to imply the rendering of Music and not "smoothing the countenance of Yahweh) and it may be that the Psalms to which this designation was attached had been taken from a collection belonging to an unknown presenter, or perhaps dedicated to him. Jeduthun, the name of a Levitical choir leader in the Solomonic period (II Chr. 5:12cf. II Chr. 35:15 as the name of the sun in Josiah's time), and also the cognomen of levitic in the time of Nehemiah (Neh. 11:17), appeared in the titles of three Psalms (39, 62, 77), and may have had some significance in connection with choral work, but this also is uncertain.

(ix) Individuals or guilds of singer appeared under various designations, one of the more common being Asaph (Ps. 50, 78-83). A prominent court-musician in the time of David bore this name (I Chr. 6:39; 15:17), and it may well be that the "sons of Asaph" in the period of Nehemiah (Neh. 7:44) were members of a musical guild that went back to the days of David and the monarchy. Asaph, in the Psalter could refer either to guild, to some member of it, or to their collection of religious poetry.

(x) Ethan, the Ezrahite: (Ps. 89) cf. I Chr. 6:44. In I Kings 4:31 Ethan is a Hebrew sage and He-man, the Ezrahite (Ps. 88 cf. I Chr. 6:33), enshrined the native Canaanite tradition of music and psalmody.

(xi) Sons of Korah: (Ps. 42, 44-49, 84-85, 88-89), may imply the existence of another musical guild whose traditional origins probably reached back to Korah, the great-grandson of Levi (Num. 16:17; I Chr. 6:31 cf. II Chron. 20:19).

(xii) Maskil: occurred in 13 titles (Ps. 32, 42, 44, 45, 52-55, 74, 78, 88-89, 142) has been interpreted to mean a "didactic" or "meditative" Psalm. The root idea of the verb appears to be that of "Prudence" or "insight" (cf. Amos 5:13), and since maskil is causative in force it might imply the conveying of insight.

(xiii) Mikhtam: is a matter of debate for several years. It occurs in six Psalms (16, 56-60), not to be translated as "golden" as done by the authorized version. Sigmund Mowinckel proposes that on the books of Assyrian term Ka-ta-mu, "to even", the word is related to the atoning or expiatory functions or associates of the Psalms concerned (but Mowinckel's idea has not been furnished with much of evidence).

(xiv) Shiggayon: (found in Ps.7 only cf. Habakkuk 3:1), may be related to Akkadian shegu or lamentation Psalm, but the actual meaning is not known.

***(D) Cultic Setting of the Psalms (Book of Psalms as Hymn Book of the Second Temple):*** Both ancient writers and critical scholars of 19th and early 20th century tended to regard the Psalms as providing evidence of private, individual devotion in Israel. Ancient authorities were, of course, bound by the traditional psalm headings; but earlier critical scholars, though rejecting the originality of these superscriptions, were still inclined to see the Psalms as individual compositions, reflecting particular historical circumstances. Even Hermann Gunkel, who played a significant role in the form critical analysis of the Psalter, failed to attain a complete cultic understanding of the Psalms. While he rightly saw that Psalmography must go back to pre-exilic times and that some of our psalms date from that period, he believed that the majority of our extant Psalms are post exilic, spiritualized imitations of the earlier cultic Psalms, and that they are derived from small, more or less private, conventicles of pious laymen. He supposed that the many references to cultic matters in the Psalter were only metaphorical.

As a result of the work of Mowinckel, however, this view is no longer generally accepted. The Psalms are littered with cultic allusions, which only make sense of they were used in public worship in the temple in Jerusalem. For example, references to the temple include Ps. 23:6; 26:8; 27:4; 63:2; 96:6; 122:1, and Psalms 24, 6, 118 and 132 make allusion to cultic processions, while similarly Ps. 48. 12 alludes to the perambulation around the walls of Mount Zion. References to sacrifices of various kinds are found, e.g. sacrif1ces generally (Ps. 4:5; 27:6), burnt offering (Ps. 20:3), a covenant sacrifice (Ps. 50:5), and a free will offering (Ps. 54:6). Mention is also made of dancing (Ps. 30:11; 87:7; 149:3; 150:4), singing (Ps. 9:11, 30:4; 33:2; 47:6-7) and various kinds of musical instruments (Ps. 33:2, 47:5; 81:2; 98:6; 150:5).

Support for the cultic interpretation of the Psalms may be found in Mishnah and other rabbinic sources, which stipulate various cultic occasions for the use of Psalms. Some of the Psalm headings also attest liturgical-usage, though they also contain some uncertainties. When we come to the late period, we actually find Psalms composed in non-cultic, pious circles, specifically the psalms of Solomon and the Qumran Hodayoth (Thanksgiving Psalms). These differ markedly from our OT Psalms in various ways, and their non-cultic orientation highlights all the more the cultic nature of the biblical Psalms.

E. S. Gerstenberger has recently argued that the great majority of the Psalms derive not from the Jerusalem temple, but primarily from small-group local community worship, mainly the synagogue of the post-exilic period. However, the grounds for this theory are not convincing, we know nothing about synagogue worship in the Persian period - it is not even certain that synagogues existed there and Gerstenberger gives insufficient weight to the indications of a temple cult origin as well as to evidence that a very large number of Psalms are pre-exilic. It should also be noted that some scholars who accept a temple setting for Psalms generally make an exception of the wisdom and Torah Psalms, locating them in a school context, but even this is somewhat doubtful.

As a book of cultic songs the Psalter has sometimes been referred in the past as 'The hymn book of the second temple' i.e.: of the Post-exilic period. This is fair enough, provided that we remember that a considerable part of it was also the 'hymn book' of the first temple, i.e.: of the Pre-exilic period. On broader terms we can say that there appears to be pre-dominance of the pre-exilic Psalms in the first two thirds of the Psalter and the post-exilic Psalms in the last third. It was fashionable at the end of 19th and early part of 20th century to regard most Psalms as late (For instance, B. Duhm, could regard the exilic Psalm 137 as the earliest Psalm), it later became generally recognized that there are a large number of pre-exilic Psalms (a trend carried to extremes by I. Engnell who regarded Ps. 137 as the latest). Although some would argue for Psalms as predominantly post-exilic (e.g. Gerstenberger, O. Loretz), most would now recognize that there are in fact a large number of both pre and post-exilic Psalms.

***(E) The Role of Psalms in the Community:*** Some Psalms take on the nature of prayer and relate private thoughts, while others take on the nature of prayer and relate public attitudes. Personal laments contain intimate descriptions of the Psalmists 'suffering, voicing the sufferers' private fears of pain and death. Such open confession offers therapeutic benefit, as does the occasional confession of sin which appears in various types of Psalms. In the following lines we will briefly discuss on the relationship between Psalms and their use in the community.

(a) Personal confession: The laments provide a format for the expression of "improper" reactions to suffering and struggle. Psalmists, like Job, frequently over self the limits of propriety based on Israel's standards as well as our own. In the framework of a lament the worshipper can voice strong expressions of God's unfairness and capriciousness. The worshipper does not fear reprisal, since the questionable attitudes remain incidental to the greater purpose of the lament. The lament achieves its purpose by festering confidence in God's eventual deliverance. Whether the worshipper intends to describe suffering to obtain forgiveness, or to release pent-up anger, the Psalmist always directs the confessions of the Psalms of God.

(b) Community unity and stability: The use of Psalms to release detrimental emotions also relates the place of the Psalms maintaining the unity and stability of the community. The Psalms absorb tensions including: (i) Contrasting feelings (in a single person), (ii) Attitudes and words unacceptable in other contexts, and (iii) God's disposition toward his people. The community gained solidarity when Psalms served as acceptable outlets for potentially damaging attitudes. Psalms provided an outlet for the individual's admixture of joy and grief, depression and confidence. They allowed that person to voice the deepest emotions in the strongest terms even when the emotions and their expressions were not socially acceptable (for example, the claim in Psalm 44 that God had wrongly punished his obedient people, or the desire to break vengeance on innocent babes in Ps. 137).

Apart from the release valve for tension, the Psalms also added to the stability of the community by identifying common foes and suggesting common goals. Common goals relate these two tasks. The identification of the type of behavior acceptable to God differentiated the community of Israel from the wicked or proud. The Psalms present widely varied portraits of God, Israel, the ideal community as a nationalistic consolidation of the nation to the ideal community as a peaceful conglomeration of all peoples, and from the world as the setting for incessant pain to the world as the medium for God's lavish blessing. These perspectives added to the unity and stability of second temple Judaism due to their eclecticism. The psalms as a whole show eclecticism rather than exclusivism. They tend to promote the broadest range of response to history rather than limiting the worshiper to a narrow band of propriety.

(c) Medium of Instruction: When Psalms serve as a medium for instruction, traits of both eclecticism and exclusivity become important.

The tension between God as an avenger and God as the redeemer of Israel remains. Each aspect provides insight into important dimensions of theology. God is depicted both as the avenger of the righteous and showing his covenant love. Moreover, God is depicted as creator and elector. The presentation of God's work in history instills a sense of identity as well as providing theological insight for the individual believer and the community.

The wisdom Psalms (the most notable tools for instruction in the Psalter) reveal this same dual identity. Torah Psalms such as 1, 19, 119 encourage devotion to God and draw attention of religious duty. The reflection they engender compares to that recommended by the Shema (Deut. 6:4-9). Maintaining a relationship with God and fellow worshippers of God involves constant meditation on the meanings and ramifications of the commitment. The wisdom Psalms, including Torah Psalms and others, concentrate on a single dynamic simply in terms of the "righteous" and the "wicked". To the contemporary ethics these decision making. On the other hand, their usefulness as basic resources for moral instruction appears clearly. All moral responsibility depends on the primary categories, "good" and "bad". This provides a foundation for the more sophisticated reflections urged in the Torah Psalms.

(d) Reconstituting reality: In contrast to the earthly concerns of the wisdom Psalms, the laments especially express the aim of reconstituting reality. This involves a denial of current negative experiences and a reimagining of the present. Laments base those attitudes on trust in Yahweh's activity in the future. From this perspective, the poetry of the Psalms aims to reconstitute present experience. As ritual documents, the Psalms enable hope amid hopelessness and justice amid injustice. A similar phenomenon occurs in the hymns (especially Zion songs) in their anticipation of an era under God's complete control. Such Psalms provided opportunity for worshippers whose current experience offered no encouragement to live in the future. They understand goals of faith as achieved in spite of situations to the contrary in the here and now.

This special philosophy of time occurs when words serve as the medium for faith. The Psalms attempt to express transcendent experience with finite communication. The Hebrew Psalmists continually stretch language out of a constant preference for God's sovereignty. Since these poems actually made God present, they also worked as effective agents to bring change to the worshipper's experience. The laments often called God to earth, which makes anything possible. So, the poetry actually changed the face of God, linking its effect directly to his identity.

***(F) The Theology of Psalms:*** Whenever Israel experienced the saving acts of Yahweh, they did not keep silent: not only did she repeatedly take up her pen to recall those acts of Yahweh in a wholly personal way she offered praise to him, and asked him questions, and complained to him about all her sufferings, for Yahweh had pot chosen his people as a mere dumb object of his will 1n history, but for converse with him. The answer of Israel's which we gather for the most part form the Psalter, is theologically a subject in itself. In the following pages we shall take up the issues in the theology of Psalms.

(a) Yahweh, the God of Israel: In the Psalter, we find not a theoretical monotheism but a practical monotheism is stressed. Israel is to worship only Yahweh cf. the echo of the beginning of the Decalogue in Ps. 81:9-10: "There shall be no strange god among you; you shall not bow down to a foreign god. I am the Lord your God, who brought you up out of the land of Egypt." This is not the same as saying that other gods do not exist. However, the post-exilic passages about the idols of the nations in Ps. 115:4-8 and 135:15-18 clearly do reflect a belief in absolute monotheism. When the existence of other gods is not denied it is Yahweh's incomparability and superiority which are emphasized, for example Psalm 95:3: "For the Lord is a great God, and a great king above all gods", Ps. 97:7 "........all gods bow down before him." Furthermore, the understanding of God of Israel, Yahweh is presented in the Psalms under various sub-headings as follows:

(i) Yahweh the creator and the Lord of History: Yahweh's creation of the world is a recurrent theme in the Psalms. Quite often it is associated with Yahweh's conflict with the chaos waters or dragon, which preceded the effective work of creation. Sometimes this event is appealed to in laments as a reminder of Yahweh's past triumphs (cf. Ps. 74:12-l7; 89:9-13), and here the dragon is referred to, named either as Leviathan or Rahab. More commonly we hear of the sea or waters subdued at creation (cf. Ps. 65:6-7; 93:3-4; 104:5-9); in Ps. 33:67 a demythologization has taken place in so far as the conflict with the waters appears to have become simply a job of work, as in Genesis l. In Ps. 29:3,10, God's supremacy over the waters is a sign of his effective lordship over the creation. This was the theme associated with Yahweh's kingship at the feast of Tabernacles. One of the passages cited, Ps. 104:5-9, forms part of a larger whole extolling Yahweh's Lordship over creation. This Psalm also shows evidence of dependence on Pharaoh Akhenaten's hymn to the sun, and in turn seems to be one of the sources underlying Genesis 1, where the order of creation is strikingly similar.

The splendor of the universe was held to declare the glory of God. As Psalm 19 declares, in words made famous by Haydn's splendid composition: "The heavens are telling the glory of God; and the firmament proclaims his handiwork". In other places in the Psalms the various parts of creation are exhorted to praise Yahweh (Ps. 96:11ff; 98:7f). It is in the hymns in the Psalter that Yahweh's creation of the world is characteristically alluded to.

The revelation of Yahweh as the God of universe is manifested in the history of his chosen people. The historical Psalms, which deal with the beginnings and early events of Israel's existence, tell of this. The great deeds of Yahweh are that to which Israel is constantly relating itself in the Psalms and on which Israel's life is based. In all these testimonies to history there is no doubt even for a moment that God's people are not relying on themselves, on their faith, on their accomplishments, but on Yahweh alone; This history is not a dumb and anonymous history of fated course of events. Rather, God personally drew near to this history of his with Israel in word that he addressed to Israel, and; he chose her to be his partner in conversation. Just as Yahweh's choice of Israel was the creative expression of his unrestricted sovereignty, so Israel's history was dependent on God's intervention an activity, which always made it possible for Israel to confront the moment and move forward. Thus it is one of the deepest mysteries of Israel's history that the presuppositions of the existence of God's people and of their course of life are based on the theme of "creation" this is expressed most clearly in the confession, "our help is in the name of the Lord, who made heaven and earth" (Ps. 124:8; 121:2; 115:15).

As mentioned above, in innumerable hymns and historical Psalms in the Psalter the deeds of Yahweh in history and creation are recited and praised in close connection with each other. Psalm 136 is the clearest example of this. Creation is seen as a work of Yahweh in history, as the first, basic deed which brought into being the area of God's activity, of his choice of Israel and his establishing the covenant, of his leading and speaking with the people, and finally and above all Yahweh's coming to the peoples of the earth.

Israel knew Yahweh as creator, not in the numinous manifestations of nature or in cosmogonic myths, but only in that he himself manifested. and communicated his name, and in the history of his speaking to his people and his saving them. "O Lord, our Lord, how majestic is thy name in all the earth!" (Ps. 8:1). "The north and the south, thou hast created them; Tabor and Hermon joyously praise thy name" (Ps. 89:12). The creator God, to whom the OT and especially the Psalter give testimony and honour is not just any supreme being, but the Lord of Israel's history, Yahweh, who has revealed himself and made himself known in the history of his deeds and self-disclosures. In their encounter with the cosmogonic myths of the religions of Israel's neighbors, Israel perceived and experienced the creative power has been specifically encountered in election and deliverance. This is clearly shown in Ps. 89. The statements about creation in this Psalm is Polemical, confessional, and doxological. But this psalm shows the soteriological understanding of creation, i.e.: the relation of creation and salvation history to each other, is also found in Isa. 40-55 and Ps. 74:12-17.

In the history of Yahweh's acts Israel experienced the absolute sovereignty of God, a sovereignty never in doubt, never involved in process of development. Yahweh's superiority in all activity. his power as the cause of everything, necessarily had its effect on creation theology. The Old Testament knows nothing of any theogonic speculations that precede the act of creation. "Before the mountains were brought forth, or even thou hast founded the earth and the world, from everlasting to everlasting thou are God" (Ps. 90:2)

(ii) Yahweh's attributes and the Presence: One image employed of Yahweh in the Psalms is that king (e.g. Ps. 24:7-10; 29:10; 48:2; 74:12; 93:3; 96:10; 97:6; 99:1). This epithet too was borrowed from the Canaanites. Some passages associate Yahweh's kingship with the victory over the chaos waters (cf. Ps. 29:10; 74:12ff; 93:1ff), which clearly derives ultimately from the Canaanite god Baal, whose victory over the god yam (sea) formed the basis of his kingship, as it is known from the myth preserved in the Ugaritic texts. The Old Testament on a number of occasions connects Yahweh's kingship with his creation of the world (cf. Ps. 74:12ff; 93:1ff; 95:3f; 96:10). As king, Yahweh was envisaged as enthroned on the cherubim in the Holy of Holies of the Jerusalem temple (Ps. 80:1), and the gods formed as it were his heavenly court (Ps. 29:1, 82:1,6; 89:5-7). It should be noted that the images of Yahweh as shepherd (cf. Ps. 23:1ff; 80:1) and judge (e.g. Ps. 82:1; 96:13) are alternative ways of referring to his kingship.

Another way in which Yahweh's greatness is indicated in the Psalms is by referring to him as the Highest (Hebrew: 'elyon, cf. Ps. 46:4; 47:2; 82:6; 87:5; 97:9). Yahweh in the Psalms is presented as a holy God. On a number of occasions, he is called the Holy one of Israel (Ps. 71:22; 78:41; 89:18). Another term used remarkably frequently of Yahweh in the Psalms is the Hebrew word hesed. Altogether it occurs there over one hundred times. It is variously translated as steadfast love, mercy, loyalty, or loving kindness etc. and denotes Yahweh's characteristic attitude towards the Israelites, both collectively and individually. Psalmists repeatedly (25:6; 31:16) and it is constantly given as a reason for praising him (cf. Psalms 117; 136). Because of his loving kindness Yahweh is a God who delivers his people, both individually and collectively. The verb yasa' ('save') is used in the imperative form in lament Psalms in appeals to the deity (e.g. Ps. 7:1; 22:21; 28:9). Sometimes the verb "redeem" is used in connection with God, also the rood go'el (redeemer) was a kinsman who redeemed a relative from slavery (Lev. 25:47-55), bought back their lost land (Lev. 25:23-34) or undertook marriage to a female relative so as to remove her widowhood (Ruth 4). As employed of God, therefore, the term had warm personal overtones. Various terms are used to give expression to the Psalmist's confidence in Yahweh. For example, God is spoken of as a rock (Heb. sela' or sur, e.g. Ps. 18:2;

31:2-3), or fortress (e.g. Ps. 94:22; 14:42) am as one under whose wings one shelters (e.g. Ps. 17:8; 63:7).

The Hebrews conceived of Yahweh as both transcendent and immanent, and this is reflected in the Psalter. He is regarded as dwelling at once in heaven and in the temple on Mount Zion cf. Ps. 11:4, "The Lord is in his holy temple the Lord's throne is in heaven........" Yahweh's presence was associated with Mt. Zion from the time of David, when he brought up the sacred Ark into Jerusalem (II Sam. 6), and with the temple in Jerusalem from the time of Solomon, when the Ark was taken up into that sanctuary. Ps. 132 indicates a repeated cultic bringing up of the Ark into the sanctuary at the feast of Tabernacles (cf. Ps. 24:7-10; 47:5, 68:1, 18). It should be noted that the Psalter suggests that God's presence was particularly apprehended in the course of worship in the temple (cf. Ps. 23:5-6; 27:4; 42:1-2; 84:1-7,10). Isaiah's majestic vision of God in Isa.6, which contains echoes of Psalm 99, was experienced in the temple. Ps.139 adequately declares, it is impossible to escape from God's presence.

(b) The Sanctuary and Its worship: In the sanctuary in Jerusalem Israel gathered as a worshipping community. In the following pages we shall consider the following things: certain concepts, expressions, and statements that are related to worship will be examined. Then the Zion theology is examined and presented followed by actual cultic practices involved in a theology of worship.

(i) The Sanctuary: The starting point must be the name of the city of God, Jerusalem. Psalm 125:2 describes its location: "The mountain, are round about Jerusalem." This mountain that surround the "city of David", situated on the southeast elevation of the later city of Jerusalem are higher than Mount Zion, the highest elevation of the city of God "Jerusalem" is the first of all the name of the city which functioned as the "property of the crown" of Davidic dynasty and as the royal capital of Judah. In the Psalms there are references to the destruction of this city and to its rebuilding (Ps. 79:1-3; 51:18). But Jerusalem is also and especially the designation of the central sanctuary of the Israelite tribes (Ps. 122:3-4). In its "midst" is the "house of the Lord" (Ps. 116:10). From his temple Yahweh shows his power over Jerusalem (Ps. 68:29). In other words, the city of Jerusalem lies within the sphere of the glory and might of the sanctuary. Thus "Jerusalem" can be used as a synonym for "Zion" (Ps. 102:21; 135:21) and also as a designation for the place where Yahweh dwells (Ps. 135:21).

The distinctive designation of the Jerusalem sanctuary, however, is the name Zion. It is found predominantly in the form of "mount Zion" (Ps. 48:2,11; 74:2; 78:68; 125:1; plurals Ps. 133:3). From Zion, God "shines forth", his theophany is manifest, help comes for the oppressed (Ps. 14:7;

20:2; 53:6), and Yahweh's blessings goes forth (Ps. 128:5; 134:3). On Zion, Israel's songs of praise ring out (Ps. 65:1; 147:12).

As the mount of Yahweh, Zion is Yahweh's holy mountain (Ps. 2:6; 3:5; 15:1; 43:3; 48:1; 87:1; 99:9), the "holy place" of the holy God (Ps. 24:3), the place where he is present and where he has "holy habitation" (Ps. 68:5, 76:2). On this "holy mountain" the temple stands, the house of Yahweh. The one praying in Ps. 5:8 proclaims, "I.......will enter thy house, I will worship toward thy holy temple." The worshipping community bows down before the temple, addressing its prayers to the house of Yahweh (Ps. 138:2), because in the temple, in the inner sanctuary Yahweh is present, "dwells", is "enthroned". Therefore, in prayer one's hands are raised towards the "most holy sanctuary" (Ps. 28:2). Temple and inner sanctuary are the "holy place". There Yahweh communicates his word (Ps. 60:6; 108:7), and from there come help and comfort for those who are oppressed and needy (Ps. 20:2). The concept of the sanctuary includes the gates of the holy area (Ps. 9:14; 87:2; 100:4; 118:19-20; 122:2) and the outer courts, and on the festival days participates in the cultic Observances entered the temple itself.

The Jerusalem sanctuary on Mount Zion was in pre-exilic times the sacred hill of the original Canaanite inhabitants, the Jebusites. The question of now cultic traditions of this Jebusite sanctuary were carried over into Zion theology of the Old Testament will be taken up later, but now we will consider another question: how Israel's sanctuary received its legitimation i.e. how Mount Zion became the central sanctuary to which the tubes of Israel, in accordance with the ordinance, were to make their pilgrimage (Ps. 122:4). In order to answer this question which is complex in nature we need to trace out some more history.

The first temple that can be identified in early Israelite times is in the Sanctuary at Shiloh. The destruction of this sanctuary sent shock waves through following centuries and had its echo in the Psalter as well (Jer. 7:12; 26:9; Ps.78:60). The function and meaning of the Ark of Yahweh are attested to in a tradition that served as the hieros logos ("sacral tradition") of the Jerusalem sanctuary, where the ark was kept. Ark was considered not only as the throne of God (I Sam. 4:4; II Sam. 6:2) who in the cult was honored as present; it was also carried into battle as the palladium of the "holy war" (I Sam. 4:3). The army welcomed this sign of Yahweh's presence with a great shout of joy (I Sam. 4:5). Where ever the Ark made its appearance it was received with fear and joy. (I Sam. 6:13; II Sam. 6:9). Burnt offerings and sacrifices were presented before it (I Sam. 6:14ff). Following this Philistines captured the Ark and in the same hurry sent it back to Israel.

After David had conquered the Jebusite city of Jerusalem, the perished Shiloh cult began to be renewed in the city of Jerusalem. The king rescued the holiest of ancient Israelite objects from its obscurity in Krirathjearim and brought it to Jerusalem. This procedure was of decisive significance (Ps. 132:5ff). By virtue of the presence of the Ark in the city of David, Jerusalem was raised to the rank of Israelite cultic center. In this way traditions and institutions of ancient Israel were transferred to Zion sanctuary. Jerusalem was now the chosen place (Ps. 78:68; 87:1; 132:13). The hieros logos ("sacral tradition") of the Ark narrative thus clearly intends to announce that the history of worship in Jerusalem is a continuation of the Shiloh tradition, the previous site of the Ark.

The warlike concepts of Yahweh, "mighty in battle" which are connected with the Ark are clearly seen in Psalm 24:7-10. In Jerusalem the "shepherd of Israel" (Ps. 80:1) "dwells" and "is enthroned upon the cherubim", and he comes to be designated by and honored with the titles "king", "judge", "mighty God", and "creator". He dwells on Zion (Ps. 9:11; 132:13-14), and his throne is in heaven (Ps. 11:4; 103:19; 123:1).

Some of the statements in the Psalms are worth examining at this point: Joy and praise of God in the sanctuary have a tendency to permeate and fill all of life: "So I will bless thee as long as I live" (Ps. 63:4). The statement, "I shall dwell in the house of the Lord forever" (Rsv. margin, "as long as I Live" Ps. 23:6), is not a mere confession of faith uttered by the Levites, but an expression of the longing of all those who have "tested" and "seen" the blessing bestowed by the holy place (Ps. 34:8), "Blessed are those who dwell in thy house, ever singing thy praise" (Ps. 84:4). However, it would be erroneous to ascribe this exaltation and ecstasy to the influence of the holy precincts themselves. The life that is exalting and enabling, filling and fulfilling, which the ancient Israelites experienced in the sanctuary, is life that comes from Yahweh, the God of life: "For with thee are the fountain of life; in thy light do we see light" (Ps. 36:9). This is a key verse for our understanding of Israel's cultic life. Fulfilled life (in the sanctuary) is not the result of some magic power, but the result of the power of the divine presence, the gift of God's steadfast love; it is blessing and shalom received from him.

(ii) The Zion Theology: In the same Psalms which contain a detail portrayal of the sanctuary on Zion, or Jerusalem, the city of God, we find also a remarkable Zion theology. The primary passages in this regard are "Songs of Zion", Ps. 46-48 and 76 as "eschatological concepts" and consequently he "eschatologized" his overall explanation of these psalms. But we are not sure of the history of the transmission of the traditions related/connected to these psalms.

In Ps. 48:2, the location of Jerusalem is described as, Mount Zion, in the far north. The Concepts, Mount Zion and north here mean: the clue is given in Isa. 14:13-14. This text contains taunt song described against the king of Babylon. He himself speaks with arrogance and hybris: "I will ascend to heaven, above the stars of God, I will set my throne on high, I will sit on the mount of assembly in the far north; I will ascend above the heights of the clouds, I will make myself like the Highest", even though this song was composed quite lately, it shows that Mount (Zaphon) was a mountain of the gods, soaring into the heavens, above clouds and stars. This sacred mountain was the throne of "God Highest" and the place of the "assembly" of the gods. It is now possible to identify Mount "Zaphon" and to locate it topographically.

As the dwelling and throne of "God Highest" the "mountain in the North", Mount Zaphon was the center of the universe, the navel of the world. As Zaphon, Zion can be termed ("Joy of all the earth" - Ps. 48:2). The majesty of the place where Yahweh sits enthroned shines out into all the world. Everywhere the beauty and splendor of the mountain of God are spoken of (Lam. 2:15). The spender of paradise came to be associated with the concept of Mountain Zaphon, and a great wealth of cultic and mythological concepts was transferred to Jerusalem, the city of God, and to Mount Zion. Yet all these concepts are merely the glorification of Yahweh, the God of Israel, or of the place where he is present.

The statement in Ps. 46:4, "There is a river whose streams make glad the city of God" is merely an embellishment in reference to Zion, but the context shows clearly that the concept of the primeval ocean, which is found also in against, also echoes here, so that we are reminded of the powers of chaos (v. 5). All the metaphors and allusions are in the service of the declaration concerning the superior power of Israel's God, the protective might of the one who is enthroned on Zion and who intervenes for his people (Ps. 46:1,3,7,11). This enunciates a further theme of the Zion theology. Enemies threaten the city of God (Ps. 46:6; 48:4; 76:5-6). In Ps. 46:3 the tumultuous, chaotic primeval floods, aroused by an earthquake, threaten the mountains symbols of all that is fived and permanent. This cosmic motif probably represents the original from the threat (cf. Ps. 93:3-4). In Ps.46:6 the destructive powers of chaos make their appearance in a "historicized" form: "The nations rage, the kingdoms totter." It is noteworthy that these enemy's powers are characterized as "kingdoms" (Ps. 46:6), "princes" (Ps. 76:12), or "kings" (Ps. 48:4; 76:12). The city of God is surrounded by hostile armies (Ps. 2:2a; 48:4ff.). The foes threaten and roar like "many waters" (Isa. 17:12f; Job 6:23). Obviously, the myth of the raging of the chaotic primeval waters has been applied specifically to Jerusalem in a historicized, political form, from which all mythological concepts and events have been eliminated. It is unlikely that this involves the cultic dramatization of a battle, as proposed by Mowinckel, rather these are ancient cultic traditions that are appropriated by Israel, given new form, and stripped of their mythological significance. It is highly significant that the historicizing of the cosmic struggle against chaos first took place during the transmission of the material in Israel.

When the foes attack, it is shown that the city of God is unconquerable. This is supported by several factors. Jerusalem is the city of God (Ps. 46:49; 48:1b; 87:3). Here is found the "holy habitation" of the Highest (Ps. 46:4b; 76:2; 87:5). The city of God is situated on Yahweh's "holy mountain" (Ps. 48:2; 87:1). On the summit of "Mount Zaphon", which reaches into the heavens (Ps. 48:2). But the decisive reason for the invincibility of the city of God is the fact that Yahweh is "in the midst of her" (Ps. 46:5; 48:3). This is no area of taboo protected by Magic, rather, "the Lord of hosts is with us, the God of Jacob is our refuge" (Ps. 46:7,11). The theme of the invincibility of Jerusalem seems to rest on a very Old tradition (II Sam. 5:6). It was a firm certainty that Zion "cannot be moved", but "abides forever" (Ps. 125:1; Isa. 26:1). When the foes attack they will be beaten back and destroyed (Ps. 76:36; 48:5,6; Isa. 17:13-14; 24:21; 29:8). Yahweh himself shatters his foe with his thunder (Ps. 46:6), with his rebuke (Ps. 76:6; Isa. 17:13), and with the "terror" of God (Ps. 46:8; Isa. 17:14). He destroys their weapons (Ps. 46:9; 76:3-6). A careful analysis of all those factors shows that on the one hand, such motifs as the "rebuke" had their origin in the stream of pre-Israelite mythological tradition, which assumed historicized form in Jerusalem. In the unconquerable city of God, Yahweh confronts his enemies as the creator God who "rebuked" the primeval waters (cf. Isa.17:13; Ps.76:6). On the other hand, the ancient Israelite traditions of holy war can be clearly recognized (Ps.46). Two streams of traditions merged.

Jerusalem, the city of God, is the abode of peace. In her the shalom of Yahweh reigns. In the Psalms the concept shalom is used in four distinct meanings. *First*, the people pray for hope for, and await shalom for the land and for the whole earth. It will be manifested in the form of fruitfulness and undisturbed growth, prosperity, and life (Ps. 72:3,7; 85:11; 147:14). *Second*, Israel prays for, hopes for, and awaits shalom for the whole nation (Ps. 29:11; 85:8; 125:5; 128:6). *Third*, shalom is the basic theme involved in the activity of the king (Ps. 72:3-7), *Fourth*, shalom is a distinctive force that is available to the city of Jerusalem (Ps. 122:6f). The people should pray for the shalom of Jerusalem. The object for which they should pray is made explicit in Ps. 122:7, "Peace be within your walls, and security within your towers."

In summary, we can say that the themes and motifs of the Zion theology have given us a profile of the cultic traditions of Jerusalem.

(iii) Worship in Jerusalem: The pilgrimage to Zion sanctuary was described one of the key elements of worship in Jerusalem. The clans and families traveled to Jerusalem, the mountain of Yahweh, with glad songs and the sound of flutes (Isa. 30:29). This arrival is described in Ps. 122:2, "our feet have been standing within your gates, O Jerusalem!" who was worthy to pass through the gates which in Ps. 118:19 are called "gates of righteousness", "He who walks blamelessly and does what is right, and speaks the truth from his heart......" (Ps. 15:2 cf. Ps. 24:3-4). In the "gate liturgies" the conditions for and mission are made known to those who are arriving to take part in worship. The marks of the "righteous" are proclaimed in the "gates of righteousness." This was a liturgical act, in which the Torah was recited. Based on Ps. 5 it is possible to understand that anyone who was unjustly accused and wanted to appeal sacral justice in the holy precincts had to undergo a preliminary examination at the gate. No one who was boastful or an evildoer was permitted to come into the presence of Yahweh (Ps. 5:4-6). If the initial questioning was decided according to "righteousness", then the accused was granted permission, but since he had not yet been declared innocent he would affirm, "But I through the abundance of thy steadfast love will enter thy house. I will worship toward thy holy temple in the fear of thee" (Ps. 5:7). The "gates of righteousness" were opened to those who were righteous (Ps.118:19). And they entered into the sanctuary (Ps. 118:20).

Immediately following the entrance ceremony of the "gate liturgy" in Ps. 24:1-6 we find the description of the entrance of Yahweh into the sanctuary (Ps. 24:7-10). It is evident that these two events were directly connected. These were the events of the first day of a festival, perhaps the feast of Tabernacles.

Ps. 95:6 contains the cultic cry, "O come, let us worship and bow down, let us kneel before the Lord, our maker." The verb "let us worship" is significant here. It denotes bowing before Yahweh, falling down and praying "towards thy holy temple" (Ps. 5:7). The goal of the procession of Yahweh and the cultic community was the great act of bowing down in the outer court of the temple before the divine king (Ps. 100:4). The community that was gathered there worshipped Yahweh "at his foot stool" (Ps. 99:5) and praised, lauded, and honored him. In this act of worship, the noble appellations of Israel's God were spoken - "Kind", "Almighty God", "Creator", and "Judge". Here music of worship was performed (Ps. 150). Israel came into the presence of Yahweh in order to praise him and give him thanks (Ps. 100:47). The worship of God at the festival began with the call, "serve the Lord with gladness! come into his presence with singing!" (Ps. 100:2). Thus worship. in Israel was characterized by joy. To serve God means in cultic terms to come before his face, to praise him, laud him, and honor him (Ps. 95:1-6). In the spirit of the universal nature of the appellations of Yahweh, Israel's adoration knowns no bounds. All peoples, the whole of creation, heaven and earth, join in the praise of the divine king and creator (Ps. 96; 97:6-9; 98:7-9; 99:1-5; 100:1). The praise of God knows no limits of time.

All the Psalms are characterized by continual, never ending adoration. Even during the night, Praise rises up (Ps. 134; 8:3; Isa. 30:29). We shall now turn to another aspect of Jerusalem worship, i.e., the sacrifice under separate sub-heading.

(c) Sacrifice in the Psalms: The presentation of the sacrifice has constituted a special theme in the cultic life of Jerusalem. But it is surprising that only a little about it is mentioned. It is appropriate to begin with the general understanding of sacrifice in the OT before dealing in particular to the Psalter.

The first type of sacrifice offered in the OT is usually called, Zebah, which etymologically means a "slaughtering" - But it is not the mere fact that the slaughtered animal is vital, but the fact that a common eating of the flesh of the slaughtered animal establishes community. Simply by the fact that they together eat the meat of the sacrifice, those who share in the meal become a community. The meaning, purpose, and effect of the Zebah is the establishment of community among those who share in it. This human community is constituted by the basic community of the people with Yahweh, who is present as a participant in the meal. The fellowship formed creates not union; it creates an offensive and defensive alliance; there is a reciprocal acknowledgment ("I will be your God, and you shall be my people" Jer. 7:23; "our God" - Ps. 95:7; 'thy people' - 79:13), one stands up for other, those involved live together in a relationship of mutual trust and faith.

The other type of sacrifice is the gift offering. This gift offering (minhah) signifies something that is "offered" or "presented". In a secular context is denotes a gift that is intended to win a favor (Gen. 32:13-21; 43:11). Someone gives a gift to another person to show his respect for the other person. It is entirely his own affair and done of his own free will.

Third type of sacrifice mentioned in the Old Testament is 'olah, usually translated "burnt offering", and in fact the gift presented as an 'olah was usually to be consumed by fire. The smoke that ascended to heaven accompanied the homage, praise, petitions, and laments of the giver. The 'olah like minhah, was designated for the exclusive use of Yahweh. In every case the shared offering and the gift offering are two totally different types of sacrifice. In the gift offering, man disposes of something which belongs to him for one reason or another. He gives. He surrenders his gift completely. He surrenders it by destroying it in the fire. He surrenders it because he seeks God's face. is forgiveness, His favor, His good will. In the gift offering he does not seek God's fellowship. The gift offering does not establish a relationship; it underlines in fact the distance between the two. It is an act of homage, a token of respect, submission, surrender to him who receives the gift.

The Psalter makes frequent references to the types of sacrifices mentioned above at several places. Zebah for instance offers in Ps. 4:5; 27:6; 54:6; 116:17, the 'olah alluded in Ps. 20:3; 66:13,25. The Psalter also mentions the thank offering (toda Ps. 56:12; 100; 107:22; 116:17), the free will offering (Ps. 54:6), minhah (Ps. 20:3; 86:8). In spite of these occurrences, the Psalter does not offer any proper theological explanation of the meaning of sacrifice. However, it does contain some interesting 'anti-sacrificial' passages, Ps. 40:6; 50:8-15; 51:116f. to which may be added Ps. 69:30f and 141:2. Anti-sacrificial passages are also found elsewhere in the Old Testament, especially in the prophets (cf. I Sam. 15:22; Isa. 1:11f; Jer. 6:20; 7:21f; Hosea 6:6; Amos 5:21f; Micah 6:6f; Prov. 21:3). In all the instances mentioned above in the Psalter, the rejection or opposition is not to sacrifice per se, but an affirmation that ethical righteousness and obedience to God are more important than sacrifices - cf. Ps. 50:8-15; 69:30f. What is reprieved is that kind of notion that Yahweh is dependent on sacrifices for food and drink (cf. Ps. 50:12-13, also the idea of feeding the deity with sacrificial meat to give strength is an idea of Canaanite sacrificial practice).

(d) Psalms and the kingship: Several songs in the Psalter celebrate the king. In the royal Psalms, the central figure is King (Ps. 2:6; 20:8; 21:1,7; 45:1: 61:6; 63:11; 72:1; 89:18). A distinctive feature is the use of the term "anointed" for the king of Israel: Ps. 2:2; 20:7; 84:9; 89:38,51; 132:10. The king is Yahweh's anointed: Ps. 2:2; 20:7; 84:9; 89:38,51; 132:10. Psalm 89:20 even declares that Yahweh himself has anointed him with the holy oil (cf. Ps. 45:7). W. H. Schmidt rightly observes that, the anointing was not the essential part of coronation ritual, but from time to time it was practiced in Egypt, Syria and even in Hittite context whenever the officials are installed. In Babylon it was believed that the Kingship came down from heaven in mystical prehistory. But in Israel, it is quite different. It is not possible to speak of kingship as such. The striking historical aspect of kingship in Israel is that Israel established this in situation only late in its history. In the Psalms, what is said of the king always involves the name David. David is the first one to be chosen (Ps. 89:3,20,35; 132:1,10,17; 144:10). The kings in Jerusalem (Ps. 144:10) are the "seed" the descendants of David, and therefore the heirs of the promise given through Nathan (II Sam.7), which promised David and his family an everlasting kingdom.

King is called "Son of God", a foreign religious influence in Israel brought in to the divine choice of king in Israel in a demythologized form. In Ps. 2:7 the ruler is declared to be the son of Yahweh. In the act of coronation, the ruler is called to Yahweh's side and is invited to take his place, "sit at my right hand" (Ps. 110:1), he can be called "the man of thy right hand" (Ps. 80:18). As the one enthroned at the right hand of God, the ruler shares in Yahweh's dignity and power as "highest" and can be acclaimed as "the highest of the kings of the earth" (Ps. 89:27). Many of these expressions are in the background of AWA court style. Filled with awe, a cultic speaker calls the king "my Lord" (Ps. 110:1), accords to him the divine designation "shield" (Ps. 84:9-11; 89:18) and even addressed him as "god" (Ps. 45: 6). But this reading of "God" is disputed because of the reason that, "it is beyond doubt that the Jerusalem monarchy, and even more, the monarchy in the states of Israel and Judah, was never regarded as divine". Furthermore, Noth translates the word "God" as "Thy throne is (like) that of God, enduring for ever and ever" (Ps. 45:6). This idea is to be firmly maintained because in Israel the king was not regarded as equal to God, and thus was never consciously addressed in theological terms as "God".

It is beyond doubt that in Israel's worship the king was not the object of veneration. Not even rudiments can be found of any veneration offered to him. At the same time the reigning king in Jerusalem exercised cultic functions. According to Ps. 110:4 the office of Priest was conferred on him. The kings were responsible for performing mediatorial functions, such as offering prayer for all cultic institutions in royal sanctuary in Jerusalem (I Kings 8:22-26), blessing the assembled people of the nation (I Kings 8:14), and on special occasions, offering sacrifices (I Kings 8:62-63). In spite of all this the role of king was limited only to a practical affair as the Priests in Israel grew more steadily.

The king of Israel received royal charisma and concrete commission from Yahweh. Prayers are offered to the king that would receive the gift of rendering justice to his people (Ps. 72:1). It was his commission to judge the people in righteousness, but above all to be the advocate and support of the weak and oppressed (Ps. 72:2, 4, 12ff). As the one who defended the divine will for justice against men of violence, the king was to carry out the office of judge - on behalf of those to whom justice had been denied. He loved righteousness and hated wickedness (Ps. 45:7). He was to intervene for the oppressed when there was no longer any other voice raised on their behalf. In Jerusalem there were "thrones for judgement........... the thrones of the house of David" (Ps. 122:5).

It is probably noteworthy in Israel is the twofold basic relationship of the royal office of judge in Jerusalem. *First*, the kings who pronounce judgement on Zion are successors of an ancient Israelite in situation, which was embodied in the office of "Judge of Israel". This "Judge of Israel" had the responsibility to know and explicate the law and to give information about it, to watch over its observance, and to be responsible for its application to new situations and thus see to it that it has further developed and validated. When the monarchy became established in Israel, the old system confronted a crisis. There is no doubt that the Davidic kings rendered the final verdict in legal cases and in the framework of their royal charisma and commission continued the old tradition and institution. (cf. II Sam. 15:1-6; I Kings 3:16-28; Jer. 21:12; Isa. 16:5; 11:3). *Second*, the judicial activity of the kings in Jerusalem is to be seen in its consistent reference to Yahweh, the God of righteousness and justice. Righteousness and justice proceed himself fully to the righteous will of God. As "righteous" (said) he stands in a right relationship to his God, a relationship in which Yahweh's own righteousness and his own justice will be able to find expression.

The influence of the monarchy operating under the authority of Yahweh went beyond the sphere of justice and the pronouncement of verdicts. I involved shalom of the land and the people. Life, bounteous harvest, good fortune and blessing in boundless measure - these are the expectations connected with Yahweh's presence with his king (Ps. 72:3) and they are not to be thought of as due to the immanent power of a "divine monarchy."

Furthermore, the charisma and commission of the king is characterized by war and conquests of all foes by the king. Yahweh himself arms his anointed when he goes to war against the foes of his people (Ps. 18:39). God intervenes for his king and aids him (Ps. 2:5; 8-9; 21:8-9; 110:2-3; 144:1-2). With the help of Yahweh, the king defeats and destroys all his enemies. They are made a stool for his feet (Ps. 110:1).

In the post-exilic period, when there was no longer an Israelite king on the throne, the royal Psalms were interpreted in an eschatological sense as referring to an ideal future ruler - whom we should call Messiah - though the OT itself employs this term only of the current King.

(e) The Psalms in the New Testament: In the New Testament the word "Psalm" is found seven times and the verb *psallein*, "to sing praise" four times. Some references are not clearly identified, but some are identified clearly. We shall make a general survey of these occurrences to begin with and then talk about their significance in this section. While studying this theme three things in specific should be kept in mind. There are: First, the context of each Psalm quotation is to be investigated to; determine the intention of its kerygma. This includes a precise determination of the place of the quotation in this specific context. Second, from the New Testament context we should identify the purpose for which the Psalm has been quoted. Then we must identify the kerygmatic scope of meaning which the Old Testament text has helped to advance. Third, we should also reflect on the character which the NT context has given to the quotation in its relationship to the way the text was understood in the Old Testament.

(i) New Testament References to the Psalms: While in Judaism the Torah is at the center of worship and life, in the early church the prophetic writings and the Psalms took on special importance. The Septuagint, the Greek translation of the OT, served as the primary source for quotations.

In Luke 20:42 and Acts 1:20 the Psalter is called "the book of Psalms." Luke 24:44 identifies a Psalm quotation as found "in the Psalms". In Acts 13:33; Ps. 2:7 is quoted with the identification "in the second Psalm." Other readings of this text (The Nestle-Aland Greek Testament) identify it as being the "first" Psalm. The term "Psalm" is also found in I Cor. 14:26. Perhaps this quotation refers to three types of Psalm poetry which were inspired by the Psalms of the OT and influenced by its language: *First*, the Jewish psalmody which is accessible in the remarkable example of the Hodayoth ("Thanksgiving Psalm") of Qumran; *Second*, the Jewish-Christian Psalmody which is seen in Luke l:46:55, 68-79; 2:29-35; *Third*, the Christian psalmody which permeates the book of Revelation (Rev. 5:9-10; 11:17-18; 12:10-12; 19:6-8). The criterion of it is appropriate to use in worship is the (oikodome), the edification of the church.

Ephesians 5:19-20 and Col. 3:16 also refer to Psalms that were sung by the early Christians or used in their prayers. The worshippers are exhorted to "be filled with the Spirit, addressing one another in Psalms and hymns and spiritual songs, singing and making melody to the Lord with all your heart" (Eph. 5:19-20). in these texts the purpose of using Psalms is kerygmatic in function. Even though Psalms are directed to God in petition, adoration, thanks, and song, they are also intended to speak to those hearers who are the same time singing and praying.

(ii) Psalms of special significance: It is clear that in early Christianity several Old Testament Psalms were extremely important. They were quoted again and again as "star witnesses" in the proclamation that the promises of God had been fulfilled. These are Psalm 2; 22; 69; 110; 118. It seems appropriate to begin with Psalm 2 and 110, two "royal Psalms", because these two songs stand at the center of the messianic message of the NT and are used as witnesses to the messiahship of Jesus of Nazareth.

Psalm 2 is quoted often in the NT, especially in the synoptic Gospels in connection with the baptism of Jesus and his transfiguration (Matt. 3:17; 17:5; Mark 9:7; Luke 3:22; 9:35). II Peter 1:17 also cites it in reference to the transfiguration. Psalm 2 is also quoted in Acts (4:25f; 13:33), in the letter to the Hebrews (1:5; 5:5; 7:28), and in Revelation (2:26f; 6:15; 11:15,18;17:18; 19:19). Two themes are stressed in these quotation in the New Testament: divine son ship (based on Ps. 2:7) and the rebellion and defeat of the hostile nations (Ps. 2:1-2, 8-9). Since particular attention has been paid to me witness to divine son ship, and the motif of the nation derives its significance in connection with the often-quoted saying in Ps. 2:7, it is appropriate to begin with the saying.

In LXX. the Hebrew text is translated by the words: "You are my son, today I have begotten you" - Ps. 2:7, It should be borne in mind that what God says, transmitted by a prophet, had its Sitz-im-Leben in the royal ritual of the enthronement (or annual festival) of the king of Jerusalem, and that the testimony given "today" is to be understood as an act of adoption, and thus as a legal act. The ruler was installed by Yahweh as his "son", that is, as the representative of divine power and majesty. Thus the adoption took on the meaning of a choosing of the king. The chosen ("anointed") is placed at Yahweh's side as the one nearest to him, as the "heir" of the realm of divine glory (Ps. 2:8-9).

We need to ask the question: How the word "today" in Ps. 2:7 was understood in the early Christian kerygma, that is, in terms of what event the elevation to divine sonship in the OT passage was understood in the New Testament. Four possibilities can be discerned in the text. *First*, the "today" is the event of baptism of Jesus. *Second*, in the miracle of transfiguration Jesus was declared to be the "son of God." *Third*, Jesus became the "Son of God" by his resurrection from the dead, *Fourth*, the ascension in to God's heavenly world elevated the one who was humbled to be God's son.

In addition to these Christological interpretations of Ps. 2:7, the early church drew attention to the relevance of two other themes in Ps. 2 for the decisive divine statement: *First*, threats against "God's anointed" by the hostile nations, and Second, the triumph over these nations and their rulers by the sound of God, who had been installed as heir and emperor. The first of these themes is developed in Ps. 1-2 and is cited in Acts 4:25-26. When the apostle Peter and John were released often their interrogation and went back to their supporters, they reported about being brought to trial before the elders and chief Priests. The community responded with the praise and adoration of God. In this context they are referred to Ps. 2:1-2, as translated in LXX. In v. 24 they praised the creator and Lord of heaven and earth and in vv. 25f., with the quotation from Psalm 2, they praised the Lord of the nations. Still, the situation described in Ps. 2:1-2 of a worldwide revolution of the "kings of the earth" and the "rulers" is not applied directly to the legal accusations that Peter and John had faced, but the judicial procedure against "thy holy servant Jesus, who thou didst anoint" (v. 27). Herod, Pilate, and the Gentiles are named. It is remarkable how immediately the application is drawn to the trial of Jesus. In this context, and in illustration of this scene, Ps. 2:1-2 is quoted. That means that it is against Jesus as the Christ that the power of the Gentile world rose in rebellion, and not have been crucified. In vain they dared to seek to dethrone "God's anointed". But if this is a repetition of threat of a worldwide revolt against God and his anointed, then the community can, in the light of the Christ event and thus in the assurance that the enemy has already been defeated pray that God will hear and rescue them out of their present perils. What they are experiencing are in reality nothing but rearguard actions. For in the trials of Jesus the fate of the nations and their rulers has already been decided. Psalm 2 as here been fulfilled as a whole. Psalm 2:1-4 is seen in the light of the eschatological enthronement of Jesus Christ. With the crucifixion, opposition and accusations have resulted in an event that was in accord with will of God, and which attained its goal in the exaltation of Christ and the defeat of the hostile forces. Jesus is the "servant of God" (Isa. 52:13ff), who astonished the nations and closed the mouths of kings (Isa. 52:15). "God was with him" (Acts 10:38). He raised him from the dead (Acts 3:26) and glorified him (Acts 3:13). Every uprising of the nations has been brought to an end in this eschatological event, an event foreshadowed in the Old Testament. The promise made implicitly in Ps. 2:1-2 is recognized as a promise in its explicitly manifested fulfillment and is proclaimed as having attained its goal. The promise of God given to David and his dynasty, with all the events involved in its accomplishment, has been fulfilled in Jesus the Messiah. From now on the hostile powers that confront the Christian community can accomplish nothing that is not the will of God. This will, was accomplished in the crucifixion. Who are attacking their uprising will therefore never achieve its purpose. Moreover, the quotation of Ps. 2:1-2 was made a part of a prayer of the community in the early church, as a promise in the context of the Davidic history (Acts 4:25), in the context of the promises given to David, to which the Messiah's community could appeal in a situation of concrete peril.

(iii) Other Psalm Texts cited or quoted: In the pericope of the "wise men from the East" (Matt. 2:1-18) the fulfillment of a prophecy found in Ps. 72:10,15 and Isa. 60: 6 is described Three things are significant in Matt. 2:11. *First*, the structure of the passage with the use of the OT materials; *Second*, the enhancing of the statements about the "wise men" by the use of Psalm 72 and its words about "kings" that come from afar, which had effects on the tradition of the church; and *Third*, the messianic understanding of the entire pericope - it is God's Messiah who is being adored. Other examples are: In the account of the temptation (Matt. 4:1-11; Luke 4:1-13) the use of the OT is quite different. Psalm 91:11-12 is quoted by the tempter (Matt. 4:6; Luke 4:10-11). Here scripture is used as a kind of lively affirmation of one's own commitment and faith to God Matt. 5:4 'Blessed are those who mourn for they shall be comforted", reminds the hearer of Psalm 126:5-6, "May those who sow in tears reap with shouts of Joy!" and also of Isa. 61:2; The Beatitude in Matt 5:8 draws on the phraseology of the Psalm that speak of a "pure heart" (Ps. 24:4; 51:10; 73:1). The recasting of the concept is interesting. According to Ps. 24:4 those who have a "pure heart" will be permitted to enter the sanctuary (Ps. 24:4), while in Matt. 5:8 the eschatological vision of God will be fulfilled of the promise. Thus the NT makes explicit in eschatological terms the old cultic formula "to see the face of God", which in the Psalms means to enter into the sanctuary, the place where Yahweh is present.

***Conclusion:*** the book of Psalms as discussed above has rich content and a variety of literary and theological categories. It was also observed that the book of psalms was freely circulated and used in local and small sanctuaries before it was used in the Jerusalem Temple. The richness of theological categories that the book has once again demonstrate that how it uses used in cultic and liturgical setting.

***2. The Book of Lamentations:*** Psalms shows the clearest similarities of the Book of Lamentations. In fact, Lamentations contains five or more Psalms, conforming to the patterns followed in the Psalter. Appropriate to the title of the work, the entire book consists of Psalms, of distress. The book of Lamentations, like the Torah and Psalms, neatly divides into five units corresponding to the chapter divisions. Within each of the first four chapters, succeeding lines begin with successive letters of the Hebrew alphabet. All poems in this book relate in theme to the fall of Jerusalem in 586 BCE and the subsequent Babylonian exile. In the following pages, we shall make a brief survey on the issues like Title, place of the book in the canon, date, authorship, form and structure, content and main theological message of the book.

***(A) Title:*** Original Hebrew title of the book is Qinoth, "dirges" or "laments", according to Rabbinic tradition. But now it is titled as 'Ekah', "Alas, how....." based on the first word of the text. LXX uses the threnoi means "lamentations", followed by Vulgate and modern translations. In LXX, Vulgate and modern translations, the book appears after Jeremiah. The superscription in LXX B (Codex Vaticanus) specifically connects the book with Jeremiah (by the words: "Jeremiah had wept and lamented"); this usage is followed by other versions. Probably due to II Chr. 35:25, which speaks of Jeremiah composing a funeral lament for king Josiah on the latter's death. This is not, however, the content of lamentations, which speak of the destruction of Jerusalem.

***(B) Place of the Book in Canon:*** This is one of the five books of Megilloth and in the Hebrew Canon it is placed in the eleven books of the third part of the Hebrew bible namely Kethubim. In Rabbinic bible the book is arranged as per the order of the festival which each of the five books of megilloth is read: Song of Songs (Passover), Ruth (Pentecost or weeks), Lamentations (9th of the month Ab), Ecclesiastes (The feast of Tabernacles) and Esther (the festival of Purim). Codes Leningradensis and Biblia Hebraica Stuttgartensia (BHS), the book is arranged according to the chronological order: Ruth (in the time of Judges), Song of Songs (in the young age of king Solomon), Ecclesiastes (in the old age of king Solomon), Lamentations (during the time of the fall of Jerusalem). In LXX and Vulgate as already been mentioned, the book is placed after Jeremiah due to the assumption that in II Chronicles 35:25. There is Jeremiah's funeral lament after the death of king Josiah, but as already stated that is not what the book is concerned about.

***(C) Date:*** Traditionally, the book is dated soon after the Babylonian exile somewhere around 586 BCE; thus the statements reflect no hope situation (Lam. 2:15a). Based on the order of the content we do have the following suggestions: According to W. Rudolph, chapter 1 is perhaps written after 597 BCE because it does not speak about destruction but only about famine and chapter 3 is considered to be the latest because the destruction is described more vividly than chapter 2 (but no strong evidence to prove this point). W. Fuerst contends that, not all chapters in this book are written at the same time, but D. R. Hillers is of the opinion that all the chapters are written and composed at the same time.

***(D) Authorship:*** Rabbinic tradition, LXX, Syriac, Tragum and Christian tradition attributed the authorship of the Lamentations to Jeremiah till 18th century A.D. But in 1712, Vander Hardt challenged Jeremiah's authorship to Lamentations by saying that chapter was written by Shadrach Daniel. Ibn Ezra later on did not deny Jeremiah's authorship, but rejected the view that it is the scroll burnt by king Jehoiakim. Moreover, in the Masoretic Text, no clue is given in the title as to say that the book is written by Jeremiah. Those who strongly argue for the Jeremiah's authorship of this book also furnish the following clues: II Chro. 35:25, Jeremiah laments for the king Josiah and in 9:1 of Jeremiah, Jeremiah weeps, perhaps lamentations 4:20 may have been referred to Josiah. If the book of Lamentations is an integral part of the book of Jeremiah why then is it separated from the latter? the reasons given to this question are: Lamentations 4:20 has a definite reference to king Zedekiah (but Jeremiah was perhaps against royal theology?); the other clues are in Lam 1:10, Jeremiah was against the temple and 2:9 there are no visions given to the prophet is in time with Jeremiah's thinking. There are other suggestions for the authorship of the book suggested by other scholars: According to F. M. Cross and N. K. Gottwald, the author of the book was a cult prophet, lay person in the royal court or even the probable idea that the book is written by many authors. The reasons for this is: in chapter 1 Hebrew ayin comes before Pe; in chapter 3 and 4 Pe comes before ayin and other reason is that chapters 1, 2, 4 are individual laments, but chapter 5 is a communal lament. Probably a redactor at a later stage compiled all these individual parts into a single unit.

***(E) Form and Structure:*** Chapter 1-4 are composed in third person in form and content. Usually the book is called acrostic poem with Qinah (used in laments, especially in funerary laments like Amos 5:1ff with 3+4 meter in

Hebrew throughout) meter. The questions why this poem is acrostic? Four reasons are furnished by N. K. Gottwald as follows: (i) belief in magical power of writing, (ii) exhibit artistic form, (iii) form by which merismus (wholeness of beginning and end) is achieved, (iv) format by which mnemonic expressions (boundless grief is expressed). The other form is found in its Chiastic Structure: Chapter I: a generalizing summary; Chapter 2: Vivid description; Chapter 3: intensified acrostic structure; Chapter 4: Vivid description; Chapter 5: Generalizing summary. The center this five-chapter structure is Chapter 3:31, 32, 33 with the theme of "assurance" in the midst of trouble.

The genre contains mixed and varied forms. On the whole the Poem contains individual and communal laments. Chapters 1, 2, 4 are individual laments and funeral dirge; Chapter 5 is a communal lament. Chapter 3 contains a mixture of genre: vv. 19-24 and 54-58 thanksgiving words; vv. 25-39: wisdom song; Chapter 4:21-22 contains mixed oracles of salvation and judgement. i.e., salvation for Zion and Judgement on Edom. 5:19 is a hymnic speech. In general, on the whole the meter of this poem is 3+2 (Qinah meter), but 4+2 (in chapter 5) and 2+2 is also present at certain places. The city of Zion is personified as virgin at least 25 times in the poem. Let us talk more on the acrostic structure of the Poem in the following lines.

Several features of this acrostic poem of Lamentations make the series unique. *First*, Lamentations concentrates on a single disaster, the fall of Jerusalem in 586 BCE along with subsequent hardships. *Second*, the book views the disaster three perspectives, including complaints from individuals, the community as a whole, and Jerusalem itself. *Third*, Lamentations shows signs of thematic development from poem to poem. *Fourth*, the acrostic structure of the units shows four variations in type in five chapters. All these unique features combine to indicate that Lamentations, unlike the Psalms, comprised a single carefully constructed unit.

The acrostic structure presents obvious evidence of the book's careful design. All five of the poems contain a number of lines divisible by twenty-two (the number of letters in the Hebrew alphabet). The lines of chapter 1 and 2 follows an AXX, BXX pattern. Chapter 3 follows an AAA and BBB pattern. Chapter 4 follows an AX, BX pattern. Chapter 5 can be designated X, X with no acrostic pattern. English translations however, indicate none of these patterns. Two features of this acrostic organization reveal a concern for the development of the book as a whole. *First*, the numbers of lines per chapter decrease from the beginning to end. Such a design may mimic the 3+2 pattern of Qinah rhythm. *Second*, the acrostic pattern reaches its climax with Chapter 3. Chapter 3 possesses three lines in succession beginning with each letter of the Hebrew alphabet. Only Chapter 3 exhibits this threefold acrostic structure. This represents the apex of the 'exiles' complaint. The third chapter deserves special attention for this reason. The following Table explains the Acrostic form in the book of Lamentations. (Table is adapted from Donald K. Berry, An Introduction to wisdom and poetry of the OT, Nashville: Broad man & Holman publishers, 1995, P. 413-415).

| Chapter | Number of Verses | Acrostic Structure |
|---|---|---|
| 1 | 66 | First letter of the first time of triple lines forms acrostic |
| 2 | 66 | First letter of first line of triple lines forms acrostic |
| 3 | 66 | First letter of all triple lines form acrostic |
| 4 | 44 | First letter of first line of double lines forms acrostic |
| 5 | 22 | No acrostic form |

The table below again shows a sense of varieties of types of units with combinations employed in the chapters. These varieties show the depth of the sense of grief and problem expressed.

| | | |
|---|---|---|
| 1 | Report of suffering and grief | (throughout) |
| 2 | Corporate confessions of sin | 3:40-42 |
| 3 | Account of the fall as a divine operation | 2:1-9 |
| 4 | Call for help | 1:22; 2:20 |
| 5 | Call for lamentation | 2:18-19 |
| 6 | Statement of trust | 3:22-29 |
| 7 | Remembrance of better fortunes | 4:7 |
| 8 | Imprecations against enemies | 4:21-22 |

***(F) Content:*** The contents are also based on the form already described in our previous section. We shall deal with the content in this section according to each chapter.

***Chapter 1:*** divides into four main parts A communal lament.

vv. 1-11: lament over the overthrow of the city, personified as a woman, the daughter of Zion, who speaks in 9c and 11c.

vv. 12-16: the personified city laments (note v. 13).

v. 17: a transition which says Zion has none to comfort her; the Lord has sent the enemies.

vv. 18-22: Zion again laments, calling on the Lord to hear her and deal with the enemy as He has dealt with her.

To be dated in 597, after the first deportation (according to W. Rudolph) or after 586 BCE.

***Chapter 2:*** a communal lament which describes vividly the fact that Yahweh became like an enemy to destroy Jerusalem. The concrete details suggest that it was composed soon after the disaster of 586.

***Chapter 3***:

vv. 1-18: the confession of suffering of an individual.

vv. 19-24: a confession of trust in Yahweh.

vv. 25-33: instruction, in the Spirit of wisdom, to wait for the help of the Lord. Note vv.31-33, which are at the center of this chapter (and the book).

vv. 34-39: Voice the doubt which afflict the people; refutes them.

vv. 40-41: call to common prayer.

vv. 42-47: prayer in the form of a communal lament.

vv. 48-66: an individual lamentation.

This poem appears to be a liturgy of lament, which seems to presuppose a cultic memorial celebration at the ruins of the temple (suggested by Zech. 7:1ff and 8:18ft).

***Chapter 4:***

vv. 1-16: descriptive lamentation over the misery of the people of Jerusalem; it is emphasized that the distress is Yahweh's punishment for sin.

vv. 17-20: lamentation in 1st person plural, pointing a vivid picture of the destruction of the city. Note v.20, describing the taking of king Zedekiah: this is an excellent summary of the Theology of kingship which gave rise to the messianic hope ("anointed" meshiah).

v. 21: Punishment of Edom in the form (Gattung) of a salvation saying, Ironic.

v. 22a: a salvation saying for Zion. Compare with Isaiah 40:1-2, unique in lament.

v. 22 b: A threat saying for Edom.

Like Chapter 2, this must be dated soon after 586 BCE.

***Chapter 5:*** A classic form of communal lament.

v. 1: Introduction, with invocation of Yahweh and the call for help.

vv. 2-28: the prayer and cry for help and deliverance.

All five of these poems witness to the crisis of faith in Jerusalem after its fall. The Royal-Zion theology of Judah stated that Jerusalem would not fall; the Davidic dynasty would not end. The songs lead the community from doubt and disappear to a lamentation and intercession. (Chapters 1-3); to the thought that Zion's suffering has redeemed its guilt (4:22a); to prayer before God.

In addition to these insights, it is interesting to note that in Chapter 4: there is a formula that presents the contrast between former glory and present shame in a "once.... now" format. The following table lists major examples from Chapter 1, adapted from D. K. Berry, An Introduction to poetic and wisdom literature of the OT, P. 416.

| Once | Now | Verse |
|---|---|---|
| Full of people | A widow | 1 |
| Princes | Vassal | 1 |
| Many lovers | No comforter | 2 |
| Many friends | All enemies | 2 |
| Festivals | Mourning | 4 |
| Foes | Masters | 5 |
| Majesty | Rules displaced | 6 |
| Precious things | Afflictions and wandering | 7 |
| Pure sanctuary | Filled with Gentiles | 10 |
| Treasures | Starving | 11 |
| Lovers | Liars | 19 |
| The "once…now" scheme | Also appears in 4:1-2 and 5:1-18 | |

***(G) Theology:*** The point discussed throughout the poem is concerning the destruction of the city, temple and the aftermath of the destruction of Jerusalem in 587 BCE. The destruction on the whole is seen as a horrible scene, but there is a realization that the punishment is deserved because of their sin (the realization is on the part of the people concerning their sin). Even the prophets and the Priests share the blame rather than people only (2:14; 4:13). There are also some references to the traditions which have been broken and this make the people very difficult to pray for Yahweh.

Another significant contribution of the book of Lamentations is concerning its reference to the Royal Zion Theology. Two things in particular are said about this. *First*, the reference to Zion past (2:15). All who pass by clap their hand by looking at the present pathetic condition of Jerusalem by remarking. Is this the city that once called the perfection of beauty, the joy of the whole earth? According to 4:12. the inhabitants of the world not believed that enemy could enter into the gates of Jerusalem; even it is mentioned in 2:4f that Jerusalem is visible. *Second*, reference to the royal past is made. According to 4:20. the anointed one of the Lord is taken away, O King. The sins of Judah were too much that the unconditional promise to Zion was written off, therefore turn to God (3:40). But there is a feeling that the punishment given to them is well deserved for what they have done but at times felt that it is too much, therefore, there is a shift in emphasis in chapter 3:31,33. God will not cast off his people forever, God doesn't afflict his chosen ones willingly. To have faith means it is waiting for Yahweh. The basic deuternomic idea that punishment is the result of sin is applicable here although this. view is dominant in the entire book.

The content of the book also relates to an annual commemoration of the fall of Jerusalem. The present day of fasting known as the ninth of Ab May have originated in such responses during the exile. These laments evolved into the current text which is mere a record of the depth of suffering than a conventional lament. These chapters survive as reminders to future generations of the absolute desperation of times.

***Conclusion:*** the book of Lamentations with its rich variety of literary expressions was a conscious document composed at a time when Israelites were totally shattered and devastated by war and destruction after the exile. As noted above one major purpose of the book may be to vividly depict the amount of disaster and lead the community into a world of hope and restoration despite the loss.

***(3) The Song of Songs:*** The book takes its name from its first two words: sirhassirim (song of songs). In Greek the title is: asma asmator; Vulgate gives the title: Cantium Canticorum. The periphrastic superlative is intended to suggest that the book is "the most beautiful (or best) Song of Solomon", who is reputed to have written 1500 songs (as mentioned in I Kings 4:32). The association of this book with Solomon is probably the real reason why the book became part of the Canon; its canonical status dates back to before the so-called Synod or Jamnia (ca, AD. 100), nor was it questioned at that time. Subsequently during the second century, doubts arose as to the propriety of its inclusion, but these were put to rest by the statement of Mishna Yadayim 3.5. Evidence for the use of the book as the festival scroll for Passover dates from the eighth century. Thus this is regarded one among the five books of Megilloth. In the following pages we shall focus our attention on this book by dealing with the issues like: the structure, form and in relation to the sitz-im-leben of the book as proposed by several scholars. Also brief consideration on the points like: authorship, date, place in the canon, interpretation and purpose.

***(A) Structure:*** There has been always a question raised concerning the structure of this book: Is it a loose connection of individual poem? Or unified compositions of five to eight poems (longer ones), with the integrity of the theme and the unity of action? N. K. Gottwald identities unity and context through the repetition of figures of speech. For instance, in 2:15 there is a description of vineyard and in 5:1 and 8:13 there is also description of garden. Both these descriptions are compared to women in 1:1-3 to chapter 8, Then there is a possibility that it may contain an inclusion. Rolf Rendtoff finds a structure or frame work of 1:2-6 and 8:8-14. It contains the following elements in a chiastic construction: *First*, declaration of love by the woman for her beloved with the invitation "Draw me alter you, let us make haste" (1:2-4); this is matched by the conversation of the lovers at the end (8:13f) which in turn leads up to the woman's invitation, "Make haste my beloved". *Second*, the depicted as the vineyard. *Third*, associated with second, the speech of her welcoming her beloved. This framework is anchored to the center of the composition by the invitation of the man of his betrothed "come with me, my bride" (4:8), which corresponds to the invitations of the woman at the beginning and at the end.

One basic dividing line is provided by the woman's appeal to the "daughters of Jerusalem." It has a twofold function in the composition. On the one-hand the phrase, 'I adjure you, daughters of Jerusalem', used four times (2:7; 3:5; 5:8; 8:4), each time marks a conclusion, so that the whole collection with in the frame work is divided into four sections, 1:7-2:7 contains three conversations between the lovers (1:7f; 9-17, 2:1-3) and a final description of the love scene with words of the woman (2:4-7) which ends with the appeal to the 'daughters of Jerusalem' 2:8-3:5 contain only words or songs of the woman; here 2:8f and 17 correspond, and in 3:1-5 again, to conclude with, there is the description of a love scene which ends with the appeal to the 'Daughters of Jerusalem'. 3:6-5:1 begin with the description of a splendid procession of king Solomon (3:6-11) and are followed with words of the man: first of all, a description of the beloved (4:1-7) and then further discourses and songs to the 'bride' (kalla, the Hebrew word only here in 4:8-12; 5:1), which ends with a conversation (4:16-5th Chapter). The section 5:2-8 serves as a transition: this time the concluding love scene does not take place, so that the appeal to the 'daughters of Jerusalem' (5:8) is at the same time an introduction to a conversation with a double question-and-answer play (5:9-16; 6:1-3). 6:4-7:10 contain descriptions of the beloved and love songs by the man (6:4-7,8-10,11f; 7:2-6,7-10); in 7:11 the woman again speaks until the concluding love scene in 8:1-4, which again ends with an appeal to the 'daughters of Jerusalem.'

Between the lost love some (8:1-4) and the final part of the framework (8:8-14) there is a concluding conversation between the lovers (vv. 5-7) which contains emphatic, reflective sayings about love ('Love is strong as death', v. 6). This forms the climax of the love conversations and songs.

The structure of the song of songs can be presented as follows: However, this is not an exclusive structure in itself. There can be modifications and variations possible. 1:2-6: Invitation to set out, vineyard metaphor, brothers (v. 5 - Daughters of Jerusalem).

| | |
|---|---|
| I:7-2:7 | |
| 1:7f | |
| 9-17 | Conversation of the lovers |
| 2:1-3 | Love Scene ('I adjure you, daughters of Jerusalem') |
| 2:4-7 | |
| II. 2:8-3:5 | |
| 2:8-14 | |
| 15 | Songs of the woman |
| 16f | Love Scene ('I adjure you, daughters of Jerusalem') |
| 3:1-5 | |
| III. 3:6-5:1 | |
| 3:6-11 | Splendid procession of King Solomon (vv. 10f. 'Daughters of Jerusalem Zion) |
| 4:17 | |
| 4:8 | (Invitation to set out) |
| 9-11 | |
| 4:12-15 | Song of the man |
| 4:16-5:1 | |
| Interlude 5:2-6:3 | |
| 5:2-8 | Delayed love scene ('I adjure you, daughters of Jerusalem') |
| 9-6 | Conversations with the 'daughters of Jerusalem' |
| 6:1-3 | |
| IV. 6:4-8:4 | |
| 6:4-7 | |
| 8-10 | |
| 11f & 7:1f | Songs of the man |
| 7:2-6 | |
| 7-10 | |
| 11-14 | |
| 8:1-4 | Invitation to the beloved Love Scene ('I adjure you. daughters of Jerusalem') |
| 8:5-7 | Concluding conversation of the lovers ('Love is a strong as death') |
| 8:8-14 | Brothers, vineyard metaphor, invitation to set out. |

There are others who comment on the structure by saying that the song cannot comprise a drama in the proper sense, due to the lack of plot. Other features associated with drama (characters, scenes, settings, action) occur frequently. However, on the basis of the vocabulary and the content of the images, the sentiment expressed in 8:6 identifies the theme: "Love is strong as death." Emphasis throughout the work is on the exclusive devotion of the couple to one another. Love remains in spite of interference (2:2), separation

(5:6), and beating (5:7). Not only does it endure, but its intensity never diminishes. Instead, its depth may actually increase from beginning to end. This tenure development offers the nearest thing to plot, making the drama something of a dramatic illustration of the moral expressed in 8:6. Based on the thematic or formal units in the Song of Songs, the following structure is proposed by D. K. Berry, An Introduction to Poetic and wisdom Literature of the OT, 1995, p.386.

| | |
|---|---|
| 1:2-4 | Love |
| 1:5-8 | Pastoral images |
| 1:9-17 | Royal luxury |
| 2:1-7 | Pastoral images |
| 2:8-17 | Pastoral images |
| 3:1-5 | Night / sleep |
| 3:6-11 | Royal references |
| 4:1-5:1 | Pastoral / garden imagery |
| 5:2-8 | Report of events (linked to 5:9-6:3 by question in 5:9) |
| 5:9-6:3 | Questions (5:9; 6:1) |
| 6:4-10 | Pastoral images (linked to 5:9-6:3 by question in 6:10) |
| 6:11-14 | Pastoral images, "looking" |
| 7:1-9 | Pastoral images, beauty |
| 7:10-8:4 | Pastoral images |
| 8:5 | (Isolated Questions) |
| 8:6-7 | Strength of love |
| 8:6-10 | Breasts / Building imagery |
| 8:11-12 | Vineyard / Solomon |
| 8:13 | (Isolated Statement) |
| 8:14 | (Isolated Statement) |

***(B) Form and Sitz-im-Leben:*** It has been recognized that the form of this book is love poetry but with different genre like: Song of yearning for love, Songs of admiration of the beloved (Therefore we find some words like: boasts, teases (teasing), descriptive forms of the physical love experiences. This type of form is found in the Arabian Poetic expression which are called Wasfs. The Wasf describes the beauty of the spouse's (or lover's) body. It typically surveys the subject's appearance from feet to head or head to feet: vv. 1-5 of chapter 4 review the appearance of her upper torso involving images listed in the following chart. This table / chart is adapted from D.K. Berry, An Introduction to Poetic and Wisdom Literature of the OT, 1995, p.393.

***Chapter 4:1-3 of Song of Songs***

| | | |
|---|---|---|
| Verse 1 | Eyes | Doves |
| Verse 1 | Hair | Flocks of Goats |
| Verse 2 | Teeth | Twins of washed sheep |
| Verse 3 | Lips | Crimson Thread |
| Verse 3 | Cheeks | Pomegranate halves |
| Verse 4 | Neck | Tower of David |
| Verse 5 | Breasts | Twin fawns |

There are similar examples too we find in the Egyptian love songs, (cf. also 6:4-9). Others call the expression of love poetry in the song as Travesties, here the lover is portrayed in a role above or below in the social ladder. For example: Lover is either portrayed as a king or as a shepherd. All these elements are combined and woven together in the entire poem, perhaps sung at the wedding ceremony in Palestine. Related to the question of form, the sitz-im-leben is very vital question we shall now discuss in brief. There are at least four important proposals in this regard made by different scholars.

*First*, according to J. G. Wetzstein, (1873), who was an anthropologist contended that the song was a marriage song, resembling Palestinian wedding customs. But this view is very old and is also disputed by the scholars because of the reason that, not all the songs in the book are marriage songs, some are Wasfs, not at all connected with any marriage occasion.

*Second*, according to Ewald (1826) who proposed dramatic theory in which he said that the Song of Songs is a plot of the drama. The "Shulamite" woman was brought before the king to be with him, but she remains faithful to her lover, who is a shepherd. But Rolf Rendtroff refutes this idea and calls it as a woman's song; the woman has the first and last words and also plays a dominant role in other respects. Her conversation partners are always the 'daughters of Jerusalem.' Her beloved, who also speaks often (mostly indirectly with in one of the woman's discourses 2:10-14; 5:2), is described as a herdsman (1:7; 2:16 etc.) who comes from out on the mountains (2:8,17 etc.). He is contrasted with king Solomon, on whom the woman looks from afar with the 'daughters of Jerusalem' (3:6-11) and chose many wives (6:8) and rich vineyards (8:11) only serve as a contrast to her beloved (6:9; 8:12). Moreover, Rentdorff says that it is not a plot, nor is it a drama.

*Third*, Meek and Miller suggests that it is a cultic drama like in the pattern of cult of dying and rising of Tammuz / Ishtari (Haller and Schmoekel also subscribe to this View). Ishtar looks for Tammuz but he is dead. This cultic drama (in the cultus) is enacted by a Priest. (Tammuz) and a Priestess (Ishtar), representing divine marriage (as in Babylon) and at the end heavens are opened and rain comes (resembles fertility cult). But scholars strongly object to these view found in the book, rather Song of Songs speaks more of a longing, physical and emotional love is more indicated rather than love in marriage.

*Fourth*, N. K. Gottwald raises the question, where is the class of origin of such a literature? Indeed, this was not originated in the context of Patriarchy. This poem speaks about woman: 2:10-14, 5:2ff etc. Then is a collection of such poems found in the Egyptian upper class, Gottwald supposes that it may be the same in the case of Israel with only the difference that like what we described in the form of Travesties, may be lower class is playing a role like an upper class here in this poem.

***(C) Authorship, Date and Place in the Canon:*** Traditionally it is believed to be written by Solomon (cf. I Kings 4:29-32 – because Solomon wrote many songs), but the superscription (1:1) may be a later addition, the lover of the girl is considered to be the king (1:4,12 due to the presence of the phrase: "king has brought me"). According to Baba Bathra 15.a, Hezekiah and his scribes may have written this song like many other songs, so also the Proverbs (Prov. 25:1ff). Some would strongly argue for the wisdom influence in the song. According to 30:19, there is an idea that, the way of the man is with woman, Song of Song: also illustrates this point very well throughout.

Concerning the date of the book, the final redaction (not actual composition) of it may have taken place after the time of Solomon, most probably the date goes back to the Post-exilic times, even as late as third century BCE. This conclusion drawn based on the image of words of Post-exilic times in the book. For instance, usage of Persian word like "Parotes" means "Orchard" in 4:13; Greek or Iranian loan word like apriyon means "chariot" in 3:9 is used; the prefix Seh is used instead of 'aser (which is normally used in other poetic texts), Moreover, several words are related to Aramaic.

The words like daughters of Jerusalem, Sharon (2:1), Hermon (4:8), Carmel (7:5) etc. indicate that this book was probably had its origin in Palestine.

The book's inclusion in the Canon is due to the reason of Solomonic authorship. For Jews this book means God's love for Israel, for Roman church Jesus' love for Mother is the theme to which the book is compared with. For Christian tradition this book is interpreted in terms of God's love for the church (the community of believers).

***(D) Interpretation and Purpose:*** From the early church father's time onwards, it was an allegorical interpretation of the text that was dominant regarding this poem.

A broad tradition of Jewish and Christian exegetes answer the question, how did a collection of love songs come to be in the canon of holy scripture? by saying that, by means of an allegorical interpretation. "may contend that the texts do not deal with the love between man and woman but with that between God and Israel or between Christ and the Church. However, it is by no means certain that this allegorical interpretation antedated the incorporation of the work into canon. Sharp criticism from Rabbi Akiba (c. CE 50-135) is reported of those who sing the Song of Songs in the taverns, so this evidently happened at that time. The Mishnah (Tractate Yadayim III. 5) hands down a rabbinic discussion about the sanctuary (i.e. the canonicity) of the Song of Songs (and Koheleth), here again Rabbi Akiba declares against those who challenge them. "All scripture is holy, but the Song of Songs is most holy."

Another leading interpretation on the Song of Songs is called Dramatic interpretation proposed by Milton, Origen and later developed by Selitzch in the 19th century. According to this interpretation, two twin characters are found in this song: Solomon and Shulamite girl, i.e., "Solomon takes her from her village and eventually marries her". Another suggestion in the same ground is made by Ewald: Solomon, Shulamite girl and shepherd lover are the main characters in the drama. However, "she (the girl) remains true (to her lover) despite the King's desperate efforts to win her." According to Wetzstein, the Song of Songs is in the form of Nuptial songs, used in the marriage with so plain and erotic meaning.

The main purpose of the book is to serve as an object lesson, an extended mashal. The Song illustrates rich wonders of human love, provides a wholesome balance between the extremities, i.e., asceticism and too much romantic outlook. Love is pure than our own thinking, and it is a deeply felt expression. The Song in its literal sense viewed as a celebration of love between man and woman, but more than that, the elevation of a love so genuine at it cannot be purchased with royal enticements. It is like divine love, given freely and unmeritorious.

***Conclusion:*** The Song of Songs was written for different purposes for any contemporary Christian community can benefit from its message. The book talks about the two extremes of too much ascetic thinking or too much romantic orientation. It calls us to balance between these two lopsided views. The book also talks about the love that is deeply felt expression and this love is also allegorically related to the love between the Church and Jesus Christ.

## *Part II - Wisdom Books in the Old Testament*

***1. The Book of Proverbs:*** Proverbs features classic wisdom vocabulary, the masal form, emphasis on common sense activity, and a tone which is neither distinctly parenetic (rules providing specific directives to fit specific situations) nor directly linked to the ethical demands of Torah. The book contains only poetic stories and didactic units (in a formalistic sense), on the other wise widely distributed among diverse biblical materials. For this book represents the commonsense approach to life and faith. It touches the shared concerns of all who are given the gift of life and struggle with how to live it. For those who are recipients of the gift of faith, this book distills the theological substance of Old Testament religion into its practical essence. In the following pages, we shall deal with the book of Proverbs in detail by concentrating on the issues like: the title and nature of the book, authorship and composition (including literary structure), date and the canonicity of the book, some literary genres and theological view point of the book (other relevant issue if there is any).

***A. Nature and Title of the Book:*** "The Proverbs of the Solomon the son of David, king of Israel" (1 :1) was very likely the original title of the book. The Septuagint (LXX) has the slightly different title "Proverbs of Solomon son of David, who ruled in Israel", whereas the Vulgate has simply "Libber 'Proverbiorum" (The Book of Proverbs). The abbreviated title "The Proverbs of Solomon" at 10:1 is a subtitle within the larger collection (Chaps. 1-24), and another title at 25:1, "These also are Proverbs of Solomon", begins the second Solomonic collection (chaps. 25-29). Many scholars assume that the title of the first collection (1:1) has been borrowed from one of the other title as the opening title, Actually the title of the first Solomonic collection may be 1:1-6, in which the author identities himself and sets forth his purpose for the book.

The basic nature of wisdom as viewed by the author of Proverbs is summed up in his statement, "The fear of the Lord is the beginning of knowledge" (1:7. cf. 9:10), that is, the fundamental nature of wisdom was theological. Thus in Proverbs the underling basis of life is one's relationship to God. Out of that relationship grow moral understanding and the ability to judge what is right (2:6-22), a proper attitude towards material possessions (3:9-10), industrious labor (6:6-11), the necessary equilibrium and sense of security for living in the world (3:21-26), and the right relationship towards one's neighbor (3:27-29), to mention only a few of the more practical benefits of that relationship.

Wisdom in the book of Proverbs capitalizes upon the horizontal dimension of life (one's relations with other human beings and the natural world) and offers instruction in affirmative and declarative tones compared to the exhortative word of the prophets. The person-to-person details of life are not dealt with in a theological vacuum, however, but are viewed within the context of the Mosaic Covenant and Law. It deals with the question: 'How ought we then to live?'

The Hebrew word mashal (means likeness or similarity), which also means a Proverb or a saying (a short pithy saying in common use), which the entire book contains. This book belongs to the general class of wisdom literature of the Old Testament (Job, Ecclesiastics and Proverbs). The book serves the purpose of education for good and profitable behavior.

***B. Authorship, Date and Composition:*** Although certain features of the book associate the name "Solomon" with discrete units, other names also occur in connection with specific sections of the book. Some textual units lack any name whatever. Furthermore, the superscriptions may derive from a time later than the actual composition of the sayings. Within a given collection The Book therefore takes the shape of an anthology, its individual components coming from various periods of Israel. At least two and Probably three, short sections contain from non-Israelite sources, making the anthology truly international. There are at least seven individual collections discerned in the book of Proverbs. We shall briefly present them as follows:

***First*:** Chapters 1-9, titled as the Proverbs of Solomon, appears to be latest collection of the entire book, this collection is predominantly a hortatory (sermonic) section, the most and highly developed literary form in the entire book in comparison with other sections. Within this block, 1:1-6 serves as a prologue to the entire book and was possibly inserted as a final redaction. The personification of wisdom in this section could have been influenced from Egypt and may not be from the Greek influence. The basic and ideal theme of this sections is: the first principle knowledge (wisdom) is to hold the Lord in awe (1:7 and 9:10). The warnings against strange women and the personification of wisdom amounts for the dating of this section in the Post-exilic period (but it 15 only a probable conclusion).

***Second*:** 10:1-22:16, titled as the "Proverbs of Solomon." Thig section, on the basis of form and content be divided into two sections; (i) Chapters 10-15; consists of proverbs in antithetic parallelism contrasting wise/ righteous with fools/evil doers. Repetition of some sayings (cf. 10:1, 15-20; 10:2;11:4; 13:14;14:27) with the replacement of "the teachings of the wise" by the phrase, "the fear of the LORD", This fact indicates of a process of gradual accumulation; (ii) 16:1-22:16: contains antithetic, synthetic and synonymous parallelism in equal shares (for the explanation of these terms see the section before on the characteristic features of Hebrews Poetry). Proverbs about the king are found here: Moreover, concern for trade and legal problems points to an upper class background in the capital city during monarchy. In chapters 10-15, Yahweh is the guarantor of the moral ordering of the world and in 16:1-22:16, Yahweh is the Sovereign ruler and the creator of the world; collection of independent proverbs in this section at times is the distinctive feature, found mostly in prose as well.

***Third*:** 22:17-24:22 titled as the "sayings of the wise" These have units with more than two lines. Here in this section antithetic parallelism disappears (thus it is argued that it is form critically later than second section). One of the interesting feature found in this section is that, there is a parallel between Prov. 22:17-23:1 and to that of Egyptian "Instruction of Amen-em-opet", both in form and content, the resemblances are found. The Egyptian Amen-em-opet is dated from 13$^{th}$-12th century BCE. Out of thirty precepts in this section of Prov. 24:17-24:22, nine of the first ten have exact parallels to that of Egyptian Amen-em-opet. This leads us to think that perhaps a Hebrew sage/scribe may have modeled his work in proverbs on the basis of Amen-em-opet; since 23:12-24:22 contains "parental instruction", this and 22:17-23:11 may have come from the monarchic period.

***Fourth*:** 24:23-34 is a small appendix to the previous section, titled as a "further sayings of the wise." This section contains sayings against corruption in courts (24:23b) against flaunting evil as good (24:24-26), on one's domestic priorities (24:27) against false witness (24:28), against the law of retaliation (24:29), and one longer passage, which might be titled the wisdom work ethic (24:30-34). The longer passages of this type in the book of Proverbs seem to be example of the teachers' exposition of shorter wisdom sayings. The present one may be a parable or the teacher's personal reminiscence. This theme appeared earlier in 6:6-11 where the conclusion is almost identical (cf. 6:10-11/24:33-34).

***Fifth*:** 25-29 chapters titled as the "Hezekiah's collection", perhaps these were also collected from the time of Solomon (Prov. 29:27), but edited later by Hezekiah's men. It may be that already existing Solomonic proverbs are collected by Hezekiah's time. Chapters 25-27 has four lines in English text and two lines in Hebrew text. The tone here is more secular and less moralizing then section two; Yahweh is mentioned only once in this section (25:22), righteous and wicked are contrasted only once. Chapters 28-29, in this block parallelism dominates, religious faith as the door to wisdom is asserted again. In this entire section (25-29 chaps) court played an important role, thus lead some scholars to develop a court wisdom genre.

***Sixth*:** Chapter 30, titled as sayings of Agur. The frame work of this section is vv. 1-14 and v.32-33 and in between section vv. 15-3l are the numerical proverbs, which has some similarities within the Ugaritic literature. The name Agur son of Jakeh is found in south Arabic inscriptions. The Septuagint translator translated Agur as a verb means "fear", moreover the arrangement of chapters is also different than the Masoretic Text (In LXX, the arrangement of Prov. 22:17-31:31 is as follows: 22:17-24:22; 30:1-14; 24:23-34; 30:15-33; 31:1-9; 25:1-29:27; 31:10-31).

***Seventh*:** Chapter 31, it contains two further divisions vv. 1-9 are the words of Lemuel, King of Massa (perhaps Massa, name of Kingdom in North-West Arabia (cf. Gen. 25: 14), nomadic or semi-nomadic wisdom is prevalent here; thus an inclusion of foreign material in the book of Proverbs may have taken place, vv. 1-9 are the words of Lemuel, King of Massa, with which his mother instructed him. Other references have been made to the teaching of the mother and its importance (Prov. 1:8; 5:20) and even when only the father's instruction is mentioned, the mother's may be included. The content of this discourse is an appropriate conclusion for a book largely written by a King and collected by one. It focuses, not upon the privileges of Kingship but upon the responsibilities of the office.

The second section is vv. 10-31, the words in praise of virtuous wife. it is an acrostic open, each new verse begins with a different letter of the Hebrew alphabet in sequence. This extended poem on the significance of the mother and wife balances out the social spectrum of the book of Proverbs very well. In the previous section (vv. 1-9) mother's teaching and in here the mention of a virtuous woman is an indication of the fact of the transmission of teaching of wisdom and the positive and affirmative role played by the women and also it indicates the matriarchal collection of material in the bible. Claudia Camp undertook an extensive study on the wisdom in the feminine in the book of Proverbs made more observations in-depth like the one mentioned above. Regarding this section C. Hassel Bullock writes positively as follows: "And lest the male-dominated language of the book appear to excuse the women of society from religious obligations, this poem puts the joyful yoke of religious observance upon women, too."

There are several problems in the exact dating of the individual components of the book. However, following suggestions can be made regarding the composition date of collections in the book. Chapters 1-24 have a framing device and cyclic composition, whereas 25-31 chapters are an additive technique. Chapters 1-9 combine two elemental or core blocks (2-4, the personal acquisition of wisdom, and 5-7 ethical advice, mostly about sex). A speech in first person (1:20-33 and 8:1-36) and a framing ring (the prologue 1:27 and the final contrasting "allegory" about wisdom and folly, 9:1-18), enclose the two kernel blocks, chapter 10 serves as an entrance way into the following collections, and chapter 15 functions as a second theological focus. Within chapters 10-15 only 14:7 uses the style of instruction, but in 26:1-22; 16 it occurs frequently (16:3; 18:22; 19: 18,20,27; 20:16; 22:6,10). Chapters 25-27 appear to be more empirical and general, whereas 28-29 contain a pronounced theological bent. A plait pattern is discernible in chapter 29, a linking of a verse with the one after its immediate sequel (land 3; 2 and 4; 7 and 9; 12 and 14; 15 and 17; 19 and 21; 20 and 22).

In the sections mentioned earlier (seven sections or collections) sections two, three and five are to be Pre-exilic and sections four, six and seven cannot be dated accurately. Section one in the Present form is to be dated as Post-exilic document, probably added to the final redaction of the book.

***C. Canonicity:*** Sparse information on the disposition of the book of Proverbs in the canonization process is found in the Babylonian Talmud. A question revolved around the alleged contradiction between Proverbs 26:4 and 26:5. "Do not answer a fool according to his folly......Answer a fool according to his folly" (KJV "as his folly deserves"). The rabbinic resolution was to view the first as a reference to matters of the law and the second to secular affairs. The doubts about the book were dispelled early in Post-exilic time, and Proverbs exercised a pervasive influence upon Judaism and early Christianity.

***D. Some Literary Genres Found in the Book of Proverbs:*** Already in our discussion earlier we have considered several literary types of wisdom and their significance in general. Here we shall once again pick up few genres in relation to the book of Proverbs;

(a) Allegory: (with metaphor as a devise in allegory) E.g. Prov. 5:15-23 (also ct. Amen-em-opet VI:1-10).

(b) Sayings: It has three sub-divisions as follows: (i) Numerical sayings; (Prov.30:18-19; 6:16-19) here there an attempt made to systematize to order things of knowledge acquired by human beings; (ii) Experiential sayings (or observational sayings) conclusions are to be drawn by the reader E.g. Prov. 11:24 and 18:26. In 11:24, the famous saying goes as follows: "One man pretends to be rich, yet has nothing, another pretends to be poor, yet has great wealth", (iii) didactic (learned) sayings. It is something that goes beyond a mere statement about reality. It is characterized in one's attitude and conduct. E.g. Prov. 14:31: one's relation to God is defined in terms of one's treatment of the poor (cf. Prov. 19:17; 22:22-23). It also has an artistic way of saying (15:23; 25:11; 26:25 cf.).

(c) Wisdom teaching: It is a systematic teaching about a specific topic, its sitz-im-Leben is the context of education (school) E.g. Prov. 1-9 chapters contain many such teachings.
(d) The Hymn: It occurs in the cosmic transcendence of wisdom, also in the sphere of creation (especially Prov. 8:22ff). The Poetic description and language is of high literary master piece type.
(e) Beatitude: The Sitz-im-leben of it is official cult E.g. Prov. 3:13; 8:32-34; 16:20 et.al.
(f) Popular Proverb: It is in a didactic form E.g. Prov. 1:17; 11:2; 13:3 etc.
(g) Command and Prohibitions: Supported by the genre of instruction. E.g. Prov. 8:33; 16:3; 16:20. These also contain motive clauses like: "because", "lest" etc. Here the teacher is engaged in persuading and convincing his disciples/students. In these sayings usually the following elements are found: (i) Call, (ii) notice, (iii) exhortation, (iv) consequence.

***E. Theological view Point:*** The book of Proverbs affirms the fact that wisdom is not primarily human achievement, yet through instruction and self-discipline it can achieved. All young men and women can receive wisdom by preparing themselves to receive it as a gift from God (Prov. 2:1-8), and for those who receive it, wisdom becomes a guide in their life. It is also stressed clearly that the fear of the Lord is the basic foundation of wisdom (cf. Prov. 1:1-5,7 and chapter 2). Wisdom is the understanding of the way of god life for human beings and of its dynamic relationship to the right order established by God as the Creator (cf. chapter 8 of the Proverbs). It is remarkable to note that the book does not mention any cultic obligation (except very rarely in 3:9-10). This is further exemplified in the contrast set between righteous and wicked, the point made here is this. It is not to be seen in the cultic regulations, nor in the law, but quality of life exhibited as a wise person is far more vital than any ritual/cultic obligation. The most important theological contribution of the book is found in chapter 8 where wisdom is seen in its nature and its origin is the cosmic principle and power. This way wisdom serves as an effective link between God and human beings.

***Conclusion:*** The book of Proverbs as noted above is a composition and compilation of smaller collections of wisdom sayings. Many of the sayings have emerged from the practical and ethical context of the ancient Israelite community. The instructions and sayings are also derived as parallels from the Egyptian and other ancient West Asian background.

***2. The Book of Job:*** This book is in the third division of the Hebrew Bible (the "writings") that recurrent the story of Job, a righteous man whose motives for being righteous are tested through a series of personal tragedies and sufferings. When three friends arrive to console him, they all engage in a dialogue focusing not only on the cause of Job's personal misfortune but also more generally on the problem of evil. Their dialogue (or "dispute"), in which Job sharply questions the nature of divine justice, ends without resolution, whereupon yet another character, the young Elihu, appears to offer his own observations on the nature of Job's predicament. Eventually God appears on the scene to upbraid Job for complaining, and to restore Job's family, property and health. We shall deal with all these issues in detail at a later stage in our discussion. We shall, in the following pages, consider the following matters in relation to the book of Job as follows: Title, Nature and Pan, date and authorship, content and structure, and main theological emphasis and other related issue as required.

***(A) Title, nature and Place of the Book in Canon:*** The book of Job, like the books of Joshua and Ruth, bears the name of its hero. The Hebrew form of the name' Iyyob was represented in Greek by Iob, and then through Latin came the English form Job. Some have connected the meaning of the name with the root' yb, to yield the meaning 'the hated one' or 'the persecuted one' or 'the hater' or even 'the aggressor' Others have looked to the Arabic' wb for the meaning, and have suggested 'the persistent one'. It is improbable we should seek a meaning appropriate to the story, and the name may have been taken over by the author from the tradition on which he based his book.

The book discusses on the problems of suffering of the righteous, the problem of theodicy, i.e., Justice of God. There is a truth in the presupposition of the wisdom, i.e., the world is governed in a rational way by divine wisdom. However, the book doesn't sustain this presupposition throughout. Moreover, there is no logical and consistent reply given to Job's question/s in the book. His questions are not resolved in a rational sphere, but are resolved in faith (i.e. in the realm of faith).

In the Hebrew canon the book belongs to the third division, the Kethubim, which contains also Psalms, Proverbs, Ruth, the song of Songs, Ecclesiastes, Lamentations, Esther, Daniel, Ezra, Nehemiah, 1 and 2 Chronicles. In some manuscripts, Job follows Psalms and Proverbs and in some it stands between them. In Syriac it stands between Deuteronomy and Joshua, doubtless coming to the fact that the scene of the book is set in patriarchal age.

In Greek manuscripts, the prophetical books were transferred from the second division of the Hebrew canon to follow the three 'poetical' books, Job, Psalms and proverbs (these three not always in the same order), and

Daniel was placed among the prophetical books, while the other books of the Kethubim were distributed, similarly the manuscripts of vulgate vary, while following the same general principle as the Greek and the English order follows what had become the prevailing order of Vulgate.

***(B) Date and Authorship:*** The book of Job has been attributed to the widest variety of dates, ranging from the Patriarchal age-due to the fact that the scene in set in that age-to the second or first century BCE. Even within the present century dates from the time of Solomon to the Hasmonaean period have been suggested. Most recent scholars argue that in its original form, the book was of Post-exilic origin, and the secondary parts of later composition. Reference has made earlier to the book of some similarities with the Deuteronomic doctrine of the rigid correlation of desert and fortune on the national scale. It is generally accepted that the Deuteronomic school flourished in the seventh century BCE and that Deuteronomic history embodied in the former prophets was composed in the seventh and sixth centuries. It was probably under the influence of the application of this principle to the individual that the hard doctrine of Job's friends became accepted in certain circles. Based on these observations, scholars date the book not earlier that 500 BCE and more probably later. The substantial Aramaic coloring of the language also some would like date it in the early fifth century.

Concerning the author of the book we know nothing apart from this book and only speculations are possible in this regard. J. P. Naish thought that the author was a disciple of Deutero-Isaiah, but without any evidence. Humbert thought that the book was composed in Egypt and E. Dhorme stresses the author's acquaintance with Egypt. F. H. Foster thought the book had been translated from an Arabic original, and Pfeiffer thinks the author was an Edomite.

It is hard to think that he was not an Israelite. That there is no reference to the land or cultus of Israel is not surprising, since the scene is set in the Patriarchal age and the person who figure in the books do not appear to be themselves Jews. The original tradition on which the book is based was probably a non-Israelite story, which the author adapted for his purpose. He was certainly a monotheist and a worshipper of Yahweh, and if he was influence by Deuteronomic and Post-Deuteronomic theory, it is hard to think to him as anything but a Jew.

***(C) Content and Structure:*** The book of Job consists of a narrative, framework and a poetic core. The prose section is divided into a prologue (1:1-2:13) and an epilogue (42:7-17), the poetry is embedded between these two together prose and poetry examine the possibility of being good without thought of either reward or punishment and explore the nature of innocent suffering, whether or not it exists, how one ought to act in the presence of misery and why such injustice occurs. The prose framework deals with loss and eventual restoration without so much as a raised voice and in its simplicity embraces and makes possible the eruption of volcanic emotions in the poetry.

Emphasizing the historical gap between the time of the hero and the subsequent narrating of the events, the narrative sets the action in (pre) patriarchal times. Job's possessions, like those of the patriarchs, consist of cattle and servants, not only his three friends but also his enemies (nomadic Sabeans and Chaldeans) come from the greater environment associated with Abraham's wanderings; The monetary unit (42:11) belongs to that ancient era (cf. Gen. 33:19); Job's life span exceeds that of the patriarchs and the sacrifice of animals corresponds to the practice prior to official priests. The name Job recalls a folk hero associated in Ezek. 14:14, 20 with Noah and Daniel, probably the Daniel of Canaanite epic texts. Although the meaning of Job's name is uncertain, similar forms are attested from early times in Egypt and Mesopotamia with the meanings "where is the divine father?" and "Inveterate Foe/Hated one," In accord with the universality typical of early wisdom, the hero seems to have been an Edomite (only a Probability), famous for the wisdom of its inhabitants and setting in the land of UZ echoes the noun "counsel" (42:1-6).

The action of the prologue (l:1-2:3) alternates between earth and heaven, the events of the latter hidden from Job. The hero, perfect outwardly and inwardly according to irrefutable testimony (1:3,8) enjoys the fruits of virtue-until God directs the adversary's attention to him, eliciting suspicion of Job's motive for being good and provoking a test to determine the truth. Calamity befalls Job without warning. Having lost his children and possessions, Job blesses the Lord as source of good and ill (1:21). A second heavenly scene ensues, with God's "I told you so" and the adversary's insistence that the real test must touch the actual person (2:3-5). God accepts once more, insisting that Job's life must not be taken. The facial scene depicts a surely afflicted Job, but one restrains his integrity despite his wife's urging to curse God and die (2:9-10). This time Job's confession takes interrogative form, but he does not curse God. Having heard of Job's misfortune, three of Job's friends, Eliphaz, Bildad, and Zophar, journey from their homes in Tennan, Shuah and Naaman respectively to offer comfort in adversity.

The conversation in the form of a poetic dialogue consist of three distinct units: Job versus Eliphaz, Bildad and Zophar (chaps. 3-37), and God's lectures to Job (38:1-42:6, with brief responses by Job in 40:3-5 and 42:1-6).

The epilogue (42:7-17) ties up all loose ends, having repented, of what. is unclear, Job intercedes on behalf of the three friends, at whom God is angry because they did not speak truth about God as Job did. A temporal connection between prayer and restoration occurs, and Job returns to his previous state, with one bonus: his three daughters losses unsurpassed beauty, besides an inheritance. Seven times the verb "blessed" occurs in the story (1:5,10,11,21; 2:5,9; 42:12), alternating between the meanings "curse" and "bless" except the last two which are reversed.

There are few elements of laments in the book which contains. petition, wish, motivation and a vocal of trust. In chapters 3 and 30 of the book, there is a threefold articulation of lament is visible.

***First*:** the lament is directed to God: ***Second***, self-lament and ***Third***, a lament about enemies E.g. chapters 3: Job cursing his birth, in vv. 3 and 10 of chapter 3, the lament is directed against enemies, v.11: is a self-lament and v. 23: is a lament to God; again vv. 24-26: self-lament chapters 29-31 genuine or true lament. In chapter 29 we find Job's retrospective look on his earlier fortune. Chapter 31 is understood as an oath of clearance or attestation of innocence. In chapter 30 the lament is threefold as mentioned above: to God, to self and against enemy.

Claus Westermann is the one who strongly argues for the elements of laments present in the book. He writes thus; "At the base of my investigation lies the simple recognition that in the Old testament, human suffering has its own peculiar language and that one can understand the structure of the book of Job (based on content as well) if one has first understood this language, namely, the language of lamentation. As lamentation, which is suffering expressed in speech, gets developed along the three axes which determine human existence in general-the self in isolation, the self over against other human beings, and the self over against God's-so the poet of the Book Job presents the suffering of Job through three representations of this threefold aspect of human existence: Job himself, the friends of Job who become his enemies, and God. This basic recognition, garnered from the structure of lamentation, provides the key that unlocks the meaning of the entire book of Job. Not only those parts which contain Job's laments, but also the whole polarity of lamentation and praise out of which the dramatic dialogue arises."

Another element in the lamentation in the book of Job is wishes and Petitions in the speeches of Job are identified by Claus Westermann. There are four such elements as follows:

***First*:** The wish to die (3:11-13, 21-22; 6:8-20; 7:15 an echo of this wish occurs in 10:18b-19).

***Second*:** The wish that God would leave Job alone, due to the reason that Job might be able to breathe freely (7:10b; 10:20b) or so that human kind might be able to breath freely (14:6, 13-15).

***Third*:** The wish that Job's cause might be heard and that he might find an advocate despite his death (16:18-22; 17:3; 19:23.24).

***Fourth*:** The wish to encounter God (23:3-12; 31:35-37 the summoning of God). Petition or something like petition intrinsically belong to the lament.

In two important parts, the book of Job's content can be neatly grasped:

***First*:** The speeches of Job: First speech begins with an apology and later contains a personal defense. Second speech begins with concurrence, no attack on the friend and in third speech, Job occupies his friends' intervention on God's behalf.

***Second*:** The speeches of God: God's answer to Job is in the form of disputation (although other varieties of forms are proposed) speech. Job's final lament ends with summoning God to a law suit, couched in die form of a wish that God would answer him. The wish is fulfilled for Job. To be sure, this answer does not correspond to what Job has expected. In this answer Job neither learns the indictment against him (31:35)-and there by the reason for God's terrible anger against him-nor finds either the advocate or the vindication for which, despite all appearances on the contrary, he had been waiting (16:19-21; 19:25). But none of that alters the basic fact that God does answer him.

God's answer to Job puts one question to Job: Who are you? (38:2) God pushes Job to the spot where Job can experience and receive the assurance of God, the intervention of God on his behalf. The question is developed from 38:12 to 41:34. If one transposes it from direct top indirect discourse it reveals itself for what it really is; Praise of God the creator. Along with disputation, praise of the creator is a motif which ties together all three characters in the drama. The whole divine speech is segmented in accord with the Psalmic motif; Praise of the creator-praise of the Lord of history. Peculiarity and uniqueness of God's speech is not its content, but rather in transformation.

Further to this God's answer Job's answer is seen in two parts. *First*: an act of silence which precedes the answer itself (42:2-6). *Second*: 42:5 contains 'solution' to the 'problem' of Job. Job now knows of God, not just one aspect of God's activity-what Job has recognized and whom he has seen remains concealed. Confession of Job concludes the drama.

***The Structure of the book:*** As we have noted above the general content of the book, the book can also be systematically divided into following units on the basis of its arrangement. Three major parts with several sub divisions in part two can be seen as follows:

***I. Prologue (chapters 1-2):*** Prose-Divine name Yahweh used. Suffering is presented as a test of a person's righteousness. A righteous person lives righteously not for the sake of reward but for the sake of the relationship with Yahweh, which endures in adversity as well as in property.

***II. Speeches (3:1-42:6) Poetry:*** Divine name Elshaddai or Eloah used (except for whirlwind speeches 38:1-42:6).

A. Chaps. 3-27: Triple exchange of speeches, beginning with Job's cause on the day on which he was born (ch. 3).

| | | |
|---|---|---|
| Job 3 | 12-14 | 21 |
| Elephaz 4-5 | 15 | 22 |
| Job 6-7 | 16-17 | 23-24 |
| Bildad 8 | 18 | 25 |
| Job 9-10 | 19 | 26-27 |
| Zophar 11 | 20 | missing |

View of suffering: suffering results from sin. Since Job is suffering, Job must be a sinner.

B. Chaps. 28: Independent poem on wisdom. It may be a latter addition to the work. Describes the search for wisdom, reading its climax in 28:28 "Behold, the fear of the Lord (not Yahweh), that is wisdom: end to depart from evil is understanding."

C. Chaps. 29-31: Job summarizes his position 29; his former happy position 30; his recent hopeless lot 31; his oath of clearance (sometimes called as "the sermon on the Mount of the Old Testament") ending with a challenge to God to answer him (31:35-37).

D. Chaps 32-37: Speeches of Elihu, argues that suffering has disciplinary value. Sees Job's suffering as the result of his self-righteousness (34:5-9), humility would bring God's blessing (36:8-12). Points out that if there were a mediator who suffers a ransom, humans would be able to pray to God and be accepted and come into the divine presence with joy (33:23-30).

E. 38:1-42:6: The speeches of the LORD (Yahweh) from the whirlwind with Job's replies. The LORD reminds Job that there are many things in creation that he does not understand. In 40:8, Yahweh reveals Job's true sin. Job, is insisting on his own righteousness, has questioned the justice and goodness of God; he has set himself up as a judge of God. Job is not vindicated, but he is accepted by the creator. The creator has entered into communion with him. This is the answer to Job's need (42:5). The just live, not by their own righteousness, but by faith. It is emphasized here that God's ways are not transparent to humans. What is questioned here is the legalistic application of the understanding of the cosmic order found in wisdom thought (and in the Deuteronomistic theology).

***III. Epilogue***: (42:7-17) Prose. Divine name Yahweh used. Job prays on behalf of his friends, who have not spoken of God what is right (vv. 7-9), Job's fortunes are restored with double restoration of goods, new children born (vv. 10-17). The view of suffering here is that the suffering of the righteous and the prosperity of the wicked are temporary, and both will pass away, leading to times of just punishment and reward.

***D. Theological View Point:*** The book of Job represents a response to the time of crisis. It is believed that the story was orally circulated and is reworked by the narrator (there is an opinion that perhaps the book was originally written and then translated into Hebrew?). Following are the important observations to summarize the theological view of the book.

***First***, the narrator wanted to stress that God is creator and also wanted to reemphasize God as provider or sustainer or God as immanent judge of his people.

***Second***, In this book we mostly find that there is a shift from communitarian concept of Israel to individualistic view (piety).

*Third*, Emphasis on God's transcendence and not insisting on God's immanence.

***Fourth***, Yahweh as the Lord over cosmic order; the design of God is not governed by a necessary law of reward and retribution; God's wisdom is of a higher order and remains a mystery.

Recently H. G. Reventlow made the following observation on the theology of the book Job. The book presents the problem of crisis of wisdom, between deed and consequence (cf. Klaus Koch's view; God, one who is involve in the human affairs of deed and consequence, not an automatic connection is operative). Similar type of crisis in wisdom is also found in Akkadian literature such as: The prayer of righteous sufferer, from Egyptian context, a man's dialogue with his own soul as to the merits of suicide as a way of escape from the miseries of life and another narrative which narrates a man's bold and persistent appeal against social injustice until his wrong were righted. In Babylonian literature we do find a parallel to Job's such as: 'A pessimistic Dialogue between a master and his servant' (W. G. Lambert, Babylonian Wisdom Literature 1960, pp.139fi), "the Babylonian Job" (Lambert pp. 21ff). God's answer to Job in 38:1ff reveals that God's act of creation human's existence is a short one and human wisdom also has limits. In reply to God's speech Job's silence is maintained because no answer will suffice. 42:5 is the key verse to the entire book, that is, the realm of faith is important, repentance is only the answer. Human wisdom can't comprehend the whole. Before the eyes of God human beings. are in any case the sinners, God's wisdom is a mystery, which no one can understand (seems to be a paradoxical answer). Norman C. Habel writes: "In a world where paradox and in congruity are integral to its design, there is no simplistic answer to the problem of innocent suffering. The baby eagle survives because another young creature dies. God does not eliminate the forces of chaos, the role of Death, or the presence of the wicked. They operate within the eternal constraints of his design, light is balanced by darkness. Each night the wicked function, but with each dawn they are exposed and contained (38:12-15). No mechanical law of reward and retribution operates in this design. The "wasted wasteland" is as much God's concern as the rain that breaks the drought (38:26-27, 37-38). For there is a celebrative aspect to the world which puts all structural and function features into perspective. In his design there is a measure of the cosmic with the controlled, the bizarre with the beautiful, the serendipitous (something happening you don't expect) with the serious. Yahweh challenges Job to show the discernment necessary to keep this paradoxical world in balance. From these parallels in the natural world Job is left to draw the necessary conclusion relevant to his personal world. Job's complaint that the innocent sufferer unjustly is never refuted. It stands side by side with the answers of Yahweh as part of the paradox of that design. Yahweh's theophanic appearance honors Job; his speech challenges Job; his enigmatic design throws Job back into a bewildering world of wonder. In that world Job reluctantly foregoes his demand for litigation."

James A. Sanders has taken to pen out few remarks recently in his what is called a recent and fresh approach, to the book of Job. He writes thus: "The question which the Book of Job passes is how to relate, the mosaic Prophetic theology of the God of Israel as a nation to the situation of Israel's dispersion, where covenant responsibility has dramatically shifted to the individual wherever he might be. The answer it offers is that the theology of the new Israel in the Diaspora, nascent Judaism, should emphasize God's transcendence a simply not insist so much on his immanence. God should be seen primarily as a creator God and less as the intruder in history who rules by his judgments... For (the Job poet) it was better to let God be God the creator, a little distant, a bit aloof, and not accountable to man for the vagaries of history and nature or a burden, to theologians to explain it all and "plead the case for God" (Job 13:8).

According to Mitchell, the voice in the whirlwind ushers Job into a new dimension of reality where his eyes light up with joy inspired by the dance of death and life. Engulfed in Primary energy, Job recognizes the triviality of his quest for justice, but J. L. Crenshaw contents that besides Mitchell's insights into the language of the biblical masterpiece, he misses its pathos. Divine perfidy and human suffering ought to evoke a loud outcry that can be heard above Job's enforced silence.

***Conclusion:*** The book of Job as discussed above comes from a time of postexilic context (if we may agree to this dating), when the individual piety was given prominence in the life of the community. Moreover, the book raises prominent theological questions in the light of retribution, theodicy and other major concerns. At the same time the book deals with the skewed social system and aberrations that are to be addressed within the question of justice of God.

***3. The Book of Ecclesiastes (Qoheleth):*** Ecclesiastes, like Job, questions the justice of life's retribution, such discussions seem as much a part of the wisdom pursuit as the corresponding endorsement of the rigid view of retribution in Proverbs. The book presents two opposing approaches to life. These exhibit no obvious connection with other Hebrew wisdom. Other wisdom books assume life's meaningfulness. The Hebrew author of Ecclesiastes called Qoheleth "the Preacher" or "Preacher", sees things from a different perspective. Qoheleth's claim that life is empty (for example 1:2-11) apparently runs counter to the books advice to fear God and enjoy life (for example 2:24-25). The memes themselves offer less difficulty than the apparent contradiction. Wisdom occasionally offer opposing truths, but it does so with proper acknowledgment and consistent advice. In the following pages we shall focus our attention on the study of the book of Ecclesiastes by paying particular attention to the following issues: The Title, authorship, date and place of authorship, background of the Qoheletlh's wisdom, content and place of the book in canon and the message of the book.

***A. Title:*** The Hebrew word used is Qoheleth (Qal feminine singular of Qahal means to assemble). This means, collector or the leader of the assembly, the word is put in the feminine because it describes an office or activity. In LXX (Greek), the title given is Ekklesiastes translated as "a member of the assembly-." In vulgate, the term "cocionator" is used to means "Preacher". Identification of Qoheleth with Solomon was deliberate because of the tradition of issuing wisdom teaching as the King's teaching (as in Egyptian "royal instructions"). This fictitious royal authorship doesn't influence the book after chapter 2 (4:13-14; 7:19; 8:2-5; 10:16-17 presupposes the point of view of a King's subject not the king himself).

***B. Date, Author and Place of Authorship:*** The book contains full of Aramaisms, using Persian loan words (for e.g. pardes translated as "park" in 2:5, pithgam translated as "decree" in 8:11). The book reflects Hellenistic ideas such as the cyclic nature of time (1:9-10) rather than Hebraic linear view of time, this is the reason the date for the book is suggested as 3rd century BCE. According to Whybry, it is most likely the time during Ptotem

II Philadelphus reign (286-246 BCE) may have been written (during this King's reign LXX was translated and he advocated the religion of tolerance, thus Greek influence in the writing is natural to expect). This reign of Ptolemy II was also a time of peace and prosperity. Zenon Archives in Egypt reflects a political situation of economic prosperity in upper class of Jewish society in about 250 BCE. According Stephen de Jong this date is probable because to him it was a time of prosperity, peace, efficient administration and economic boom. It was a time of great ambition and optimism. This is the time 'the preacher' proclaims his message thus middle of third century BCE may be the probable date.

The book usually seen as the work of one author. The superscription 1:1 and epilogue 12:9-14 are considered redactional 12:12-14 of the book in particular looked upon by many scholars as an attempt to criticize the book from a mere "orthodox" point of view, and to reinterpret it. Some would accept the epilogue as the work of Qoheleth himself (It is best "fear God and keep his commandments, for this is the duty of the whole man" 12:13). According to H. G. Reventlow, it seems that is, this idea is much against the tone of Qoheleth on the whole, because Qoheleth is against traditional understanding of wisdom cf. chapter 3 in this regard and other passages as well. Qoheleth is not a nick name for Solomon and that the author sought to inform us of that by means of the enigmatic name that he chose and the unusual phrase "king in Jerusalem." Nevertheless, he assumed the personality of Solomon as a literary device to convey his ideas. According to Robert Gordis (Koheleth-The Man and His world, Texts and studies of the Jewish Theological Seminary of America. vol. 19. 2nd enlarged, New York: Bloch, 1955, p. 194) "The book of Koheleth is not a Pseudepigraph, which the author seeks to attribute to Solomon, like "the wisdom of Solomon." He impersonates Solomon only in the opening section because he wishes to prove that both wisdom and pleasure are worthless as goods in life (1:16-18; 2:1-12) and Solomon had the reputation of possessing both in superlative degree."

The book was probably originated in Jerusalem, Alexandria, Jewish circles in Phoenicia have also been suggested.

***C. Place of the Book in Canon:*** Ecclesiastes occurs among "writings" the third part of Hebrew Bible. It is one among five books of megilloth which was read during the feast of tabernacles. The fourth position of the book in the megilloth was may be due to the fourth festival, the feast of Tabernacles in the calendar of the synagogue. Fragments of Qoheleth have been found out in the fourth cave of Qumran (5:13-17; 6:3-8; 7:7-9 for instance, one single manuscript of Qoheleth was found at Qumran dated in the middle of 2nd century BCE). The Synod of Jamnia (approx. 100 BCE) included the book in the list of holy scriptures, the school of Shammai Questioned the canonical value of Ecclesiastes but the school of gate; accepted it. It is generally held that the book gained the canonical status because it was attributed to Solomon, but this generalization may not be true because even other "Pseudepigraphs" in the name of Solomon like, wisdom of Solomon or the Odes of Solomon could not get canonical status. However, the book's inclusion in the canon is justified based on the words found in the epilogue (12:9-14) which removes the stings of skepticism and advocates traditional beliefs of the book towards the end.

***D. The Background of the Preacher's Wisdom:*** It is observed that wisdom in Israel was not an isolated phenomenon but had developed through the same phases as its West Asian neighbors. The fact that the empire of Ptolamies were dominating at the time of Qoheleth, the Greek influence on the book, no doubt, was found. Aristotelian, Stoic and Epicurean Philosophies seem to have been directly influenced in the book of Qoheleth. Many scholars dismiss the book as parallel with Greek literature, not from one period and from one philosophical system, could be claimed as a whole makes the basis of Qoheleth's teaching. In the Hellenistic Period, certain terms are introduced to serve as intermediaries between God and human beings such as: the name, the word, wisdom and spirit. Numerous angles and archangels made their appearance in Greek literature (thus the development of angelology in ihe several places of the intertestamental literature are seen). The influence is clearly seen in the book of Tobit (ca. 200 BCE). In the midst of such a tremendous influence of Greek philosophies, the book of Ecclesiastes still holds to the idea of remoteness of God.

There are more similarities in some Mesopotamian texts with Qoheleth's ideas. For instance, in Gilgamesh epic, Gilgamesh was advised to enjoy wife, fine cloths and tasty food. This may be similar to Qoheleth's idea of advising to eat, drink and enjoy. Themes such as, death and memory of ones' name after death are also dealt in Gilgamesh epic. In another document namely, "I will praise the Lord of wisdom" has similarities with Qoheleth who holds that divine laws are not known to human beings and they are hidden (3:11; 8:12-14 and 8:17).

"Babylonian Theodicy" and "The dialogue between Master and His slave" also have some similarities with Qoheleth (although these are more nearly paralleled to Job). According to Loretz, there are similarities between Mesopotamian literature and Qoheleth with regard to the concept of theodicy, retribution and so on. But Loretz feels the difficulty is no one is able to explain how these types of literature reached Qoheleth.

The late Egyptian texts like: papyrus Insigner and "the instructions of Onkshashongy" refer to the hiddenness of God and similar fate explained in Qoheleth. "The dialogue of a Man with his soul" remains Qoheleth's preoccupation with death. The protest against the traditional (old) wisdom and its values which are not valid practically is opposed by the Teaching of Anii. According to the story, Anii's father forces him to obey the old (traditional) wisdom, but he protests against it. As all the neighbors of Israel has some similarities to the Qoheleth's made of thinking, it is possible to say, it is not that they are depending on each other in writing their material (although that factor cannot be ruled out) but all of them are simply independent expressions of a widespread human mood.

Qoheleth's relationship with other Old Testament traditions reveal some important points too. Archie Lee has worked on the comparative traditions between Qoheleth and the book of Job. He has taken the issue of divine retribution and limit of wisdom. He opines that Qoheleth is a "critique of foundation" in Hebrew wisdom tradition. He further contends that both Job and Qoheleth call into question the doctrine of retribution and the foundation of wisdom heritage itself. Qoheleth talks on retribution but comes out with a negative result. But Job's discussion on reiteration is resolved finally in the realm of faith. It capitulates wisdom of God is higher than the human wisdom.

R. N. Whybray has dealt more extensively with the question of relationship between Qoheleth and the Old Testament tradition in general. According to him Qoheleth has both traditional and anti-traditional materials. Moreover, the anti-tradition materials in Qoheleth have their counterparts throughout OT material even from the earlier times. Further, Whybray thinks that like all other OT texts, Qoheleth believes there is one God who created the world (3:1) and has sovereign power over it (3:14; 6:10; 7:13; 9:1 and 11:15). Whybray cites J. L. Crenshaw who has referred God as an "oppressive presence" by quoting the story of sacrifice of Isaac (Gen. 22) Where God is indifferent to the torment which he is inflicting on his faithful servant Abraham. In another example of Qoheleth 6:7-8, in v. 7 it is written: "All human toil is for the mouth, yet the appetite is not satisfied" is a traditional wisdom saying like any other wisdom observation. However, v. 8 reads thus "For what advantage have the wise over fools? And what do the poor who know how to conduct themselves before the living?". This saying is clearly the expression that may be termed as anti-traditional material, which is the innovation (contribution) of Qoheleth himself. Thus Qoheleth while affirming the old traditional concepts of wisdom radically questions them too.

***E. Literary Form and Structure of the Book:*** Some of the literary forms found in the book are common to other parts of OT and to wisdom literature, while some forms are special to Qoheleth himself.

(i) Synonymous couplets: Here the second line echoes the first line Eg. 1:15,18; 7:7; 10:8,9,18; 11:4.

(ii) Antithetical couplets: Two opposites are contradicted with implicit approval of one of them Eg. 2:14; 7:14.

(iii) Non parallel couplets: Two lines of which the second line completes the thought of the first. Sometimes it is also called as Synthetic parallelism Eg. 4:5; 10:3,5.

(iv) Couplets declaring A to be preferable to B: The so called better sayings these are common in wisdom thinking, more special to Qoheleth's thinking. Eg. 4:6,13; 6:9; 7:2,5; 9:17.

(v) Metaphor: This form is a force comparison of image and reality, found usually in proverbial and other old wisdom materials Eg. 7:26.

(vi) Parable: The preacher uses small stories for teaching to express an idea that wisdom is useless. Eg. 9:13-15.

(vii) The Rhetorical Question: The question presupposes the answer Eg. 8:4.

(viii) Allegory: Translates every picture into reality, a series of metaphors appear in the form of allegory in 12:3-4.

(ix) Malediction and benediction: is also juxtaposed in 10:16-17.

Concerning the integrity of the book, Crenshaw raises four important concerns as follows:

***First***, the author writes the bulk of the book, with editorial glosses entered in the book at a later stage.

***Second***, the author cites traditional wisdom and refutes it.

***Third***, the author enters into a dialogue with an interpret be it real or imagined figure.

***Fourth***, the book reflects a single author's changing view points over the years, as well as life's ambiguities, thus we have varied opinions and thought forms with a single writing.

Several scholars proposed several structural arrangements for the book of Ecclesiastes, but the structure proposed by Sphinx and Skehan seems to be better. It is as follows:

Introduction: 1:1-11 (Prologue)

I. Qoheleth's investigation of life. 1:12-6:9
   - A. Double introduction 1:12-15, 16-18
   - B. Study of pleasure seeking 2:1-11
   - C. Study of wisdom and folly 2:12-17
   - D. Study of the fruits of toil 2:18-6:9

II. Qoheleth's conclusion 6:10-11:6

A. Introduction 6:10-12.

B. A man cannot find what is good for him to do; critique on traditional wisdom; on the day of prosperity and adversity 7:1-14.

a. on justice and wickedness 7:15-24
b. on women and folly 7:25-29
c. on the wise man and the king 8:1-17

C. Man does not know what will come after him 9:1-11:6

a. He (man) knows he will die, the dead know nothing 9:1-6
b. There is no knowledge in Sheol 9:7-10
c. Man does not know what will happen 9:13-10:15
d. He does not know what evil will come 10:16-11:2
e. He does not know what good will come 11:3-6

D. The joy of Youth and Old age 11:7-12:8

Conclusion 129-14 (Epilogue)

***F. Content and the Message of the Book:*** The book of Ecclesiastes contains reflections, confessions, proverbs and meditations of various kind. All these center around one problem i.e. the problem of death. Everything is "Vanity of vanities" (1:2) better translated (based on the Hebrew word Hebel) as "nothing but vanity." Even wisdom, the divine cosmic power which rules the universe is justice and in vain (1:18). Pleasure, works, riches, fame all likewise are vain, for all leads to death "A living dog is better than a dead lion" (9:4b).

However, Qoheleth doesn't affirm atheism either theoretically or practically. He affirms the power of God over against the weakness of human beings. God's purposes endure, even if human hope and glory crumble to dust.

Most important to Qoheleth's vocabulary is Hebel (as mentioned above), which is translated differently as follows; futility, absurdity, nothingness etc. According to Whybray, this word may not have negative connotation, but it means more than a 'mystery' or 'impermanence.' To enjoy is God's gift, take life as it comes and enjoy because, we can't change the fate which God has chosen for us and we can't know what God has instore for us. Wisdom is gift, but there is a wide gap between God and human beings and human beings are kept ignorant (same as Job at this point), every human action is futile because God holds the card and death cancels everything.

Qoheleth taught by means of various literary types that earlier optimistic claims about wisdom's power to secure one's existence have no validity. No discernible principle of order governs the universe, rewarding virtue and punishing evil. The creator, distant and uninvolved, acts as judge only (if at all) in extreme cases of flagrant afferent (for example, reneging on religious vows). Death cancels all imagined gains, rendering life under sun absurd. Therefore, the best policy is to enjoy one's life (see above for the same idea) with one's wife, together with good food and drink, during youth for old age and death will soon put an end to this "relative" good. In short, Qoheleth examined all of life and discovered no absolute good that would survive death's effect. He then proceeded to report this discovery and to counsel young people on the best option in the light of stark reality. It follows that Qoheleth bears witness to an intellectual crisis in ancient Israel, at least in the circles among whom he taught.

All that is mentioned above can be recaptured under the five-point structure (i) Death cancels everything (2:17); (ii) Wisdom can't achieve its goal (3:11); (iii) God is unknowable to human beings (3:15); (iv) World is crooked (v) Pleasure commend itself.

***Conclusion:*** Among the other books of Wisdom literature, Qoheleth stands distinct due to its background from the Hellenistic context. The book also departs from the usual and mechanical understanding of retribution and radically questions that life is not governed by the mechanical and preconceived notion of justice of God. However, the book affirms that it is the fear of God that overtakes all other equations in the rhythm of life.

Chapter 8

# Dalit Sages and their Relevance to the Ancient Hebrew Sages

***Introduction:*** Dalit sages, poets, and reformers voiced truth that arise not from institutional privilege but from embodied suffering, social resistance, and deep communal reflection. Their teachings are not abstract or speculative; rather, they emerge from the soil of daily struggle and carry the weight of ethical urgency. These teachings do more than challenge dominant Brahmanical ideologies—they preserve and transmit a wisdom that is lived, ethical, and profoundly experiential. In this way, Dalit sages function as wisdom figures, offering guidance, critique, and hope grounded in everyday realities. Their insight, like that of sages in other cultural traditions, grows from experience, observation, struggle, and the search for meaning amid oppression.

While classical Indian philosophy celebrates sages such as Yajnavalkya and Patanjali for their metaphysical and textual sophistication, figures like Ravidas, and Chokhamela are often dismissed as merely devotional or "folk" voices. This dismissal is not due to a lack of philosophical depth but reflects the caste-based hierarchies that govern epistemic legitimacy. Philosopher Sundar Sarukkai critiques this disparity, calling for a democratization of philosophy that values the knowledge systems of those historically excluded from formal intellectual spaces.[1] Though Dalit sages may not have authored Sanskrit treatises, their insights carry metaphysical and ethical clarity that continues to resonate and challenge.

We can talk about Dalit sages in the broader light as pointed above and every word they uttered have critically analysed the skewed social and

1 Sundar Sarukkai, *Philosophy for Everyone* (Oxford University Press, 2020), 73-75.

political system in the Indian context as was done by the ancient Hebrew sages. In the course of our discussion we shall explain more convergences between Hebrew and Dalit sages.

Among these voices, Ravidas (1398-1540, though the exact date of his life span remains controversial and no exact dates are thus ascribed to him) stands out as a 15th-century saint born into the Chamar caste, traditionally leatherworkers and deemed untouchable within the Brahmanical order. Despite such marginalization, Ravidas became a revered Bhakti poet-saint, and his teachings boldly confronted caste discrimination through a vision of spiritual and social liberation. In his vision of Begampura, a city without suffering or caste—he reimagined moksha not as a mystical escape but as a form of collective, this-worldly justice:

> "Begampura sheher ka naam, dukh andohu nahi jismein kaam."
> *(Begampura is the city free from sorrow, where suffering has no place).*[2]

This was not an individualistic liberation, nor a retreat from worldly concerns, but a radical reordering of the world itself. Ravidas's wisdom lies in his hopeful realism, an ethical imagination that dares to envision what justice could mean for the oppressed. As Maren Bellwinkel-Schempp observes, Ravidas's teachings became the spiritual and ethical foundation for later political mobilizations.[3] His wisdom is hopeful realism, a vision of what justice can look like for the oppressed.

Chokhamela - A 14th-century saint from Maharashtra born into the Mahar caste, one of the most stigmatized untouchable communities. His abhangas (devotional verses) reflect his dual experience of deep devotion and caste-based exclusion:

> "Cane is crooked, but its juice isn't crooked.
> The bow is crooked, but the arrow isn't crooked.
> The river is twisting, but the water isn't crooked.
> Chokha is ugly, but his feelings aren't ugly.
> Why be fooled by outward appearance?"[4]

This poetic reflection affirms the moral and spiritual dignity of the oppressed and critiques the shallow markers of purity and status. It is a

---

2 Cited in J. S. Hawley, & M. Juergensmeyer, *Songs of the Saints of India* (New York: Oxford University Press, 2004), 111–114-.

3 Maren Bellwinkel-Schempp, "From Bhakti to Buddhism: Ravidas and Ambedkar," Economic and Political Weekly 42, no. 50 (2007): 106–113. https://www.jstor.org/stable/4419688.

4 Cited in Eleanor Zelliot, "Chokhāmeḷā: Piety and Protest," *Bhakti Religion in North India: Community Identity and Political Action* (1995): 212.

profound statement on the nature of truth and human worth, spoken from the underside of society. His wife and fellow saint, Soyarabai, adds another powerful voice to this wisdom tradition. In defiance of purity codes that excluded her body from sacred space, she declared:

> "Even if my body is impure, my mind holds God."

These affirmations elevate inner life as the true space of the sacred, challenging traditions that associate divine proximity with birth, caste, or ritual. Their voices reflect a wisdom born of struggle and affirmation, where ethics triumph over ritualism.[5]

Jyotirao Phule - Born in 1827 in a Mali caste family in Maharashtra, traditionally gardeners and considered Shudras, Phule was among the first anti-caste intellectuals to systematically challenge Brahminical supremacy. He founded the Satyashodhak Samaj and reconceived Indian history through a Dalit-Bahujan lens:

"The Brahmin's pen has caused more destruction than the sword of the conqueror."[6]

Gail Omvedt writes that Phule's reinterpretation of Indian history laid the foundation for modern anti-caste historiography.[7]

Periyar - born in 1879, known as the 'Father of the Dravidian movement,' born in a Naicker caste in Tamil Nadu, aligned himself with Dalit struggles and is venerated as a radical anti-caste thinker. His declaration of atheism and critique of religious exploitation energized the Self-Respect Movement:

> "There is no god, there is no god, there is no god at all. He who invented god is a fool…"[8]

His critique of religion as a Brahmanical invention to enslave the masses catalyzed a movement toward atheistic humanism. For Periyar, liberation meant eradicating caste through education, reason, and self-

---

5 Eleanor Zelliot, "Chokhamela and Eknath: Two Bhakti Modes of Legitimacy for Modern Change," in Tradition and Modernity in Bhakti Movements (Leiden: Brill, 1981), 139–156.

6 Jotirao Govindrao Phule, *Slavery (in the Civilised British Government under the Cloak of Brahmanism)*, trans. P. G. Patil (Bombay: Education Department, Government of Maharashtra, 1991), 27.

7 Gail Omvedt, *Cultural Revolt in a Colonial Society: The Non-Brahman Movement in Western India* (Bombay: Scientific Socialist Education Trust, 1976), 88–95.

8 Periyar E. V. Ramasamy, *Collected Works of Periyar E.V.R.*, Compiled by Dr. K. Veeramani (Chenni: The Periyar Self-Respect Propaganda Institution, 2019), 232.

respect.[9] Although Periyar was not a Dalit sage his reforms and initiatives were far sighted that are still followed in Tamilnadu even today. He is now considered as iconic figure for the entire Dravidian movement which puts emphasis on the equality of all people beyond caste differences.

Dr. B. R. Ambedkar - Born into the Mahar caste, Ambedkar faced untouchability from childhood. He became the chief architect of the Indian Constitution and the foremost theorist of caste abolition. His work fused legal, social, and religious critique:

> "Religion must mainly be a matter of principles only. It cannot be a matter of rules."[10]

Rejecting Hinduism's hierarchical cosmos, Ambedkar embraced Navayana Buddhism as an ethical system that promotes equality, reason, and compassion. In his seminal work, *Annihilation of Caste*, he exposed Hindu theology as a source of systemic violence.

Gurram Jashuva (1895–1971), This wisdom tradition continues in the works of poets and thinkers like Gurram Jashuva, who, writing in early 20th-century Andhra Pradesh, reclaimed the sacred through literature. Born into the Madiga caste, Jashuva gave voice to those denied access to temples and scriptures. In his celebrated poem *Gabbilam*, the bat becomes a symbol of the Dalit soul—unwelcome in spaces of worship yet reaching out with longing and moral clarity:

> "న శరీరములో పపములేమియున్న, పలనలేని బ్రహ్మణు నపై తలవంచె."[11]

*(Though my body holds no sin, the uncontrolled Brahmin still looks down upon me.)*

Jashuva's verses are not only lyrical but deeply theological, expressing a longing for divine presence from the margins. His poetry reflects a contemplative wisdom shaped by exclusion but aimed at reconciliation and dignity. It is the voice of one who sees clearly because he has stood in the shadows.

Katti Padma Rao, A Dalit scholar and revolutionary from Andhra Pradesh, he hails from the Madiga community. Rao's work emphasizes the power of language and the subversive nature of Dalit speech:

---

9 V. Geetha, and S. V. Rajadurai, *Towards a Non-Brahmin Millennium: From Iyothee Thass to Periyar* (Calcutta: Bhatkal & Sen, 1998), 163–175.

10 B. R. Ambedkar, *Annihilation of Caste*, Annotated Edition by Arundhati Roy (Navayana, 2014), 23.

11 Gurram Jashuva, *Gabbilam* (Hyderabad: Andhra Pradesh Sahitya Akademi, 1941), 16–18.

*(Every word a Dalit speaks is history; their silence is a lie).*[12]

He viewed Telugu Dalit literature as a vehicle for asserting voice, identity, and truth against centuries of suppression.

Kancha Ilaiah, born into a Kuruma (shepherd) caste, Ilaiah identifies as a Dalit-Bahujan thinker. He calls for epistemological revolution rooted in labor and dignity:

"We are the producers of food, the creators of goods, but denied recognition as thinkers."[13]

He distinguishes between spiritual knowledge rooted in oppression and productive knowledge rooted in labor. For Ilaiah, the theology of Dalits is embodied in daily struggles, what he calls a "living philosophy" tied to work, ethics, and justice. Although Kancha Illaiah comes from shepherd community (golla caste) he voiced his concerns for Dalits through his writings and strong support for Dalit cause and through his wisdom sayings in our contemporary times.

These sages were not merely contemplatives but also community leaders whose teachings inspired ethical solidarity and transformation. The philosophies articulated by these sages meet the essential criteria of intellectual rigor. They are rational, coherent, and oriented toward moral universality. These teachings question karma as an ideological tool of subjugation and reconceive moksha as collective liberation rather than individual transcendence. Kancha Ilaiah Shepherd describes this as "productive and pragmatic knowledge," a living philosophy embedded in labor, struggle, and community.[14] To continue privileging only Brahmanical texts as the sole repositories of Indian wisdom is to ignore the plural and contested nature of Indian intellectual history. The voices of Dalit sages, though shaped by different methods, languages, and social locations, are equal in depth, moral vision, and philosophical substance. Their experiential wisdom, articulated through poetry, resistance, theology, and ethical reflection, forms a transformative framework for understanding truth, justice, and human dignity.

When we look at the converging points between Dalit sages and ancient Hebrew sages, the following concluding observations can be made:

First, both Hebrew and contemporary Dalit sages are committed to shake the foundations of their socio-economic and political structures as

12 Katti Padma Rao, *Dalit Voice and Language Politics (interviews and essays)* (Hyderabad: Dakkhina, 2002).

13 Kancha Ilaiah, *Why I Am Not a Hindu: A Sudra Critique of Hindutva Philosophy, Culture and Political Economy* (Calcuttta: Samya, 2005), 2.

14 Kancha Ilaiah Shepherd, *Post-Hindu India: A Discourse in Dalit-Bahujan, Socio-Spiritual and Scientific Revolution* (SAGE Publications, 2017).

well as their religious institutional value systems. While the ancient Hebrew sages are very subtle in this venture, the contemporary Dalit sages are forthright.

Second, through education and appropriate instructions Dalit and Hebrew sages conscientized the communities of faith to walk in righteous paths for progress and development. Through their wise instructions the sages of both periods stimulated and encouraged the communities to make difference in their socio-political and religious life situations.

Third, through their religious and social teachings the sages of both periods revolutionized and demolished the age old practices of religious superstitions and think in terms of progress for all human beings beyond class and caste. These sages also created awareness towards created order in a way that sustains the future generations in the entire cosmos.

Chapter 9

# Exegetical Study on the Selected Psalms

***Introduction:*** In the previous chapters considered thus far, we had dealt elaborately on several issues of poetic and wisdom literature in the Old Testament (Canonical books). Several background materials related to poetic and wisdom material has been presented. Then we also undertook a survey of all the six books belonging to the poetic and wisdom literature.

In this present chapter, we will focus our attention on the exegetical analysis on the selected psalms, the selection is done randomly of the psalms belonging to different categories. Before the reader comes to this chapter on specific psalms, detailed reading of the book of Psalms presented above should have been completed reading because there several general things related to psalms and the book are elaborately presented.

### *(1) Psalm 2: Yahweh's Anointed and the Nations*

A survey on the exegetical details are presented from selected psalms is mostly reflected from the reading: Hans-Joachim Kraus, Psalms 1-59 and 60-150 (2 volumes Trans. Hilton C. Oswald, Minneapolis, Augsburg Publishing House, 1988, along with other important commentaries and articles in Psalms. For each psalm, the following pattern/scheme is followed. The text (to be followed RSV/NRSV) by the reader, form (including structure), setting, interpretation, intention or application).

***(A) Form:*** In the collection of the Psalter, Psalm 2 originally was counted as Psalm 1 and Psalm 1 was considered a preamble. The following structure can be found for this psalm vv. 1-3: we hear of the world revolution of the foreign nations (against Yahweh and his anointed one) vv.4-6: the reaction of Yahweh to this revolt mentioned in vv. 1-3; vv. 7-9: the calling of the King to his investiture, vv. 10-12: the effective power of the king, the wrathful intervention of Yahweh and an ultimatum served to the rebellious kings. The speaker implied in this psalm is the king enthroned on Zion. In the psalm, formal statements are combined that the king still had to proclaim, that is, promulgate at an occasion still to be determined.

Psalm 2 belongs to the thematic form group royal psalms. The royal psalms, clearly designated a special group in Ps. 45:1, have as their common theme the term "King".

***(B) Setting:*** The singer and the speaker in this psalm is the king only. Moreover, it is the ritual expression of the of the statement that the Jerusalem King, because of Yahweh, is unassailable and invincible; Therefore, we have in vv. 1-3 the contrast of a renewed chaotic revolt of the nations, but one which because of Yahweh's subduing of the chaos of nations is indeed doomed to fail from the start. But the reference to the investiture formula for the enthronement allows us to think also of another connection as the "sitz-im-leben" i.e., the annual enthronement festival after the manner of Sed festival which was for a time celebrated every 30th year in Egypt or of a royal Zion festival. The era of Jerusalem monarchy in Judah could be the time for the origin of this psalm with the caution that in the history of tradition and transmission some statement could have been intruded or expanded and even modified.

***(C) Interpretation:*** v. 1 begins with the question, because the psalmist is astonished and surprised that the foreign nations (a presupposition according to v. 3) up to now had been subject to the King of Jerusalem, are risking a revolt. This astonishment arises from the knowledge about the sovereign power of Yahweh (v. 3), who indeed has given the foreign nations into the power of his chosen king (v. 8). Therefore, how can those powers dare to rebel against Yahweh and his 'anointed one' (v. 2). Three things are to be made clear concerning the king or the dominion of a Judahite king: *First*, in Israel of the Kingdom of David that was expanded to universal propositions. For Judean kings the model of world empire is the empire of David. *Second*, in the ancient West Asia, the ruler is "divine king" and for that reason also ruler of the world. *Third*, in the AWA the ruler is "divine king" in the sense of the mythical sacral pretenses of the time, but the ruler on Zion is Yahweh's chosen king. His world dominion can be understood only from the viewpoint of the creator and Lord of the world, Yahweh.

In vv. 2-3, the poet of Psalm 2 visualizes the hostile kings and "dignitaries" (technical word used same as in Judges 5:3; Isa. 40:23; Hab. 1:10), as plotting together in the great world revolution against the world dominion of Yahweh and his anointed one. The word "anointed" is the king of God who has been embarked by anointing and who is untouchable (I Sam. 2:10, 35; 12:3,5 and often Ps. 18:50; 20:6; 28:8; 89:38,51; 132:10,17). The words "bonds" and "cords" represent their subjugation and subordination, the foreign power want to be free and independent of Yahweh and the one who represents his lordship.

In vv. 4f God laughs at the wicked designs and plans of the hostile powers and rebels (ps. 37:13; 59:18). This anthropomorphic presentation characterizes Yahweh as the God who experiences a lively reaction to the goings-on the earth and enthusiastically takes part in them. According to H. D. Preuss, Yahweh's laughter is an expression of his sovereignty, majesty, and loftiness. In v. 5, Yahweh does not let things go their own way. He hides his time (Isa. 18:4) but will "in good time" (v. 5) in his anger come face to face with the rebellious forces and terrify them with a sudden eruption of his message. In v. 6, it is stated that Yahweh himself has "established" the king enthroned on so on (the Hebrew word used here ask means, "pour out a libation", or "dedicate". God professes his loyalty to his chosen king before all the nations.

v. 7 crucial to the entire Psalm which talks about the ruler enthroned on Zion proclaims the investiture under which even now his kingly authority may be seen and understood. "I will announce Yahweh's enactment" (the Hebrew word used here carries the sense of sacral royal law). It also denotes the document of legitimacy, the royal protocol that was written down at the enthronement and thereafter identified the legitimate ruler. In the AWA context similar laws are found. For example, in Egyptian ritual of the king, Amen-Re of Karnak says to Hatsheput "My dear daughter... I am your dear father. I confirm your position as ruler of both countries. I am writing your portal for you". In Egypt (i) the king is chosen and designated as the ruler of the divinity on its own throne, (ii) the ruler is given power to subjugate all foreigners.

The statement, "you are my son, I myself have begotten you today." This statement fixed by protocol, has solemnly been communicated to the king at the enthronement (carried out some times ago or just now); to it the ruler appeals in view of the world revolution. The phrase: "a first-born son statement of Yahweh". Should be discussed to some length. In AWA, it was a common idea that the king is "God's son". In Egypt, it is understood as mythological, in Babylonia and Assyria, the king is understood as to be a servant called, installed, and empowered through a "statement" by the gods. In Israel, this concept reveals itself as a creative word, one that originates a new existence, the chosen king is drawn to the side of God, he becomes the heir and representative of his rule. 2:7 contains an act of God's choosing the king (that is what adoption means, "today" means in this solemn moment of the enthronement.

In vv. 8-9, Yahweh intends to transfer to the chosen king "the nations" as an inheritance and "the ends of the earth" as his possession. In.v. 9, the picture of dashing pottery to pieces has a far reaching significance. In the Egyptian coronation and jubilee rituals the earthen vessels that bore the names of foreign nations or by symbolic shooting of four arrows into four directions of the heavens. Thus, this concept both in Egypt and in Israel leads towards, "universal, judiciary absolute power."

In vv. 10-12, after the king of Jerusalem has given notice of his installation and investiture (protocol in vv. 7-9), he presents an ultimatum to the revolting foreign powers:" Now then, you kings, act wisely! Be warned, you judges of earth!" What should then the kings of foreign powers do? The answer is in v.11, to serve Yahweh in fear. The son directs the foreign powers towards the "Father" he does not claim honor for himself. Kissing the feet is a sign of servile subjection (Isa. 49:23), based on the Ugaritic root, the phrase is translated as "Kiss the pure one", or "Kiss the shining one." All who seek shelter in him (trust in him), who seek protection in him will be blessed.

***(D) Purpose and Application:*** According to von Rad, the royal Psalms depict the kingdom and office of the anointed one according to his skill hidden-divine doxa (glory), which for them he now already has, and which may at any moment become manifest. The aim of the message of Psalm 2 could be summarized thus: The revolt of the nations and kings against the universal lordship of God and his anointed one is a senseless undertaking- the rebellion is viewed here only with amazement. And immediately, in view of the universal power of God and the effective investiture of his king, an ultimatum calls people to rethink the situation. The NT citations (Acts 4:25f; 13:33; Rev. 2:26-27; 19:15) also aim in the direction of this appeal, since indeed Jesus Christ is seen as God's eschatological King.

### *(2) Psalm 8: The Glory of the Creator and the Role of Human Beings*

***(A) Form:*** Psalm 8 belongs to the group songs of praise, which is entirely formed and molded by addressing Yahweh in the second person. This hymnic style of direct address is relatively rare (cf. Exod. 15:1-18) and according to H. Gunkel, first penetrated the Israelite hymn only at a late time. The real principle subject of the Psalm can be called "hymn of an individual." This song of praise of an individual is framed by a choral refrain (vv.1a and 9), so that, a cultic antiphonal song may have been at the base of it. But in the "hymn of the individual" the rhetorical question (v. 4) forms the context. There are other. suggestions as well regarding the form of this psalm: elements of lament and thanksgiving (H. G. Reventlow), features of wisdom (W. H. Schmidt). There are also similarities of this psalm with other texts like Ps. 90 (v. 12) and Gen. 1:26ff.

***(B) Setting:*** There is an assumption that this Psalm has cultic "sitz-im-Leben", may be a festival at night during which the song of praise Was intoned antiphonally (cf. Ps. 134:1; Isa. 30:29; I Chron. 9:33). According to J. Hempel, Ps. 8 is based on a Canaanite song that was Sung by the royal representative of the cultic congregation (perhaps in honor of hadad) but then in Israel applied to human beings. Also this Psalm has reference to Gen.1:26ff. In its text the Psalm is later than Gen. 1:26ff due to its usage of the word, adoneynu (our Lord in vv. 1 and 9) which occurs only in post-exilic times (Neh. 10:30; Ps 135:5; 147:5). An "exemplary I" would have been assumed as the one who raises his voice in a song of Praise, framed by the choral song of the congregation, also this phrase may have been in the wisdom reflections. But it is reasonable to conclude that this psalm had its "Sitz-im-Leben" in the worship of the post exilic sanctuary.

***(C) Interpretation:*** Yahweh is called "our Lord" which is characteristic address in the OT for kings (1 Kings 1:11, 43, 47). In other context of Psalms other titles used such as: Yahweh is the Lord of all the earth in Ps. 97:5. The Lord of Israel is Lord of creation (Ps. 135:5 and 147:5). He is the universal ruler (Ps. 2:4). Psalm 8 is not talking about the glory of creation but about the glory of the Lord of Israel. The word "name" in v.1 preserves the exclusiveness of his might and thereby also the uniqueness of the revelation of glory which is the self-presentation to Israel had become the basis of the knowledge of God. In a very astonishing way, the Psalm establishes the immeasurable power of the God who has decided to make the chosen people the realm of his rule and recognition of God self-presentation in the whole creation (cf. ps. 76:1). According to R. Tournay, the name (of Yahweh) as the embodiment of the revelation and presence of Yahweh in his people decodes the mystery of the creation. The glorification of the God of Israel as the Lord and creator of all the world is from certain given cultic data. In Sumerian myth for E.g. the weather God Ishkar could be addressed in song in as follows: "Father Ishkur, Lord, you who ride on a storm wind, your name extends to the end of heaven. Father Ishkur, you who ride on a great storm wind, your name extends to the end of heaven.

The content of v. 2 does not have even any remotest parallel in the OT. The questions raised from this verse are, Did children sing along in this song of praise? or does the singer have something like a parable or even an episodic conception in mind? According to Gunkel, God performs his great deeds through apparently insufficient means, so that his power may be revealed all the more plainly (cf. also I Cor. 1:27). Two things stand distinct at this point: *First*, the presence of despisers and enemies of God is in the creation hymns perceived as a piercing cacophony. The theme, the end of all anarchy in God's realm of creation is worthy of our attention (cf. Ps. 104:35;

97:3,4). *Second*, the termination of all enmity in God's creation is by way of the mouth of children. Here wisdom reflection may be involved in that it shows how power of enemies is broken by the voice of weak children (cf. Matt. 21:6, the praise of children, Ps. 8:2 is quoted there).

vv. 3-4 depicts Yahweh's work in the creation. Yahweh has created heaven (Ps. 33:6; 95:5 102:25; 136:5). It is "the work of his fingers", i.e., all of it bears the "personal mark" of God's creating and working. (Gen. 1:17; Isa. 40:26 for instance). The word "man" often games the connotation like here, of a frail, impotent being (Ps. 9:20; 90:3; 103:14) and "son of man' designates the earth born (from ground/dust). The weak human being, lost under the lofty heaven of God is in comprehensibly the pardoned, accepted human beings (Ps. 144:3 cf. Job 7:17; 14:3). But the fact that God "thinks of", human existence and "takes care of" it is grounded in a long standing and ever-valid act of the creator.

vv. 5-6 is the expansion of the thought found in v. 4. The Psalmist reminds himself of a basic arrangement of God, according to which human beings have their place in creation, this place given to human beings by God is placed immediately below the heavenly beings that surround Yahweh's royal throne (I Kings 22:19; Job 1:6; Isa. 621-3). Even the dominion over all the works of the creator is assigned to the human being. The creator and world ruler Yahweh assigns the world of the human being is markedly distinguished from that of a regent. The King has peoples and enemies of the historical area subjected to him (Ps. 110:1). Man has animals subordinated to him (Gen. 1:28fi). Here no "sacral king ideology" is unfolded, but the hidden backgrounds of everyday human life are revealed. The shepherding and the slaughtering of animals, the hunting and catching of wild game and flesh is a sovereign right emanating from God by which the superiority of the human beings over all created things-even more, their elohim-stature-is revealed.

In vv. 7-8, the psalmist examines with elation the area of human jurisdiction, similar to the King's singer. Not only the domestic animals Serve human beings, even "beasts of the field" (wild animals) belong to this area of rule. V. 9 is a refrain of v. 1. According E. Baumann, this refrain is inherent in the train of thought of the Psalm, i.e., the thoughts of the Psalmist in vv. 2-8 essentially deal only with the earth.

***(D) Purpose and Application:*** Psalm 8 deals with the glory of the creator and the dignity of the human beings. In the adoration, life. determining perceptions are revealed. The world and the human beings are permeated by the radiating power of divine creation and ordaining. This Psalm also reveals the basic fact that, Human beings belong to God's world. God has blessed them with incomprehensible rights to rule and they are crowned with honor and glory. To sum up, two specific things can be mentioned about this Psalm: *First*, Humans are destined to praise God. The man in Psalm 8, who discovers his superiority in the world, is unable to express this fact through praise of himself, he can only find words of praise addressed to God; *Second*, Human beings are destined for ruling. This obviously does not mean that human beings can exploit and destroy animals, plants others riches/resources in the creation. God appointed human beings to rule over the creation means to be steward over the world (in view of his minuteness in relation to the universe and his pitiable need of providing care), to be a responsible care-taker of God's wonderful creation to sustain it, to replenish it and to maintain it in order.

### *(3) Psalm 15: Who May Enter into the Sanctuary?*

***(A) Form:*** Ps. 15, listed among the Psalms of David in the collection of the Psalter, is very clearly laid out in its arrangement. The question asked in v.1 is answered in vv. 2-5, In v.1, Yahweh is addressed, and to him the question is put. According to H. Gunkel, Ps. 15 is based on the conception of the Torah-consultation customary in Israel. A person goes to the priest and asks him for an "instruction" transmitted in the name of Yahweh. Such examples found in the OT are: Zech 7:1ff; Hag. 2:1ff; II Sam. 21:1ff. The question is addressed to Yahweh and the answer is given in the name of Yahweh. But here in Ps. 15, no individual is consulting, and vv. 2-5 enumerates number of stipulations of OT divine law, obedience to which the presupposition for participation in worship directs. The process of Torah-consultation has accordingly been transferred to a ritual of the worship community thus, the designation from "Torah liturgy" is being expanded to "entrance liturgy."

***(B) Setting:*** The setting of Ps. 15 can be reconstructed on the basis of its combination with Ps. 24. At the time of entrance into the sanctuary in Jerusalem, a liturgical act took place. The participants in the worship standout the portals of the worship area and ask the question: "O Yahweh, who may sojourn in your tent, who may dwell on your holy holy"? From the inside a priestly speaker answers them with the declaration of the conditions of entrance. Ps. 15 belongs to the tradition of Jerusalem temple ("Your holy hill", "Your tent"-15:1). Its composition and use in the pre-exilic cultus can hardly be doubted. In the AWA, the conditions to the cultic participant had to know at the entrance to the sanctuary is noted. For instance, in a holy area in Egypt the inscription is found: "who enters here should be clean, and he should cleanse himself the way he cleanses himself for the temple of the great god." Above all, "clean hands" of the cultic participant are required.

***(C) Interpretation:*** At the beginning of Ps. 15 the question of who may enter the sanctuary and sojourn there is addressed to Yahweh. The pilgrims who stand at the gates of the sanctuary turn to Yahweh himself. The God present in the temple alone decides who may appear before him. The verbs "abide" and "dwell" in v. 1 refer to the conception that the participant in worship who has been admitted to the sanctuary is under the protection of God (Ps. 61:4) and receives "citizen's rights" in the sacred precincts (cf. NT passages. Eph. 2:19; Phil. 3:20). Where Yahweh is present, there "devouring fire" (Isa. 33:14) reigns. The place of the presence of Yahweh is indicated by the terms "tent" and "holy hills" are in relation to the tradition of the tent sanctuary of Yahweh (II Sam.7:6, holy Hill-Ps. 2:6; 3:4; 48:1 et.al).

To the liturgical question of the congregation praying for entrance vv. 2-5 now give the answer. The cultic attendants announce the conditions of entry in the name of Yahweh, as statements of the Old Testament divine law are proclaimed. The liturgical question in v. 1 is in essence answered in v. 2. Here the condition for the sojourn in the holy place is identified in three very basic words (i) "one who walks blamelessly" refers to one's being tied into the life of a community in whose ordinances a blameless walk is required. (ii) "And do what is right" is the central formulation of the Psalm who is righteous, who lives according to the covenant and keeps the ordinances of the mutual relationship between Yahweh and his people may enter the sacred precincts of temple. (cf. Ezek. 18:5-7 for more details on the term sadiq) (iii) This irreproachable conduct vis-a-vis the ordinance of the covenant ordained by Yahweh is aimed at a person's innermost being "speak truth from their heart". This expression reveals the innermost movements of thought and directions of the will "faithful" and "reliable". The word Assyria even upto 50% of loan interest is charged. Such unjust enrichment is not to be possible in the community constitution of Israel. Bribery is refereed in the OT divine law in Exod. 23:8; Deut. 16:19; 27:25, the condition of the entry into sanctuary depends in the correct way of behaving in everyday communal life. The participant in worship on Zion before Yahweh, who is a God of justice and aid, shows his "righteousness" in the hidden deals and business transactions which are not accessible to the intervention of any judicial agent. The gift of salvation in the OT cultus is not a magic center of power and it is not dispensed in impersonal fullness at every festival. Every visitor of Zion is asked to give a declaration of loyalty, the word "to serve" here does not refers to cultic skills and special arrangements, to ritual conduct and esoteric rules, but to one's entire life (Josh. 24:15, 21,23).

***(D) Purpose and Application:*** Yahweh who is enthroned on Zion, is a God of all that is right. Yahweh's cult is not naturalistic, magical grant of power to the assembled community. whoever enters the realm of God's presence is interrogated regarding his everyday manner of behavior and is called to account. Not those who say, Lord, Lord, but the ones who do the will of God have familial privileges and rights with him. According to Martin Luther, the Psalmist in this Psalm does not say 'he who speaks, thinks and hears of righteousness' because not 'hearers, but doors of the law will be justified'.

### *(4) Psalms 42 and 43: Longing to be in the Presence of Yahweh*

***(A) Form:*** Psalms 42 and 43 together forms a unit. The reason for this is the refrain in 42:5,11 and 43:5 attests to this fact. Also the close relationship between 42:9 and 43:2 reveal the same togetherness of these two Psalms. Therefore, following structure can be seen in these Psalms: 42:1-5; 6-11 and 43:1-5. The form of these Psalms is assigned to a category of Prayer songs and details of the situation reveal the descriptions of the distress. Not until Psalm 43 do the supplications clearly emerge while in Psalm 42 the self-revelation of the soul pining for the living God stands in the foreground. Time and again through the refrain, consolation and exhortation to be patient addressed to one's own spirit, emerges. At the same time the petitioner looks forward to "truth" penetrates to the innermost recesses of human existence (cf. Duet 6:4), the whole person is undoubtedly involved. von Rad remarks that if a person was a 'Sadiq' (righteous), he was not so in an inchoate or approximate way, but he was so completely. If the declarations mentioned in v. 2 are right, then Psalm 15 would be a perfect model of a' legalistic piety that makes perfect obedience the presupposition for the reception of salvation. But as von Rad rightly thinks that it does not mean in Israel fulfilling commandments was in principle antecedent to the reception of salvation in the cult. Those who are seeking entry into the temple are not coming before Yahweh for the first time, but they are asked to declare their loyalty to Yahweh's will for justice (von Rad, OT Theology vol. I P. 378). In Israel worship and life are intimately associated. Already in most ancient times the customary covenant responsibility culminates in a confession that applies to the whole life (Josh. 24:15, 21,24). The law of God was in Israel originally the essential content of worship.

Beginning from v. 3, the assertions in v. 2 are now explained. Individual concrete ways of behavior in everyday life are mentioned and called to remembrance for the participants in worship as the acknowledged law of God. Ps. 15 is related to the apodictic law of God, for the apodictic commandments apply to deeds and areas of life that do not become judicial cases, or which, under certain circumstances, do not come under the purview of jurisdiction. According to v. 3 the 'righteous' does not make "rounds" in order to slander he does nor do to his neighbor what is evil, and he does not bring shame on his neighbor by false rumors or wicked machinations. Here, in daily life, irreproachable conduct-the practice of righteousness and purity of inner impulses-proves itself. In v.4, the subject is on thoughtless, vain swearing by which one intends to accomplish some injustice (cf. Lev. 5:4).

In v. 5, the subject is traffic in money. The Sadiq does not enrich himself in a dishonest way. On money loaned he does not impose usurious interest, and he does not take bribes. The lending of money according to OT law is understood exclusively as a service assistance. Exod. 22:24; Lev. 25:36f; Deut. 23:20. In AWA, high interest rates are charged on loans. In Babylonia 33.3% was demanded, in the moment of thanksgiving for the excuse already accomplished ("I will still thank him, the help of my countenance and my God). The petitioner "sings" a "prayer". Therefore "prayer song" is appropriate form, but earlier it is also called "individual lament" is also worth noting.

***(B) Setting:*** The place of origin of the Prayer song is indicated precisely in Ps. 42-43. The precise description in 42:6 is unique the Petitioner is at the sources of the Jordan, why the singer of the lament is found in this region (outside the territory of Israel-Ps. 43:1). We are not told. There is no information given about the person of the lamenting singer. The question about the life situation of the lamenting poet cannot be answered conclusively. Destructive powers want to kill him (Ps. 42:7). He must go about in mourning (Ps. 42:9; 43 :2), Yahweh had "forgotten" him (Ps. 42:9) and "cast him oft" (Ps. 43:2). Reviling enemies surround him (Ps. 42:9f; 43:1,2). From this distress, forsakenness, and oppression the lamenting singer songs for the place of God's presence. The origin of this prayer song can hardly be determined. Concerning the transmission of the Psalm is concerned, we can assume that the singer of the prayer song brought the text (cf. "scroll of the book" in Ps. 40:7) to the temple after his rescue; there it may well have been preserved in the temple archives.

***(C) Interpretation:*** The first verse of the Prayer song begins with impressive comparison. As a "hind" parts over the water brooks so the lamenting poet parts for Yahweh. For the simile in Ps. 42:1 there is an Ugaritic parallel. The animal yearning and crying for water is an effective picture of the torment and the consuming desire with which the Petitioner stretches out towards Yahweh. His nepes (literally "gut" or paraphrased as soul/being). "thirsts" for God (Ps. 63:1). The word nepes in this unit of Psalms denotes "the self of the needy life, thirsting with desire." The expiring nepes cries for living God. In God people in prayer look for the fountain of life (Ps. 36:9). Life knows that it is dependent on him (God), and sustained and determined by him (Ps. 42:8). This God is present in the sanctuary. Therefore, the petitioner is looking (longing) for a moment when he will enter the holy precincts. Nothing is said about the ultimate reason for the suffering from a dreadful disease (but no evidence for this). The Petitioner encounters a question from the enemies: "Where is your God now?" (42:3) also cf. Pss. 79:10; 115:2; Joel 2:17). It is to be noted that this question is often asked at a time of struggle. they question the existence and effectiveness of Yahweh. But the Psalmist, by remembering the festival days of joy wants to restore himself. He does not want to forget what good things Yahweh has bestowed on him (Ps. 103:2).

In v. 5, the phrase 'questioning heart' is interesting to note. Similar prayers are found in Mesopotamia. But like Mesopotamia, OT lacks all signs of quietening oneself that operates with magic incantations. The comfort addressed to the dissolving, disintegrating power of "being" has its origin in the assurance (v. 4).

In 42:6, the prayer begins anew. The Psalmist describes the disintegration of his nepes, i.e., the dissolution of his vital power. May be a serious sickness is assumed. In his distress, the singer "thinks" of Yahweh. (The word zqr has the meaning "to stretch out towards" in prayer: Ps. 63:6; 77:3; 119:55; Ezek. 6:9; Zech. 10:9; Neh. 4:8). The supplication originates from a specific places the land of Jordan, the entire range of mount Hermon to Paneas. Accordingly, the geographical area specified would be the headwaters of the Jordon. in the Hermon range. In his desperate state the sufferer now looks towards Yahweh and waits for his intervention. The Psalmist feels death in his bones. Here too we could think of a mortal sickness. In this distressing and dissolution of physical strength, there is a heard the incessant taunt of the enemies.

In Ps. 43:1ff it becomes evident that the Petitioner is also persecuted with charges and accusations. There must be reason for the dissolution of Physical strength-that is logic of the hostile accuser. In this plight the persecuted Psalmist appeals to Yahweh the judge and pleads for his intervention (cf. Ps. 7:8f; 9:4; 26:1). The Psalmist is sure that he is "cast off". Now in v. 3 he pleads for Yahweh's intervention. Yahweh's "light" is a protective and guiding force that accomplishes the righteous (cf. Job 29:2ff); Yahweh's "faithfulness" is the proof of the constancy oil his healing. Both these "light" and "faithfulness" are two forces for protection and healing, sent by Yahweh as "guides" are to lead the Petitioner and bring him to Yahweh's sanctuary. The Psalmist has a clear conception of the entrance to the sacred area, based on what he experienced earlier (Ps. 42:4); he wants to approach the alter of Yahweh and in this place of thank offerings joyfully exalt and sing his song of thanksgiving.

***(D) Purpose and Application:*** The Psalmist in these Psalms, who from the dark valley of his sufferings looks up to those heights of life. The prayer song is permeated-as has been clear from the beginning-by motives of the songs of Zion. All the longing of the thirsty and languishing petitioner is directed to Zion, to the place Yahweh has chosen to bear witness to his presence there. It is this height, and therefore not any of the "heights of life." for which the heart of the petitioner longs. The election of Zion as the place of God's presence has in the NT been transferred to Jesus Christ and his community. In the light of fulfillment, we recognize a new that only in the place of God's presence and the assembled congregation are life and salvation to be found. Apart from this reality a consuming sadness operates.

### *(5) Psalm 48: The Glory of the City of God*

***(A) Form:*** The structure of this Psalm is easily recognized. The laudatory significance (glorification) of the city of God (vv. 1-3) is followed by a description of an attack of the nations and their defeat (vv. 4-7), vv. 8-11 deal with the astonished acknowledgment of the power of Yahweh on Zion and in the world. While vv. 12-14 are to be understood as an invitation to join a procession. Increasing importance is given on the question whether Ps. 48 should be understood as a song organized by strophes. According to L. Krinetzk and M. Palmer, Ps.48 is a 4-stophe poem in which each strophe refers to one of the four points of the compass: north, v. 2; east, v. 7; South. v. 10; west v. 13 with this conjecture of "theological geography", Jerusalem is indicated as the "navel of the world". But these suggestions remain only a speculation, because the north turns up in connection with a very definite statement about Zion, the east as the "east wind" (v. 7), the south and the west not at all in so many words. H. Gunkel considered Ps.48 a hymn. And yet, based on Ps. 46, this Psalm too belongs to the thematic form group, songs of Zion.

***(B) Setting:*** Since vv. 4-7 deal with an attack against the city of God and with the repelling of this attack, therefore the question about the situation of the psalm presupposed in these verses arises again and again. While earlier scholars thought of the wondrous rescue of Jerusalem of the events of the year 701 BCE (under Sennacherib, the Assyrian King), H. Gunkel opines that Ps. 48 is an "eschatological" psalm. In this light the descriptions of the final attack of the nations were prophetic and visionary. But others refute this idea saying, these are not the visions of the future but traditional glorifications of the city of God, its impregnability and its heavenly splendor are reflected in the conceptions of the hymnically expressed song of Zion. Age-old traditions (cultic traditions) have been applied to Jerusalem, however, the mythical elements are involved. From v. 9 onwards the "sitz-im-leben" emerges clearly "inside the temple" Yahweh is honored as a mighty king, and his "royal city" (v. 2) is glorified. From v.12ff, the invitation to walk about the city of God, we learn that a procession has joined in the prostration before the God present on Zion. In view of this invitation, we might even conclude that the song of Zion, Ps. 48, had its "sitz-im-leben" immediately before this procession. This introduced the solemn "instruction in viewing" which was to be received in the walk around the city of God Also Ps. 48 is to be dated in the pre-exilic times.

***(C) Interpretation:*** vv. 1-3 deal with the beauty and praise worthiness of the city of God on Mount Zion. Here Yahweh reveals himself as great (cf. Ps. 96:4; 99:2; 145:3 and great King in 47:2). The city of Yahweh is situated on Zion, the "holy hill" (cf. Ps. 3:6). In v. 2, four assertions are made concerning the holy mountain and the city of located there First: the hill is rising beautifully (cf. Ps. 50;2; Lam. 2:15); The hill of God is praised as a place of perfect beauty; Second: the holy hill has a location that blesses the whole world and is central; and its brightness makes the earth rejoice; paradisiacal conceptions are evoked here; third Zion is described as a hill; Fourth: Zion is the city of great King; Yahweh is the "great king" the "world ruler" (cf. Ps. 47:2; 95:3). All these assertions place Zion in the light of universal glorification. In the city of God, the king of the entire world rules. Yahweh is the one that here proves to be the protection. He is the one who gives to the city of God its invincibility (cf. Ps. 46:5,7).

vv. 4-7 reports the attack on the city of God. Here the kings conspire and march up to the city of God. What is involved here is a historicizing variant to the primordial battle of chaos in creation myths. But the attacking enemy "look up"-and immediately they become numb with fright and confusion (v. 5). But what do they lock up at? Why do they become numb with fright? In Ps. 77:16 it is the waters of chaos that tremble because they get to see Yahweh. That may be the reason here also for the paralyzing fright of the nations and their kings. They behold the "great king" who appears in his "glory" before the enemies (Isa. 66:18) and as "the lofty one" (Ps. 46:10) is about to break up (Ps. 46:9) the levy of the forces of chaos. The fear created by "God's fright" paralyzes and confuses the enemy (Ps. 46:6,8; I Sam. 14:15; Isa.8:9; 17:13; 29:5; 33:3). The picture given in v. 7 of the ships of Tarshish smashed by the "east wind" is unusual. The parable belongs to the Phoenician-Syrian area and would be suitable for Mount Zaphon there, for the "ships of Tarshish" are the splendidly equipped (Phoenician) transmarine ships that sailed all the way to Tartessus in Spain (Jonah 1:3). The term "east wind" is also a technical term for every heavy wind that packs destructive force (for actually the heaviest storms in the Syrian-Canaanite area come from the west. 'East wind' can also be involved an element of myth (Isa. 27:8; Jer. 18:17; Ezek. 27:26; Job 27:21).

If we assume that the description in vv. 4-7 is from cultic tradition, thus graphically presented to the assembled congregation by a single speaker, then vv. 8-11 would be a hymnic response, a continuing statement by that cultic community. v. 9 speaks of the completion of the cultic act which is to be presupposed as the "sitz-im-leben" for the glorification of

Yahweh and his city. The community "compares", it illustrates Yahweh's loving kindness. The concentration here entirely on the name of Yahweh (v. 10). Yahweh, the God of Israel, is God highest and great king over all the world. His name and fame extend to the ends of the earth. Yahweh bestows his power of salvation in beating down the chaos of the attacks of nations (vv. 3-7) and thereby creating a universal kingdom of Peace (Isa. 2:2f). Mount Zion rejoices, and the "daughters of Judah" (the cities of the country, Numb. 21:25; Josh. 17:16), shout for joy (v. 11).

V. 12 calls for a procession. This in connection with the glorification of the temple (v. 9) a solemn procession around the city of God must have taken place. In the Egyptian context we know that at Sed festival a procession round about the walls took place. By this procedure the temple area of the deity was consecrated. An OT parallel to this ceremony of consecration could perhaps be found in Neh.12:27ff. But such a kind of procession is not intended in Ps.48. Rather, one gets the impression that the glory and invincibility of Zion are being celebrated when the towers and citadels "are examined". Like Egyptian celebration, no magical element is involved here in this Psalm.

In vv. 13-14 we find that the counting towers (v. 12), carefully studying the glacis (v. 13) and examining the citadels-all this is to provide an indelible impression of the strength and protective power of the city of God. Succeeding generations are to hear about this (Ps. 102:18). Yet all glories of Zion point to Yahweh (v. 14). The concluding verse then looks into the future and expresses the confidence that Yahweh will always remain the same. In his invincible power he will "lead" his people. The verb "lead", the local tradition word of Jerusalem is transferred to the historical dimension of Israel. Yahweh will (like a shepherd) precede his people (ps. 78:52; Deut. 4:27; Isa. 49:10; 63:14).

***(D) Purpose and Application:*** Inside the temple the OT community, by prostration and the glorification of Yahweh, emphasizes for itself the world power of its "great king" (v. 9). The place where Yahweh is present is called the "delight of the world", Yahweh's renown spreads from here to the ends of the earth. The forces of chaos in the arena of history that rise up against the "great king" are in numbing fright cut down at his appearance. The invincibility of the city of God rests alone on the fact that Yahweh is in her midst (v. 3 cf. also ps. 46). The protective power of God is proved and unchallenged. The NT community will try to understand Ps. 48 in view of Matt. 16:18. It will however, have to keep strict watch that the sovereign majesty of Yahweh is not overshadowed by the immanent splendor of any "churchliness" that is present. Also consideration will have to be given to the fact that all bestowals of God's protection and salvation have universal significance. The "great King", who is present in the community of Israel and protects the city of god, at the central site of the earth guard's creation against the incursion of chaos which is released in the form of the uprising of nations. His judgements are a guarantee for the salvation of the world. The joy over this universal protective and saving power is in Ps. 48 not eschatological but cultically present. The ultimate reality of the world is, as in a parable, visible to worshipping faith in a fully this-worldly way.

### *(6) Psalm 51: Prayer for Forgiveness of Guilt and Renewal of the Heart*

***(A) Form:*** An analysis of this Psalm yields the following structure: vv. 1-2: title; vv. 1-2: The Petition; vv. 3-6: acknowledgment of guilt; vv. 7-9: plea for the deliverance from sin; vv. 10-12: Prayer for a clean heart and a willing spirit; v. 13: a vow to praise and teach; v. 14: a petition; v. 15: Prayer to make praise possible; vv. 16-17: thoughts about the right offering; vv.18-19: intercession for Jerusalem. H. Gunkel remarks concerning vv. 18-19: A later, timidly legalistic pious person who was not able to grasp the lofty sense of the Psalmist quietly took offense at the fact that the Psalmist spoke so freely of sacrifices, which after all prescribed by God's law. Ps. 51 belongs to the form-group, prayer songs, in which the descriptions of distress and petition dominate, but in which the prospect of the hour of thanksgiving is then also entertained (vv. 13,15f).

***(B) Setting:*** The Petitionary prayer is customarily presented before Yahweh in the area of the sanctuary. In v. 7, the singer prays for purgation "with hyssop", rituals of cleans of the cultic site are being referred to. But what is the petitioner's situation? What distress does he have to suffer? It is explained that the confession of guilt always is connected with the petition for healing from a serious illness. Because the physical suffering always precipitates the question of guilt as the cause and this is a first inducement for a confession of guilt. This fact is further confirmed according to H. Gunkel, the mention of "broken bones" in v. 8. But F. Notscher opines that v. 8 as an expressive illustration of inner suffering and refers the thought to a sickness. We need to be careful in any case that not all psalms of confession should necessarily have the connection between sickness and guilt. But according to J. J. Stamm, v. 8 is concerned more about being freed from his suits rather than the restoration of health.

Concerning the date of the Psalm, the title gives no clue about the author and the historical occasion (except the addition of superscription by the composer at a later stage). The Psalm is unthinkable for the time of David. Clues for a time setting of Ps. 51 is to be found in the content itself. Two important observations are made on this: First: The prayer for a clean heart and a "spirit of obedience" (vv. 10-12) reminds of Jer. 24:7; 31:33;

33:39; Ezek. 36:25ff. Second: the thoughts about the value of sacrifices system (Amos 5:22; Isa.1:11; Jer. 6:20 and others). Based on this scholar would like to date Ps. 51 later than Ezekiel 36, even other would date it as far as the time of Nehemiah. But even earlier dates are also possible if we consider vv.18-19 are expansion of the Psalm at a later stage.

***(C) Interpretation:*** In vv. 1-2, in his distress the Petitioner and singer of Ps. 51 appeals to the goodness and mercy of Yahweh. The real wrong with which Ps. 51 has to do is "breaking away from God", the revolt of the human will against the divine will." This guilt stands between god and man-heavy and burdensome (cf..Ps. 32). In v. 1b, the underlying conception obviously is that the sin is registered. Are we talking about specific rites of cleansing here by way of saying that the sins are removed by blotting out (Num. 5:23; Isa. 43:25; Ps. 109:14). The Babylonians speak of tablets on which sins are registered, and they ask that these tablets are broken. In v. 2 the concepts for guilt are varied. *wn*, has the meaning "perversion", "distortion". This word also expresses the intention not in accord with God's will and other word *ht'* denotes "failure", "miss". The word *kbs* is a very strong verb which can have the meaning "to full". The Petitioner is pleading for a thorough cleansing of his guilt, which is basically represented as defilement, as filth and defect. The guilt is intolerable; it must not only be softened and diminished but must be eliminated completely; blotted out, washed away, made to disappear from the sight of God. This act is only possible by God.

vv. 3-6 deals with the recognition of guilt. The petitioner confuses that he clearly sees his offense. "The subject is emphatic." The words: "Against you, you only have I sinned" in v. 4 has resulted in heated debate. The questions raised here are: Has the petitioner of the psalm sinner against Yahweh himself through idolatry or is guilt where against human beings viewed as sin against God? All sin, also all against human beings is only an insult to God, is a distortion of the text. v. 4 is viewed as an element of the so called "court doxology" He who has committed sin is called on to "give honor to" Yahweh (cf. Josh 7:19). In a confession of guilt over against God himself, the petitioner submits to the righteous judgment of Yahweh. The basic declaration of the judgment doxology in v.4 is further expanded by means of a profound insight into man's fateful deterioration into guilt as it is expressed in vv. 5-6. The guilt and the sin have from the hour of birth been the determining forces under whose signature life began. The petitioner wants to say that the primordial cause, the root cause of my existence, is interwoven with corruption. However, it must be noted that the statements like these (in vv. 5-6) are neither as genetically caused nor one-sidedly moral and sexist. The total depravity that is determinative for humans from the beginning is here acknowledged (Gen. 8:21; Job. 14:4; 15:14f;

25:4; Ps.143:2; John 3:6). But this passage is not a proof text for the later development the church doctrine of original sin. On the contrary, the OT emphasizes the total depravity, the degeneracy of guilt of human existence with an altogether different force than the church's doctrine of original sin. In v. 6, the relations to OT wisdom is discernible (Job 14:4; 15:14f; 25:4f). And yet the insight into the hidden depths of the degeneracy of guilt is not the result of human contemplation, but a gift of divine communication and revelation (cf. Job. 11:6).

In vv. 7-9, the Psalmist prays for absolution and pardon. v. 7 refers to an ancient ceremonial cleansing. The word 'Hyssop' indicates a whisk of hyssop shrubs was made with which water or blood was sprinkled on the Penitent to indicate absolution. Cleansing power was attributed to the shrub as such. In Babylonian prayer to Marduk the sinner prays: "May the tamarisks cleanse me, the.........growth cleanse me, the palm pulp blot out my sins; may the basin of holy water of Ea and Asariluchi bring me good luck!" vv. 8-9 Petitioner would like to hear the exultation and the shouts of joy of the one who has experienced Yahweh's salvation. But pardon would mean that Yahweh has "let his countenance shine" and "has lifted it up". Yet, for a time God hides his countenance in view of the sins (v. 9). Dark and threatening, the guilt stands between Yahweh and the petitioner.

In vv. 10-12 we see that the petitioner brings only an act of God, only his intervention can turn all things around. In these verses, the psalmist prays for new creation in his depraved innerself (v. 5). The word bara (create) is surprisingly used here. This word in the OT is strictly reserved for the creative work of God only; it is never used in reference to a human undertaking. God alone is always the subject of this verb. The "clean heart" one cannot provide for oneself, no rite can bring it to life. Only God's independent, creative act can renew a person's heart. It is not for cleansing heart that the Psalmist pray but also for a "steadfast spirit" which also in the future is redeemed from all in constancy and fickleness (cf. Ps. 78:37; 112:7). The word leb (heart) in the OT denotes the center of human existence as the seat of all feeling, thinking, and will (cf. Ezek. 36:26f). The 'holy spirit' (ruah qados) in Ps. 51 v. 11 is the power of God that selects, cleanses, and in the innermost being motivates a person obediently to nothing short of the guarantee of belonging to Yahweh and being in communion with him. The Psalmist in these verses is worried that Yahweh could cast him away and remove the Holy Spirit from him. But the pardon would mean that the "joy of salvation" returns again (cf. v. 8a). In v. 12b, the Psalmist prays to God for "supporting spirit of willing obedience" (cf. Jer. 24:7; 31:33; 23:39; Ezek. 36:25f). However, Jeremiah and Ezekiel believes that Yahweh himself will put the word (instruction) in to the heart of a person and thus create joyous, willing obedience through his "spirit". But here the Psalmist awaits a support to consolidate his life. Thus the Psalmist goes beyond the prophets even while using their categories.

In vv.13-17, there is a vow (v.13), petitions (vv.14-15) and thoughts about the right, God-pleasing sacrifice (vv.16-17). In his vow the Psalmist declares that he wants to teach the "transgressors" the ways of Yahweh (cf. Ps. 22:22). The authority of him who teaches has its foundation in the living experience of the salvation of Yahweh. in v. 14, the petitioner wants to praise God's righteousness which shows itself in new help for him, a guilty human being. In v.15, the psalmist prays that Yahweh may empower him to proclaim the glory of the creator as in Ps. 40:3, the Psalmist wait on inspiration. He knows that he is completely dependent on God. Also the testimony to Yahweh's great deeds can succeed only if Yahweh "opens" the mouth of the speaker.

Thoughts about sacrifices in vv.16-l7 are intimately connected with the vow spoken in v.13. It was customary for the one who prayed and presented petitions to bring sacrifices after his rescue (cf. Ps. 54:6). But the rejection of sacrificial system by the prophets (Amos 5:22; Isa. 1:11; Jer. 6:20) is taken up here and followed obediently. But in v.17 the Psalmist declares, "My sacrifice is a broken spirit." The Petitioner therefore brings no substitute sacrifice, but he offers himself as the sacrifice. Human beings with a broken and contrait heart are seized with a deep despair about themselves. The brokenness of their natural confidence in life and self-points to a condition of frightful anguish and despair vis-a-vis God (cf. Ps. 34:18; Isa. 57:15; 61:1).

vv.18-19 according to some scholars is ascribed to the time of Nehemiah (cf. Ps. 102:13,16; 147:2; Jer. 31:38; Isa. 26:1; 33:20; 62:6). The author in v.19 apparently is thinking of an inner reformation of the sacrificial system that no longer falls under the prophets' protest.

***(D) Purpose and Application:*** At the time of reformation Ps. 51 was among the influential biblical texts to which Luther appealed in his doctrine of justification. But, this is "over interpretation" of the Psalm, however, the essential statement in the Psalm was rightly grasped by Luther and Calvin. The Psalmist knows that he is entirely dependent on the merciful activity of God. Only God can eliminate the threatening, dark wall of separation, sin that separates God and human beings and blot out what is intolerable. Only by God's creative, renewing power can the heart be cleansed and led to a new obedience. Also the future is in the hands of God alone. If God sends the spirit of willingness and constancy, then the Psalmist is saved from fickleness and unfaithfulness. Even the witness of thanksgiving (v. 15) is exclusively left in the hands of powers furnished by Yahweh. Everything is God's act. The sola gratia shines forth from every verse. No gift, no condition comes between God and human beings. No sacrifice has an effect on Yahweh. Only the pleading and trusting human being is the sacrifice, he who with body and life surrenders himself to God, who has nothing else to offer but a heart that is bruised and broken (v. 17). The human being presents himself to God as what he is. For him nothing remains except to plead for forgiveness and to confess his guilt. In its extreme of knowledge and wisdom (v. 6) which has been won from the prophetic word of the OT, Ps. 51 stands out in the Psalter. Its peak statements are unique. And its fullness of insight is incomprehensible. According to H. Gese, based on form criticism and an analysis of structure, the ontology presented in this psalm distinguishes very sharply between an outward world of appearances and an inner, true existence that is hidden.

### *(7) Psalm 73: "You Have Taken Hold of my Right Hand"*

***(A) Form:*** It is usually held that Ps.73 is a "didactic poem" originating in the traditional area of wisdom. It was thought that one could recognize as the theme of this "didactic poem" the "dogma of retaliation" or the "question of the theodicy" or even the "problem of the moral natural law." The correct elements in these statements is no doubt that the whole psalm has a didactic character and is related to Psalms 37 and 49, which can more accurately be determined to belong to the genre "wisdom poetry." However, it is not enough to say that Ps. 73 is a "didactic poem". M. Buber correctly declares that the psalm contains "description, report, and confession". E. Wurthwein has observed that v. 1 contains elements of the "song of thanksgiving" (cf. Ps. 106:1; 107:1; 118:1; 136:1). But also v.28b points to a report of the experience the one who gives thanks. Therefore, the description of events, or the report of experiences, as a component part of Ps. 73 must receive strong emphasis. Ps. 73 is in the first place narration (in v.28) and only in the second place teaching. At the same time beside the intention of the thanksgiving liturgy, the expressions of trust (vv. 23ff), and also the Protestations of innocence (v. 13) should not go unnoticed. But how is the "component of experience" to be understood? It is significant for the didactic wisdom poems that they are characterized by autobiographical stylization (cf. Prov. 24:30-34; Sir 51;13-16; 33:16-19). According to von Rad, concerning Ps. 73. "Here we definitely have, rather, a traditional stylistic form in which the teacher could from time to time, cloth his instruction, and which also allowed of being extended into larger units. Our modern interest in the biographies of biblical authors should not, therefore, be misled for here we are scarcely dealing with genuine experiences, at any rate they appear in a highly conventionalized form."

***(B) Setting:*** The singer of the Psalm is a person suffering heavy afflictions (vv. 14,26). In his torments he who is severely tried must behold the well-being of the ungodly and wicked and experience bitter questioning in his trust in Yahweh (vv. 2ff). The profession of innocence in v. 13 permits us to learn that the Psalmist belongs among "righteous". Why must the "righteous" suffer while the "wicked" enjoys prosperity? This was the incalculably difficult question that raised bodily suffering to the point of intolerability. In this affliction the sufferer took refuge with Yahweh (v. 28a), he became to the proximity to God (v. 28b) the sanctuary (v. 17a). Here the "end" (v. 17b) was proclaimed to him who was tormented. And at the same time a certainty was granted him that overcame all affliction and temptation. Ps. 73 reports this wondrous event under the signature of thankfulness and with the purpose of proclaiming the victory over the great threat against faith by confession and teaching. The Psalm is to be assigned to a rather late date (Jer. 12:1ff: might indicate the terminus aqua). We do have a parallel for this Psalm from AWA literature, especially from the Egyptian "literature of discussion."

***(C) Interpretation:*** Ps. 73 begins with a confession thankfully proclaimed v.1 anticipates not only the theme but also the conquest of the tensions and temptations described in the Psalm. All who torment themselves with the thoughts and considerations of the Psalmist (vv. 2ff) should know from the beginning: Only goodness does Yahweh bestow on the "righteous", who in v.1 are called "upright", "who are of a clean heart". M. Buber calls attention to the fact that "heart" is the dominating word of the whole Psalm (vv. 1,7,13,21,26). The Psalmist penetrates to the innermost and most secret recesses of human existence. The confession spoken in v. 1 proclaims the salvific reality that was gained from the experience of suffering and is always valid. Under the confession of the constantly effective perfection of the goodness of Yahweh, the narrative concerning the heavy threat to and the questioning of reliance on God now begins in vv. 2ff. Ps. 73 does not contain a theoretical doctrinal essay on the "retribution", on the "question of the theodicy" on the "moral world order". Here a human being tells us how he was under threat of losing confidence in the perfection of Yahweh's goodness vis-a-vis the one who is righteous. Yahweh did not let him fall! in this he has let his goodness shine in the midst of all changes, of which the Psalm will now Speak.

In vv. 3-9, the reason for the great threat is delineated by the introduction of Particle (ki=because in v. 3). Incomprehensibly, Yahweh's goodness, which favors the "upright" (v. 1) in the form of extensive good fortune of life (shalom) became the prerogative of the God forsaking wicked ones (cf. Jer. 12:1ff; Job 21:7). That is what the Psalmist was worked up about, for his body is racked with sickness and suffering (vv. 14 and 16). But the "wicked ones" do not suffer; they are healthy and sleek. Life's hardships they do not know (v. 5). From their innermost being wicked schemes and acts continually emerge (v. 7). For the words "mouth", "tongue" has the same meaning as "word" (v. 9). H. Ringgren calls attention to a Ugaritic text based on v. 9. "A lip towards the earth a lip towards the heavens the tongue towards the stars". But demythologization took place in Ps. 73.

In vv. 10-12, the wicked ones, who are arrogant and talk "down from heaven" are successful (v. 10). The "people" become their followers and avidly take in their snobbish world-conquering words. In v. 11 it is implied that God does not take cognizance of the bustle on earth-he does not react (Isa. 29:15; Ezek. 8:12; Ps. 10:11; 94:9). In vv. 6-11, the picture of unbounded hubris is delineated of the "wicked ones" is painted. In v. 12 the description of the riotous ways the "wicked ones" is brought to a close. Now the Psalmist turns to his own fate.

In vv.13-16, the righteous, living according to the ordinances of God, has no answer. In his life Yahweh's goodness does not appear in the form of shalom. Rather it is empty, futile and without effective encouragement and without any noticeable intervention does the obedience of the "righteous" remain. The protestation of innocence with the renewed reference to "heart", to the cleanness of heart (cf. v. 1), intensifies the question into an intolerable burden; where is the goodness of God? The Psalmist has obviously demonstrated by means of an oath of cleansing that his oppressive suffering (v. 14) is not to be attributed to a failure on his part. He is suffering in innocence (cf. Ps. 17:3ff; 26:6ff). The sufferer cannot break away from the indisputable reality of God's Slavic activity in Israel (cf. Ps. 22:4f). Thus the action of Yahweh becomes an inscrutable mystery. To think about it constitutes unbearable torment (v. 16). All intellectual exertions are hopelessly shattered.

In vv. 17-21, the turning point is reached in the sanctuary of God, the place of the nearness of God (v. 28a). In the areas of sanctuary (cf. Ps. 68:35; Ezek. 21:7; 28:18). Psalmist has entered in order to receive an explanation in the abode of God's presence (v. 28a). Will the good fortune of the "wicked ones" last forever, and will there be no end to the torment of the "righteous"? This is the question with which the sufferer enters the sanctuary. He is looking for the "end". The reference to "end" means the final outcome, the final event that explains everything, the visible appearance of a situation now still veiled (cf. Lam. 1:9; Deut. 32:28f; Isa. 47:7). This revelation the Psalmist anticipates attentively (v.17b). Now the knowledge which the sufferer has gained (vv. 18-20) is full of assurance. The "wicked ones" no matter how self-assured and haughty they appear (vv.6ff) are on "slippery ground". They stand before an immediate, terrible downfall (cf. v. 2). Their good fortune is a fool's paradise. Before the brightness of God's reality, the assured life conditions of the "wicked ones" suddenly disappear. The secret of Ps. 73 is that there is information and direction concerning the righteous rule of God on the basis of a new dimension. What in this world can no longer be demonstrated empirically is cleared up prophetically? Ps.73 prophetically proclaims, on the basis of the "end", a final certainty no longer visible (cf. vv. 25ff).

Although vv. 21-22 (like v.16) again speak of the torment of thinking about the unfathomable mysteries of the hiddenness of God, we should not relocate these verses. v.16 aims at the disclosure concerning the "wicked ones" in vv. 18-20; vv. 21 and 22 are oriented to the great assurance which the Petitioner gains for himself. The embitterment of the inner being, the self-consumption of the contemplative middle of life, and the dark deafness of him who threatens to lose his mind (v. 22).

In vv. 23ff. a world-conquering trust now speaks the word. The phrase in 23a: "But I am always with you," in the sanctuary, the place of the Presence of God (vv. 17a, 28a), the Psalmist becomes aware of an unchangeable fact, (cf. v. 1): I belong to you. "You have taken hold of my right hand." Initially v. 23b states: Yahweh has palpably drawn near to him who considered himself lost and forsaken; He has let him recognize the certainty of belonging to God and the saving way of clutching Him just before his slipping away (v. 2). But there is more to this phrase: Taking hold of right hand manifests a position of honor such as befitting the ruler in ancient West Asian royal ritual. The great king was taken by the hand of the Deity (Is. 45:1). With Deutero-Isaiah, this phrase is applied to the servant (Is. 42:6, 41:13). The Psalm singer in Ps. 73 takes up this expression. The singer knows that in all the visible "injustices" that assail confidence he is led by his God (v. 24). Taken by the hand (v. 23b) and directed according to Yahweh's plan (which surpasses all human thought, Is. 55:88), the sufferer goes to meet his glorious destiny. And now the petitioner of Ps. 73 is sure that all his distresses and torment will "at the end" be set aside by sudden intervention of God. M. Buber states: "The Psalmists have transplanted the term from the area of story of miracles into that of personal piety and their personal expression." v. 25a is like a confession. Besides Yahweh, there is in the divine realm of heavenly world no helper in time of need for the petitioner. Now the Psalmist declares in v. 25a that he desires nothing on earth besides Yahweh. With this confession, all expectations of Shalom (cf. vv. 3ff.) are rejected.

v. 26 is very impressively sung by the Psalmist. The truth has come from the end, and all imminent blessings are thereby made relative (of. Ps. 63:4). The futility (in v. 13a) is replaced by the fullness of communion with God which breaks up every trace of worldliness. Now he, who is in heavy suffering, now no longer waits for healing; he waives every manifestation of clemency that might be produced in this world (v. 2b); beyond all physical deterioration he looks to the end, which beams forth with an indestructible certainty of communion with God in present time: "My rock and my portion is Yahweh." The word portion originally meant portion of ground (Deut. 10:9; Num. 18:20). When it is related to Yahweh it takes on the general meaning of the basis of life, life's subsistence (Ps. 16:5). Yahweh has become the petitioners' reason for existence that does not waver but remains stable.

vv. 27-28 contain the synopsis of the knowledge certainty won in two passages vv. 18-20 and 23-26. The "wicked ones", who retreat and apostatize from Yahweh, perish. But the "righteous" thankfully praises the nearness to God and communion with God that has become apparent in the sanctuary (v. 17a).

***(D) Purpose and Application:*** According to B. Duhm, the purpose of the whole Psalm is: "Psalm 73 shows that for the ordinary understanding the problem of retribution could hereby be solved only by the aid of the thought of immortality ..." But this will shift the real purpose of the Psalm we have been considering in the interpretation section. It is not concerned about the problem of immortality which a wise person here dealt in theoretical deliberations. What is intellectual is brought to the center of attention; the nature of events is not recognized. The occurrence narrated in Ps. 73 is overlooked. After all, there is a report of a life affliction that intensifies to the point of insanity. In helpless isolation and final loneliness, a human being is struggling towards the certainty of communion with God. Do I belong to God? Does God answer my obedience and trust? This is the decisive question which surges violently through the whole Psalm. If the afflicted person looks around in the circle of life that may be surveyed, he may become aware of a distribution of destinies that almost makes him lose faith in God. Good fortune falls to the lot of the base fools and those who haughtily despise God while the servant of God has to bear oppressive torments. The entire Visible world is a single contradiction against the righteous God. But the Psalmist does not join the chorus of the frivolous scorners (vv. 11, 15). He takes refuge in the place of God's presence (v. 28) in the sanctuary (v. 17). Here the final truth of God that overturns everything is revealed to him: Those who haughtily scorn God fall into ruin, but I belong to my God; and even when body and soul faint away, I am most intimately joined to God and look forward to the removal to "glory". Here Ps. 73 breaks through a barrier that is otherwise definitely set up in the OT; The "end" is not only the "Solution of problem" but also the end determined and modified by Yahweh's deed, which produces a term of change in the aspects of reality. Ps. 73 is an "exemplary life" (M. Buber) presenting itself to didactic poetry in Biographical stylization. And this "exemplary life" dovetails into the constant salvific faithfulness of God (W. and 15b) which is effective in Israel and has demonstrated its power even in the depths of despair. the Psalmist has become aware of certainty of this, that he may remain with his God, that Yahweh is his permanent source of life, and that he. remains so till his death. Even death cannot destroy the communion of life given by Yahweh.

The New Testament reads this Psalm and understands its view of the fact that Jesus Christ is the "place" of God's presence (v. 28). In Christ, the Christian experiences the miracle of communion with God which overcomes all affliction, yes, even death (Rom. 8:35-39).

### *8. PSALM 80: "O Yahweh Sebaoth, Restore Us"*

***(A) FORM:*** The outward form of Psalm 80 is characterized by the refrain in vv. 3,7 and 19 (also in 14 in some commentaries, but this is different based on the strophes found in the Hebrew text). This Psalm belongs to the category of community prayer songs (thus opines H. Gunkel, J. Begrich). In v. 4, the Psalm is expressly called "Prayer". In this Psalm vv. 3, 7 & 19 give the community prayer song the structure of a liturgy. According to Beyerlin, this Psalm is called as "Petitionary Prayer", an integral ingredient of the community prayer song. Based on v. 17, this Psalm is pointed out as intercession for the king.

***(B) SETTING:*** "Prayer songs of the people" were, in times of particular distress, intoned in the holy place. Presenters (priests) presented the lament and the petition for the assembled community, and the multitude again and again interrupted with audible supplications (vv. 3, 7, 14, 19). Two questions concerning Psalm 80 have been asked again and again

i. Where was the prayer song presented?
ii. To which particular emergency do the complaints of the people have reference to?

First a few thoughts about the historical situation: From v. 2 it is clear that the reference is to a serious threat to the northern Israelite group of tribes in Central Palestine: Ephraim, Manasseh and Benjamin. Psalm 80 also indicates that Israel uniformly belongs to the past. The terminus quo therefore is undoubtedly the year of the division of the Kingdom of Israel one year after the death of Solomon. But this declaration is only the beginning of the problems. In the last 150 years, this Psalm is dated from the 8th century BCE. until the time of the Maccabees. According to E. Koenig, heard on v 2. the peculiar reference of the poem to Ephraim, etc., is warrant for the conclusion that the poet was looking at a catastrophe of the Kingdom of Samaria. Moreover, E. Koenig is of the opinion that the Psalm was sung in Judah: The distress of the northern tribes of Israel was self-evidently a matter of sorrow and intercessory prayer also for the patriots in Judah, therefore in time of 732 and 722 BCE. as the time of this Psalm, but taking into account the title "Yahweh Sabaoth" E. Koenig localizes the prayer song in Northern Israel, which originated in Shiloh.

But it is difficult to give a documented answer to historical questions. The distress of the 3 tribes (cf. v. 2) cannot be identified in detail from the Psalm. The reference to I Kings 15:29, 22:29 to a situation in the time between 732 and 722 BCE. is an attempt at interpretation which has no support in the text. On the other hand, it would also be possible to emphasize the restoration of Israel prayed for in the refrain. Then a later time would be under consideration (after 722 BCE). The distress of the northern tribes would then be actually that of the exile, or complete subjugation in the formal tribal area, now under Assyrian administration. This may call attention to the time of Josiah. In these years we see a time in Judah in which the idea was strong that Israel, the old union of the twelve tribes, must be restored. Josiah crosses the border to enter the territory of the tribes of Ephraim, Benjamin and Manasseh. To this king also the intercessory prayer in v. 17 could apply. Also the declaration of loyalty in v. 18 could fit well into this time of reform.

O. Eissfeldt associated Psalm 80 closely with Ps. 89:40ff. The result: In Ps. 89 the intercession very definitely applies to the reigning Davidite (vv. 38ff.), whereas Ps. 80 prays for Yahweh's support for one who is protected by Him and who has been made strong by Him, one who, without any traditional authority, is dependent on God's support. This would fit well with the usurper Hoshea ben-Elah, about whom II Kings 15:30 reports he murdered his predecessor on the throne of Israel, Pekah ben-Remaliah, and became king in his stead. But this is yet another bold presentation of the matter. Beyerlin tries to distinguish various strata is Ps. 80 and to find traces of contemporizing. But then he writes "Much argues for the hypothesis that the stratum of text Ps. 80:4 6;16b-18 should first and foremost be derived from the days of Josiah" (W. Beyerlin, "Schichten im 80 Psalm", Festschrift fuer G. Friedrich (1973) 9 24 cited in H. J. Kraus, Psalm 60 150, p. 141).

***(C) INTERPRETATION:*** The address in v.1 is aimed at the shepherd of Israel. The underlying metaphor (God, our Shepherd, cf. Ps. 23:1, 78:52, 121:4; Gen. 48:15, 49:24) provides a characteristic expression for the close God-people relationship and emphasizes the lordship of the guiding God over His people. Israel refers to the 12 tribe confederacy, the entirety of Israel (cf. vv. 8ff.). The concept of God enthroned on Cherubim is originally

Canaanite; it applies to the Lord of heaven enthroned above the clouds (of. Ps. 68:4). The Yahweh Sabaoth revered in Shiloh was in Israel describes as "The one enthroned above the Cherubim" (cf. I Sam. 4:4). But this conception then went with the ark to Jerusalem (II Sam. 6:2) and is to be found in the cultic tradition of Zion (Ps. 18:10, 97:2, 99:1). The refrain in v. 3 prays for the restoration of Israel. The assembly prays to the God called "Yahweh Sebaoth" at the amphictyonic sanctuaries Shiloh and Jerusalem. Letting the face shine is a sign of gracious attention and blessing.

In vv. 4-7, the wrath of God (v. 4) has brought on the distress of the people of God. It has been active a long time already. All petitions are in vain. The expression "Prayers of your people" is an exact designation of the category "Prayer songs of the people". In v. 6 the suffix for the first person plural is now used because the territorial possession of all Israel is now involved, which has been lost due to the subjugation of the Northern tribes (v. 2). v. 6 could well refer to the time of decline of the Assyrian empire, when the neighbors and the enemies of Israel contend for the supremacy in the areas formerly ruled by the Assyrians. The enemies scoff at the impotence of Israel. But the community prays for Yahweh's intervention and the restoration of Israel (v. 7).

In vv. 8-15, there is a description of the dark catastrophe of the present in front of the bright background of the of the first, fundamental salvific deeds of Yahweh. Israel is compared to a grapevine, from v. 12 to a vineyard (cf. Hos. 10:1, Jer. 2:21). This allegory is related to the people of God. v. 8a alludes to the Exodus tradition (cf. also v. 1). The grapevine was "lifted up" out of Egypt. In vv. 8-9, an image beautifully illustrates Israel's right of ownership in its own land; at the same time there is an excellent description of the possession of the territory that gradually encompassed the entire area. The sovereign control of the entire land in expressed in v. 10. v. 11 speaks of the powerful extension. Here the thought is of the great empire of David, which extended from the Mediterranean to the Euphrates. The Psalm, therefore in its petition for restoration (vv. 3, 7, 19) recalls the original assets of Israel at the time of David and now in vv. 12ff. begins a lament about the dissolution of the God-given arrangement. v. 13 describes the damage by wild beasts (some would however ascribe this to Egypt). This section closes with the plea addresses to Yahweh that He would return (from hiddenness) and mercifully look down from Heaven. In v. 15 (in accordance with the transition from the grapevine metaphor to the vineyard image) the land of Israel is compared to a garden which Yahweh has planted and should now restore.

Verse 16 prays for Yahweh's intervention against the enemy. "Before the threats of your face!" is the presence of God in the judgment of His theophany. Associated with the prayer for defeat of the enemy is the intercession for the king. "Man at your right hand" (v. 17) is not an "allusion to Benjamin" but a honorable reference to the king who sits at the right hand of Yahweh (cf. Ps. 110:1). The intercession for the king in v. 17 could apply to Josiah. He comes into the area of the tribes of middle Palestine and brings with him all the hopes of Israel for a renewal of the time of David. From him a restoration of Israel was awaited. According to Claus Westermann v. 18 shows a remarkable likeness to the promise of the people at the convocation at Shechem in Josh. 24:16 18. In any case, this is a declaration of obligation such as was customary of the God-people relation carried through Israel (cf. I Kings 23:3). v. 19b is to be understood as a vow of thanksgiving.

***(D) PURPOSE AND APPLICATION:*** The prayer song of the community prays for Yahweh to come forward and make an appearance. The petitioners are sure that their God has absolute power. He is enthroned over the cherubim. The distress of the people torn apart under the wrath of God and abandoned without protection determines their complaints. And yet the community looks back to the great foundational salvific deeds of the "Shepherd of Israel" who has led His people out of Egypt and has given the land to it. The Psalm prays for the restoration of Israel. What Israel is and should be is determined from the basic history. From this perspective the petitions are determined. Israel is God's planting. It is remarkable how the founding of the people, its history of liberation and guidance is understood exclusively on the basis of sovereign activity of Yahweh. He it was who took up and planted (v. 8f). He drove out the nations and made room (vv. 9f). Here we cannot fail to notice the universal placement and mission of the people of God (vv. 10ff). The real distress which is revealed in the prayer song lies comprehended in the awful fact that has come its way in the world of peoples. For that reason, in no phase of the calls of distress and petition is the restitution of the racial and national existence as such the chief matter of concern, but the restoration as the people of God as the planting of God in the nations. The prayer song has a "messianic" component insofar as the heroic power of Yahweh Sebaoth (vv. 2f), in the "man at the right hand" (v. 17, Ps. 110:1), in the "Son of Man", is expected as present and active.

### *9. PSALM 104: GOD THE CREATOR AND SUSTAINER*

***(A) FORM:*** The extensive song belongs to the category of the hymns of an individual. The individual voice clearly emerges in vv. 1, 33 and 35 (cf. Ps. 103 & Ps. 8:3ff). Numerous verses of the Psalm are given as reports in a hymnic address. vv. 8b, 9, 20, 24b, 26b, 28 30. The theme of the Hymn is Yahweh's creation. Formally, the characteristics are the hymnic participles, which surely must also be seen in v. 5 & 19. An analysis of the structure according to form and content provides the following picture: vv. 1-4, praise of God who is above all worlds; vv. 5-9, conquest of the primeval flood and founding of the earth; vv. 10-12, springs and brooks; vv. 13-18, refreshment proceeds from Yahweh's rains to all lands; vv. 19-24, night and daybreak; vv. 25-26, the sea; vv. 27-30, all life depends on Yahweh; vv. 31-35, hymnic conclusion.

***(B) SETTING:*** In connection with the question of the "setting" of Psalm 104, the scholarly discussion always comes up with three questions:

i. What is the relation between Psalm 104 and pre-Israelite poems and transmissions?
ii. How are we to interpret the Psalm's allusions to Genesis 1?
iii. What should we consider the relation of Psalm 104 to the festival cults of Israel?

When we try to answer these points, the following observations can be made: First, when at the excavations at el-Amarna the hymn to the sun of Amenhotep IV (Akhenaton) was discovered, the connections with Psalm 104 were immediately noticed. Perhaps the elements of Akhenaton hymn impinged first on the Canaanite songs that praise the "God's Highest" and "Creator" (cf. Gen. 14:19). Israel would then have assimilated these materials and motifs. In addition to the allusions to the sun hymn of Akhenaton, still other themes would have to be named that point to a pre-Israelite time. Thus Psalm 104 is saturated with conceptions of the encyclopedic science of lists that can be documented in the natural science of the Egyptians. Also motifs of the Syro-Canaanite primeval flood myth have to be considered. All these alien elements flowed into Israel because of the contact with the Canaanites. Second, on the relation of Psalm 104 to Gen. 1, only loose allusions are pointed out. In vv. 6f, 14, 19 & 25 references to the priestly teaching of creation may be documented. But the singer of Ps. 104 plucks a number of strings of primeval themes of tradition rather freely, and these are registered also in Gen. 1. Third, the praise of the Creator will certainly have had its "sitz-im-leben" in the homage before "King Yahweh" in the worship of Israel, not related to any enthronement festival (as proposed by S. Mowinckel). The date of origin of the Psalm cannot be determined. A pre-exilic date is not out of the question.

***(C) INTERPRETATION:*** In vv. 1-4, the hymn describes the creation of Heaven. Yahweh stretches out the heaven like a tent (cf. Is. 40:22, Jer. 10:12). This section has motifs of theophany and kingship of Yahweh. Two kinds of theophanies are noticed in general; they are storm theophany and earthquake theophany. The storm theophany is from the northern kingdom, which has strong links with the Baal tradition. Earthquake theophany is connected with the southern Kingdom and identified with El. Yahweh as the one who stretches out the heaven imagery is borrowed from El in the Ugaritic text. The palace above the celestial water (Ps. 104:3, cf. 29: 10) is derived from the Baal-Canaanite tradition: So here, El and Baal traditions are blended together. The words chariots, ministers, messengers all imply the kingship motif in the psalm. The passage affirms that creation is not itself God, but belongs to God. He is the one who stretched out the heaven. Light is His garment, water is His foundation on which beams of His chambers rest, clouds are His chariots, wind is His messenger, fire and flame are His ministers. So human beings cannot treat nature as their own possession. The ownership of the land is affirmed by the priestly tradition in Lev. 25:23. Scripture affirms that earth is the Lord's and everything in it, the world and those who live in it, for He has founded it on the seas and established it on the rivers (Ps. 24:1-2).

In vv. 5-9, the idea of Hebrew three-tier cosmos is presented. The flat earth resting on the foundations, a deep sea or sheol beneath the earth and firmament above the earth (Ps. 148:1,7). Yahweh creates earth out of chaos. He makes an ordered cosmos in which human beings can live (Is. 45:18). He establishes the right order. God's struggle against chaos and subsequent creation highlights both the issues of ecology and justice.

vv. 10-13 & 16-17 depict the picture of God watering the Whole earth. The thirst of wild animals is quenched (v. 11), plants are watered (v. 12), and the earth is satisfied. vv. 16-17 seem to be an elaboration of v. 12. Trees are watered by the river and the birds make their habitation there. The water is from the valleys (v. 10) and also from above (v. 13). This may refer to springs and rain. Life on earth depends on natural resources and natural resources belong to God. The Psalmist acknowledges this fact.

In vv. 14-15 and 18-23, relationships between human beings and nature is the main concern. vv. 14-15 talk about human beings and plants. After grass for animals, the Psalmist describes the relationship between human beings and plants. Human beings cultivate plants, plants in turn give food, wine and bread to human beings. This gives satisfaction to the humans, gladdens their hearts and strengthens them. These verses highlight the interdependence of human beings on plants as well as the stewardship attitude of human beings towards plants. vv. 18-23 talk about the relationship between human beings and animals. The life in God's earth is regulated by earth and moon. The Psalmist declares that the moon is made for marking seasons. This has similarity with the priestly tradition where the sun and moon are created for signs and seasons (Gen. 1:14). Wild goats from mountains, conies from rocks and lions from the den, all creep out in darkness for their food and withdraw in the morning with the rising of the sun. Human beings go out for their labor in the morning and withdraw in the evening. Here the time is shared among the living beings for their respective work in God's world.

In vv. 24-26 we find the main theme as wisdom and creation. The Psalmist praises Yahweh's wisdom that is revealed in His creation with astonishment (v. 24). In the following verse the Psalmist describes the sea creatures, ships and Leviathan that sport about in the sea. The Psalm as a whole was influenced by the wisdom tradition. The term hokma (wisdom) is found in this section (v. 24). The Psalm portrays that everything fulfills its purpose. The singer points out the beneficial effects of water. There is a whole chain of consecutive purpose (vv. 13-15, cf. Prov. 16:4). There is also a reference to times and seasons (vv. 19-23). Here Leviathan becomes a sea creature among other creatures. von Rad also affirms the influence of wisdom in this Psalm.

In vv. 27-30, the creator God is described as the provider of food and life. H. J. Kraus observes the influence of Egyptian hymn at this point: "When thou hast risen they live: when thou does not sit they die." The passage gives equal status to all living beings as formed by the breath of Yahweh and return to the dust in the end (In Yahwist's account of creation story in Gen. 2:7, Yahweh formed man out of dust and breathed into his nostrils, and in Gen. 3:19 it is described by Yahwist that in death man would return to dust). B. W. Anderson interprets this passage as God's continuing activity of sustaining creatures.

In vv. 31-35, the concluding section of the Psalm, God seems to be rejoicing over His creation. In Gen. 1:30-31 God saw that everything He had made and that it was good. v. 32 has an allusion to theophany; trembling of the earth and smoke on earth. Perhaps the influence of Sinai tradition can be found in the background (cf. Ex. 19:16-21). According to Kraus v. 35 is to be interpreted in relation to new creation. In the presence of the creator, the wicked has lost their right to existence in the creation that is open before God, guilt has no place. Here radiates 1 faith in creation, a world that is free from guilt and failure.

***(D) PURPOSE AND APPLICATION:*** This Psalm highlights the major aspects of creator, creation, human beings and non-human creation. Four distinctive points can be summarized when we talk about God the creator and sustainer in this Psalm:

*First*: God and creation God is the creator and sustainer. All the creation belongs to Him and is related to Him at an equal level. All creation is good. All things in creation are mutually dependent and together they depend on God who not only created them but sustains mom.

*Second*: Human beings are one among the diversity of God's creation. They are the stewards of nature and nature responds to them by her provisions.

*Third*: Chaos is an enemy to creation and God, and an oppressive power over the weak. God overcomes the chaos to bring out the creation and vindicate the right of the oppressed. Sin causes fragmentation, pollution and alienation that results in disharmony and chaos. Presence of that is a reality and elimination of that is a desire of a true worshipper. This is coo-spirituality that expects a just and ecologically balanced cosmos.

*Fourth*: Wisdom connects social order with natural order and thus serves as a valuable paradigm to address the issues of ecology and justice.

### *10. PSALM 116: "I LIFT UP THE CUP OF SALVATION"*

***(A) FORM:*** The fact that the Psalm singer has experienced Yahweh's help and is appearing before Him to give thanks is clearly evident in vv. 1, 2, 12-14, & 17-19. It belongs to the category of thanksgiving songs of an individual. With the exception of v. 8, vv. 1-15 stay with the third person for Yahweh. vv. 13-19 are to be understood in the light of the thought that the vow of thanksgiving has now been paid. The situation of distress is still noticeable in the Psalm. Descriptions of distress, petitions and expression of trust are recapitulated. In the process traditional, conventional forms of expressions have been adopted.

***(B) SETTING:*** The song of thanksgiving is intoned during the great festivals in the presence of the whole community (cf. vv. 14, 17). Those giving thanks appeared in the courts of the temple of Jerusalem (v. 19) a paid the vows (vv. 14, 18) once made in great distress. From v. 11 we could infer that the Psalmist was surrounded by liars and slanderers. vv. 3 & 15 suggest that death stared him in the face Details cannot be discerned. H. Schmidt attempts to combine Ps. 116 & 117 to re-construct a "liturgy for a festival of thanksgiving for vows" in which two petitioners are supposed to have been the speakers (cf. Ps. 107). A late post-exilic date for the Psalm is assigned on the basis of the Aramaism in vv. 7, 12 & 16. We may also assume that the Psalm was available as a formulary in the cultic area.

***(C) INTERPRETATION:*** In vv. 1-2 the Psalm singer looks back to the fact that Yahweh has heard and bent down His ear to the petition. Thus the rescue already accomplished is taken for granted (cf. Ps. 28:6, 30:1). The petitioner bears witness to his intimate connection and attachment to the God of his salvation, whom he loves (cf. Ps. 5:11, 31 :33, 40: 16, 69:33, et.a1). Yahweh has heard and lamented "on the day when he cried" (Ps. 20:9, 138:3). This "day" is the subject of v. 4.

In vv. 3ff the one who is giving thanks looks back to his time of distress. This is customary in the thanksgiving song of an individual. The sufferer, about whose specific distress nothing is said at first, was destined for the "realm of death." Sheol was casting its "bands of death" into his life and placed the Psalmist in bitter distress and despair. The conception of the prison of death as a prison is customary in the ancient world. In the worst distress the oppressed person called on the name of Yahweh. The formula "call on the name of Yahweh" here refers to the prayer of lament but in vv. 13 & 17 it is in connection with the proclamation of thanksgiving. v. 4b contains a short lament: "on the day when I cried" (v. 2b) while vv. 5 & 6a show the nature of a confession of a general kind. v. 6b applies the salvific activity of Yahweh to the specific weakness suffered in one's own body.

vv. 7-9 speak about the present condition. v. 7 contains address to one's own soul, as it is familiar from Ps. 42:5 & 103:1f. By virtue of Yahweh's bountiful deeds, the oppressed and despairing "soul" (v. 3) can return to rest again. Yahweh has saved the "soul" from the realm of death. All suffering and danger is turned away (cf. Ps. 56:13). From the realm of "sheol" the Psalmist has been transported to the "land of living". The reference is of course to the land in which the living people have their being. The idea of life in the Old Testament is described by the expression: "Life before Yahweh". "Life in the presence of God" is life in the fullest sense of the word life that knows it is God's gift and that is always hidden in God.

vv. 10-11 are from a retrospective narration. In all suffering the petitioner has been firmly anchored in Yahweh, therefore he can now (without reservation) speak about his former condition. In vv. 10b & 11 we have an admission concerning the former despair. v. 11 is an expression of absolute despair in the face of slanderous accusations and lying snares. Even the friends and relatives desert the sufferer (like the thought of Lamentations). He is forsaken by all people. The Psalmist wants to express how great the distress was (cf. v. 3).

In vv. 12-14 the Psalmist is ready to give thanks. It is a matter of rounding out the song of thanksgiving. The bountiful deed of Yahweh is immeasurably great. In this song, the name of Yahweh is "called on". To call on the name of Yahweh now has the meaning: to confess the salvific presence of Yahweh in a proclamation before all the people. In the presence of the festival assembly, the one giving thanks praises the salvation of Yahweh as he narrates and confesses (cf. Ps. 22:22, 25).

The meaning of the term "cup of salvation" should be considered briefly: According to H. Schimdt, cup of salvation is a cup that has provided the rescue. At a festival of thanks offering the "cup of salvation" must have played a special role in the ceremonial (Ps. 23:5). We should take note of a votive stele of Yehawmilk, king of Byblos (5th Cent. B. C.). In a picture above the text one recognizes the king, who stands in front of the goddess Ba'alat of Byblos and lifts up a libation shell that he is presenting. The text reads: "I, Yehawmilk, King of Byblos, have made (these things) for my mistress, the lady (Ba'alat) of Byblos, for I called my mistress, the lady of Byblos, and she heard my voice and treated me kindly" (ANET p. 221). The one giving thanks lifts the cup, perhaps here too in Ps. 116 for a libation (cf. Exod. 29:40f; Num. 28:7).

vv. 15-16 contain confessions full of trust. v. 15 says that Yahweh does not let His "saints" die (cf. Ps. 162101), He saves them from death (v. 8). In other words, Yahweh sees to it that those that are His do not dwindle away into death. The singer in v. 16 declares that he is the servant of his savior (cf. Ps. 143:12). "Son of the maid" (cf. Ps. 86:16; Exod. 23:12) is in the legal terminology the slave born in the household, who has neither claim nor prospect of emancipation. This relation the Psalmist transfers to his relation with Yahweh in order to show that he is the lowliest servant and slave.

The last verses, vv. 17-19 clearly show the situation of the thanks offering. The name of Yahweh is "called out". The vows are fulfilled (cf. Ps. 61:8, 66:13). v. 19 indicates the place at which the torah is publicly presented.

***(D) PURPOSE AND APPLICATION:*** The song of thanksgiving leads the hearer to the depths of vulnerability and lets him recognize to what unplumbed depths of despair the Psalmist found himself. Helpless, he was caught in the realm of death and God-forsakenness (v. 3). He was encompassed by a web of lies which people had woven about him. But Yahweh rescued him from the realm of death, had regard for the "Saint" and showed him grace and mercy (v. 5). Therefore, the one that has been rescued from forsakenness can enter the great festival assembly and witness His love (v. 1) and his thanks in the presence of all people. The Psalm presents the idea that death is active where the fears of the underworld (v. 3) have taken hold of the human being, where the fetters of the final imprisonment become noticeable (vv. 3, 16). The land of living (v. 9) as the area of salvation is nowhere else so urgently experienced as in the courts of the temple.

## *11. PSALM 121: "HELP COMES TO ME FROM YAHWEH"*

***(A) FORM:*** Difficulties stand on the way to analyze this psalm on the basis of form and structure. Obviously, there is a dialogue form in the Psalm. But with whom? According to F. Noetscher, the dialogue is with one's own soul. Does the one who asks the question in v. 1 himself give the answer in v. 2? But, how would the section in vv. 3-8 then be viewed? Does the Psalmist address himself? or even another person? Some efforts have been made to overcome these difficulties by changing these suffixes in vv. 2ff. The dialogue in the Psalm is clearly recognizable: In v. 1, a lay person speaks; in v. 2, the priest answers; in v. 3, the lay person again speaks; in v. 4, the priest responds. Then the second part of the Psalm can also be understood to be the words of the priest (structure altered according to H. Gunkel).

We can call v. 1 an inquiry such as is addressed to the priest at a question-answer period. In v. 2 the answer is given in the form of a confidential confession. vv. 3-8 are a consolation the intention of which is either that of an "oracle of salvation" or that of a blessing. Another question: is Ps. 121 a liturgy? Or are we to assume that it is a simple dialogue that could possibly have taken place at a son's departure from his father?

***(B) SETTING:*** The solemn and formal administration of the blessing and the consolation of salvation in vv. 3-8 gives precedence to the supposition that Ps. 121 contains a cultic dialogue between a pilgrim and a priest. What is the occasion that we are to assume? H. Schmidt places Ps. 121 next to Ps. 15 and 24; in other words, he considers the liturgical dialogue of Ps. 121 a part of gate liturgy in the wider sense. It would be better to think of ceremony of dismissal that has taken place at a farewell from the sanctuary. The date of origin of Ps. 121 can hardly be determined. By no means it is self-evident that the Psalm is postexilic. Still the reference to the expression of trust in God the Creator in v. 2 could be an indication that the theology of Deutero-Isaiah had asserted itself more and more.

***(C) INTERPRETATION:*** In v. 1 there are two possible interpretations. If we assume that Ps. 121 is a ceremonial of dismissal at the gates of the sanctuary, it is conceivable that the departing pilgrim looks with anxiety at the hills that surround Jerusalem and rise above it (cf. Ps. 125:2). The hill country to the east of Jerusalem is especially dangerous (cf. Lk. 10:30). Here a pilgrim might suffer a misfortune. Thus we would imagine that after the days of festive seclusion in the sacred precincts a person might ask questions about support and safe conduct in the rugged hills. The answer of the priest given in vv. 2-8 would suit such an anxious inquiry especially well. But another explanation would also be possible. In Palestine the hilltops are the shrines and haunts of the gods. The question could be raised in this way: From which of the heights does help come to me? E. H. Blakeney even thinks of the time of reform of King Josiah, when the decision had to be made where Yahweh is present and where alone He had to be worshipped. But we have no evidence from the text for this historical answer.

v. 2 could be understood as the priest's answer to the inquiry of v. 1. The priest expresses a trusting confession. There is an emphasis on the phrase: "My help...". Thus the one giving the answer points to his own trust (cf. Ps. 91:1ff). In the protective area of Yahweh, the priest is safe. For this fact he provides a testimony. Here age-old cultic traditions of the Jerusalem sanctuary are addressed. "Yahweh is the maker of heaven and earth" (cf. Ps. 115:15; 124:8, 134:3).

In vv. 3-8 the priest, speaking words of comfort and blessing, addresses the one saying farewell. The foot of the pilgrim will not waver and slip. Yahweh will accompany him as his "keeper" and follow every step in wide-awake attention (cf. Ps. 18:46). The vegetation gods of the cultivated land, by contrast, die at the change of season. They sleep (cf. I Kings 18:27). The "keeper of Israel" is the keeper of the individual, just as in Ps. 23 the "Shepherd of Israel" is the keeper of the individual. The protective presence of God in v. S promised to the wayfarer is standing figures of speech of the language of the Psalms. Yahweh is his "shade" (cf. the term "shadow of the wings" in Ps. 17:8, 36:7, 57:1, 63:7, 91:1 and in Num. 14:9; Jer. 48:45; Lam. 4:20). At the "right" stands the helper and supporter (Ps. 16:8, a 09:3l, 110:5). The stinging sun cannot strike him (v. 6; on the danger of sun-stroke cf. II Kings 4:19; Jonah 4:8). The moon too cannot threaten the human being. In the Babylonian world disastrous effects are ascribed to the moon god. Fever and leprosy are caused by him. Moonstruck is also understood to be possessed by demons (cf. Mt. 17:15). The priest who pronounces the blessings sees the life of the departing person exclusively in the order of regular pilgrimage (cf. Ps. 15:5).

***(D) PURPOSE AND APPLICATION***: As we read this Psalm, three distinctive promises are given in the realm of Yahweh's power and goodness.

*First*: Yahweh is the creator of heaven and earth (v. 2); His power as creator is effective in His salvific activity.

*Second*: Yahweh is the "keeper of Israel", He watches without ceasing over all the members of His people, and in His salvific activity. He does not ease up even for a moment.

*Third*: Yahweh is keeper of the individual members of the peole of god, who walks a difficult way in worry and doubt, in all his ways this keeper is present and helps against all harm. But the life of the human being who departs under the promise and blessing (vv. 2-8) at all times remains related to the place of the people of God (v. 8) - finally and decisively, however', to God Himself, who in Israel has proved Himself to be the living God.

## *12. PSALM 132: "THE ELECTION OF DAVID AND OF MOUNT ZION"*

***(A) FORM:*** H. Gunkel calls it a "highly peculiar Psalm". He divides the Psalm into two parts (vv. 1-10 and 11-18). In vv. 1-10 couched in the form of a prayer, the story is told of David's transferring of the ark. vv. 11-18, by contrast, contain two oracles of God (vv. 11f: about David and his descendants; vv. 13f about Zion). Gunkel thus classifies this Psalm as "Songs of Zion". The following picture emerges as regards to the structure of the Psalm: vv. 1-2 begin with a challenge to recall an oath. The petition is addressed to Yahweh; the oath was once spoken by David in the presence of Yahweh. In vv. 3-5 the contents of the oath are noted. v. 6 serves as an interlude; v. 7 calls for a procession, the summons is addressed to the community. v. 8 then turns to Yahweh and asks Him to enter the sanctuary together with the ark. The conduct of priests and worshippers is demanded in v. 9, while v. 10 asks for a king (of the lineage of David) and again (as in v. 1) recalls David, the patriarch of the dynasty. v. 11 introduces the reader to an oath of Yahweh. Yahweh vowed the continuity of the dynasty of David for all time. v. 13 interrupts and, like a confession, establishes one fact: "Yahweh has chosen Zion". The contents of the fundamental "declaration of election" are proclaimed in W. 14-18. It may belong to "songs of Zion" also dominating themes established, the category of "Royal Psalms."

***(B) SETTING:*** S. Mowinckel was the first one to recognize the cultic connections of this Psalm. He saw the bringing of the ark to the sanctuary and the reference to the prophecy of Nathan (II Sam. 7) in the framework of the festival of the postulated enthronement of Yahweh. According to H. Gunkel who writes on the "sitz-im-liben" of this Psalm: "From Ps. 132 we can deduce that there was a festival that was dedicated to the memory of the establishment of the royal house and its sanctuary…". Further he writes: "On the commemoration of the founding of the sanctuary a liturgy is performed in which the first of all there is a dramatic presentation to show how ancestor David brought the ark of Yahweh over to Zion and in which an oracle of Yahweh is then heard in which God promises to bless David and his house in this place;" "we should perhaps think of an annual festival of dedication of the sanctuary..." According to H. Gese the date of the Psalm is pre-exilic because the vocabulary is clearly pre-Deuteronomic.

According to H. J. Kraus the setting of this Psalm could be "Royal festival of Zion." For the festival assembly gathered in Jerusalem for the feast of Tabernacles, on the first day of the festival, in a solemn entrance ceremonial, the election of Mount Zion as the central sanctuary of the twelve tribe confederacy is demonstrated. At the same time, it made reference to the principal figure of the hieros logos, David: Yahweh has chosen David and his dynasty.

***(C) INTERPRETATION:*** The Psalm begins with a petition, an appeal to Yahweh. The address also recalls the events of the time of the founding of the Jerusalem sanctuary. In II Sam. 7:1ff. and Ps. 132:1ff David is the cultic founder of the Jerusalem temple sanctuary. He is the initiator. Solomon is later the organ that carries things out, very likely this is a piece of etiology which the hieros logos of the royal private temple deliberately wants to emphasize: David is the real founder. The building of the temple goes back to his vow and his enthusiasm for Yahweh. The temple dedication (I Kings 8) does play only a secondary part. But who uttered these verses? The speaker could be a king, a descendant of David. A single speaker appears in vv. 1-5.

Abruptly in v. 6 a choir appears which represents David and his retinue (cf. I Sam. 7:17; II Sam. 6:2). This dramatic element corresponds to the manner in which everywhere in the ancient world the cultus was carried on (cf. Exod. 12:1ff). The festival is a living actual verbum visible into which the participant is immediately placed.

In vv. 7ff, immediately there is a call for the entrance of the ark. The "dwelling place", i.e. the temple, is therefore built. In a festal procession the foundational event which II Samuel 6 reports is repeated. The entry into the temple reaches its climax in prostration before Yahweh (cf. Ps. 95:6, 100:4, also Ps. 24). The cultic call in v. 8 probably represents not only a reflective allusion to the ark saying in Num. 10:35f., but the incorporation of the old war call into the cultic ceremonial. here the thought of an enthronement of Yahweh is completely out of place. According to Ps. 132:8b (and in II Sam. 6) Yahweh already enters into the sanctuary with, or over the divine throne of the ark. An act of enthronement is nowhere traceable in the OT. It would contradict the institutional and religious presuppositions that were obtained in Israel. Ps. 132 is clearly dominated by the entry of Yahweh and the election of the sanctuary.

In vv. 10-14 the festival act of procession of the priest in a "sphere of salvation" is meant. The priests are "bearers of salvation". To them "the oracle of salvation" is entrusted. They dispense "the righteous" in the name of Yahweh. "Saints" refer to the cultic community that is walking along in the procession. jubilation and shouts of joy are to accompany the entry. But the attention belongs to the king. He assumes the position of David V. 10 is to be understood in immediate connection with v. I.

In vv. 11 & 12 reference is now made to a foundational oath of Yahweh. Valid ordinances and supporting presuppositions are appealed to in Ps. 132. Yahweh has "sown" to David. It could be worded as oath to fidelity. In v. 11 the subject is above all the continuance of the dynasty. According to Yahweh's basic determination no change is to take place, no lineage is to rule in Jerusalem. But v. 12 is in casuistic form, which imposes an obligation on the descendants of David which can be nothing short of a prerequisite for the fulfillment of the basic promise and the continuance of the dynasty. Covenant fidelity and the obedience of the Davidites are accordingly the prerequisite for the fulfilment of the basic promise.

From the election of David and his dynasty the Psalm in v. 13 now again goes back to the theme of "election of Zion". v. 13 addresses the most heartfelt desire of Yahweh (cf. Ps. 78:68, 87:2). In vv. 14-15 the word of Yahweh is now quoted which serves as a foundational declaration. Yahweh has appointed mount Zion forever as His "resting place". That is where the dwelling place and throne are henceforth located. The sanctuary is the fountain of life because Yahweh is now present here (cf. Ps. 36:8ff). He equips the priests and cheers the community. Above all, He provides the throne of David with a great promise. For David, "a horn" is to sprout on Zion (v. 17). The "horn" is a symbol of invincible power. Therefore, Yahweh promises that a powerful descendant will sit on the throne of David - a king who will live to see the conquest of all foes (v. 18, cf. Ps. 110:1 - prophecies of this kind are the fountain of messianic expectation).

***(D) PURPOSE AND APPLICATION:*** Concerning the two central themes of the O. T. - faith, kingship and cultus - the ritual sampler of Ps. 132 provides us with a number of decisive statements. The events of the time of David are the foundations of the O.T. royal cult. Yahweh has chosen His king. Together with the election of the king, the election of the sanctuary is celebrated. This double theme bears witness to the presence of God in Israel. It underscores the sovereign liberty in which Yahweh chose thus king and this place in order to let His power and grace appear in the chosen people and before all the world. At the vanishing point of the history of this election of the place and person the presence of God stands as Jesus Christ. According to the N.T., in Him the promises of God are fulfilled (cf. II Cor. 1:20; Acts 2:30ff; Lk. 1:69).

### *13. PSALM 148: "THE PRAISE OF HEAVEN AND EARTH"*

***(A) FORM:*** Ps. 148 is a song of praise. This Psalm belongs to the category of imperatival hymns. According to F. Cruesemann, "The simple naming of those who are invited to praise has developed into a long, artistically constructed catalog." The structure of this Psalm is clearly discernible and transparent. The two main sections, vv. 1-6 (praise of Yahweh "from heaven") and vv. 7-14 (praise of Yahweh "from the earth"), basically contain addresses and calls to glorify Yahweh. The main themes are relatively extensive. In vv. 5 & 13 the hymnic introductions in each case end in the comprehensive statement: "They shall praise the name of Yahweh". In addition to basic elements of the hymn, the enumerations serially presented deserve special attention. Here there are components of "natural wisdom" that has its prototype in the Egyptian study of lists.

***(B) SETTING:*** Precise clues for determining the cultic situation of the Psalm are not given, but Ps. 148 should probably be thought of as a hymn for public worship. The post-exilic era is to be considered as its time of origin. (Some similarities of this Psalm with the Song of the Three Holy Children 26-68, in the Apocrypha according to W. O. E. Osterley). Also the relation of the Ps. 148 to the "Song of the Three Young Men" is sought. From all these observations, Ps. 148 could be a "mixed form between a hymn and nature wisdom." The Psalm is to be dated in the post-exilic period.

***(C) INTERPRETATION:*** The Psalm begins and concludes with a cry of praise (Hallelujah). LXX again provides (along with Ps. 146 & 147) the explanation that the Psalm is to be associated with Haggai and Malachi. The first part of the Psalm (W. 1-6) exhorts the heavenly world to praise Yahweh. From the very beginning we should bear in mind that this inclusion of the superworld in the praise of God neither has its source in the "enthusiasm of soul" (H. Schimdt) nor represents a "primeval verification of nature" (H. Gunkel). Rather, in imitation of lists of nature wisdom that were native to Egypt, the entire stock and store of the world is taken up and called and placed into the service of praise of the God of Israel. The list of science of nature first came to light through the teaching of Amenmope. This encyclopedic work provides an "instruction about everything created by Ptah, about heaven and its appurtenances, about the earth and what is in it." From this cosmological inventory, that catalog of lists goes over to an enumeration of Persons and offices. A "hierarchy of being" is laid out in a prosaic compilation. G. von Rad has now shown that this type of encyclopedic list has been adopted also in the O.T. The outstanding examples are: Job 38, Ps. 148, and in Apocrypha, Sirach 43 and the "Song of the Three Young Men." A comparison of the encyclopedic enumerations shows surprising agreement in layout and development of this sapiential science of lists. As in the teaching of Amenmope so also in Psalm 148 we find the series: heaven – sun – moon – stars – sea of heaven – primeval waters – fire (lighting) – hail – snow – storm – mountain – hill – trees – animals – offices – group of people. The peculiarity of Ps. 148 consists of the fact that here the total inventors, of the created world is invited to praise God.

The praise of Yahweh is to "resound from heaven". In v. 2 the heavenly powers are addressed. In v. 3 the heavenly bodies are directly enlisted in the "army of Yahweh" (cf. Is. 40:26). They are thought of as animate beings. In vv. 1-4 we can recognize a "gradation" in the appearance of the heavenly world. Above the heavenly powers and constellations stand the "heaven of heavens", very likely the higher sphere of heaven, above which the waters of the ocean of heaven are stored. In v. 5 we have transition to the first main theme. All elements and beings of the heavenly world shall praise the "name" of Yahweh. In the hymnic main theme introduced by "for" the creation is praised by the efficacious word of Yahweh (cf. Ps. 33:9, 147:18). At the same time the unshakable duration of what has been created has been emphasized (v. 6a, cf. Ps. 93:1, 96:10). The creation is enveloped and defined by a firm foundation "order" (in v. 6b) denoting the legitimacy that controls and governs all that has been created (cf. Gen. 8:22; Jer. 31:35f, 33:25; Job 28:26f, 38:8ff; Sir. 43: 10). The thought is especially of the boundary that by means of "order", that "which has been set" has been established against the chaotic incursion of the waters of the ocean of heaven (cf. Job 38:8ff).

In the second part of the Psalm (vv. 7-14) the invitation is given to praise God "from the earth". First in v. 7, the aspects of the three stories worldview of ancient tomes make their appearance over against the "waters of heaven" (v. 4). There are the abysmal primeval waters. "Monsters" recalls the mythological monsters that symbolize the sea of chaos (cf. Ps. 74:13; Is. 51:9; Jer. 51 :34). "All the waters" are the primeval waters (Akkadian Tiamat) that rest beneath the earth (cf. Gen. 49:24; Ps. 36:6). Of course, it could also be that in v. 7 the thought is only of the sea (cf. tehom in Ps. 107:26) in which the great sea-animals live (Gen. 1:21). In v. 8 the meteorological phenomena are first lined up: fire (lightning?), hail, snow, fog and storm; (smoke also means fog here but Greek reads it as "ice"). The storm is looked upon as the messenger who carries out Yahweh's words (cf. Ps. 103:20f; 104:4). v. 9 then mentions the hills and trees, whereas in v. 10 the animals are enumerated according to the most basic genera. Both the wild as well as domesticated (tamed) animals are mentioned here. Also the "creeping things" refer to reptiles and also the mention of the flying (winged) birds (cf. Gen. 1:21ff). It is clearly seen here that the science of lists tries to comprehend the living beings by means of genera designations. As in the teachings of Amenmope groups of human beings are also included in the encyclopedic series. It is not "the human being" who appeals here as a single unit, but here too a hierarchical order is introduced. The first classification refers to offices, the second in v. 12 to the generations. In v. 13 the invitations then cease and (as in v. 5) lead over to the main theme. The praise is for the name of Yahweh, the manifestations of the deus praesens. In the reason for praise introduced by "for", the conception of Yahweh, the king enthroned above the heaven and earth, makes its appearance. Incidentally, the sequence "earth and heaven" occurs, in addition to P 3. 148: 13, only gen. 2:4; in Psalm 148 it corresponds to the layout of the hymn (vv. 1, 7). As a deed of Yahweh, the raising of a "horn" is mentioned in v. 14. "Horn" is in the O. T. a divine symbol of "strength" (cf. Ps. 75:5, 10; 89:17, 24). There is hardly an answer to the question as to what, specifically, is being referred to.

***(D) PURPOSE AND APPLICATION:*** Like a double choir, heaven and earth are situated over against each other in Psalm 148. Both areas are called on to praise Yahweh. The universe is to resound with praise and homage before the creator (v. 5) and king (v. 13b). Motifs of "Yahweh as King" hymns (cf. especially Psalms 96 and 98) have been fused together with the encyclopedic enumerations of nature wisdom. Here we can observe how elements of ancient science were blended into the praise of Yahweh. Decisive is the "name". In His name, Yahweh has proclaimed himself as creator and King of the universe. The New Testament Church confesses that the name to which all of creation is related is that of Jesus Christ (cf. Col. 1:15ff, Heb. 1:3f).

### *14. PSALM 150: "THE PRAISE OF GOD WITH SACRED MUSIC":*

***(A) FORM:*** The Psalm belongs to the category of the songs of praise. The structure of the Psalm is determined by the imperatival hymn. Ten imperatival appeals follow one another. The actual carrying out of the song of praise for which the appeal is made is only hinted at. "The character of the appeals themselves…leaves no more room for verbal completion" (F. Cruesemann).

***(B) SETTING:*** Especially through the Chronicler's history do we learn in the O. T. that in the post-exilic community sacred music played an important role. It probably was that way in more ancient times too. The community assembled in the sanctuary praised God to the accompaniment of musical instruments. Ps. 150 is an exhortation to engage in the praise that was heard in the holy place and probably should be dated in a later time. The praise of Yahweh is intoned to music and dance.

Sacred music slayed an important role also in the cultus also in the AWA. From Egypt and the area of Mesopotamia illustrations and texts are known which confirm the presence of sacred music. We will refer here to only one song addressed to Ianna and Iddindagan from ancient Sumer:

> "The sacred algor instrument they play to her –
> appear before Holy Ianna.
> The great Queen of heaven, Ianna. I want to greet!
> The sacred Drum, the sacred timbrel they beat for her –
> appear before the holy Ianna.
> The great queen of heaven, Ianna, I want to greet!
> The sacred lyre, the sacred timbrel they beat for her –
> appear before the Holy Ianna.
> The great daughter of Su'an, Ianna, I want to greet!"

(cf. A. Falkenstein and W. von Soden, Sumerische und Akkadische hymnen und Gebete (1953), p. 911).

The method of playing and singing is still a great problem. Naturally, clear indications are missing. In general, it is assumed that the pentatonic system, without half-steps, was predominant, but various ways of singing and making music are considered possible. It is conceivable that individual instruments, thus, e.g. the horn, only had the significance of signaling the praise, while the other musical apparatus principally performed rhythmic leading tones.

***(C) INTERPRETATION:*** Psalms 146-150 begin with the word "Hallelujah", and with the same call of praise they also close.

At the holy place, heaven and earth touch each other. For that reason, the heavenly world is repeatedly drawn into the hymns. In v. 1 the appeal makes its way into the heavenly sphere (cf. also Ps. 29:9, 148:10. "The song of praise is to penetrate heaven and earth" remarks H. Gunkel. The great deeds of Yahweh which otherwise are enumerated in the main theme, are in Psalm 150 interwoven in the imperatival appeals. The reference is to the mighty deeds of Yahweh in creation and history. At v. 3 we begin the enumeration of the musical instruments which are to intone and accompany the song of praise. The "horn" in the Old Testament is a typical instrument for giving signals (of. Josh. 6:4; Neh. 12:35; I Chron. 15:24, 16:6; II Chron. 29:26). The tone of the horn is heard at the onset of the battle and on festival days. At the song of praise the function of giving a signal would probably have to be assigned to this "horn". The players were hardly able to produce a series of tones that could have served as accompaniment for singing. The stringed instruments mentioned in v. 3 need to be explained more precisely. The word mbl is translated as "the lyre with a slanting yoke", knor is translated as "the lyre with sounding box". The translation therefore is in need of corrections in view of depictions of artifacts recovered from archaeological discoveries; toph the little hand drum, is used primarily in the round dance (cf. Ps. 149:3; Ex. 15:20), while mnim (Ugaritic mnm) in a comprehensive sense refers to string playing (v. 4). wgb is the name for the shawm, a straight flute which was played without mouthpiece by blowing across the edge of the upper opening. This instrument is verified, especially, from Egypt. v. 5 speaks of two kinds of "cymbals". The cymbals found at excavations at Tell-Abu-Hawam permit us to make the deduction that there were various kinds of cymbals. v. 6 is a final, especially loud cry which stands alone. All of creation is called on to join in the great praise of God.

***(D) PURPOSE AND APPLICATION:*** Here something has to be said about the importance of the musica sacra in the praise of God by the assembly. Music provides the singing with a special power which is appropriate for the majestic greatness for the God of Israel. But all singing and music making is directed to Yahweh by means of the tenfold repeated "Halleluiah"; it points to His exalted person. By that the magic is musical is broken through. "All that has breath, praise Yahweh! Hallelujah!"

Chapter 10

# General Conclusion

We Began The work of this project with the description of prophecy and prophetic movement in ancient Israel in its first part and concluded with the section on Dalit prophets and its relevance to Hebrew prophecy and *vice-versa*. In the second section of this project we discussed on various concerns in the Hebrew Wisdom Literature and concluded with the relevance of Dalit sages to Hebrew wisdom and *vice-versa.* In order to conclude our work, a brief concluding summary is provided in this chapter.

First, Hebrew prophecy has a long historical and sociological background. So also the wisdom tradition in ancient Israel too has long history although it started after the prophetic movement. In many ways both the prophecy and the wisdom are interconnected with one another and at times overlap with each other while maintaining their distinctiveness. In matters of justice and righteousness their interrelatedness is obviously noticed. Wisdom writers call the pupils whom they trained and instructed to observe the Torah and its principles for a successful living. At least some prophets come from the wisdom background, especially the eighth century prophets as they insisted on the tribal ethos in the community during the transition period from tribal to monarchic period.

Second, the prophetic activity before the monarchy was very sporadic and non-literary mainly depending on the oral instructions. However, it was a foundational period for more systematic movement of prophecy. Moses, for example, although not a full-pledged prophet, was considered prophet par excellence and his activities are very much prophetic to nurture the community of Israel.

Third, prophecy during the monarchic period has taken definite shape with the emergence of literary prophets, whose writings are collected and circulated. On account of the change of administration, the social system and economic operations have drastically changed and the prophets too got involved in the affairs of the kingdom in order to critique and set-right the anomalies in the skewed social and economic system.

Fourth, during the exilic and postexilic prophecy, a period of turmoil in the kingdom, prophets played a significant role to appraise the rulers and the people to surrender to the will of Yahweh who, through the 'foreign' powers will guide the people of Israel. However, the people will be delivered and they will return to their homeland.

Fifth, when all that exilic and postexilic prophets predicted has not been fulfilled, the apocalyptic thought emerged through some prophetic sayings as a hope for the future restoration of the community.

Sixth, the prophetic movement in ancient Israel was heavily influenced by the ancient West Asian prophecy as we note several parallels between them. It is also observed that the prophetic material was well established after a long period of its redaction and literary activity.

Seventh, Dalit prophets like the Hebrew prophets emerged in our contemporary context in order to voice against their concerns of justice and order in the society. In most cases, Dalit prophets protested against the practice of caste oppression based on its religious legitimization.

Eighth, Hebrew sages employed various literary and professional methods to instruct the rulers and the people to walk in the ways of justice and righteousness in order to maintain order in the society.

Ninth, the poetic literature in the Hebrew Bible has contributed immensely for the development of the community of ancient Israel. Through their creative poetic sayings and by using effective devices and techniques, these writings communicate the in depth emotions and feelings of God towards the people. Book of Psalms is an invaluable source of poetic literature in ancient Israel which also has wisdom features which gives an opportunity for the people to come closer to God.

Tenth, the canonical wisdom literature books of Job, Proverbs, and Ecclesiastes are the rich responses and resources for the faith community of Israel to understand the depth of God's restoration purpose. Moreover, these books give enough guidance and instruction to see the realities of human life and suffering and thus make their life based on wisdom and cope with various odd situations. These books eventually affirm that fear of God is the source of all knowledge and wisdom.

Eleventh, wisdom in Israel is not an isolated phenomenon, rather it stands very much in parallel with the ancient West Asian wisdom. Israelites have borrowed the sayings and instructions from their West Asian neighbors. Some parallels from Egypt and Babylon are exact in content and form on many occasions.

Twelfth, wisdom tradition in ancient Israel is environment friendly. It emphasizes that God is the creator of order and well-being and all the creatures and the entire cosmos should be sustained in order to maintain the created order of God. For a just and peaceful living on this earth for all creatures and for sustaining an orderly life wisdom gives priority to balance the ecosystem.

Thirteenth, even though wisdom is given high priority in the Hebrew Bible in the latter period of history, nevertheless it is not to be considered as divine. Wisdom is created by God and it is to be operated under the guidance of God, who is the creator of all things including wisdom.

Fourteenth, Dalit sages can be compared on par with Hebrew sages as the latter, through their wise and erudite sayings led the Dalit community in a right path. Their instructions on both cases are guiding light to the oppressed community. Dalit sages in particular demonstrated their shrewdness and skill in order to work towards the progress of Dalits, through education, organization and revolution as B. R. Ambedkar has proposed.

Lastly, both prophets and sages in ancient Israel and in our contemporary Dalit context are the great resources for all human communities to live in a life filled with justice and righteousness and to envisage and achieve a community beyond caste, color, gender and creed. We will conclude this project with the words of prophet Amos 5:5-6 "Seek me and live, do not seek Bethel, do not go to Gilgal … Seek the LORD and live."

# Selected Bibliography


Anderson A. A. *The Book of Psalms*, Vol.1 & 2 New Century Bible, London: Oliphants 1972.

Crenshaw J. L. *Old Testament Wisdom, An Introduction*, Atlanta John Knox press 1981.

Crenshaw J. L. *Ecclesiastes: A Commentary*, London, SCM Press 1988 (OT Library)

Crenshaw J. L. *Urgent Advice and Probing Questions*: Mercer: University Press, 1995.

D. K. Berry, *An Introduction to Wisdom and Poetry of the Old Testament*, Nashville: Broadman & Holman, 1995.

Day J. *Psalms* (OT study guides) Sheffield: JSOT Press, 1992 (Reprint 1993).

Habel, N. C., *The Book of Job*, London: SCM Press 1985 (Old Testament Library).

Kraus, H. J., *Psalms 1-59: A Commentary*, (Vol: ITrans. Hilton C. Oswald) Minnepolis: Augsburg, 1988.

Mckane, W. *Proverbs: A New Approach*, London, SCM Press 1970.

______ *Psalms 60-150; A Commentary*, (Vol: II) Trans H. C. Oswald Minneapolis: Augsburg, I989.

______ *Theology of Psalms*, (Trans. Keith Crim) Minnepolis: Augusburg Publishing House, 1986.

Von Rad, G. *Wisdom in Israel*, London: SCM Press 1972.

Westermann, *Praise and Lament in the Psalms*, Atlanta. John Knox Press 1981.

# Author Index


**A**

A. Klostermann, 74
A. Robert, 242
A. Weiser, 242
Ackroyd, 114
Adele Berlin, 195
Albright, 4

**B**

B. Duhm, 88
Baba Bathra, 226
Beyerlin, 354

**C**

C. H. Cornil, 4
Childs, 70
Claus Wertermann, 83, 243, 312

**E**

Ewald, 300

**F**

F. Cruesemann, 368
F. Noetscher, 363
F. M. Cross, 291

**G**

Gunkel, 241-242
Gurram Jashuva, 328

**H**

H. Gese, 349, 366
H. Gunkel, 334, 337, 342, 345, 354, 364, 366, 369, 372
H. J. Kraus, 355, 360, 366
H. Schimdt, 362
H. W. Wolff, 51
H. D. Preuss, 333
H. G. Reventlow, 315
Hans Joachim Kraus, 241
Hans-Joachim Kraus, 243
Hanson, 106
Herman Gunkel, 241

**J**

J. Hempel, 335
J. G. Wetzstein, 300
J. J. Stamm, 345
Jerome, 63
John Wesley, 8
Julius Wellhausen, 13

**K**

Kancha Ilaiah, 329
Katti Padma Rao, 328
Klaus Koch, 66, 99

**L**

L. Krinetzk, 342
Loretz, 271

**M**

M. A. Cohen, 19
M. Palmer, 342
Maren Bellwinkel-Schempp, 326
Martin Luther, 339
Martin Noth, 19
Mitchell, 316
Mowinckel, 91, 241-242
Mueller, 98

**N**

N. K. Gottwald, 222, 224, 291

**R**

R. B. Y. Scott, 12

R. L. Smith, 121
R. Tournay, 335
Ralph W. Klein, 73
Robert Gordis, 318
Robert Wilson, 19, 22
Ronald Heifetz, 8

**S**

S. Mowinckel, 242
Sabourin, 243
Sigmund Mowinckel, 241, 246, 270
Stephen de Jong, 318
Stuhlmueller, 98

**V**

Von Rabenau, 76
von Rad, 257-258, 334
von Waldow, 83

**W**

W. O. E. Osterley, 368
W. Rudolph, 291, 293
W.H. Schmidt, 73, 284, 334
Weiser, 242
Westermann, 83
Wetzstein, 300
Whybry, 317
William Gesensius, 5
William McKane, 251

# Biblical Index


1 Chr.29:29, 17
1 Kings 1:11, 43, 47, 335
1 Kings 1:11-14, 17
1 Kings 10:11, 253
1 Kings 11:29-39, 18
1 Kings 11:38, 19
1 Kings 11:38, 39, 19
1 Kings 12:1-15, 18
1 Kings 12:15, 19
1 Kings 12:22-24, 18
1 Kings 12:28, 34
1 Kings 14:l-16, 18
1 Kings 14:1-18, 19
1 Kings 14:18, 5
1 Kings 15:29, 19
1 Kings 17-19, 19-20
1 Kings 18:17-18, 20
1 Kings 18:19-46, 20
1 Kings 18:17, 20
1 Kings 18:19-46, 20
1 Kings 19:16-21, 21
1 Kings 19; 19-21, 21
1 Kings 20:35, 13
1 Kings 20:35-43, 13
1 Kings 21:26, 21
1 Kings 22:20-23, 31
1 Kings 22:4-28, 22
1 Kings 2-6, 13
1 Kings l7:1, 20
1 Sam. 10:19, 13
1 Sam. 10:5, 11
1 Sam. 10:5,10, 13
1 Sam. 15:1-13, 11
1 Sam. 19:1ff, 20
1 Sam. 2:12-36, 10
1 Sam. 2:11,18, 21, 58
1 Sam. 3:11-14, 11
1 Sam. 3:20, 11
1 Sam. 9:9, 5
2 Chr. 9:29, 17
2 Chronicles: 18:3-27, 22
2 Kgs 14:25, 26
2 Kings 13:20-21, 22
2 Kings 14:23-29, 28
2 Kings 17:7-18, 18
2 Kings 17:4, 38
2 Kings 17:7-41, 49
2 Kings 18:13, 44
2 Kings 18:1f, 9, 44
2 Kings 2:19-22, 21
2 Kings 2:23-25, 21
2 Kings 2:7, 13
2 Kings 20:12-19, 48
2 Kings 2-13, 21
2 Kings 24:10-17, 81
2 Kings 4:42-44, 13
2 Kings 4:38, 42-43, 13
2 Kings 4:8-17, 22
2 Kings 4:8-37, 22
2 Kings 5:1-19, 22
2 Kings 6:8-7:20, 22
2 Kings. 9:1-10, 22
2 Sam. 7:4-17, 16
2 Sam. 7, 16
2 Sam.7: vv 5,8,17, 17
Acts 1:20, 287
Acts 10:38, 289
Acts 13:33, 287
Acts 2:30ff, 368
Acts 3:13, 289
Acts 3:22-23, 182
Acts 3:24, 11

Acts 3:26, 289
Acts 4:25, 289
Acts 4:25-26, 288
Acts 4:25f, 334
Amos 2:11-12, 4, 12
Amos 2:6, 26
Amos 2:7-9, 26
Amos 2:7a, 26
Amos 2:7b, 25
Amos 3:10,12b,15b, 25
Amos 3:15b, 25
Amos 3:3-6, 8, 223
Amos 3:3-8, 209
Amos 3:8, 5, 133
Amos 3:9, 25
Amos 4:1, 25
Amos 4:1, 25, 134
Amos 4:1-3, 33
Amos 4:24-25, 25
Amos 5:10, l2, 25
Amos 5:11b;, 25
Amos 5:13, 270
Amos 5:18-20, 67
Amos 5:1ff, 161
Amos 5:21f, 284
Amos 5:22, 346, 348
Amos 5:23, 25
Amos 5:24, 191
Amos 5:5-6, 375
Amos 6:12, 191
Amos 6:4, 6, 25
Amos 6:4b, 25
Amos 6:5, 25
Amos 7:10-13, 132
Amos 8:2, 212
Amos 8:4, 26
Amos 8:5a, 25
Amos 8:6, 26
Amos l:3-2:8, 254
Amos. 1:3ff, 133
Col 1:9, 183
Col 3:16, 183
Col. 1:15ff, 371
Col. 3:16, 287
Dan 12:7-10, 253
Dan 5:12, 253
Dan 8:23, 253
Dan 1:4,17,20, 220
Daniel 12:4, 76
Daniel 8:26, 76
Deu.18:15-18, 182
Deut 15:12, 61
Deut 16:3, 97
Deut 23:1, 105
Deut 27:25, 338
Deut 30:15, 61
Deut. 10:9, 353
Deut. 13:1-5, 60
Deut. 16:19, 338
Deut. 18:18, 7
Deut. 23:20, 340
Deut. 24:1-4, 100
Deut. 26:5-10, 208
Deut. 32:1, 157
Deut. 32:1-43, 208
Deut. 32:28f, 351
Deut. 32:7a, 212
Deut. 33:1, 5
Deut. 34:10-12, 6,7
Deut. 34:5, 7
Deut. 34:9, 220
Deut. 4:27, 344
Deut. 4:4-7, 221
Deut. 4:6, 222
Deut. 6:4-9, 273
Deut.3:l7, 23
Deut.34:10-12, 6
Duet 28:37, 251
Duet 6:4, 339
Eccl 12:8, 213
Eccl. 1:12-15, 16-18, 254
Eccl. 1:12-2:26, 260
Eccl. 1:5a, 213
Eccl. 12:1-6, 257
Eccl. 12:9-14, 254
Eccl. 3:10, 260
Eccl. 5:1-7, 8-9, 183
Eccl. 4:8, 260
Eccl. 5:18, 260
Eccl. 8:9-9:1, 260
Eccl: 1:2, 213
Eccles. 11:9-12:8, 257
Ecclesiastes 12:1-6, 257
Echa Rabbati 1:1, 253
Eph 3:5, 99
Eph 4:11, 183
Eph. 2:19, 338
Eph. 2:20, 183
Eph. 5:19-20, 183
Ephesians 5:19-20, 287

Ex. 15:20, 372
Ex. 19:16-21, 360
Exod 3:14, 40
Exod 31:6, 220
Exod 4:14-23, 7
Exod. 12:1ff, 367
Exod. 13:2,15, 11
Exod. 14:21-29, 97
Exod. 14:31, 7
Exod. 15:1-18, 208
Exod. 15:8, 208
Exod. 20:17a,b, 55
Exod. 20:3, 220
Exod. 22:24, 340
Exod. 23:12, 363
Exod. 23:8, 338
Exod. 29:40f, 363
Exod. 33:18, 7
Exod. 34:10, 7
Exod. 34:29-35, 7
Exod. 4:l9f, 5
Exod. 4:10ff, 7
Exod. 5:1, 7
Exod.12:11, 97
Exod.15:1-18, 208
Exod. 32:1, 7
Exodus 7:1-2, 5
Eze. 24:1, 75
Ezek 1:1-3:15, 136
Ezek 11:9, 79
Ezek 16:44, 218
Ezek 18:2, 218
Ezek 18:2-3, 251
Ezek 18:5-9, 190
Ezek 2:3-3:11, 31
Ezek 20:11, 193
Ezek 24:25-27, 132
Ezek 27:8, 240
Ezek 28:3, 240
Ezek 33:21-22, 132
Ezek 33:7, 108
Ezek 5:6-7, 193
Ezek. 12:21-12:23, 135
Ezek. 12:21-28, 132
Ezek. 12:22-23, 251
Ezek. 14:14, 20, 311
Ezek. 14:8, 251
Ezek. 15:16, 257
Ezek. 16:44, 251
Ezek. 17:1-10, 253
Ezek. 17:1-10:19:1-14, 257
Ezek. 17:1-10, 251
Ezek. 18:2, 252
Ezek. 18:2-4, 100
Ezek. 20:45-49, 251
Ezek. 21:7, 351
Ezek. 24:3-14, 251
Ezek. 27:26, 343
Ezek. 3:17, 108
Ezek. 34:1-10, 108
Ezek. 34:4-6,8, 187
Ezek. 36:25f, 346
Ezek. 44:13, 106
Ezek. 6:9, 341
Ezek. 8:12, 351
Ezek.17:1-10, 257
Ezek.18:5-7, 338
Ezek.19:1-9, 257
Ezek. 3:22-27, 132
Ezek. 31:1-18, 257
Ezek. 36:25ff, 346
Ezra 2:59-63, 105
Ezra 5:1, 115
Ezra 6:10, 104
Ezra 6:14, 115
Ezra 6:8, 104
Ezra 7:14, 104
Gen 10:9, 251
Gen 16:11-12, 208
Gen 2:23, 208
Gen 28:13, 34
Gen 3. 37:5-11, 257
Gen 37:40-41, 253
Gen 49:24, 167
Gen. 1:14, 359
Gen. 1:2, 213
Gen. 1:21, 370
Gen. 1:21ff, 370
Gen. 1:26ff, 334
Gen. 1:30-31, 360
Gen. 10: 9, 222
Gen. 14:19, 358
Gen. 2:4, 370
Gen. 2:7, 360
Gen. 25: l4, 306
Gen. 28:9, 268
Gen. 3:19, 360
Gen. 32:13-21, 287
Gen. 33:19, 311
Gen. 37-50, 217

Gen. 41:38, 217
Gen. 41:38-39, 153
Gen. 42:18, 217
Gen. 43:11, 287
Gen. 48:15, 355
Gen. 49:24, 167
Gen. 8:21, 346
Gen. 8:22, 370
Gen.1:17, 336
Gen.1:28fi, 336
Hab 1:4, 192
Hab 2:4, 71
Hab. 1:10, 332
Hab. 2:1, 70
Hab. 2:6, 251
Hab. 2:6-8, 251
Habakkuk 3:1, 270
Hag. 2:10-14, 104
Hag. 2:1ff, 337
Hag. 2:20-23, 115
Haggai 1:13, 5
Heb. 1:3f, 371
Hos 10:4, 192
Hos 5:1, 193
Hos 5:8-9, 46
Hos. 1:4, 95
Hos. 10:1, 192
Hos. 10:12, 192
Hos. 8:5f, 33
Hos. 9:7-8, 4
Hos.12:10,13, 4
Hos.6:5, 4
Hos.9:76, 132
Hosea 2:1-3, 209
Hosea 4:6, 222
Hosea 4:9, 223
Hosea 5:14b-15a, 211
Hosea 5:15-6:6, 249
Hosea 5:8, 213
Hosea 6:5, 99
Hosea 6:6, 284
I Chr 25:l-3, 13
I Chr. 6:33, 269
I Chr. 6:39, 269
I Chr. 6:44, 269
I Chr. 6:31, 270
I Chr. 9:22, 11
I Chro. 15:21, 269
I Chron 16:6, 372
I Chron. 15:24, 372
I Chron. 9:33, 335
I Chronicles 15:20, 268
I Cor. 12:1-10, 183
I Cor. 12:8-11, 183
I Cor. 13:2, 183
I Cor. 14:26, 287
I Cor. 14:6, 37, 183
I Cor.1:27, 335
I Kings 10:1-5, 252
I Kings 11:29ff, 131
I Kings 15:29, 19, 355
I Kings 18:27, 365
I Kings 20:11, 251
I Kings 21:1-19, 186
I Kings 22:11, 131
I Kings 22:19, 336
I Kings 22:29, 355
I Kings 23:3, 357
I Kings 3:16-28, 286
I Kings 3:5-14, 218
I Kings 4:29-32, 302
I Kings 4:29-34, 225
I Kings 4:31, 269
I Kings 4:32, 256
I kings 4:32-34, 256
I Kings 4:5, 17
I kings 5:10, 240
I Kings 8, 367
I Kings 8:22-26, 285
I Kings 8:62-63, 285
I Kings 9:7, 251
I Sam 10:11, 251
I Sam 10:12, 252
I Sam 16:7, 252
I Sam 17:22-23, 209
I Sam 17:24-27, 209
I Sam 2:27-28, 11
I Sam 23:6, 237
I Sam 24:13, 251
I Sam 24:1f, 268
I Sam. 1:20, 10
I Sam. 10:5, 12
I Sam. 10:5 ff, 13
I Sam. 10-5-13, 12
I Sam. 14:15, 343
I Sam. 15:13-23, 11
I Sam. 15:22, 284
I Sam. 19:18-20, 13
I Sam. 19:1ff, 268
I Sam. 19:8f, 268

I Sam. 2:10, 35, 332
I Sam. 2:22-25, 10
I Sam. 21:10, 267
I Sam. 21:10f, 267
I Sam. 21:10ff, 276
I Sam. 22:1, 268
I Sam. 22:1f, 276
I Sam. 22:6f, 276
I Sam. 23:14f, 276
I Sam. 24:1f, 276
I Sam. 27:1ff, 276
I Sam. 3:19-4: l, 11
I Sam. 4:3, 278
I Sam. 4:4, 278
I Sam. 4:5, 278
I Sam. 6:13, 278
I Sam. 6:14ff, 278
I Sam. 7:17, 367
I Sam. 9:6, 5
I Sam. chapter 3:1-21, 11
I Sam. 4:4, 278
I Sam: 9:9, 131
I Samuel 16:1-14, 267
I Samuel 2:4-9, 209
I Thes. 5:19-20, 183
I Tim 1:18, 183
I Tim 4:14, 187
II Chr 35:25, 59
II Chr. 29:25, 17
II Chr. 35:15, 269
II Chr. 5:12cf, 269
II Chro. 11:18, 269
II Chro. 35:25, 291
II Chron. 20:19, 290
II Chron. 20:7, 96
II Chron. 29:26, 372
II Chron. 9:14, 252
II Chron. l:7-12, 218
II Chronicles 35:25, 291
II Cor. 1:20, 368
II Kings 10:1-28, 12
II Kings 15:30, 355
II Kings 18:13-18, 49
II Kings 18:1f, 52
II Kings 24:8 20, 75
II Kings 24:16, 74
II Kings 25, 75
II Kings 25:1, 75
II Kings 4:19, 365
II Kings 4:38, 74
II Kings 4:9, 5
II Kings 6:2ff, 74
II Peter 1:17, 287
II Sam 15:1f, 268
II Sam 20:18, 222
II Sam 20:25, 223
II Sam 23:1-7, 209
II Sam 5:8, 252
II Sam 8:17, 223
II Sam. 10:15f, 268
II Sam. 10:1f, 268
II Sam. 11:1f, 268
II Sam. 15:1-18:33, 268
II Sam. 15:1-6, 286
II Sam. 21:15f, 268
II Sam. 5:17f, 268
II Sam. 5:6, 281
II Sam. 6:2, 279, 356, 367
II Sam. 7:1ff, 366
II Sam. 8:1f, 268
II Sam. 8:3f, 268
II Sam. 21:1ff, 337
II Sam. 6:9, 279
II Sam.7:6, 338
II Sam. 20:22, 220
II Samuel 1:17-27, 209
II Samuel 14:1-20, 211
II Samuel 20:16-22, 211
II Tim 1:14, 183
Is. 40:22, 358
Is. 40:26, 369
Is. 42:6, 352
Is. 45:18, 359
Is. 51:9, 370
Isa 1:17, 21, 192
Isa 10:15, 223
Isa 10:2, 192
Isa 10:8, 213
Isa 11:2, 222
Isa 19:11, 168
Isa 19:11-15, 218
Isa 19:16-24, 48
Isa 2:4ff, 67
Isa 20:1-6, 223
Isa 20:3, 23
Isa 21:6, 70
Isa 24:6, 211
Isa 28:14-22, 49
Isa 28:23-29, 153, 218
Isa 29:14, 220

Isa 3:13-15, 86
Isa 30:1-5, 52
Isa 30:17, 223
Isa 31:1-3, 48, 223
Isa 32:15-17, 187
Isa 33:20, 348
Isa 33:22, 212
Isa 37:10-13, 50
Isa 4:4, 193
Isa 40:13-14, 218
Isa 43:1,5, 98
Isa 44:26, 4
Isa 44:2ff, 98
Isa 45:1, 113
Isa 47:10, 220
Isa 5:7, 192
Isa 5:8, 51
Isa 53:9b, 92
Isa 56:1, 190
Isa 58:1-14, 109
Isa 59:8-9, 194
Isa 6:10, 36
Isa 6:21, 213
Isa 6:8-10, 31
Isa 60:7,13, 108
Isa 61:1, 348
Isa 61:6, 108
Isa 62:6, 348
Isa 62:9, 108
Isa 63:14, 344
Isa 63:7-64:12, 109
Isa 7:9a, 47
Isa 8:10, 188
Isa 8:16-18, 132
Isa. 1:10, 95
Isa. 1:11, 284
Isa. 1:11f, 284
Isa. 1:15, 110
Isa. 1:2, 134
Isa. 1:20, 5
Isa. 1:27, 195
Isa. 1:3, 195
Isa. 10:14, 49
Isa. 11:4, 192
Isa. 14:13-14, 279
Isa. 16:5, 286
Isa. 17:12f, 280
Isa. 17:13-14, 281
Isa. 17:14, 281
Isa. 17:1-6, 46
Isa. 18:4, 333
Isa. 19:1-15, 223
Isa. 2:2f, 344
Isa. 21:5, 212
Isa. 22:12-14, 49
Isa. 26:1, 281
Isa. 27:8, 343
Isa. 28:4b, 256
Isa. 29:15, 351
Isa. 30:29, 281, 283, 335
Isa. 32:6, 251
Isa. 33:14, 338
Isa. 37:36, 50
Isa. 39, 48
Isa. 40:1-8, 136
Isa. 40:23, 332
Isa. 40:26, 336
Isa. 43:25, 346
Isa. 44:28, 113
Isa. 47:7, 351
Isa. 49:10, 344
Isa. 5:10, 136
Isa. 5:1-7, 257
Isa. 52:13ff, 289
Isa. 52:15, 289
Isa. 56:1-8, 107
Isa. 56:3-5, 105
Isa. 56:9-12, 108
Isa. 57:15, 348
Isa. 59:1-15a, 109
Isa. 60:6, 289
Isa. 61:2, 289
Isa. 65:8, 111
Isa. 65:8-16, 111
Isa. 66:18, 343
Isa. 7:13-17, 133
Isa. 7:4, 47
Isa. 7-8, 135
Isa. 8:11, 134
Isa. 8:1-14, 47
Isa. 8:16, 134
Isa.1:11, 346
Isa.10:15, 223
Isa.17:13, 281
Isa. 29:16, 257
Isa. 30:29, 281
Isa. 30:8, 134
Isa. 36:4-20, 50
Isa. 45:9, 257
Isa. 49:23, 334

Isa. 5:8-10, 188
Isa. 6:1-10, 182
Isa. 61:1-2, 182
Isa. 8:1, 133
Isa. 8:9, 343
Isa. 9:8ff, 133
Isa: 10:13, 220
Isa: 41:10,13, 98
Isaiah 1:1, 44
Isaiah 40:1-2, 294
Isaiah 5:1-7, 215
Isaiah 5:8ff, 187
Jer 1:4-10, 31, 136
Jer 1:6, 36
Jer 15:1, 11
Jer 15:19, 5
Jer 15:2, 249
Jer 16:4, 63
Jer 19:7, 64
Jer 22:13-19, 191
Jer 26:9, 279
Jer 29:29, 67
Jer 3;8, 100
Jer 31:29, 100
Jer 31:33, 345
Jer 33:25, 370
Jer 33:39, 346
Jer 34:20, 64
Jer 35:10, 12
Jer 5:1, 193
Jer 52:28:30, 81
Jer 7:12-15, 95
Jer 7:21f, 284
Jer. 10:12, 358
Jer. 12:1-2, 223
Jer. 12:1ff, 350
Jer. 13:23, 223, 252
Jer. 14:2, 249
Jer. 18.1-11, 257
Jer. 18:18, 254
Jer. 2:21, 356
Jer. 20:14-18, 223
Jer. 20:9, 133
Jer. 20-7f, 233
Jer. 21:12, 286
Jer. 22:19, 170
Jer. 23:1-4, 108
Jer. 23:1-7, 187
Jer. 23:39, 347
Jer. 23:9, 135
Jer. 24:7, 345
Jer. 24:9, 251
Jer. 26:17-19, 52
Jer. 26:18, 52
Jer. 28:8, 78
Jer. 3:2, 214
Jer. 31:29, 100, 252
Jer. 31:31-34, 79
Jer. 31:33, 345
Jer. 31:35f, 370
Jer. 31:38, 348
Jer. 46:12, 213
Jer. 48:45, 365
Jer. 49:1, 211
Jer. 49:8, 211
Jer. 51:34, 370
Jer. 6:17, 108
Jer. 6:20, 284, 346
Jer. 7:12, 278
Jer. 7:23, 283
Jer. 7:33, 63
Jer. l:17, 5
Jer.18:17, 343
Jer. 24:7, 276
Jer. 26:l8, 51
Jer. 4:5ff, 133
Jer. 6:20, 284
Jeremiah 2:1-3, 215
Jeremiah 36:39b, 135
Jeremiah 49:7, 239
Jn 9:17, 182
Jn. 4:19, 182
Jn. 4:44, 182
Job 1:6, 336
Job 11:5-9, 224
Job 11:6, 220
Job 12:13, 220, 224
Job 13:8, 316
Job 14:3, 336
Job 14:4, 347
Job 15:14f, 346
Job 18:5-21, 255
Job 19:1-12, 223
Job 20:4-9, 255
Job 20:10,16, 24-25, 255
Job 21:7, 350
Job 21:7ff, 223
Job 25:4, 347
Job 25:4f, 347
Job 27:11-29, 251

Job 27:21, 343
Job 28:12, 20, 23, 224
Job 28:23, 220
Job 28:26f, 370
Job 28:28, 221
Job 28:36, 258
Job 29:2ff, 341
Job 3:20, 212
Job 3:3, 223
Job 32:8, 222
Job 33:14-15, 254
Job 38:36, 220
Job 38:8ff, 370
Job 5:17, 255
Job 5:19-22, 254
Job 6:23, 280
Job 7:17, 336
Job 9:16, 211
Job. 11:6, 347
Job. 14:4, 346
Joel 2:17, 340
Joel 2:18, 110
Joel 2:21-23, 192
Joel 2:23, 192
Joel 2:3-5, 209
Joel 4:13, 268
John 3:6, 347
Jonah 1:17, 257
Jonah 1:3, 343
Jonah 2:10, 257
Jonah 4:5-11, 257
Jonah 4:8, 365
Joseph 1:2-2:7, 210
Josh 3:10, 35
Josh 7:19, 346
Josh. 17:16, 344
Josh. 24:16, 8, 357
Josh. 24:15, 8
Josh. 24:15-27, 8
Josh. 24:16, 8
Josh. 24:19, 8
Josh. 24:20, 8
Josh. 24:21, 8
Josh. 6:4, 372
Josh. 24:15, 21,24, 339
Judg 5:15, 9
Judg 5:21-31, 9
Judg 5:28-30, 10
Judg. 14:10-18, 253
Judge. 14:10-18, 252
Judges 14:10-18, 222
Judges 14:14, 253
Judges 5:3, 332
Judges 9:7-12, 237
Judges 9:7-15, 222
Judges 9:8-15, 209
Lam 1:10, 291
Lam 4:15, 213
Lam. 2:15, 281
Lam. 2:15a, 291
Lam. 4:15, 211
Lam. 4:20, 365
Lam. 5:7, 100
Lam.1:9, 353
Lam. 2:15, 280
lamentations 4:20, 291
Lev. 19:13, 55
Lev. 25: 47-55, 276
Lev. 25:23, 276
Lev. 25:23-34, 276
Lev. 25:36f, 340
Lev. 7:11, 10
Lev. 5:4, 339
Levi 4:1-6, 210
Lk 13:33, 182
Lk 9:8, 183
Lk.1:69, 368
Lk.10:30, 364
Lk. 24:19, 182
Lk. 3:10-14, 182
Lk. 3:2-18, 182
Lk. 4:16-21, 182
Lk. 4:24, 182
Lk.7:16, 182
Lk. 8:10, 182
Luke 2:29-35, 287
Luke 20:42, 287
Luke 24:44, 287
Luke 3:22, 286
Luke 4:10-11, 289
Luke 4:1-13, 289
Luke 9:35, 287
Luke l:46:55, 68-79, 287
Mal 3:5, 193
Mal. 1:2-6, 120
Malachi 1:11, 122
Mark 9:7, 287
Matt 17:5, 287
Matt 21:11, 180
Matt. 2:11, 289

Matt. 2:1-18, 289
Matt. 3:13-17, 186
Matt. 3:17, 287
Matt. 4:1-11, 289
Matt. 4:6, 289
Matt. 5:4, 289
Matt. 5:8, 289
Matt.13:10-11, 182
Matt.13:57, 182
Matt.16:14, 182
Matt.16:18, 342
Matt. 21:6, 336
Matt. 3:1-2, 182
Matt. 7:29, 182
Micah 1:1, 51-52
Micah 1:3-4, 210
Micah 2:4, 251
Micah 3:12, 52
Micah 6:1-5, 86
Micah 6:6f, 284
Micah 7:8-20, 249
Micah 7:8ff, 99
Mk. 1:4-8, 182
Mk.4:10-12, 182
Mk. 6:15, 182
Mk. 6:4, 182
Mk 8:28, 182
Mt. 17:15, 365
Nah 3:1-3, 210
Neh. 11:17, 269
Neh. 12:35, 372
Neh. 4:8, 341
Neh. 7:44, 269
Neh. 8:7-9, 223
Neh.10:30, 335
Neh.12:27ff, 344
Num. 10:35f, 367
Num. 14:13-25, 7
Num. 14:9, 365
Num. 16:17, 270
Num. 18:20, 353
Num. 28:7, 363
Numb 10:35-36, 208
Numb 12:3, 7
Numb 21:27-30, 208
Numb 23:7-10, 208
Numb 24:3-9, 208
Numb 3:11ff, 11
Numb. 10:33-35, 96
Numb. 12:6-8, 7
Numb. 21:25, 344
Numb. 22:21-35, 257
Numb. 23:7,18, 251
Numb. 25:10-13, 109
Numb. 5:23, 346
Numb.12:6, 7
Numb.12:6-8, 6
Numb. 24: 4-5, 126
Numb. 24:3-24, 251
Numbers 6:24-27, 208
Phil. 3:20, 338
Prike Aboth 5:1, 254
Prov 16:3, 308
Prov 6:16-19, 254
Prov. 9:10, 221
Prov, 13:24, 212
Prov. 1:1-5,7, 308
Prov. 1:17, 308
Prov. 1:6, 252
Prov. 1:7, 221, 224
Prov. 1:8, 306
Prov. 10:1, 251
Prov. 10:1ff, 254
Prov. 10:2, 254
Prov. 10:26, 254
Prov. 10:6,11, 252
Prov. 11:24, 307
Prov. 12:11, 254
Prov. 15:32, 212
Prov. 17:15, 92
Prov. 17:21, 255
Prov. 19:17, 307
Prov. 2:1-8, 308
Prov. 2:31-33, 218
Prov. 21:3, 284
Prov. 24:30-34, 254, 349
Prov. 25:1, 254
Prov. 25:21-22, 254
Prov. 29:27, 305
Prov. 3:13, 308
Prov. 3:19, 220
Prov. 3:9, 254
Prov. 30:4, 213
Prov. 5:15-23, 257
Prov. 6:27, 254
Prov. 6:20-21, 23, 254
Prov. 6:27-28, 218
Prov. 7:21-23, 256
Prov. 7:6-23, 256
Prov. 8:22, 221

Prov. 8:22ff, 308
Prov. 8:23, 221
Prov. 8:27, 147
Prov. 8:33, 308
Prov. 8:34, 221
Prov. 9:13-18, 221
Prov.16:20, 308
Prov.18:26, 307
Prov. 2:6, 220
Prov. 22:17-23:1, 305
Prov. 22:17-31:31, 306
Prov. 24:17-24:22, 305
Prov. 24:30-34, 260
Prov. 25:1ff, 301
Prov. 8:1-36, 210
Prov: 10:1, 212
Proverb 16:10, 254
Proverb 22:29, 254
Proverb 25:2, 254
Proverbs 10:1-22:16, 224
Proverbs 11:2, 252
Proverbs 13:3, 252
Proverbs 22:17, 235
Proverbs 22:7-23, 238
Proverbs 24:34, 236
Proverbs 26:4, 307
Proverbs 26:5, 307
Ps 51:116f, 284
Ps 100:4, 278
Ps 103:19, 279
Ps 103:1f, 362
Ps 104:5-9, 274
Ps 107:22, 284
Ps 108:7, 278
Ps 110:2-3, 286
Ps 112:7, 347
Ps 116:17, 284
Ps 118:19-20, 278
Ps 119:55, 341
Ps 121:4, 355
Ps 122:1, 270
Ps 122:2, 202
Ps 123:1, 279
Ps 124:8, 275
Ps 125:1, 277
Ps 125:5, 287
Ps 127:1, 211
Ps 128:6, 287
Ps 132:1,10,17, 284
Ps 132:10, 284
Ps 132:13, 279
Ps 132:13-14, 279
Ps 134:3, 278, 265
Ps 135:15-18, 274
Ps 135:21, 277
Ps 135:5, 335
Ps 137:3,8, 211
Ps 138:3, 361
Ps 14:42, 277
Ps 141:2, 284
Ps 142:2a, 212
Ps 144:10, 284
Ps 144:1-2, 286
Ps 145:3, 343
Ps 147:12, 267
Ps 147:13b, 211
Ps 147:14, 281
Ps 147:18, 369
Ps 147:2, 348
Ps 149:3, 271
Ps 15:1, 278
Ps 150:4, 271
Ps 150:5, 271
Ps 19:8ff, 212
Ps 20:2, 277
Ps 20:7, 284
Ps 21:8-9, 286
Ps 22:21, 257
Ps 26:1, 341
Ps 26:6ff, 351
Ps 26:8, 270
Ps 27:4, 270, 277
Ps 27:6, 270, 284
Ps 28:9, 268
Ps 29:5, 343
Ps 29:8, 281
Ps 3:5, 278
Ps 30:1, 271
Ps 30:4, 213
Ps 31:33, 361
Ps 31:2-3, 277
Ps 33:2, 271
Ps 33:3, 277
Ps 36:5, 212
Ps 36:7, 365
Ps 40:16, 361
Ps 42:1-2, 277
Ps 42:4, 244
Ps 43:1,2, 340
Ps 43:3, 278

Ps 47:2, 276
Ps 47:5, 271, 277
Ps 47:6-7, 271
Ps 48:1, 278, 281
Ps 48:1b, 281
Ps 48:3, 281
Ps 48:4ff, 281
Ps 48:5,6, 281
Ps 50:8-15, 284
Ps 51:10, 289
Ps 51:18, 277
Ps 53:6, 278
Ps 54:6, 270
Ps 57:1, 365
Ps 59:18, 333
Ps 63:2, 270
Ps 63:7, 277
Ps 66:13, 363
Ps 66:13, 25, 284
Ps 68:1, 18, 277
Ps 69:30f, 284
Ps 69:33, 361
Ps 73:1, 256
Ps 73:11, 256
Ps 74:12ff, 276
Ps 74:2, 277
Ps 76:12, 280
Ps 76:2, 278, 281
Ps 76:3-6, 281
Ps 76:9, 47
Ps 77:3, 341
Ps 78:2, 251
Ps 78:41, 276
Ps 78:52, 344
Ps 78:68, 277
Ps 80:1, 276, 279
Ps 81:2, 271
Ps 82:1,6, 276
Ps 82:6, 276
Ps 84:1-7,10, 277
Ps 84:9, 284
Ps 85:11, 281
Ps 85:8, 281
Ps 86:8, 284
Ps 87:1, 278-279
Ps 87:2, 278, 367
Ps 87:3, 281
Ps 87:5, 276
Ps 87:7, 271
Ps 89:17, 24, 370
Ps 89:18, 276, 284-285
Ps 89:20, 284
Ps 89:38, 51, 284
Ps 89:5-7, 276
Ps 89:9-13, 274
Ps 9:4, 341
Ps 90:3, 336
Ps 91:1, 365
Ps 93:1ff, 276
Ps 93:3-4, 274
Ps 94:9, 351
Ps 95:3, 274, 343
Ps 95:3f, 276
Ps 96:10, 276, 369
Ps 96:13, 276
Ps 96:6, 270
Ps 97:2, 356
Ps 97:3,4, 336
Ps 97:6, 276
Ps 98:6, 271
Ps 98:7f, 274
Ps 99:1, 276, 356
Ps 99:2, 343
Ps 99:9, 278
Ps. 100:2, 282
Ps. 100:4, 278
Ps. 100:47, 282
Ps. 102:13,16, 348
Ps. 102:18, 344
Ps. 102:21, 277
Ps. 103:2, 341
Ps. 103:14, 336
Ps. 103:20f, 370
Ps. 104:3, 335
Ps. 104:4, 156
Ps. 105:22, 222
Ps. 106:1, 349
Ps. 107:26, 370
Ps. 11:4, 277, 279
Ps. 110:1, 284-286, 336, 357
Ps. 110:4, 285
Ps. 113:8, 211
Ps. 115:15, 275
Ps. 115:4-8, 274
Ps. 116:10, 267
Ps. 118:1, 208
Ps. 118:19, 282
Ps. 118:20, 282
Ps. 122:2, 278, 281
Ps. 122:3-4, 277

Ps. 122:4, 278
Ps. 122:5,6, 211
Ps. 122:6f, 281
Ps. 122:7, 281
Ps. 125:1, 277
Ps. 125:2, 277
Ps. 127:5, 253
Ps. 128:5, 278
Ps. 132:1ff, 366
Ps. 132:5ff, 279
Ps. 132:8b, 367
Ps. 133:3, 277
Ps. 134:1, 335
Ps. 135:21, 277
Ps. 135:5, 335
Ps. 138:2, 278
Ps. 143:12, 363
Ps. 144:10, 284
Ps. 144:3, 336
Ps. 147:5, 251
Ps. 148:1,7, 359
Ps. 148:10, 372
Ps. 149:3, 372
Ps. 15:2, 282
Ps. 15:5, 365
Ps. 16:5, 353
Ps. 16:8, 365
Ps. 17:3ff, 351
Ps. 17:8, 277, 365
Ps. 18:10, 356
Ps. 18:2, 276
Ps. 18:39, 286
Ps. 18:46, 365
Ps. 18:50, 332
Ps. 2:1-2, 287-289
Ps. 2:2, 284
Ps. 2:2a, 280
Ps. 2:4, 335
Ps. 2:5, 286
Ps. 2:6, 278
Ps. 2:7, 284, 287-288
Ps. 2:8-9, 288
Ps. 20:3, 270, 284
Ps. 20:9, 361
Ps. 22:22, 348
Ps. 22:22, 25, 362
Ps. 23:1, 355
Ps. 23:1ff, 276
Ps. 23:5, 362
Ps. 23:5-6, 277
Ps. 23:6, 195, 279
Ps. 24:1-2, 359
Ps. 24:3, 278
Ps. 24:3-4, 282
Ps. 24:4, 289
Ps. 24:7-10, 276-277, 282
Ps. 28:2, 278
Ps. 28:6, 361
Ps. 29:1, 276
Ps. 29:10, 276
Ps. 29:11, 281
Ps. 29:3,10, 274
Ps. 29:9, 372
Ps. 30:11, 271
Ps. 33:2, 271
Ps. 33:6, 336
Ps. 33:67, 274
Ps. 33:9, 369
Ps. 34:18, 348
Ps. 34:8, 279
Ps. 36:6, 370
Ps. 36:8ff, 368
Ps. 36:9, 279, 340
Ps. 4:5, 270, 284
Ps. 40:3, 348
Ps. 40:6, 284
Ps. 40:7, 340
Ps. 42:1, 340
Ps. 42:5, 362
Ps. 42:7, 340
Ps. 42:8, 340
Ps. 42:9, 340
Ps. 42:9f, 340
Ps. 43:2, 340
Ps. 45: 6, 285
Ps. 45:6, 285
Ps. 45:7, 285-284
Ps. 46:10, 343
Ps. 46:3, 280
Ps. 46:4, 280-281
Ps. 46:49, 281
Ps. 46:4b, 281
Ps. 46:5, 281
Ps. 46:5,7, 343
Ps. 46:6, 280-281
Ps. 46:6, 8, 343
Ps. 46:7, 11, 281
Ps. 46:8, 281
Ps. 46:9, 281, 343
Ps. 47:2, 343

Ps. 48:2, 279-281
Ps. 48:2,11, 277
Ps. 48:4, 280
Ps. 49:4, 255
Ps. 5:11, 361
Ps. 5:4-6, 282
Ps. 5:7, 282
Ps. 5:8, 278
Ps. 50:12-13, 284
Ps. 50:5, 270
Ps. 50:8-15, 284
Ps. 54:6, 270, 284, 348
Ps. 55:12,13, 213
Ps. 56:12, 284
Ps. 56:13, 362
Ps. 60:6, 278
Ps. 61:8, 363
Ps. 63:1, 340
Ps. 63:4, 279, 352
Ps. 63:6, 341
Ps. 65:1, 278
Ps. 65:6-7, 274
Ps. 68:29, 277
Ps. 68:35, 351
Ps. 68:4, 356
Ps. 68:5, 278
Ps. 69:30f, 284
Ps. 7:1, 276
Ps. 7:8f, 341
Ps. 71:22, 276
Ps. 72:1, 285
Ps. 72:10,15, 289
Ps. 72:1-3, 192
Ps. 72:2, 4, 12ff, 285
Ps. 72:3, 286
Ps. 72:3,7, 281
Ps. 74:12-17, 274
Ps. 74:12ff, 276
Ps. 74:12-17, 275
Ps. 74:13, 370
Ps. 75:5, 10, 370
ps. 76:1, 335
Ps. 76:12, 280
Ps. 76:36, 281
Ps. 76:6, 281
Ps. 77:16, 343
Ps. 78:2, 252
Ps. 78:37, 347
ps. 78:52, 344
Ps. 78:68, 279, 367
Ps. 79:1-3, 277
Ps. 8:1, 275
Ps. 8:3ff, 357
Ps. 80:1, 276, 279
Ps. 80:18, 284
Ps. 80:19, 35
Ps. 80:4 6, 355
Ps. 81:9-10, 274
Ps. 82:1, 276
Ps. 84:4, 279
Ps. 84:9-11, 285
Ps. 86:12, 214
Ps. 86:16, 363
Ps. 87:5, 276
Ps. 89:12, 275
Ps. 89:3, 20, 35, 284
Ps. 89:40ff, 355
Ps. 9:11, 196, 279
Ps. 9:14, 278
Ps. 9:19-20, 246
Ps. 9:20, 336
Ps. 90:2, 276
Ps. 93:1, 369
Ps. 93:3-4, 280
Ps. 94:22, 277
Ps. 95:1-6, 282
Ps. 95:6, 282
Ps. 95:7, 283
Ps. 96:4, 343
Ps. 97:5, 335
Ps. 97:9, 276
Ps. 99:5, 282
Ps. 18:2, 23
Ps.10:11, 351
Ps.102:25, 336
Ps.104:35, 335
Ps.104:5-9, 274
Ps.107:1, 349
Ps.109:14, 346
Ps.110:1, 284
Ps.118:1, 349
Ps.118:19, 282
Ps.132:10,17, 332
Ps.136:1, 349
Ps.136:5, 336
Ps.14:7, 277
Ps.143:2, 347
Ps.147:5, 335
Ps. 2:6, 278
Ps. 20:2, 278

Ps. 22:4f, 351
Ps. 24:1-6, 282
Ps. 28:8, 332
Ps. 3:6, 343
Ps. 37:13, 333
Ps. 37:25, 260
Ps. 42:4, 341
Ps. 43:1, 340
Ps. 43:1ff, 341
Ps. 46:6, 280-281
Ps. 48:2, 277
Ps. 61:4, 338
Ps. 62:1f, 254
Ps. 76:6, 281
Ps. 78:60, 278
Ps. 8:2, 336
Ps. 89:27, 285
Ps. 89:38, 51, 284
Ps. 9:3f, 246
Ps. 95:5, 336
Ps. 96:11ff, 274
Ps. 97:7, 274
Ps. 37:30, 213
Ps. 122:5, 285
Psa 99:6, 11
Psalm 104:27-28, 244
Psalm 126:5-6, 289
Psalm 24:7-10, 279
Psalm 37:16, 255
Psalm 40:13-17, 264
Psalm 89:8, 248
Psalm 91:11-12, 289
Psalm 95:3, 274
Psalms 119:7-14, 224
Pss 115:2, 340
Pss 78:2, 251
Pss. 79:10, 340
Pss. 49:4, 251
Qoh. 12:1, 259
Qoh. 9:7, 259
queen of Sheba - 10:5, 253
Rev 11:17-18, 287
Rev 12:10-12, 287
Rev 19:15, 334
Rev 19:6-8, 287
Rev 2:2,6,14,15, 20, 184
Rev. 5:9-10, 287
Rev. 2:26-27, 334
Rom 12:6-8, 183
Rom. 8:35-39, 354
shēlēm: 5:22, 35
Sir 47:17, 252
Sir. 43:10, 370
Sir. 51:13-22, 260
Sirach 1:10, 222
Sirach 11:26-27, 224
Sirach 23:16, 254
Sirach 25:7-11, 254
Sirach 26:5, 254
Sirach 33:16-18, 260
Sirach 39:3, 252
Sirach 50:25-26, 254
Testament of Simeon 2:1-4, 210
Wis 8:8, 252
Wisdom of Solomon 2:1-20, 210
Wisdom of Solomon 7:17-20, 258
wisdom of Solomon, 1:4, 222
Zebach: 4:4, 35
Zech 7:1ff, 337
Zech 7:5-9, 190
Zech. 1:1, 115
Zech. 10:9, 341
Zech. 6:10,14, 67
Zech. 7:12, 5
Zech. 9:2, 240
Zech. 7:1ff, 294
Zech. 8:18ft, 294
Zeph 1:7-13, 67
Zeph 3:5, 99
Zeph l4-l8, 67
Zeph. 1:12, 252